Macau
History and Society

Macau
History and Society

SECOND EDITION

Zhidong Hao

Hong Kong University Press
The University of Hong Kong
Pok Fu Lam Road
Hong Kong
https://hkupress.hku.hk

© University of Macau 2020

ISBN 978-988-8528-37-0 (*Paperback*)

All rights reserved. No portion of this publication may be reproduced or transmitted in any form or by any means, electronic or mechanical, including photocopying, recording, or any information storage or retrieval system, without prior permission in writing from the publisher.

British Library Cataloguing-in-Publication Data
A catalogue record for this book is available from the British Library.

Digitally printed

I dedicate this book to all those who have worked hard
to make Macau a better place.

Contents

List of Figures	viii
List of Plates	xiii
List of Tables	xvi
Acknowledgements	xvii
Introduction: Macau History and Society	1
1. Portuguese Maritime Expansion and the State of Aomen: How Macau Came into Being	9
2. Macau's Politics: Then and Now	18
3. Macau's Economy: Making a Living	52
4. Social Interaction: The Clash of Civilizations and Cultures in Macau	81
5. Religion and Social Development in Macau and China	115
6. Literature and the Arts in and about Macau	138
7. Social Issues and Problems in Macau	160
8. Conclusions: Toward a Macauan Identity	207
Appendix: A Chronicle of Events in Macau History and Society	225
Notes	232
Selected Bibliography	279
Index	301

Figures

Figure 1.1	Statue of Álvares in Macau. Photo by Wang Xin and Zhang Kai.	10
Figure 1.2	A map of Macau and Hong Kong with Tunmen and Nei Lingding (Ling Ting) Island (close to Tunmen on its left). Rui Manuel Loureiro, *Em Busca das Origens de Macau*, Macau: Museu Maritimo de Macau, 1997, p. 13.	11
Figure 1.3	Shangchuan, Langbaijiao, Macau, and Hong Kong. 中國第一歷史檔案館、澳門一國兩制研究中心,《澳門歷史地圖精選》, 北京: 華文出版社, 2001, p. 91, with English names added by Benny Tam.	13
Figure 1.4	A contemporary map of Macau. Wong Chao Son, Deng Hanzeng, and Huang Junxin, *Macau Atlas*, Macau: Macao Foundation, 1997, p. 2.	14
Figure 1.5	A map of Macau in the early 20th century. *Atlas of Macao*, Macau: Cartography and Cadastre Bureau of Macao Special Administrative Region Government, 2003, p. 63.	14
Figure 2.1	Part of Yuan Ming Yuan after being looted and burned in the Second Opium War. 黃韜朋, 黃鍾駿, 圓明園, Hong Kong: Joint Publishing Co. (HK), 1985, p. 26.	25
Figure 2.2	The ancient City Hall 議事廳, in Yin Guangren and Zhang Rulin, *Aomen Jilue Jiaozhu*, pp. 218–9.	34
Figure 2.3	The remaining wall of Qian Shan Zhai in what is now Xiangzhou, Zhuhai. 珠海市文物管理委員會, 珠海市文物志, Foshan: Guangdong Ren Min Chu Ban She, 1994, p. 2.	35
Figure 2.4	A map of the buildings at the time, including the Chinese Christian church in the middle of the map. Ho Weng Hong, *The Past of Macau*, Macau: Macao Foundation, 1994, p. 14.	37
Figure 2.5	Amaral's portrait. Courtesy of Oxford University Press.	39

Figures   ix

Figure 2.6a	The Border Gate, at Love Food blog at http://hk.lovefood.cc/2015/11/blog-post_6.html, accessed August 11, 2019.	40
Figure 2.6b	The dates inscribed on the inside and front of the walls, at Memory Macau blog at http://memorymacau.blogspot.com/2012/03/blog-post_14.html, accessed August 11, 2019.	41
Figure 2.7	The border gate. Lei Kun Min and Lam Fat Lam, *Macao in Postcards*, Macau: Macao Association for Historical Education, 2008, p. 33.	43
Figure 2.8	Confrontation between the police and union members that led to the 12-3 Incident. Li Hongjiang, *Danzai Qinghuai* (Taipa remembrance) (Macau: The Civic and Municipal Affairs Bureau, 2001), p. 188, cited in Ruan Zirong and Li Jinglin, "Aomen koushu shi: 'huo huashi' de huiyi" (Macau oral history: "the live fossil" remembers), September 23, 2018 at Pengpai News, https://www.thepaper.cn/newsDetail_forward_2463790, accessed October 9, 2018.	43
Figure 2.9	The Portuguese Macau government accepted all the conditions raised by the Chinese community. Chief among the Chinese community leaders receiving the agreement and apology were Ho Yin (何賢, Edmund Ho's father, second from left) and Ma Man Kei (馬萬祺, sixth from left). Chen Shurong, *Yishiting Qiandi* (The Lea Senado Plaza) (Macau: Jun Liang Tang Press, 2013), p. 59.	44
Figure 2.10	The protests against the possible legislation of Article 23 in Hong Kong in 2003. Fu Hualing, Carole J. Petersen, and Simon N. M. Yong, *National Security and Fundamental Freedoms*, Hong Kong: Hong Kong University Press, 2005, cover page.	50
Figure 3.1	Mount Fortress (大炮臺) in Macau with its cannon. Photo by Wang Xin and Zhang Kai.	53
Figure 3.2	A Portuguese ship. Yin Guangren and Zhang Rulin, *Aomen Jilue Jiaozhu*, p. 233.	54
Figure 3.3	The view of Praia Grande, or Grand Beach. Lei Kun Min and Lam Fat Lam, *Macao in Postcards*, Macau: Macao Association for Historical Education, 2008, p. 105.	55
Figure 3.4	Opium smoking. Geoffrey Gunn, *Aomen Shi* (Encountering Macau), Beijing: Central Compilation and Translation Press, 2009, p. 128.	56

Figure 3.5	An opium smuggling ship off the coast of Macau in the late 19th century. 孔繁壯, 陳伯良, 劉雅煌, *Macau*, Macau: 澳門出版社, 2002, p. 47.	57
Figure 3.6	Coolies in rebellion. Edgar Holden, *Harper's New Monthly Magazine*: A Chapter on the Coolie Trade 29 Vol. Harper & Brothers, 06/01/1864. Web. November 20, 2015. 1–10, at http://scalar.usc.edu/works/the-voyages-of-the-clarence/norway-2, accessed October 9, 2018.	58
Figure 3.7	A sedan chair for women. Yin Guangren and Zhang Rulin, *Aomen Jilue Jiaozhu*, p. 232.	62
Figure 3.8	A pirate ship. Courtesy of Oxford University Press.	63
Figure 3.9	Queen of Pirates. Courtesy of Oxford University Press.	64
Figure 3.10	A firecracker workshop, a traditional handicraft in Macau. Ruan Zirong, "Aomen Koushu Shi: Huo Huashi de Huiyi" (Macau oral history: The memory of a "living fossil"), at https://www.thepaper.cn/newsDetail_forward_2463790, accessed October 9, 2018.	69
Figure 3.11	Street vendors. Photo by Ou Ping. *A Voyage in Time*, Macau: Museu de Arte de Macau, 2005, p. 47.	70
Figure 3.12	Chinese grocery stores. Photo by Raymond Wong.	70
Figure 3.13	Market-place in front of Largo do Pagode do Bazar. Ho Weng Hong, *The Past of Macau*, Macau: Macao Foundation, 1994, p. 164.	70
Figure 3.14	A *fantan* saloon in old Macau. Macau Data website: http://www.macaudata.com/macauweb/book114/, accessed February 16, 2005.	73
Figure 3.15	Playing *fantan* in a gambling den in Macau. Benjamim Videira Pires, "The Chinese Quarter One Hundred Years Ago," Macau Cultural Affairs Bureau at http://www.icm.gov.mo/rc/viewer/20007/867, accessed October 9, 2018.	73
Figure 3.16	Casino Lisboa. Photo by Wang Xin and Zhang Kai.	74
Figure 4.1	Shoe-mender (approx. 1890) with his shoulder pole and baskets. Ho Weng Hong, *The Past of Macau*, Macau: Macao Foundation, 1994, p. 160.	91
Figure 4.2	Along the docks of the Inner Harbour (approx. 1920). Ho Weng Hong, *The Past of Macau*, Macau: Macao Foundation, 1994, p. 119.	98

Figure 4.3	Portuguese missionaries clad in Chinese costume in Macao in the early 1900s. 林明德, 澳門的匯聯文化, Taipei: Chinese Folk-Arts Foundation, 1997, p. 21.	99
Figure 4.4	José Luis de Sales Marques, the then chairman of the Macau Municipal Council before the handover. Leal Senado de Macau, *Relatorio de Actividades de 1997*, Macau: Leal Senado de Macau, 1997, p. 5.	105
Figure 4.5	A section of the old European city wall that still remains today. Photo by Vincent Ho.	107
Figure 5.1	Nezha Temple. Photo by Jerry Wu.	117
Figure 5.2	Santa Casa da Misericórdia (仁慈堂). Photo by Jerry Wu.	120
Figure 5.3	Igreja de Sao Lazaro (聖望得堂, also called 望德聖母堂). Photo by Wang Xin and Zhang Kai.	120
Figure 5.4	St. Lawrence Church (風順堂街聖老楞佐堂). Photo by Jerry Wu.	120
Figure 5.5	St. Dominic's Church 板樟堂 (又名玫瑰聖母堂). Photo by Wang Xin and Zhang Kai.	121
Figure 5.6	The outside of St. Augustine's Church (聖奧古斯丁教堂). Photo by Jerry Wu.	121
Figure 5.7	The inside of the Church of St. Anthony (聖安多尼堂). Photo by Jerry Wu.	122
Figure 5.8	The Cathedral of Macau (主教堂). Photo by Jerry Wu.	122
Figure 5.9	Chapel of Our Lady of Penha (主教山小堂). Photo by Jerry Wu.	122
Figure 5.10	Chapel of Our Lady of Guia (聖母雪地殿堂). Photo by Jerry Wu.	123
Figure 5.11	The Morrison Protestant Chapel (馬禮遜基督教堂). Photo by Wang Xin and Zhang Kai.	124
Figure 5.12	Robert Morrison translating the Bible with his Chinese helpers; painting by Chinnery. *Review of Culture* N°58, Macau: Instituto Cultural de Macau, 2006, p. 28.	132
Figure 5.13	Yung Wing. 錢鋼 胡勁草, *Chinese Educational Mission Students* (大清留美幼童記), Beijing: Contemporary China Publishing House, p. 2.	134
Figure 5.14	Students sent to the U.S. 錢鋼 胡勁草, *Chinese Educational Mission Students* (大清留美幼童記), Beijing: Contemporary China Publishing House, p. 47.	134

Figure 5.15	St. Mary stepping on the head of the dragon. Photo by Wang Xin and Zhang Kai.	135
Figure 5.16	The Temple of Nu Wa. Photo by Wang Xin and Zhang Kai.	136
Figures 6.1a–c	The Camões Garden (白鴿巢花園) today. Photo by Jerry Wu.	145
Figure 6.2	Going to watch Guangdong Yue opera. *Review of Culture* N°10, Macau: Instituto Cultural de Macau, 1992, p. 73.	147
Figure 6.3	Part of the façade of St. Paul's College and cathedral built in 1620. Photo by Wang Xin and Zhang Kai.	150
Figure 6.4	Corruption in Macau. Courtesy of Chou Cheong Hong.	151
Figure 6.5	Henrique de Senna Fernandes. Goodreads at https://www.goodreads.com/author/show/781735.Henrique_de_Senna_Fernandes, accessed November 6, 2018.	152
Figure 6.6	Adé. Christina Miu Bing Cheng, "The Son of Macao and the Mandarin's House" at the website of the Cultural Affairs Bureau, MSAR, http://www.icm.gov.mo/rc/viewer/40052/2215, accessed November 6, 2018.	154
Figure 7.1	Class identification by occupation.	170
Figure 7.2	Class identification by monthly income (MOP).	171
Figure 7.3	Class identification by education.	172
Figure 7.4	World heritages. Courtesy of Chou Cheong Hong.	204
Figure 8.1	A *pailou* built in front of Leal Senado in Macau to celebrate the Chinese national holiday in the 1960s, courtesy of *Macao Daily*, September 25, 2004.	222

Plates

After page 114

Plate 1.1 India, Malacca, and South China. Maria do Carmo Maia Cadete, *Museu de Macau*, Macau: Pro-Jardim, 1999, p. 40.

Plate 1.2 Temple of Goddess A-Ma in 1842. This is a later model of the temple the Portuguese saw when they first came here. It was almost three hundred years later, but one may still have an idea of what it might have been like at the time. 霍啟昌, 蘇慶彬, 鄭德華, *澳門歷史實驗教材*, Macau: 澳門大學實驗教材編寫組, 1998, p. 6.

Plate 1.3 The memorial rock in A-Ma Temple commemorating the arrival of Portuguese ships. Photo by Jerry Wu.

Plate 1.4 A historic map of Macau in the 18th century. Isabel Leonor da Silva Diaz de Seabra, *Relacoes entre Macau e o Siao*, Macau: University of Macau, 1999, p. 24.

Plate 2.1 Statue of Amaral. Photo by Raymond Wong.

Plate 2.2 The First Opium War. 孔繁壯, 陳伯良, 劉雅煌, *Macau*, Macau: 澳門出版社, 2002, p. 47.

Plate 2.3 The Senate building. Photo by Jerry Wu.

Plate 2.4 Mesquita, and his statue standing opposite the Leal Senado and being pulled down in 1966. Lei Pang Chu, *Macao China*, Macau: Macao Daily News, 1999, p. 65.

Plate 2.5 The Governor's Mansion, and now part of the Chief Executive's Office. Photo by Jerry Wu.

Plate 3.1 Fulong Xin Jie where brothels were located. Photo by Jerry Wu.

Plate 3.2 A fisherwoman, painting by George Chinnery (1774–1852). Rosmarie W. N. Lamas, *Everything in Style: Harriett Low's Macau*, Hong Kong University Press, 2006, Fig. 12.

Plate 4.1 Chinese and Westerners in Macau. Macau Data website: http://www.macaudata.com/Macau/draw/pic/02_17.html, accessed on February 19, 2005.

Plate 4.2 Chinese Boxers fighting the Eight-Nation Alliance (English and Japanese soldiers depicted), http://en.wikipedia.org/wiki/Boxer_Rebellion, accessed on October 8, 2009.

Plate 4.3 A portrait of Harriett Low. Chen Jichun, 錢納利與澳門 *Qian Nali yu Aomen*, Macau Foundation, 1995, p. 197.

Plate 4.4 Rua da Guimarães 海邊新街, approx. 1890. Ho Weng Hong, *The Past of Macau*, Macau: Macao Foundation, 1994, p. 163.

Plate 4.5 Monument commemorating the war on Luhuan (Coloane). Photo by Wang Xin and Zhang Kai.

Plate 4.6 *The Trail of Tears*. Robert Lindneux (1942), The Granger Collection, New York.

Plate 4.7 A picture of the city in 1635 with the city wall seen, Liu Yuelian, Zhang Tingmao, and Huang Xiaofeng, *Aomen Lishi: Chuzhong buchong jiaocai* (Macau history: A supplementary textbook for middle school students) (Macau: Macau Education and Youth Bureau, 2006), p. 18.

After page 205

Plate 5.1 How Mazu saves people on the sea. 劉曉艷, 墉城妙韵, Beijing: 宗教文化出版社, 2008, p. 191.

Plate 5.2 Puji Chanyuan, one of the major Buddhist temples in Macau. Photo by Wang Xin and Zhang Kai.

Plate 5.3 Pictures of St. Mary and Jesus Christ in St. Dominic's Church in Macau. Photo by Jerry Wu.

Plate 5.4 Matteo Ricci and Xu Guangqi 利瑪竇與徐光啟. *Review of Culture* N°21 English Edition, Macau: Instituto Cultural de Macau, 1994, p. 103.

Plate 6.1 Rickshaw men in Macau. Ho Weng Hong, *The Past of Macau*, Macau: Macao Foundation, 1994, p. 162.

Plate 6.2 A contemporary scene of a Catholic procession. Photo by Raymond Wong.

Plate 6.3 Chinese opera singers. Photo by Pan Iok Kin. Camara Municipal das Ilhas, *Retrato das ilhas*, Macau: Camara Municipal das Ilhas, 1995, p. 34.

Plate 6.4 Two examples of the calligraphy as art at A-Ma Temple. Photos by Choi Lap San.

Plate 6.5 Wu Li's Lake, *Sky and Spring* 吳歷《湖天春色圖》. *Review of Culture* N°40 & 41, Macau: Instituto Cultural de Macau, 2000, p. 32.

Plate 6.6 One of the earliest Chinese painters of Western style. Wong Yan-Tat, *Macau, As Time Goes By*, Sunbright Publishing Co., 1999, p. 115.

Plate 6.7	*The Bewitching Braid*《大辮子的誘惑》. Wu Zhiliang and Ieong Wan Chong, *Enciclopedia de Macau*, Macau: Macao Foundation, 1999, p. 112.
Plate 6.8	The Camões Garden by William Daniell where Luis de Camões once worked. Luis Sa Cunha, *Macau di nos-sa coracam*, Macau: Macao Foundation, 1999, p. 2.
Plate 6.9	A portrait of George Chinnery. Wu Zhiliang and Ieong Wan Chong, *Enciclopedia de Macau*, Macau: Macao Foundation, 1999, p. 75.
Plate 6.10	Dr. Thomas R. Colledge and his patients. Chen Jichun, 錢納利與澳門 *Qian Nali yu Aomen*, Macau Foundation, 1995, p. 194.
Plate 6.11	The ruins of St. Paul's Cathedral and the vicinity by William Heine (1858). Lei Pang Chu, *Macao China*, Macau: Macao Daily News, 1999, p. 7.
Plate 6.12	A-Ma Temple by William Heine (1896). *Review of Culture* N°33, Macau: Instituto Cultural de Macau, 1997, p. 129.
Plate 6.13	Access to the Taipa island (1960s). Camara Municipal das Ilhas and Associacao de Historia de Macau, *Fotografias Antigas das Ilhas da Taipa e de Coloane*, Macau: Camara Municipal das Ilhas and Associacao de Historia de Macau, 1994, p. 49.
Plate 8.1	The rent receipt given to the Portuguese officials by the local Chinese government in Xiangshan. 孔繁壯, 陳伯良, 劉雅煌, *Macau*, Macau: 澳門出版社, 2002, p. 38.
Plate 8.2	The return of Macau to China. 兩國總理在交換簽署文本後握手致賀, ("Two premiers shake hands after exchanging the signed agreement") April 13, 1987. *Macao Daily News*, 澳門歷史的見證, Macau: Macao Daily News, 1987, p. 3.

Tables

Table 7.1 Population change around the handover between 1997 and 2011   162
Table 7.2 Number and percentage of government officials in 1997 and 2013 by ethnicity   163
Table 7.3 Class distribution in Macau in 2006, 2007, and 2012 (%)   173
Table 7.4 Percentage of legislators in different categories of occupational background, 1976–2013   175
Table 7.5 Major social protest movements between 1989 and 2013   180–183
Table 7.6 The number of religious and non-religious middle schools and their students 2015/2016   190
Table 7.7 The distribution of countries and regions where graduating high school students enrolled in colleges and universities from 2012/2013 to 2016/2017 academic year   194
Table 7.8 Higher education institutions (HEIs) in Macau in 2006 and 2016   197

Acknowledgements

This project, both the first and the second editions of this book, was sponsored by a University of Macau Research Grant. I would like to thank the University Research Committee for its support. Vice Rector Rui Martins' and Associate University Librarian Raymond Wong's efforts in facilitating the publication of the book are greatly appreciated.

Two anonymous reviewers for Hong Kong University Press and another two for the Publication Center of the University of Macau offered valuable suggestions for revision of the first edition. Professors Cathryn Hope Clayton and William Guthrie read parts of the previous book draft and made suggestions for revision as well. I am grateful for all their advice, based on which the book is greatly improved.

Much of chapter 3 on Macau's economy was first published in *Aomen Yanjiu* (Journal of Macau studies), No. 37 (December, 2006): 72–86. Much of chapter 6 on literature and the arts was first published in the *Journal of Macao Polytechnic Institute*, 2008 Issue (Serial No. 2): 78–96. Much of chapter 7 on social issues and problems was first published in an article entitled "Social Stratification and Ethnic and Class Politics in Macau before and after the Handover in 1999" in *China: An International Journal*, 13(1) (2015): 66–92. I would like to thank the journals for allowing much of the contents of these articles to be republished here, although many changes have also been made to the current book.

Quite a number of student assistants from the University of Macau helped me research the book in the past years, and the students who took my course in Macau history and society from 2004 to 2016 also helped me further think about the issues and revise the book accordingly. The students who were involved in my projects on middle and post-secondary education in Macau deserve a special thank-you. Raymond Wong, Associate University Librarian, and my research assistants Wang Xin, Jerry Wu, and Berry Tam helped me especially with the images. I owe my gratitude to them all.

I would like to thank the editors at Hong Kong University Press, without whose professional help the book would not have been able to reach the standard it has achieved now. All errors are, of course, mine.

Finally, my deep appreciation goes to Professors David Brookshaw of the University of Bristol, Jonathan Porter of the University of New Mexico, and Wu Zhiliang of the Macau Foundation for their endorsements of the first edition of the book. I would like to copy their endorsements here to help the reader approach the book.

Brookshaw: *"Most social and political histories of Macau have relied almost solely on Portuguese or other Western sources. This book corrects the imbalance in its extensive use of Chinese source material, and is written from a Chinese postcolonial perspective. It is therefore an important contribution to the ongoing story of Macau."*

Porter: *"Blending history and sociology, Zhidong Hao offers a frank and innovative analysis of Macau's past, present, and future. Going beyond the traditional view of the city as meeting place between East and West, this fascinating multidimensional approach links the study of Macau to the understanding of China's future."*

Wu: *"Hao's book provides a comprehensive narrative and profound analysis of Macau's politics, economy, social interaction, culture, literature and the arts, as well as the opportunities and challenges it is facing. This is a book for those who wish to explore the context in which the unique local identity is formed."*

I hope you will like it.

Zhidong Hao
Alameda CA, USA
August 20, 2019

Introduction
Macau History and Society

> Bourgeois society replaces the relatively autonomous local communities characteristic of prior types of society by a division of labor which draws the disparate cultural and even national groupings which formerly existed into the same social and economic system. At the same time as it expands the range of human interdependence, the spread of bourgeois society sweeps away the particular cultural myths and traditions under which men have lived from the beginning of time. Ultimately, bourgeois society brings the whole of mankind, for the first time in history, within the purview of a single social order, and is genuinely "world-historical."
>
> Anthony Giddens explaining Karl Marx's theory of capitalist development[1]

> If policies are altered, China can become the leader of all nations; if policies are not altered, she will become the servant of all nations.
>
> Robert Hart, Inspector General of China's Maritime Customs (1863–1911)[2]

It is true that China still faces many problems, including the gap between the rich and the poor, and the continuing lack of human rights and democratization. But China is now the world's second largest economy, and with increasing authoritarianism, it is exerting great political powers all over the world. When the capitalist world-system began to spread throughout the world about 450 years ago, first in the forms of merchant capitalism and colonialism, China faced a dilemma about whether and how to change.[3] Gradually, China did change, and it has changed so much so that it is becoming one of the world's superpowers; the concern now is whether a rising China will turn out to be peaceful or bellicose.[4]

To understand this change and where it may lead, it is helpful for us to understand Macau first.[5] Macau used to be the most important meeting place between the East and the West, and it played an instrumental role in China's confrontation with the West, especially in the 16th, 17th, 18th, and 19th centuries. Since then, Macau has evolved into a place with its own political, economic, and social characteristics.

Thus the study of Macau history and society is not only a study of Macau itself, but also a study of China's transformation in the past 450 years, and its possibilities in the future.[6] At a time when Macau is becoming more and more like mainland China and Hong Kong is becoming more and more like Macau, what happens in Macau is indicative of what happens in Greater China in general. Hence the importance of Macau studies.

The Political Context in Which Macau Was Brought into Being

In reading China's history in the early part of the last 450 years, from 1550 on, one cannot help but find that the Western powers, the Portuguese, the Dutch, the English, the French, and later the Americans, repeatedly wanted to establish trading ports in China and have formal relations. But repeatedly, the Chinese government turned down that kind of request or otherwise wanted to channel those relations into its tributary system with the surrounding countries. So if any other relations were eventually established with the West, they were often after wars and skirmishes between China and the Western powers. The trade war between China and the US at the time of writing seems to be doing the same thing.

Although China seemed to be reluctant to engage the outside world, especially the West, it had not always been the case. In the early years of the Western Han dynasty (206 B.C.E–25 C.E.), Panyu (Canton or Guangzhou now) was already a trading metropolis between China and Southeast Asia. In the Tang dynasty (618–907), Guangzhou, Quanzhou in Fujian, and Yangzhou on the Yangtze River had already become large trading ports. Foreign traders, mostly Indian, Arab, and Persian, regularly lived in settlements in Canton called *fanfang* (蕃坊). In the Song dynasty (960–1279), they were able to select their own *fanzhang* (蕃長), the community leader. The first Bureau of Trading Junks was established by the Tang dynasty in the 8th century, registering foreign ships and collecting duties and freight charges for the central government.[7]

The Ming dynasty (1368–1644), especially in the Yongle emperor's reign (1403–25), even sent seven maritime expeditions between 1405 and 1431, led by Zheng He (1371–1435), a eunuch.[8] The fleet reached Southeast Asia, the west coast of India, the Persian Gulf, and the east coast of Africa. But these expeditions were discontinued because they turned out to be too expensive, involving 50 to 300 ships each time and as many as 27,000 men, and the emperor was too busy with the northern defenses. More importantly, the expeditions were meant to advance the tributary system rather than active international politics or commerce. So even though they might exchange goods and ambassadors with the countries they visited, the relationship was pretty limited. So the empire stopped such expeditions after 1433.[9]

Soon after 1500, while the Ming dynasty lacked interest in maritime trade and turned largely inward-looking, as did the later Qing dynasty, the Western traders, armed and aggressive, came to the coast of China after undermining the Arab, Persian and Indian Muslim trading powers. Inevitably conflicts occurred. These conflicts made Macau possible, a Macau that was a window through which the Chinese and Westerners could interact with each other.

Macau's Intriguing Characteristics

When describing Macau, words like these come to mind: "seedy," "sleepy," "thoughtful, amiable, gentle"; "ambiguity," "indetermination," "marginality," "uncertainty," a "riddle"; "the wickedest city of the Far East," "a city of sin," "the Monte Carlo of the East," a "famous and wealthy city," a "mass of contradictions," a "rich and tightly knit community," a "Catholic place," "a city of culture," a "bridge between China and Europe," an "unpolished diamond."[10] Indeed, as Cremer points out, people tend to be uncertain about many things in Macau: its origins, historical significance, political status, culture, population, the languages spoken, and its economic situation and potential.[11] Its geographical location seems to be the only fair certainty or that it is the gambling mecca of the world; all the other aspects of Macau are still matters of debate.

For example, how do we assess the economic history of Macau? If regular trade can be considered "normal," there is also the coolie trade, the opium trade, and the gambling industry. These economic activities on which Macau has relied at one time or another certainly look morally ambiguous, or at least "marginal" vis-à-vis the "mainstream" trade of, say, silk and porcelain and tea. Somehow, the city has indeed existed "on the edges of nations, oceans, cultures, languages, economies, and civilizations."[12] It is sometimes viewed as "a city of sin," and other times viewed as "a city of culture."[13] Or maybe it is really "a mass of contradictions."[14]

It is mostly a "Catholic place"[15] for the Macanese, whom we will discuss in chapter 4, but not for the Chinese. It is a "rich and tightly knit community"[16] for the Portuguese and Macanese, and for the upper classes of the Chinese, but not for most people in Macau, who are middle and lower-class Chinese. Is it the religiosity of the Portuguese and Macanese or the silence of the lower classes of the Chinese that makes Macau a "thoughtful, amiable, and gentle place"? Or is it really what some might claim to be the integration of Chinese and Portuguese cultures that has made Macau what it is now?

The question of Macau's own personality, culture, and identity, that is, a Macauan identity, follows the same line of thought.[17] Out of the integration of Chinese and Western cultures has grown a characteristic some label 和而不同，多元共生,[18] i.e., a culture that has multiple components which have learned to live together without much killing of each other. Where Macau culture is concerned, we are more likely to encounter some kind of propaganda rather than a rigorous analysis—"more a mutual agreement to disagree than, properly speaking, a cross-cultural dialogue."[19]

However it does not mean that Macau culture cannot be defined or developed. One of the aims of this book is precisely to explore the possible contents of that culture and of a Macauan identity. We will set out to solve the "riddle" of Macau.[20] If Macau is "an unpolished diamond,"[21] we want to polish it and allow others to appreciate it. If Macau can serve as a "bridge between China and Europe,"[22] we want to see how and whether Macau can become a city of "determination," rather than one of "indetermination,"[23] a "city of culture," rather than a "city of sin."

The Structure and the Themes of the Book

Chapter 1 discusses Macau in the shadow of China, how Macau came into being. Beginning with the Portuguese maritime expansion and the earlier conflicts between China and the West which made Macau possible, I will explore the origins by giving a brief history of the establishment of Portuguese settlements.

Chapter 2 discusses political transformation, first looking at Macau and China in international conflicts, including the conflicts between the Portuguese and the Dutch, and among the Portuguese, British, and the Chinese, which culminated in the First Opium War. Then I will consider the development of Macau's political system, including the Senado period and dual jurisdiction, the colonial period, and the true Chinese period. We will see how different systems have worked, and look closely at the issues of sovereignty and democratization.

Chapter 3 examines the economic lives of peoples in Macau—cannon building; trade in the 16th and 17th centuries; the trade in opium and coolies; the life and work of pilots, compradors, slaves, coolies, servants, and prostitutes as well as fishermen and fisherwomen. Moving on to more recent times, we will study the rise of the modern Chinese working and capitalist classes, the growth of the gambling industry, including the reasons and developments, and the repercussions for Macau's economic future.

Chapter 4 examines the way people have interacted with each other since the West met the East in the 16th century. Emphasizing the significance of the Macanese community, we will examine the tale of one city and two cities, the Macau model of the clash and cooperation of civilizations, and how we might improve it.

Chapter 5 looks into the religious lives of people in Macau, whose existence owes much to the Catholics' desire to use it as a base to spread their religion to the rest of Asia. Many inhabitants also have a religious life. In a place with some 660,000 people and an area of close to 32 as of 2018 square kilometers, there are 19 Christian churches and 34 Buddhist and folk religion temples, according to the *Encyclopedia of Macau* (1999). We will reflect on the different religions represented in Macau, Daoism, Buddhism, Catholicism, Protestantism, and other folk religion, as well as the relationship between church and state, the Controversy of Rites, and the contribution of the missionaries in the East-West cultural exchange.

Chapter 6 explores literature and the arts in Macau. Throughout history, Chinese and Portuguese have written poetry and stories in and about Macau, and depicted it in paintings and drawings. This chapter will echo the theme of the clash and integration of civilizations of the preceding chapters. Both chapters 5 and 6 demonstrate that Macau's culture is very rich indeed.

Chapter 7 examines ethnic and class stratification and politics, middle and postsecondary education, casino-related crime and deviance, and Macau's civil society and public sphere. We emphasize the importance of the social and structural bases of these problems; the social responsibility of the government, the corporation, social organizations, and the individuals; and the importance of building a civil society and public sphere in Macau.

Looking to the future, chapter 8 questions the political, economic, cultural, and social identities of Macau. Can Macau become a "gaming" town rather than a "gambling" town? Is there a difference between the two? Can Macau become a model federal or confederal state of China? Is Macau going to be a model of social and ethnic harmony?

There are three major themes that run throughout the book. First, Macau and China are tied together in history, and we cannot understand one without understanding the other. Macau has always had plenty of autonomy and played important roles in China's development. It has the potential to continue to do so. But as Macau is becoming more and more mainlandized, it is gradually losing that potential. This is a matter of success or failure of the "one country, two systems" principle and some hard thinking needs to be done and really hard efforts to be made to preserve Macau's autonomy.

Second, this is a study of the clash and integration of civilizations and cultures, critically engaging Huntington's theme of the clash of civilizations. I am arguing that Huntington has a point to make: it is indeed difficult for cultures and civilizations to integrate with one another. But it is a project that needs to be done, however difficult it is, if we want to prevent the world, China and Macau included, from degenerating into tribalism, authoritarianism, and dictatorship.

Third, there is a Macau model of clash and integration of civilizations and cultures characterized by a set of unique features and an attitude of "I don't bother you and you don't bother me." But it is a problematic model. Much needs to be done in negotiating differences and building a new cultural, political, and economic identity of Macau. As Francis Fukuyama (2018), a student of Huntington, points out when discussing identity politics in today's world, some larger and more integrative national identities have to be defined while taking into consideration different cultures and civilizations. That is what I am trying to do in this book.

The Difficulties of Studying Macau History and Society and Our Methodology

First, the further one goes back into history, the fewer records are available. Many things are lost or have not been recorded at all. The 12-3 Incident in 1966, for example, destroyed an estimated one third of the documents stored in the National Library in Macau.[24] Second, even when there are records, they have been kept by the elites of society, who selected what to write and what to keep. That selection was constrained by the writers' own class, gender, race, and other political statuses. For example, most of the earlier records are in Portuguese, and were written by the Catholic Church.[25]

The earliest records, especially the Chinese records, tend to be few and sketchy. In the Chinese literature, for example, Pang Shangpeng 龐尚鵬 in 1564 discussed the earlier years of Macau, and the *Annals of Guangdong* (廣東通誌) in 1602 discussed how the Portuguese borrowed Macau to dry their goods. Both are, however, sketchy. *The History of the Ming Dynasty—The Story of Portugal in Macau* (明史・佛郎機傳), an official record finished in 1735, runs only about 2,500 words. Yin Guangren 印光任 and Zhang Rulin 張汝霖 wrote *The Annals of Macau* (Aomen Jilue or 澳門記略) in 1751, the first encyclopedic work of Macau, indicating the beginning of the study of Macau, but that was about 200 years after the Portuguese came to Macau.[26]

The earliest records in the Portuguese language were by Fernão Mendes Pinto in both 1555 and 1614, where he described Macau as a wasteland before the Portuguese came. Later records became more detailed, and they recounted the relationship between the Portuguese and the Chinese officials as well as the geography, history, and society of Macau and China. But the earliest full study of Macau began with Anders Ljungstedt's work in 1832, *An Historical Sketch of the Portuguese Settlements in China*, and it was in English. (Ljungstedt disputed the Portuguese claim that they had sovereignty over Macau, which somewhat embarrassed the colonial government.)[27]

In the 19th and 20th century then, more historical studies of Macau were published, including Montalto de Jesus's 1902 work *Historic Macau*, and de Jesus's and J. M. Braga's 1949 work, *The Western Pioneers and Their Discovery of Macau*. Austin Coates's *Macao and the British 1637–1842: Prelude to Hong Kong* (1966) and his *A Macao Narrative* (1978) provide vivid pictures of Macau history and society. Works in Chinese include Zhou Jianglian's 周景濂《中葡外交史》(The history of Chinese-Portuguese diplomatic relations) (1937), and Zhang Tianze's 張天澤 "Sino-Portuguese Trade from 1514–1644," a Ph.D. dissertation he wrote in Holland in 1934. The study of Macau flourished in the twentieth century,[28] and even more so at the turn of the twenty-first century. Many of these later studies are also cited in this book.

However, as mentioned above, scholars are constrained by their own background limitations. What they see and record is bound to be biased to some degree. All written materials are but a glimpse of a certain part of history and society; it can never be a full record. Every work adds to our overall understanding. It is with this humble ambition that I write this book.

This book mainly uses the historical-comparative method along with the interpretive method, drawing upon existing studies, diaries, journals, newspaper articles, interviews, and statistics. It is a sociologist's understanding of Macau's historical development. Like a historian, I also tell a story. But I am using a sociological perspective, focusing on sociopolitical issues, especially the fate of the little people and the downtrodden, and an explanation of the influencing factors. I examine especially the historical circumstances and social interaction among contemporaneous players in explaining historical and contemporary events.

A Few Words on the Second Edition

In this edition, I have deleted some information which I think is either outdated or not as important now as before. Meanwhile, I have updated and added some information which I believe to be of interest. For example, chapter 7 on social issues and problems is overhauled. Some parts are deleted and new research findings are included regarding ethnic and class stratification and politics, middle and postsecondary education, and casino-related crime and deviance.

I have also corrected a few errors and clarified some places to make the reading smoother. Furthermore, I have added a few pictures and replaced others since I think these pictures or drawings are more illuminating and enlightening.

Equally important, in writing the second edition, I have benefited from three book reviews of the first edition: César Guillén Nuñez (2012), Richard Loius Edmonds (2011), and Chan Kwok Shing (2011). One of them says that this reads like a textbook. Indeed, my intention is to make it into a textbook as well as a research project that has a theme and a set of arguments. I have strengthened the good points they commented on and tried to overcome the shortcomings. I hope I am successful in most of these efforts. I hope the reader will like the new edition.

Conclusion

A study of Macau history and society goes beyond the city itself. As Margaret MacMillan, an accomplished historian, says, in a summary by Kennedy, "history's ultimate utility does not lie in its predictive or even its explanatory value, but in its ability to teach humility, to nurture an appreciation of the limits on our capacity to see the past clearly or to know fully the historical determinants of our own brief passage in time."[29]

Macau is an intriguing place, with many processes, complexities of development as well as implications for China's evolution from a traditional society into a modern one. This study is not only about China's modernization processes in the world-historical transformations but also has implications for the clash and integration of civilizations and cultures in today's world, and for the humble limits of human capacities.

It is not an easy task to sort out all the intricacies, but the efforts are worth our while. The process itself is rewarding. Only through an exchange of ideas can we better understand the issues of our concern, individual or collective.

1 Portuguese Maritime Expansion and the State of Aomen

How Macau Came into Being

> In the morning of the following day we departed the island of Sanchan [Shangchuan] and arrived at sunset at another island called Lampacau [Langbaiao], six leagues distant on the northern coast, the place where the Portuguese entered into commerce with the Chinese, a practice that was continued until 1557 whereupon the Mandarins of Canton, at the request of the merchants, gave us the port of Macau where the commerce is now carried on, and at which place (otherwise deserted) we have strongly populated, and where can be found buildings worth three or four thousand ducats, along with a Cathedral, a priestery and its beneficiers. What is more, this colony supports its own governor, its auditor and its officers of justice, and which, it might be added, all live in security as if they were most peaceful part of Portugal.
>
> Fernão Mendez Pinto, in his *Perigrinacam* published in Lisbon in 1614 describing the Portuguese settlement in Macau[1]

While the entering into Macau by the Portuguese in Pinto's description sounds fairly peaceful, the Portuguese encounter with the Chinese in the earlier years was not so. The Portuguese who tried to settle on the China coast encountered fierce resistance, which finally led them to Macau.

Portuguese Maritime Expansion and China's Encounter with Portugal

While the Ming government was retreating from its maritime expeditions, some European countries were entering a period of merchant capitalism. Capitalist expansion began around the 16th century and continued to the late 18th century, followed by colonialism that peaked between 1850 and 1900.[2] The latter period was when China was most seriously challenged. The events of the colonial era that began with Portuguese merchant capitalism became a catalyst for Chinese nationalism, and still resonate in today's China.

The Portuguese maritime expansion began in the 15th century, when the North African Moorish city of Ceuta was conquered by Henry the Navigator (Prince Dom Henrique) and his royal brothers in 1415.³ Then the Portuguese mariners reached Madeira in 1420, Cape Bojador in 1434, Cape Branco in 1441, Cape Verde in 1445, and Gambia in 1446. Diogo Cao arrived at the mouth of Zaire in 1485, and Bartolomeu Dias sailed around the Cape of Good Hope in 1487. Vasco da Gama arrived in Calicut on the Malabar coast of India in 1498. Afonso de Albuquerque conquered Ormuz and Goa of India in 1507 and 1510 respectively. Then he took Malacca in 1511, by which he gained access to the China sea.⁴ (See Plate 1.1 for a map of the East Indies.)

In 1513, Jorge Álvares set foot on the China coast from Malacca, and his ship anchored in Tunmen (屯門, Tuen Mun or Tāmāu or Tāmão) in what is now a western part of the New Territories, Hong Kong. Álvares then based himself in Nei Lingding Island (內伶仃島) in the estuary of the Pearl River, close to Tunmen, and erected a landmark there.⁵ (See Figures 1.1 and 1.2.) As business representative of the Portuguese king, he sold spices to the Chinese, made a huge profit and left. Then in 1515, Rafael Perestrelo made the second Portuguese mission to China from Malacca, and it was equally successful. But the situation changed with the next missions.⁶

In 1517, the viceroy of Goa, Lopo Soares de Albergaria, sent a fleet of eight ships to China, led by Fernão Peres de Andrade. This was a successful expedition and the Portuguese were able to establish good relations with the Chinese, even though

Figure 1.1
Statue of Álvares in Macau. Photo by Wang Xin and Zhang Kai.

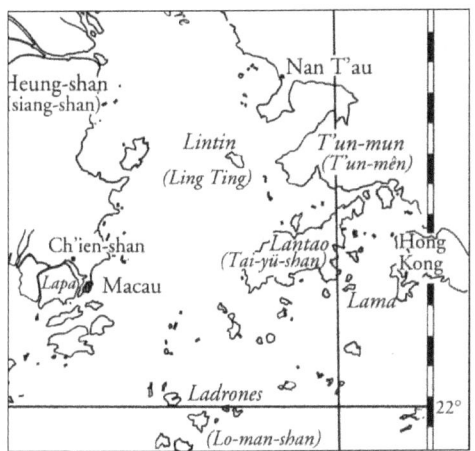

Figure 1.2
A map of Macau and Hong Kong with Tunmen and Nei Lingding (Ling Ting) Island (close to Tunmen on its left). Rui Manuel Loureiro, *Em Busca das Origens de Macau*, Macau: Museu Maritimo de Macau, 1997, p. 13.

there was some serious misunderstanding at first. When he arrived in Canton, Andrade announced his arrival by cannon fire in the harbor, contrary to Chinese customs. But he explained to the Chinese officials that these were signs of peace and goodwill. His personality and integrity finally convinced the Chinese that he meant no ill will.[7]

Along with the fleet was Tomé Pires, whom Andrade left behind after he sailed back for Lisbon in the same year. Pires came as an ambassador to Beijing to negotiate trade terms and settlements with China. He did make it to Beijing, but the mission failed because first, while Pires was in Beijing, the dethroned Sultan of Malacca also sent an envoy to Beijing to complain to the emperor about the Portuguese attack and conquest of Malacca. Malacca was part of China's suzerainty when the Portuguese took it. The Chinese were apparently not happy with what the Portuguese did there.

At the same time, the Portuguese stationed in Tunmen began to set up fortifications, attacked and looted Chinese ships, and kidnapped Chinese men and women. But the main problem may be the Portuguese purchase and enslavement of Chinese children, who had been most likely kidnapped by local criminals. The purchase and enslavement were done by men led by Andrade's younger brother, Simão de Andrade in 1518–19.[8] By that time, Fernão Peres de Andrade had already returned to Lisbon with triumph. So the Chinese arrested Pires on his way back to Guangzhou, and he died in prison there in 1524.[9] The Portuguese were eventually expelled from Tunmen in 1521 and the authorities in Beijing and Guangzhou announced a ban on trade with the Portuguese.

This ban was followed by bloody encounters between the Chinese and Portuguese. A Portuguese fleet of several ships came to China again in April or May of 1521. The Ming court ordered the Guangdong authorities to expel the Portuguese. Led by Wang Hong 汪鋐, the Ming naval forces engaged in battles against the Portuguese and won. Many Portuguese were captured and endured horrific execution, rather than surrendering. More ships came in the following months and fought the Chinese, but failed. In the end of October, they retreated to Malacca after many casualties. This was the Battle of Tunmen (屯門海戰).[10]

In 1522, a fleet of six ships and 300 men led by Martim Afonso de Melo Coutinho came to China. They encountered and fought the Chinese naval forces in Xicaowan, an area in Xin'an county in what is Bao'an county of Shenzhen close to Hong Kong. In the military conflict with the Chinese, however, dozens of them were captured, and some were executed.[11] The Battle of Xicaowan (西草灣之戰) frustrated the Portuguese so much that they decided to try other places. These are the places mentioned by Pinto in the quote at the beginning of the chapter: Shangchuan (or Sanchan), Langbaiao (Lampacau), and finally Macau.

Portuguese Arrival in Shangchuan and Langbajiao before Macau

Shangchuan Island (上川) is part of what is now the city of Taishan. As seen on the map in Figure 1.3 of Shangchuan, Langbaijiao, Macau, and Hong Kong, it is one of the two islands below the city. This is where the Jesuit St. Francisco Xavier stayed for a short while. He hoped to go to the mainland, but died of illness in 1552 and was initially buried on the island.[12] His corpse was later transferred to Goa in 1554. It is still on view there—allegedly incorrupt—in a transparent casket. On Shangchuan the Portuguese traded with the Chinese from 1549 to 1553 despite the government's ban on trade.[13] Bribery of the Chinese officials played a role in the practice.[14]

Langbajiao (浪白滘, sometimes as Langbaiao 浪白澳; Lampacau or Lampakau in Portuguese) was another trading place for the Portuguese from 1553–57. It was in what is now Nanshui Zhen (南水鎮), a town in the south-west of Zhuhai, and west of Sanzao in Zhuhai, 30 miles from Macau, and closer to Macau than Shangchuan. By 1555, there were already 400 Portuguese and five priests in Langbajiao.[15] At the same time that the Portuguese were in Langbajiao, they also visited Macau. Hence the story of Macau.

The Name, Place, and People of Macau in Earlier Times

The story goes that when the Portuguese traders first came to Macau in 1553, they encountered some local people and asked what this place was called. The locals thought that they were asking about the temple, and told them it was "Ma Kok," or "Ma Kok Temple." (See Plate 1.2 for a later version of the temple.)[16] So "Ma Kok" in Fujianese became "Macau" in Portuguese, according to most accounts.[17] "Macau" at the time refers to the Macau peninsula, not including the islands of Taipa and Coloane. Plate 1.3 depicts a giant rock inside the Temple of Goddess A-Ma, engraved with an ancient Chinese ship. This is regarded as testimony to the Portuguese landing in Macau; some call it the "landing point of Westerners."[18]

Portuguese Maritime Expansion and the State of Aomen   13

The map in Plate 1.4 depicts the shape of the peninsula in the eyes of foreign visitors in the 18th century. Compare it with the map of Macau in the 20th century in Figure 1.4, which already includes the two outlying islands connected to one another (see Figure 1.5), and one will see how much the shape and land area of the city have changed. Apparently, when the Portuguese landed in Macau, it was a much smaller place. Much of the land we see now is the result of either the accumulation of silt from the Xijiang (or the West River) and the Pearl River, or land reclamation.[19]

Situated at the south-western tip of the mouth of the Pearl River, Macau provides an excellent gateway to Guangzhou. It is also close to Xijiang, another waterway to the inner cities like Zhaoqing in Guangdong, where the Jesuits later established a base for the missions in China. Xijiang also leads to various other parts of Guangxi.[20] (See Figure 1.3.) In addition, the waterways also connect to Dongjiang (the East River) and Beijiang (the Northern River), which lead to other parts of southern China. Indeed, it is not only a gateway to Guangdong, but to the most prosperous parts of China as well.

Another reason for the Portuguese to like Macau is its other name, *shi zi men* or 十字門, i.e., "the gate of the cross." This refers to the geographical formation of the waterway with the big and small Hengqin Islands on the west and the Islands of Taipa and Coloane to the east. The waterway formed a cross, which is the Chinese

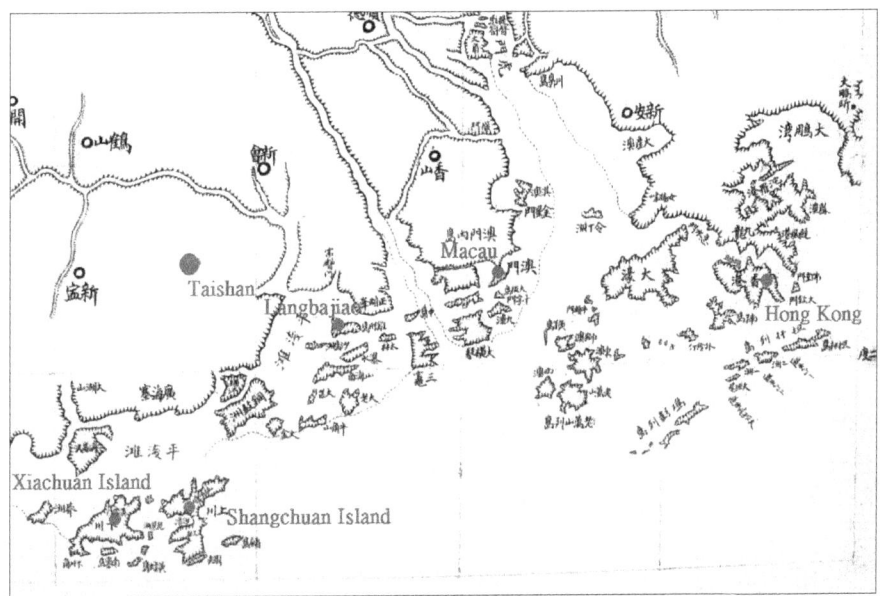

Figure 1.3

Shangchuan, Langbaijiao, Macau, and Hong Kong. 中國第一歷史檔案館、澳門一國兩制研究中心,《澳門歷史地圖精選》, 北京: 華文出版社, 2001, p. 91, with English names added by Benny Tam.

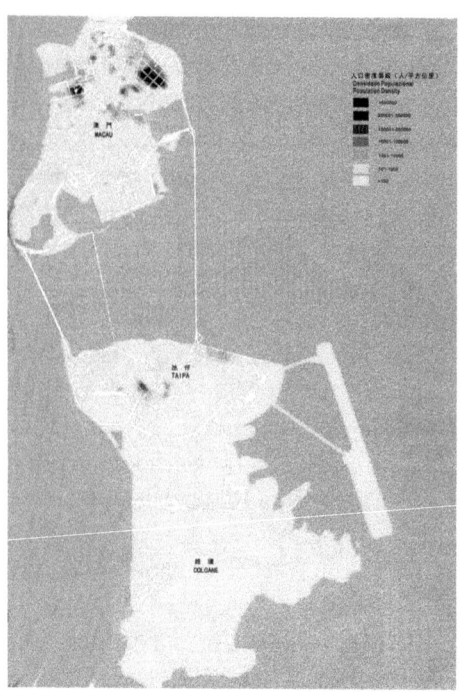

Figure 1.4
A contemporary map of Macau. Wong Chao Son, Deng Hanzeng, and Huang Junxin, *Macau Atlas*, Macau: Macao Foundation, 1997, p. 2.

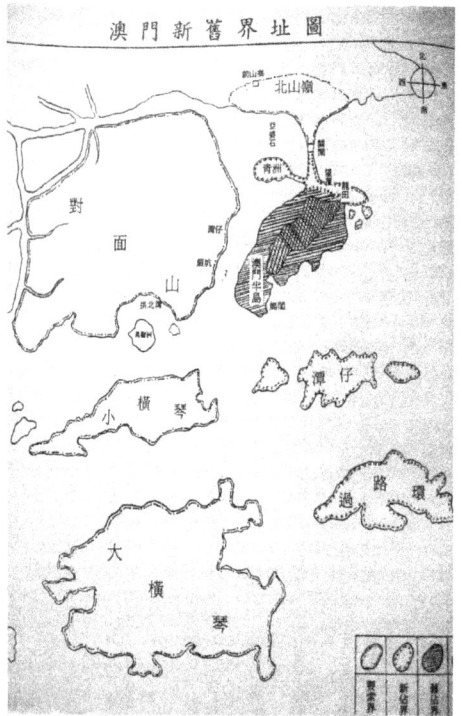

Figure 1.5
A map of Macau in the early 20th century. *Atlas of Macao*, Macau: Cartography and Cadastre Bureau of Macao Special Administrative Region Government, 2003, p. 63.

character 十. (See Figure 1.5.) This cross is also an emblem of Christianity, a suitable symbol for the Portuguese coming to Macau, as if it was a God-chosen place for them.[21]

Archeological findings indicate that there had been Chinese people and human activities since the Han dynasty (206 B.C.E.–220 C.E.) in the peninsula and the two islands, Taipa and Coloane. According to Jin Guoping and Wu Zhiliang, the aborigines of Macau should be the Yao (傜) people, with two branches, She (佘) and Dan (蛋 or 蜑).[22] The Dan people lived on the waters and made a living by fishing.

In addition, when the Mongols conquered China and established the Yuan dynasty (1206–1368), the remnants of the Song dynasty (960–1279) fought the Yuan army over the waters of Taipa in 1277. Here is a poem that was written by a Ming dynasty (1368–1644) scholar Huang Yu 黃瑜 depicting the battle and the tragedy of the events at the time.[23]

悲井澳 (The Sorrow in Jing Ao)
白雁過，江南破，更無一寸土可坐。自閩入廣隨波流，氣塵暗天天亦愁。
黃蘆霾岸風颼颼，上有井澳，下有仙女澳，漁舟不往禦舟到。風吹禦舟，
力排舁，嗟嗟悲哉誰與告。……

The poem relates the story of the emperor of the South Song dynasty in his last days. It says that the land was lost and the emperor did not have a place to stay. His ships drifted to the waters of Macau from Fujian and Guangdong, being chased by the Yuan army. It describes the misery and the sadness of the day, with the wind beating the ships and men struggling to hold it stable. The poet laments that the emperor's ships came to a place where the fishermen's boats might not even want to go.[24] (That is, of course, exaggeration, as there were fishing people.)

You might notice that the poet uses "jing ao" to refer to Macau, which was one of the Chinese names for Macau. It was only later that the Chinese name became *ao men* (澳門), or the gate of *ao*, or *shi zi men* (十字門), which refers to the formation of the islands of the big and small Hengqin, Taipa, and Coloane that resembles a gate, as mentioned above. "Ao" here means a port. So literally *ao men* means "port gate," or the "gate of the port."[25]

Wen Tianxiang 文天祥 (1236–83), a famous poet, patriot, and general, wrote the famous poem while fighting the Yuan army in this area, "Guo Lingding Yang" (過零丁洋, Passing the Lingding ocean) in 1279:

辛苦遭逢起一經，干戈寥落四周星。
山河破碎風飄絮，身世沉浮雨打萍。
惶恐灘頭說惶恐，零丁洋裏歎零丁。
人生自古誰無死，留取丹心照汗青。

He is depicting the last days of the Song dynasty with him leading the last few battles. The poem illustrates his determination to serve the emperor and the Chinese nation until his death, even if he was faced with a broken country, personal misfortunes, and an uncertain future. He was captured after a battle and, refusing to surrender, he was executed a few years later. Since then the poem, especially the last two lines, "From time immemorial is there anybody who would not die? But one's death is worthwhile if his valor and loyalty can be recorded in history," has become one of the most remembered poems in China, and Wen one of the most celebrated Han Chinese national heroes.

In a word, when the Portuguese came to Aomen, there were already inhabitants who had an interesting history as part of Xiangshan county.[26]

The Establishment of the Portuguese Settlements in Macau

The Portuguese traders who came to Macau were able to establish a settlement, even though the Chinese government banned trade with foreigners and expelled them from Tunmen and other areas of China. Chinese history books record that Portuguese traders came to Macau in 1553 and asked the authorities to allow them to dry their cargos here. Given the restrictions they faced at the time, they had to bribe the chief official Wang Bo 汪柏 to be allowed entry (although there are disputes as to whether Wang accepted the bribe).[27] The bribe eventually became a yearly rent of 500 silver dollars, according to some historical records (see Plate 8.1). More and more Portuguese came, and they established a "colony" of some kind.

However, the reasons for allowing the Portuguese to stay were more than just bribery,[28] as there were political, military, and economic considerations. Politically, it would make sense to allow the Portuguese to stay so that they could become a force in helping the Chinese government deal with other foreigners and the pirates in the area.[29] As Coates observes, "the Portuguese were installed at the mouth of the river somewhat in the capacity of a filter, without passing through which no outsider could make contact with the Chinese."[30] As for the pirates, the report by a French royal official and scientist who traveled in this area in the late 1700s says, "The Chinese armed a fleet together with the Portuguese force but simply remained spectators. The Portuguese won battle upon battle, and finally purged the area of the fearsome pirates."[31]

Militarily, the Chinese were already very weak at the time, and it would have been hard to really expel the foreigners out of China. They were here to stay and the Chinese had to find a way to accommodate them. The Ming dynasty was especially weakened by the military conflicts with uprisings of Bai Lian Jiao in Shandong, with Mongolians in the north-east of China, as well as with Japan over Korea.[32]

Economically, the taxes from foreign trade had been an important source of government income. Indeed, in 1535, the Ming government had already stationed officials in Macau to take care of foreign trade. So the Chinese ban on trade had to be more in name than in reality. One more important reason that may be related to "economy" was the emperor's needs of ambergris (龍涎香), which was used as a component for Chinese medicine of longevity. The most effective way to obtain ambergris was from the Portuguese.[33]

The Portuguese had an economic reason, too. As Pires points out, the "driving forces behind the establishment of the Portuguese empire were of a religious and of an economic nature."[34] Economically, there were huge profits to be made in the China trade. Despite the dangers, risks, labor, violence, deprivation, disease, and the Chinese suspicion of all things foreign, the Portuguese felt that life was better here than the misery and poverty of the kingdom of Portugal. One Portuguese document of 1566 said that the region was extremely fertile, rich, and provided plenty of opportunities. In addition, the missionaries who came along with the traders had a mission here in Macau, and in China, to accomplish.[35]

So between 1553 and 1557, the Portuguese traders and missionaries established themselves in Macau. Thus began the cooperation and conflicts among the Chinese, Portuguese, Dutch, British, Americans, and others in the following years.

Conclusion

Merchant capitalism came to China in the 16th century unlike any other forces in the past. The Chinese were learning to cope with armed and aggressive traders from the West. To use Teng's and Fairbank's words, "faced with the aggressive expansion of the modern West," China was trying to "understand an alien civilization and take action to preserve their own culture and their political and social institutions."[36] As the quote we cited at the beginning of the Introduction says, the bourgeois society was to make a huge impact on traditional societies everywhere.

A Macau Chinese historian, K. C. Fok, uses the term "Macau formula" to refer to the strategy the Ming dynasty used to control foreigners and at the same time profit from foreign trade. On the one hand, the foreigners were confined to a small area so that it was easier for the Chinese government to deal with them: they could just close the border and the foreigners would have to yield to their demands. On the other hand, the foreigners could still do their business in Macau and the Chinese could still get tax incomes.[37] The idea of "using barbarians to control barbarians" (以夷制夷) was both a defensive and passive model. It worked to some extent but was not liked by foreigners other than the Portuguese. It is different from the Macau model we will develop in chapter 4 regarding the social interaction of civilizations, although one might argue that there is a relationship between the two models. This Macau model would turn out to be a better one for the Chinese than the Hong Kong model, as we will see in the next chapter. At any rate, more serious challenges lay ahead, and the Macau experience was only the beginning of the troubles for the Chinese.

2 Macau's Politics
Then and Now

In the park of a residential neighborhood behind Lisbon airport, one comes across the bronze statue of a man on horseback. [See Plate 2.1 for the statue when it was in Macau.] The horse is rearing and the man, with a fierce expression, has his left arm twisted across him in a fighting pose. The statue is far too grand for its locale.... The statue bears a plaque that reads: *João Maria Ferreira do Amaral / (1803–1849) / Illustrious soldier and Governor of Macau from 1843 to 1849 / Killed on 22 August 1849, near the gates of the Siege in Macau/ Made by Maximiliano Alves, the Statue was unveiled on 24 June 1940 / and removed from Macau in November 1991 / It represents Ferreira do Amaral defending himself from his aggressors....* Originally, however, it contained the figures of two Chinese men, represented in a smaller scale, just as they were being thrown to the ground by the Governor's spirited response.

João de Pina-Cabral on the symbolism of the statue of Amaral[1]

As Pina-Cabral observes, "In the 1940s and 1950s, Ferreira do Amaral took on the role of founding martyr for the Macanese," since he represented their claims to sovereignty over Macau. But at the same time, for the Chinese, he personified all that was wrong in the early modern Chinese history, that is, colonial aggression and domination against the Chinese by the Westerners.[2] (See Plate 2.1 for the statue.) Indeed, in the few centuries after the Portuguese established themselves in Macau, there were more political struggles among the Chinese, Portuguese, English, and other Western powers, regarding the control of Macau.

In 2004 in campaign stops for re-election to his second five-year term as the chief executive of the Macau Special Administrative Region (MSAR) of the People's Republic of China, Edmund Ho commented that in the last five years, he had been thinking about the difference between his administration and the preceding Portuguese administration. (He was unopposed in the election.) He wanted to find a way to really implement the principles of "one country, two systems" (一國兩制), "Macau governed by Macau people" (澳人治澳), and "a high degree of autonomy" (高度自治) for the MSAR. He wanted a clearer relationship between the government and the various community groups. He wanted everybody to be clear about their obligations and responsibilities.³ The legislators, on the other hand, would also like to see more coordination between the executive branch and legislative branch of the government.⁴ Ho said that he would like to work with others on such matters and even develop a theory about them.

Another fifteen years have passed, and the second chief executive is now near the end of his second term, but the problems Ho raised remain unsolved. The new head of Macau was again "elected" without a competitor. The pace of democratization is still very slow. Indeed, the purpose of this chapter is to continue to tackle Ho's questions, by examining how the politics in Macau has evolved in the past 450 years among all the players in the region. Although the current "Macau governed by Macau people" is widely preferred to the preceding colonial governments, much more needs to be done.

Macau and China in International Conflicts

Portuguese Conflicts with the Dutch

Peace dominated the first 50 years of Portuguese settlement in Macau. Then in 1601, a Dutch fleet of six ships came to Macau. Surprised to see a city with "Spanish style" buildings, they sent a boat to investigate. The Portuguese captured the boat and the 11 sailors on it. The Dutch sent another boat, and again the sailors were captured. The Portuguese then executed 17 of the captives, even though the latter tried to save their lives by becoming Roman Catholic converts at the eleventh hour. Only three were released. Since then the two countries became enemies; whenever they met on the sea, there would be a battle. In 1603, the Dutch captured *Santa Catarina*, a 1,500 ton Portuguese boat loaded with Chinese silk and porcelain, in Malacca. The sale of the goods later in Amsterdam caused quite a scene in Europe. In July of the same year the Dutch came to Macau and made a surprise attack on a ship loaded with goods. They took away with them both the boat and its cargos.⁵

In the following years, similar skirmishes continued. The most famous battle between the two was in 1622. The Dutch wanted a foothold in China, and the occupation of Macau would enable them to have a secure market around the area. They attacked Macau in 1622 with 600 men, while defending Macau were only about 150 Portuguese and Eurasian musketeers under the command of António Rodriguez. Musketeers were fighting the invading army, who boldly marched "in orderly array and with even steps along the field which borders the foot of the hill of Nossa Senhora da Guia, firing their muskets with such precision and dexterity that they aroused great admiration amongst our people in their respect," said a Jesuit eyewitness.⁶ But the Portuguese cannon shots were directed at the Dutch ships. One of the cannon shots, fired by Italian Fathers Christoforo Borri Bruno and Girolamo Rho, hit an ammunition ship. In the battle, 136 Dutch died and 126 were wounded. The Dutch retreated, and no longer attacked Macau in the following years.[7] They went on to Taiwan.

But that victory did not guarantee Macau's prosperity, and the Portuguese-Dutch conflict was more than economic. From 1580 to 1640 Portugal was under Spanish rule. The Dutch, who were largely Protestant, were at war with the Spanish, who were largely Catholic. In this political context, the Dutch took a number of Portuguese colonies including areas of Brazil, Angola, and Malacca, as part of the Dutch maritime expansion. They finally seized Malacca from the Portuguese in 1640, which greatly frustrated Portuguese trade links with Goa and leading to difficult times for the Portuguese.[8] Meanwhile, the Dutch went directly to Beijing and negotiated a trade agreement with China, although the latter allowed only one ship every eight years![9] The rivalry between the Dutch and the Portuguese did not end until the War of Spanish Succession (1702–14), when Holland and Portugal became allies. Dutch ships began to call at Taipa regularly, and Portuguese vessels were able to sail to Timor and India without the fear of a Dutch attack.[10]

Conflicts among the Portuguese, English, and Chinese

In June of 1637, the first British fleet of four ships led by Captain John Weddell came to Macau and anchored around what are now Taipa and Coloane, then rocky and grass-covered islands.[11] The English came to meet the Portuguese on the Macau peninsula. They marveled at the magnificent, newly built St. Paul's Cathedral, and were impressed with women wearing Malay sarongs of splendid colors and designs or kimonos, reflecting Portuguese trade and contact with Malacca and Japan. There was only one Portuguese woman in Macau at the time.[12] But the English were not impressed with the Portuguese captain-general's reply that they could not assist the English in their intended trip to Canton to obtain a trade license.[13]

Weddell decided to take matters into his own hands, and sailed without pilots up north. They came to Humen (Bocca Tigris) only to be informed by the Chinese officials that they had to go back to Macau to apply to the Chinese officials there for permission to go to Canton for trade purposes, or at least they had to wait there for them to report to the higher authorities. They waited and were served *cha* or tea, probably the first time they tasted something that would become a major item in international trade. But permission still did not come, so the English decided to push their way up. The Chinese stationed at the fort opened fire, but they were overpowered by the English. Several skirmishes like this happened in the following months. The English delegations finally met the Chinese authorities, and some trade was done. When the English stayed in Humen, they seized junks, raided villages for livestock and provisions, and murdered a number of Chinese. The Portuguese again got involved in the negotiations with the Chinese, and the latter blamed the former for allowing the English to come in. But all was to no avail. The English finally left China and Macau in December. The first English trading voyage to China did not achieve much.

While the Portuguese might have had an interest in protecting its monopoly over the China trade, the Chinese simply wanted no more foreigners in China. For several decades thereafter, China would see only a few English voyages. The most notable was the voyage of the English ship, *Defence*, led by William Heath, which came to Macau in 1689 and clashed with the Chinese. In the skirmish, one person from each side died, and some were wounded.[14]

In 1685, Kangxi, the Qing emperor, decided to open China's ports to foreigners, and in an edict in 1692 he also tolerated Christianity. Both edicts were probably a result of influence from Jesuit fathers. Father Adam Schall von Bell tutored Kangxi when he was a still a boy. Schall von Bell's successor, Father Ferdinand Verbiest, became the president of the Board of Astronomy in 1676 and also had some influence on the emperor. The British East India Company saw that there was some opening in China trade and sent their ship *Macclesfield* to the Pearl River in 1699. Thereafter the East India Company sent more ships to Canton, Xiamen (Amoy), Fuzhou (Foochow), and Ningbo. Their tonnage dues were determined at Macau, and they mostly sold woolen cloth and bought silk.[15]

In 1733, however, the emperor Yongzheng wanted all foreign trade again to go through Macau. But he died in two years and it would take some time for his son Emperor Qianlong to make a decision. Meanwhile, a British warship led by Captain George Anson came to visit Macau in 1742 and wanted to sail upstream for repairs. The Portuguese in Macau refused Anson's passage, citing that they needed to pay dues and seek permission from the governor of Guangdong. Anson refused to follow their instructions, and got his provisions and repairs twice in the few months in the Pearl River.[16]

In 1792, the British sent George Macartney as an ambassador to China. He was to ask the Chinese for rights similar to those enjoyed by the Portuguese in Macau, including the cession of an island at Zhoushan (Chusan) in Zhejiang province.[17] He was also to ask for free trade at Canton, including purchasing Chinese goods at market price from whomever they chose. He did meet Qianlong, but he got nothing from him except a gift of his calligraphy work. At that time, the Chinese empire still did not accept the idea of an embassy. Qianlong warned the British not to think of taking possession of any Chinese land.[18]

But the British refused to give up. At one point in 1801, the British were thinking about asking the Portuguese to surrender Macau to them. When that idea was dropped, the British troops forced their way into Macau in 1808, led by Rear-Admiral William Drury, in the name of protecting their interests in China, and of "defending" Macau from possible French and Spanish attacks. The Portuguese thought that it would be futile for them to fight the British so they allowed them to station in Macau but under the condition that the Portuguese flag would fly. The Chinese government was not happy, and was preparing its troops to fight the British. Meanwhile, the Chinese in Macau also fled the city. Drury was thinking about fighting his way to Canton, but abandoned the idea under pressure from the East India Company, for they were afraid of losing their interests in China with such a war. Drury finally withdrew his troops from Macau. A war between the Chinese and the British was avoided, and the Portuguese Macau survived.[19]

The First Opium War

When the opium crisis came, things were beginning to change in some ways. Opium was made contraband in 1729 and 1799 by Emperors Yongzheng and Jiaqing respectively.[20] But Britons, Americans, Portuguese, and other Europeans continued to deal in it, and the Chinese officials continued to share privately the profit made in it while openly condemning the drug. Meanwhile, more Chinese were smoking opium, and the demand far exceeded the supply. Both the Americans and the Britons developed new fast vessels to meet the need. Macau and the islands in Lingding became opium depots for the merchants and the amount of opium reaching China by 1838 increased to 40,000 chests from 20,486 in the 1833–34 season. High government officials like Lin Zexu clearly saw a danger brought forth by opium in national health and morality and in the drain of silver. They submitted memorials advocating the ban of opium. After some hesitation, Emperor Daoguang decided to take action and appointed Lin Zexu as the imperial high commissioner for the job.

Lin then ordered the foreign merchants to surrender all their opium and sign a bond pledging not to bring any more opium to China. Everyone, including the Americans, signed the bond except the British led by Charles Elliot. Elliot, however, did make British merchants surrender more opium than the latter would have liked. But he did not want to sign the bond, knowing that it would be impossible for the British not to continue with the drug trade.

Lin finally threatened that if the British did not sign the bond, he would attack their ships in the Hong Kong harbor. At that time, although no houses were built in Hong Kong, the British had already used it as a place to anchor their ships. Lin said he would surround the British houses in Macau as well. Elliot led two warships to Humen, demanding that the Chinese withdraw their threat. Having not received an answer from the Chinese, Elliot decided to attack the Chinese naval force led by Guan Tianpei. The First Opium War thus broke out in 1839.

In the first engagement in Humen near Canton, or the Battle of Chuanbi (Chuenpe, 川鼻), several Chinese war-junks were sunk, and the British withdrew to Macau to evacuate the British there as well as those in Kowloon to islands off the waters of Hong Kong. The Portuguese governor of Macau refused to allow

British goods to be stored there, and allowed Chinese posters in Macau inciting the Chinese to kill Britons. Lin Zexue, now succeeding Deng Tingzhen as the governor of Guangdong and Guangxi, began to train his soldiers and build up arms for more engagement with the British.

Meanwhile, London sent to Elliot a reinforcement force of 3 battleships, 14 frigates and sloops, 4 armed steamers, and about 4,000 British and Indian troops conveyed aboard 27 troopships, a force led by Sir James John Gordon Bremer.[21] In June 1840, Bremer declared a blockade of Canton, sailed northward to take Dinghai (Tinghai) of Zhoushan (Chusan) Islands in Zhejiang, came to Tianjin, and presented to Qishan, the governor of Zhili, the British dispatch for his transmission to Beijing. The emperor agreed to negotiate with the British in Guangzhou, and the British agreed to withdraw their troops except those in Zhoushan. Lin Zexu was dismissed for his radical measures to deal with the British, which caused them to go north to threaten Beijing. Qishan took his place and was given the difficult task of negotiating with the British, with Lin as one of his advisors, although he might not have listened to his advice.[22]

In the negotiations, Elliot again demanded the cession of an island, but was refused. So he launched the second Battle of Chuanbi at Humen in January 1841. In this battle 18 Chinese war junks were sunk, 500 Chinese soldiers were killed, and 300 wounded, while the British had only 38 wounded and none killed.[23] (See Plate 2.2 for an example of the battle in the First Opium War.) The Chinese offered the cession of Hong Kong to the British and an indemnity for the seized opium, but the British would still have to pay dues to the Chinese empire upon the commerce there. However, neither the British merchants nor the Chinese authorities were happy with the terms. So a third Battle of Chuanbi broke out in February 1841. A large number of Chinese were killed, including Admiral Guan Tianpei. Qishan was dismissed and led in chains to Beijing. The British advanced close to Canton and were ready for a full assault on the city. The traders and opium ships followed. In the ensuing battles, over 100 Chinese war junks and fireships were sunk. This led to the signing of the Treaty of Canton, under which the Chinese had to pay over $6,000,000 for the ransom of Canton and as an indemnity for British losses.

This was when the village peasant uprisings, represented by those in Sanyuanli, occurred. Some British troops went into the villages to the north-west of the city and looted for food and provisions. They broke into houses, attacked women, and even opened tombs. Thousands of peasants went up in arms in spears, shields, and swords. Only one British soldier was killed, although a dozen were seriously wounded.[24]

Knowing that the cession of Hong Kong would not be approved by the emperor, Elliot did not raise the issue in the Treaty of Canton. Instead, when he returned to Macau, he encouraged the British to move to Hong Kong and settle there, as if he had already obtained the place. He began to sell the land in Hong Kong to traders.

Despite the strike of malaria in June and a big typhoon in July of 1841 that blew the roof tops off all their houses, the British stayed.

But London was not satisfied with the Treaty of Canton, thinking that the indemnities were not large enough to cover their losses in the surrendered opium. "Even the Queen expressed surprised amusement that her representative in China should have presented her with a scarcely-populated, barren granite rock."[25] So Elliot was dismissed, and his successor, Sir Henry Pottinger, launched another battle to take over Xiamen (Amoy), Chinhai, Ningbo, and Zhoushan in August 1841. This was a bloody process. In Ningbo, for example, the British "scoured the countryside, … put houses to the torch, … brought suspects back tied together by their tails.… Whole sections of the city were gutted; the rest assumed a more and more desolate and abandoned air."[26] In one occasion, "Two British sailors and a soldier about fifty yards apart from each other formed the points of a triangle, in which some six or eight Chinese were running helplessly about over the paddy fields, some disarmed and others with swords in their hands. Our three men were loading and firing at them as coolly as if they were crows, and bayoneting to death those who fell wounded." When one officer tried to stop them, they did not pay attention. Another soldier came up, took a shot himself, and said, "If we don't kill them now, Sir, they will fight us again, and we shall never finish the war."[27]

By April 1842, the British troops occupied Wusung and Shanghai. In July they captured Zhenjiang on the Yangtze River, and continued to Nanjing. The Chinese troops had put on a fierce fight in Zhenjiang. They would have rather died than surrender or run. With bodies lying about the streets, the English soldiers looted and partially burned the city. Local Chinese also joined in the looting and burning. When the troops left, "the desolation and the stench of death far exceeded anything experienced at Ningbo or at any other place."[28] The Chinese failed again. In August 1842, the Treaty of Nanjing was signed, ceding Hong Kong to the British, no taxes or dues to be paid to the Chinese, and opening the ports of Canton, Xiamen, Fuzhou, Ningbo, and Shanghai. In addition, an indemnity of $21,000,000 was to be paid to the British by the Chinese government. The First Opium War ended.

The Second Opium War

The Second Opium War broke out in 1856 and lasted until 1860 between China on one hand and the British and the French on the other, with the close support of the United States and Russia.[29] The Western powers "demanded eleven new treaty ports, unlimited travel in the interior, the right of envoys to live in Peking, more territory near Hong Kong, the legalization of opium, the protection of missionaries, and the inevitable indemnities."[30] They seized the Dagu (Taku) forts close to Tianjin in 1858 and negotiated the Treaty of Tianjin with the Chinese. But Emperor Xianfeng (Hsien-feng) rejected the treaty upon his advisors' suggestions and decided

Macau's Politics

Figure 2.1
Part of Yuan Ming Yuan after being looted and burned in the Second Opium War. 黃韜朋, 黃鍾駿, 圓明園, Hong Kong: Joint Publishing Co. (HK), 1985, p. 26.

to fight the allied armies. The Chinese failed again and the allied soldiers advanced to Beijing unopposed. The emperor fled Beijing, and the invaders decided to put torch to the 200 pagodas and pleasure pavilions of Yuan Ming Yuan as a punishment for him (see Figure 2.1). "The fires burned across those ten square miles of the Summer Palace for two days, and the skies over Peking grew black with the pall of smoking lacquer."[31] A British chaplain serving the expedition wrote, while justifying the barbarity: "whenever I think of beauty and taste, of skill and antiquity, while I live, I shall see before my mind's eye some scene from those grounds, those palaces, and ever regret the stern but just necessity which laid them in ashes."[32] The treaty was finally ratified.[33]

The Reasons for China's Defeat

Why did China not force itself upon Europe in the Ming dynasty with its superior civilization, technology, and commerce, rather than being forced upon by the Europeans?[34] First, the forces of merchant capitalist expansion were one of the main reasons for the Westerners to come to China and want to stay. (The same is still true today.) But not actually knowing what was happening in the world, the Chinese were not ready to accommodate the new world situation. It is true that during the

Yongle reign of the Ming dynasty, the Chinese were able to send enormous fleets to Southeast Asia, India, and East Africa. Kangxi was also open-minded when he hired Jesuits in his court, allowed foreign trade, and tolerated Christianity. But these seemed to be only moments of openness in the several hundred years of the Ming and Qing history, rather than a long-term policy, nor were they far-reaching enough.

Since the mid-Ming court, the Chinese "maintained an inward-looking and defensive posture with regard to foreign relations and was uninterested in the opportunities for trade and diplomacy abroad that the early Ming had begun to explore." That was why Liu Ta-hsia (1437–1516), one of Ming's ministers of war, had copies of Zheng He's expeditionary charts burned.[35] If the knowledge Zheng He accumulated regarding seafaring and foreign matters was not lost in society, it was certainly not used much. This inward-looking mentality and defensive posture largely continued in the Qing dynasty, except for the previously mentioned moments in Kangxi's reign. The following message Emperor Qianlong sent to Britain's King George III is very illuminating:

> We possess all things. I set no value on object strange or ingenious, and have no use for your country's manufactures…. It behooves you, O King, to respect my sentiments and to display even greater devotion and loyalty in future, so that, by perpetual submission to our Throne, you may secure peace and prosperity for your country forever.[36]

In Fairbank's and Reischauer's terms, this is a mentality of Chinese cultural superiority combined with a Chinese ethnocentrism and xenophobia. While the Chinese closed themselves off from the world, the West was going through a dynamic rise: "the Renaissance, the Reformation, the growth of national states, their expansion into the New World and over the earth, followed by the French Revolution and the Industrial Revolution."[37] As Coates comments, "while Europe had been steadily rising, China was standing still."[38] This mentality effectively kept China in the dark of what was happening in the rest of the world. Indeed, the Westerners found that they had to convince the emperors that "Zhongguo," or "the middle kingdom," was actually neither the center of the world nor the only civilized nation in the world.[39] They cannot treat others as barbarians, as the word *yi* or *fan* (夷 or 蕃) indicates they did.

But because of this mentality, China's strategy in dealing with the Westerners was to keep them away as far as possible. When the Chinese found that it could not totally expel the Portuguese, they decided to allow them to stay in Macau. They would manage them as they did the *fan fang* (蕃坊) in the past. This was a smart move for some time. The Chinese way of "using barbarians to control barbarians" seemed to work. Indeed, if the Portuguese had not been in Macau in the early 17th century, the Chinese would have had to deal with a possible Dutch invasion. It was not clear if the Chinese would have won as the Portuguese did. But the Macau model was only a defensive one.[40]

As it turned out, the Macau model would not satisfy all the Westerners. Other Western powers wanted to break the Portuguese monopoly and to trade with China directly, rather than through Macau, in what they believed to be equal terms. Like Tomé Pires, the Portuguese representative to China in 1517, they wanted to send an embassy to Beijing. But like Pires, they also failed. The British wanted a place like Macau, and they failed. Finally the Opium Wars forced China to open its doors, and the Western powers obtained what they wanted. The two wars resulted in not only the cession of Hong Kong, but also the renting of many other small Macaus, called "concessions," in the mainland port cities. China thus went through a long and painful learning process of several hundred years,[41] during which both wars with the foreign powers and the civil wars plagued the county. It was not until the end of the 20th century that China had begun to merge with the world in some serious ways.

The second most important reason for China's failure in the Ming and Qing dynasties was apparently structural. The monarchical system was so corrupt that it was impossible for it to make effective decisions and carry them out. The Chinese law, at least as it appeared to the British, was rudimentary, and was enforced with whims and caprice. When it was applied to foreigners, it would cause a lot of resentment among those whose laws were different, especially when it concerned a death penalty.[42]

Taking bribes so as not to strictly enforce rules, for example, in the opium prohibition campaign, was the norm.[43] That was one of the reasons why the Yongzheng and Jiaqing emperors' orders made little or no effect. As Teng and Fairbank comment, in such a political structure, officials "were more interested in profit to themselves than progress for their country."[44]

The Daoguang emperor's appointment of Lin Zexu as the imperial high commissioner might be one of the few good decisions. Lin did an effective job by vigorously studying Western things[45] and seriously carried out his mission. But the Qing army was unable to fight an effective war. They lacked both weapons and training. While the English soldiers used guns, many Chinese soldiers still used bows and arrows, spears and halberds. If they used muskets, these were crudely made and of small caliber. The gunpowder was coarse and inferior. More importantly, the organization of the armies was problematic: there was no clear chain of command.[46] The military and political systems were both corrupt.

Speaking of the lack of ships and guns, Lin Zexu lamented in one of his letters to a friend:

> I recall that after I had been punished two years ago, I still took the risk of calling the Emperor's attention to two things: ships and guns. At that time, if these things could have been made and prepared, they still could have been used with effective fight against the enemy in Zhejiang last fall [1841].... After all, ships, guns, and a water force are absolutely indispensable. Even if the rebellious barbarians had fled and returned beyond the seas, these things would still have to be urgently planned

for, in order to work out the permanent defense of our sea frontier. Moreover, unless we have weapons, what other help can we get now to drive away the crocodile and to get rid of the whales?[47]

Of course, Lin still possessed the Chinese mentality of cultural superiority, but his strategy to build up arms was an important one. The emperor, however, did not think the same. Lin was dismissed, rather than promoted, for his role in the campaign to suppress opium. Later, Empress Dowager even used the money meant for building a navy to build her enormous garden, Yi He Yuan. It is true that the higher officials like Li Hongzhang and Zhang Zhidong made great efforts to build up arms in the self-strengthening movement after the Opium War. But all was too little and too late.

Scholars like Feng Guifen (1809–74) also advocated learning from the West, especially solid ships and effective guns, and treating "barbarians" with sincerity and respect, since they were persons of good faith.[48] Not that they are naturally trustworthy, but they appeal to reason and understand the importance of faith. As Guo Songtao, a diplomat and ambassador to Britain in 1877 and the first ambassador to the West, wrote in 1884 about foreigners and the Chinese attitudes toward them,

> We have noticed that they do not speak lightly of war but argue with us back and forth, leaving themselves ample leeway to seek in each instance some advantage. If, on account of the fact that they do not speak of warfare easily, we goad them into acting with outrageous violence, then there will be a great deal of harm. Once warfare has been resorted to, the military expense they incur will eventually be sought from us as an indemnity ... Of all the officials in and outside the capital, there is not a single one who is versed in foreign affairs. All they do is cautiously watch the intention of the court and show their zeal for war. The officials in charge of frontier troops are also accustomed to the old habits of military camps and make falsely exaggerated reports, which are all mere fabrications that avoid mentioning defeat but report success without a single sentence that can be verified.[49]

Guo might be too idealistic about foreigners, but the problems he illustrated seem to reflect fairly well what frequently happened in China's interaction with the West.[50] By the end of the Qing dynasty, China's Maritime Customs revenue was fully used to pay foreign loans and indemnities.[51] The modernization achievements made by Robert Hart,[52] the former inspector-general of the Maritime Customs, were now used to meet the needs of foreigners rather than those of the Chinese. But Guo was dismissed for his politics.[53] So politically the monarchical system was as corrupt as the military. In fact, some of the same problems still plague the Chinese government now over 150 years later, though to a much lesser extent than before.

The realization that China must learn from the West and strengthen itself in every way came very late, and the efforts China took to transform the system were too little to avoid further humiliations in the 1895 war against Japan, which resulted in the cession of Taiwan to Japan, and the 1900 war of the allied forces marching into Beijing to suppress the Boxers. These losses contributed to the rationale for the Nationalist revolution led by Sun Yat-sen in order to establish a democratic republic and Communist revolution led by Mao Zedong. Only 150 years after the Opium War would China appear strong enough to merge with the world economy and compete with other world powers and global trends, although its political system remains plagued by similar problems. We will now come back to the example of Macau in the global context.

The Senado Period and the Dual Jurisdiction (1583–1783)

There are three main periods in discussing the political history of Macau in the context of international conflicts examined above: 1) the Senado, or the Senate, period (1583–1783); 2) the colonial period (1849–1976); and 3) the Chinese Macau period (1999–present).[54] Two issues stand out in these periods of Macau's history: prolonged dispute on the issue of sovereignty, and consistent development toward a more democratic form of government.

Sovereignty and Democratization in Macau

Sovereignty is a complex issue with internal and external dimensions. Internal sovereignty refers to a state's power and authority to control its population and borders, to set policies regarding development, and to determine exchange rates and taxation policies within the state. External sovereignty refers to the state's power and authority to represent the state in international organizations, establish diplomatic relations with other countries, and negotiate and sign treaties.[55]

Some say that sovereignty is absolute, and like individual freedom, cannot be shared.[56] Others say that sovereignty is always relative, so there can be joint or shared sovereignty. David Held says that "the operation of states in an ever more complex international system both limits their autonomy (in some spheres radically) and impinges increasingly upon their sovereignty."[57]

The history of Macau's sovereignty question is what Clayton calls "a long tangle of disputed claims and unspoken assumptions that have sometimes resulted in military showdowns, but more often been swept under the rug of diplomacy."[58] Portugal's history books used to maintain that China had ceded Macau to Portugal in return for the latter's military assistance in fending the pirates in the area. It was said that there was even some kind of tangible proof, like a golden plate, or an engraved stone tablet, or an illuminated scroll, or a silk banner that the emperor gave the Portuguese granting the land to them, but that it was somehow lost in history.[59] The Portuguese Constitution of 1822 also claimed that Macau was an integral part of Portugal's territory,[60] or at least the Portuguese thought they had sovereignty over Macau after the 1887 treaty, when China gave Portugal the right for perpetual occupation and governance.

The Chinese also claimed that they had sovereignty over Macau before, but lost it after 1887.[61] Indeed, the Portuguese government had governed Macau, at least tried to, as if it had sovereignty over the land.

The typical Portuguese opinion now, however, seems to be that by and large Macau's sovereign status was ambiguous. The Chinese had always had sovereignty over Macau, but the Portuguese managed the city. Or from 1974 on, the Portuguese gave up sovereignty over Macau and retained only the right to manage it. Macau then ceased to be a colony. But up until 1999, the Macanese had been citizens of Macau, not of China. Or from the signing of the 1887 treaty to the 1999 return of Macau to China, Portugal had more sovereignty in Macau, but other than that, Portugal had mainly only some administrative power.[62] Overall the sovereignty of Macau was divided, to say the least, and therefore ambiguous.

This somewhat converges with the dominant Chinese opinion that China never gave the sovereignty of Macau to the Portuguese. In the Senado period, for example, Chinese exercised, to a great extent, rights over the land use, administrative rights, legal rights, and the customs rights. Even after the 1887 treaty when China gave Portugal the power and authority to govern the land permanently, and the latter seemed to have *de facto* sovereignty, Portugal still had only the right to administer the people on the land, but not to own the land. The border delineation was never done, and the Chinese government managed to influence Macau in one way or another. The Portuguese did not have full control of Macau. Another way to put it is that China always had sovereignty over Macau but Portugal largely had the administrative rights.[63] That may be too simple, but it does explain much of Macau's history.

But can sovereignty and administration really be separated? Isn't it empty sovereignty if there is little or no administration? Fairbank's and Reischauer's comments on the foreign concessions in China's coastal cities seem to apply here: "Under extraterritoriality they also exercised legal jurisdiction over their own nationals, and by degrees developed taxation, police forces, and other features of municipal government. Thus China's sovereignty, without being destroyed, was largely in abeyance in the foreign quarters of the major ports."[64] That was largely the case in Macau as well, especially during what we call the colonial period, although at one time or another, the Chinese government had more control in Macau than they did in the foreign concessions.

The complexity of the sovereignty question in Macau suggests that the Chinese and Portuguese shared Macau's sovereignty before 1999.[65] Chapters 1 and 2 so far have already demonstrated that China's sovereignty had been increasingly impinged upon since the 1500s by the Portuguese, English, French, Japanese, etc.[66] In the colonial period of Macau, China had the lesser control in Macau, therefore the lesser sovereignty, and Portugal had more of it. On the other hand, if the Portuguese had sovereignty over Macau, even after the 1887 treaty, it was never absolute either. So sovereignty in fact had been shared between China and Portugal in one way or another, with one party having more at one time than the other.

Democracy, briefly stated, is a system where "its most powerful collective decision-makers are selected through periodic elections in which candidates freely compete for votes and in which virtually all the adult population is eligible to vote."[67] In a democracy, there will also be checks and balances among the executive, the legislative, and the judicial branches of government. And there is also freedom of speech and an independent press.

Such a democracy is viewed by many to be a better way to deal with political, economic, and social conflicts. It is not perfect, and indeed it has many problems, as we can see from the history of the American or Taiwan model. But one can argue that it is better than a monarchy, warlordism, dictatorship, or an authoritarian government in fairness in political procedures, economic activities, and social welfare. The system provides an opportunity for most citizens to vote for the chief executives of the government, and replace them if necessary. The checks and balances in the government and the freedom of speech in society are better mechanisms to guarantee that the government performs at its best possible level.

To what extent is Macau and the "one country, two systems" formula democratic? Thirty years after the Portuguese settled in Macau, they found a way to govern themselves with the consent from the Indo-Portuguese government in Goa (or the viceroy of India) and the Portuguese government in Lisbon. If the Portuguese system had some democratic elements in the first 400 years, it took on more such characteristics in the 1970s. The MSAR government seems to have made further improvement on democratization though very much limited in degree and scope.

The Portuguese Political Structure in Macau

Politics concern the regulation and coordination of group interests. As far as the Portuguese in Macau are concerned, they had to regulate and coordinate the interests of the Portuguese, the Chinese, and other foreigners. In the Senado period, the major players in the Portuguese political structure were the captain-major, captain-general, or later governor-general (the latter tending to have more power than the former), the Senado or the Municipal Senate, the chief judge (for some time), and the bishops in Macau.[68]

The captain-major (capitão-mor) since 1557, that is, 兵頭, who became governor and captain-general, or simply governor (總督), after 1623, was appointed by the viceroy of Goa colonial government and approved by the royal court in Lisbon. The position was a lucrative one. In fact, the original name of the position was captain major of the Japan voyage.[69] He would decide which traders would go on voyages with the well-armed government fleet, for which he would get a gift or a percentage of the profit, so the position was "generally reserved for friends or relatives of the Viceroy."[70] Since the first appointment of captain-general in 1623 until 1999, there were altogether 128 persons appointed to this position, all across the four historical periods in Chinese history: the Ming dynasty, the Qing dynasty, the Republic of China, and the People's Republic of China.[71]

He was, at first, supposed to be the military officer of Macau and should not interfere with the government affairs. But he could do much more than that. According to Ljungstedt,[72] he had the power to intervene if he found the Senate not in accordance with the orders from Lisbon or Goa. His main job, however, was to recruit an army of about 400 men (240 in 1834), often from India as well as from Macau. He would man the six fortresses with 130 cannons. The captain-majors served on a one-year term, while the captain-general served on a three-year term. Since 1623 when the first governor and captain-general was appointed, he was gaining more and more power vis-à-vis the Senate. When Amaral became governor in 1846, the new governor had almost all the power.[73]

The Senate (議事會), first started in 1583, was composed of six representatives elected by the Portuguese citizens in Macau. This was the virtual government of the Portuguese Macau. There are different accounts as to how the senators were selected.[74] But according to most accounts, the selection process is reminiscent of some of the contemporary Chinese practices in Macau. The citizens would elect six electors, who would then select the senators or vereadors (*weiliduo* 委黎多 or 唩嚟哆, the term the Chinese used to refer to them, especially to the prosecutor below, or procurador).[75] Among the elected officials, three would be aldermen, each of whom would serve as the chair of the Senate for one year. There would also be two judges, one prosecutor, and a secretary. The Senado was invested with political, judicial, and administrative powers concerning everyday life in Macau including commerce and security. The prosecutor (*lishiguan* 理事官 as is called in Chinese) was in charge of collecting taxes and maintaining relationships with the Chinese government as well as taking care of some judicial matters. He was even "conferred by the imperial court the grade of mandarin 2nd class with jurisdiction over the steadily increasing number of Chinese living in Macau."[76] He became independent of the Senate in 1865.[77] The election was held every three years.[78] (See Plate 2.3 for the Senate building in the 20th century.)

The chief judge (王室大法官), known as an *ouvidor*, representing the royal court, presided over the elections and made judicial decisions. The first appointee was Rui Machado in 1580. Because of his conflicts with the Senate and the captain-general, the position was suspended in 1642 and resumed in 1702.[79] But the position was suspended again some years later. Here we can sense the desire of the royal court to control matters in Macau by its own representatives and the difficulties of doing so. The chief judge was to take care of the judicial matters in Macau, and even local Chinese would go to him for disputes with the Portuguese.[80] He was also to act on the captain-general's behalf in his absence and take care of the customs. But since there were already judges in the Senate, his responsibilities might conflict with those of the senators, which led to the Senate's request to get rid of the position.[81]

Because Catholicism was the religion of the state, all the Senate members had to be Catholic. So the roles of the bishop and the high clergy in municipal matters were crucial, and sometimes decisive, if they chose to intervene (more on religion in chapter 5).[82]

Although it was by no means a democracy but more like a plutocracy, this political arrangement did have an element of democracy, since the members of the Senate were indirectly selected by the Portuguese populace in Macau. But the Senate was the legislature, the government, and the judicial body all in one. The captain-general and the chief judge were not always happy to have their roles restricted, so there was some inherent tension among the three.

Problems occurred. In 1710, Diogo de Pinho Teixeira 戴冰玉, the captain-general, took the initiative to punish a soldier who raped a black slave, in disregard of the Senate's protest of his interference in their affairs. Moreover, he cancelled the periodic election of the Senate. When the latter protested, he ordered to put the senators in jail. When the senators hid themselves in St. Paul's College, he bombed the college with his cannon from Mount Fortress despite the efforts of reconciliation proposed by the bishops and the chief judge. A battle between his soldiers and the armed citizens resulted in the surrender of the senators. The captain-general got his way.[83] António José Telles de Menezes, another captain-general appointed in 1747, even flogged one of the judges for his negligence on the job.[84]

At the best of times, however, the captain-general and the senate worked together to have things done. If they had disputes, they would resort to the help of the bishops, or call a meeting of the voting public and put things to a vote.[85] An incident may show the seeming checks and balances of the political system. In 1773, the emperor Yongzheng was suggesting informally that all foreign trade go through Macau. The Senate was willing to accept the offer, but the bishop of Macau was not, fearing that the Europeans would corrupt the city's morals, especially because most of them would be Protestant. The Portuguese viceroy of India supported him, for different reasons, and the offer was put on hold.[86] Thus in the Portuguese rule in Macau, democracy and dictatorship alternated.

The Chinese Political Structure

When the Portuguese traders first came to Macau, they had to pay rent to Chinese officials, a symbol of Chinese sovereignty. In the Ming dynasty, Macau was viewed as part of Xiangshan County (which is the city of Zhongshan today) and was governed by the Chinese officials stationed there.[87] When they came to Macau, they would meet the Portuguese officials in *casa da câmara*, or the city hall in Macau, 議事亭 (*yi shi ting*, see Figure 2.2). When the higher officials came to Macau, they stayed here too.[88] In addition, the Chinese government set up a border station at Guanzha and built a wall and a gate to control the flow of people and goods to and from Macau.[89]

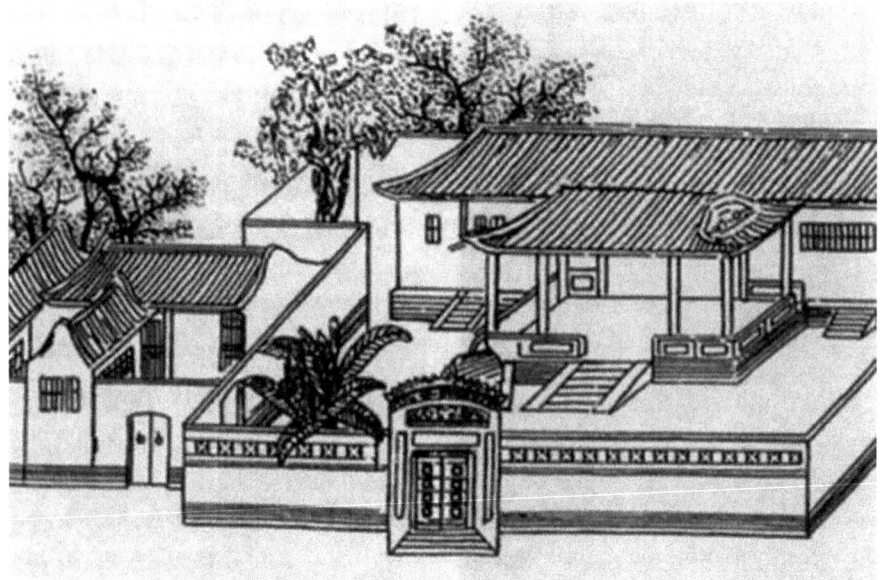

Figure 2.2
The ancient City Hall 議事廳, in Yin Guangren and Zhang Rulin, Aomen Jilue Jiaozhu, pp. 218–9.

The ancient city hall was the place where the Chinese officials would discuss with the Portuguese officials affairs concerning the city, including trade matters. Some important rules and regulations made by the Chinese government that would apply to both the Chinese and Portuguese were inscribed on the four stones and placed right in the city hall, which were another symbol of Chinese sovereignty. These would include the prohibition of slavery, human trafficking, smuggling, etc. But other than collecting taxes on foreign traders, the Chinese control of Macau was mainly symbolic. The rules were not always followed, as we will see below, and conflicts abounded.[90]

During the Qing dynasty, the Chinese set up a local government in 1731 headed by *xian cheng* (縣丞, the title of office) in Qian Shan Zhai (前山寨) or what is now Xiangzhou, Zhuhai, under Xiangshan county, to manage the affairs in Macau, both Chinese and Portuguese, again a symbol of sovereignty (see Figure 2.3). Twelve years later, the *xian cheng* government was moved to Wang Xia Village (望廈村), or Mong Ha, in Macau. From 1731 to 1906, 57 *xian cheng* were appointed and instituted. In 1744, the Chinese government added another layer of government above the county, Macau Coast Military and Civilian Government (澳門海防軍民同知), which governed the four counties of Panyu, Dongguan, Shunde, and Xiangshan. The chief official was called Tongzhi 同知. The authors of *The Annals of Macau* (澳門記略), Yin Guangren and Zhang Rulin, were the first and third officials to hold

Figure 2.3
The remaining wall of Qian Shan Zhai in what is now Xiangzhou, Zhuhai. 珠海市文物管理委員會, 珠海市文物志, Foshan: Guangdong Ren Min Chu Ban She, 1994, p. 2.

the position. From 1744 to 1910, 64 persons were appointed to the position.[91] They stationed in Qian Shan Zhai, where the *xian cheng* used to be.[92]

Now the Chinese government set up more rules for people living in Macau. For example, foreign ships must be piloted by the Chinese into harbors along the Pearl River. The building of ships and houses had to be recorded with the Chinese government. Also the Portuguese could not entice the Chinese to believe in their religion.[93]

Chinese soldiers were stationed in both Qian Shan Zhai, at one time about 2,000, and in Macau, about 200. They joined in the Portuguese army in military actions in the area, as we will discuss now about the conflicts and cooperation between the Chinese and the Portuguese.

The Clash and Cooperation of Two Political Structures

Both sides were trying to gain as much control as possible over the land, but neither side had complete control of it, hence the term "shared sovereignty." The establishment of a local Chinese government in and of Macau indicates that the Chinese were trying to exercise as much sovereignty as possible. The Portuguese acquiescence to Chinese control indicates that they knew sovereignty was not completely theirs. Both sides found it acceptable since the Portuguese could benefit from the trading port, and the Chinese could benefit from taxes. Besides, neither side had the power to change the status quo. That was when things were largely calm. But events did happen.

One of the constant conflicts concerned judicial matters. A famous example was about the handling of two Chinese vagrants, Li Tingfu 李廷富 and Jian Ya'er 简亞二, by the Portuguese soldiers in 1747. The two were abused and beaten to death. The Chinese officials, led by Zhang Rulin, came to Macau and wanted both the dead bodies and the culprits, but António José Telles de Menezes, the captain-general, did not want to hand them over. The Portuguese Senate also intervened, but Menezes did not budge. The Chinese officials decided to close the border gate and cut off supplies from the mainland, on which the Portuguese depended for their daily lives.[94] Some Chinese also evacuated from Macau, and Chinese troops were sent in. The captain-general finally exiled to Timor the two soldiers involved in the murder. The Senate (or the Church and businessmen) bribed Zhang Rulin for a solution, according to one assumption, and the latter acquiesced. The border gate was opened in three weeks. Zhang Rulin was demoted after the event, since the emperor was not happy with the way he handled the incident.

However, Zhang did set up 12 rules in 1749 for the Portuguese to follow: no deportation of criminals; registration of boats and ships; no credit for black slaves when they purchased any goods; no private detention or abuse of Chinese if the latter mistakenly entered Portuguese private places; non-Chinese criminals would be tried by both the Chinese and Portuguese officials; no private detention and punishment of Chinese who owed Portuguese debts or violated the latter in any way—rather they should be sent to the Chinese officials; no building of houses without permission from the Chinese officials; no buying or selling of Chinese children; no theft by black slaves; no sheltering of Chinese criminals; no allowing foreigners to go out of Macau to the Chinese territories to disturb the Chinese; and no preaching of religion to the Chinese people. Whether these rules could be followed was another matter, but they were inscribed on stones both in Chinese and in Portuguese. The Chinese version was placed in the Xiangshan *xian cheng* government seat in Mong Ha in Macau, and the Portuguese version was placed in the Senate building.[95]

On another occasion in 1773, a Chinese was killed by an Englishman, and the Chinese officials wanted the culprit. They again threatened to cut off supplies if the Portuguese did not comply. The latter did, and the Englishman was executed by the Chinese government.[96] The close economic ties between Macau and the mainland was a key factor in their relationship. That is true today as well.

Another matter of serious contention between the two sides concerned the Portuguese conversion of Chinese to Catholicism. The Chinese government's position on this issue varied during the 400 years; in the early days of the Kangxi era at the beginning of the Qing dynasty, the government was tolerant. By 1735, there were 300,000 Catholics in mainland China. Some Catholic priests even became government officials in Beijing. But factions within the Catholic Church disagreed over their policies in China, and whether to allow Chinese Catholics to worship their ancestors and Confucius. The Vatican decided against it in 1704, which enraged Kangxi, who then decided to forbid Chinese to believe in Catholicism.[97]

It is in this context that the Chinese officials, this time the governor-general of Guangdong and Guangxi, decided to close Nossa Senhora do Amparo, the Church of Our Lady of Defense, a Chinese Catholic Church (唐人廟), in 1749. The event was triggered by the Chinese officials' search for somebody who hid in the church (see Figure 2.4). The Chinese priests refused to hand him over, and instead transported him elsewhere. The Chinese officials threatened again to cut off supplies to Macau. The Senate finally decided to hand the entire church to the Chinese, which was then closed. The Chinese officials set up more rules and regulations for the Portuguese and Chinese in Macau. Montalto de Jesus laments that it was a shame on the part of the Portuguese to surrender to the Chinese officials so easily.[98]

Although conflicts abounded, cooperation was also consistent between the two sides, especially when Macau was faced with outside threat. Two of the major threats were from the Dutch and the British. The Dutch tried several times from 1601 to 1688 to take over Macau from the Portuguese either by tricks or by force but failed.[99] Although the Chinese did not especially get involved in fighting the Dutch, they did not help them either in the Portuguese-Dutch conflict. The Dutch finally decided to go to Taiwan instead, as we mentioned earlier. From 1623 to 1840 the British, like the Dutch, also wanted to set foot on Macau, and they tried over a dozen times by trade or by force.[100] The Portuguese often sought help from the Chinese, and the latter sometimes threatened with war with the British. After repeated failures to take Macau, the British made their ambitions at Hong Kong. This time they won. But

Figure 2.4
A map of the buildings at the time, including the Chinese Christian church in the middle of the map. Ho Weng Hong, *The Past of Macau*, Macau: Macao Foundation, 1994, p. 14.

the cooperation between the Portuguese and the Chinese in defending Macau when faced with outside threat was fairly successful.

So politically, Macau weathered all the storms in the 16th, 17th, and 18th centuries under the dual jurisdiction of the Chinese and the Portuguese and with a shared sovereignty. The political arrangements, with some limited democratic elements in Macau, seemed to have largely worked. Although conflicts were constant, the Chinese and Portuguese were able to cooperate when faced with outside threats. The 19th century, however, would bring Macau some fundamental change in its political arrangements.

The Colonial Period (1849–1976)

This period is characterized by the declining significance of the Senate and the increasing power of the captain-general, now called governor-general. Chinese control of Macau was also by and large phased out, and what we may call a true colonial rule was instituted. Pina-Cabral calls this period "colonial" for two reasons: "the formal terms of government were phrased in typical colonial manner, and ethnic relations in the city acquired a distinct 'colonial' tone."[101] Scholars largely agree that this is the colonial period and the Chinese sovereignty over the land was indeed mainly nominal. More conflicts occurred during this period.

The Perpetual Occupation and Management of Macau by Portugal

The move toward the colonial rule rather than continuation of dual jurisdiction happened along with changes both in Portugal and in China.[102] In Portugal, the constitutional monarchy was established in 1820 and a constitution was passed to include all Portuguese colonies as part of Portugal. In 1869, Macau and Timor became one province and a governor-general of the province was appointed. This position was empowered with administrative duties as well as military affairs, although he should still consult with the Senate in matters related to Macau. The latter was now the administrative council in charge of public affairs and it was part of the administration with the governor-general as its head.

The Opium Wars revealed China's weaknesses, and the Portuguese government in Macau felt that this was an opportunity for them to change Macau's status just like that of Hong Kong. In 1843, they sent a letter to the imperial commissioner Qiying arguing that since Hong Kong was ceded to the British, it would not make sense for them to pay for the lease of Macau. They also wanted to include Taipa as part of their controlled territories. Following the British, they also made more requests about trading terms. In other words, the Portuguese wanted full sovereignty over Macau and its surrounding waters and islands. But Qiying did not agree with them.[103]

Figure 2.5
Amaral's portrait. Courtesy of Oxford University Press.

Then in 1846, Lisbon appointed a strongman, João Maria Ferreira Amaral, as the new governor of Macau (see Plate 2.1 and Figure 2.5).[104] He was asked to assert Portugal's absolute sovereignty in the settlement. So Amaral began a series of actions to limit the Chinese government's presence in Macau. Considering the competition from Hong Kong, he made Macau a free port. He shut down and destroyed the Chinese customs houses and removed the Chinese officials. He started collecting taxes from the Chinese living in Macau and brought them under Portuguese legal institutions. Both the Senate and the bishop, Jerónimo da Mata, disagreed with Amaral, arguing that the Chinese had never been under the Portuguese control. But Amaral would have his way. When the Chinese protested by shutting all their shops and stopped bringing provisions to the city, he threatened that he would order the guns at the Monte to open fire on the market area and raze all the buildings to the ground. The Chinese complied and opened their markets.[105]

In addition, he annexed the island of Taipa and suspended Macau's annual lease payment to China, which was now 10,000 silver dollars.[106] He pulled down houses, asked the Chinese to remove their ancestors' graves, and destroyed small farms in order to build new roads.[107] He took away the stone inscriptions from the Leal Senado that laid down the rules for the Portuguese. These were serious violations of Chinese interests and of the Chinese sense that this land was theirs. They constituted a challenge.

The Senate secretly petitioned the minister of colonies about the danger of this anti-Chinese policy:

> It is thus important to understand that, for the moment, we can only count on the usufruct [dominio until] of this territory on the basis of the agreements that exist between ourselves and the Chinese; and attempting to transform it into absolute ownership [dominio directo] by means of force would be not only an effort vastly superior to our forces but also a most unfair and disloyal gesture, if we take into consideration the varied attentions we have always received from the Chinese.[108]

But Amaral's response was to disband the Senate, branding the senators as unpatriotic.[109] He told the Chinese that when the Chinese officials came to Macau, they would be received as visiting representatives of a foreign power. Amaral's policies aroused much resentment and he was assassinated by some angry Chinese led by Shen Zhiliang on August 22, 1849.[110] Three days later on August 25, a young officer, Vicente Nicolau de Mesquita (see Plate 2.4), led a small group of armed Portuguese/Macanese men and attacked the Chinese troops north of Macau. They overpowered the latter and took their fort. Mesquita became the Macanese hero who redeemed Amaral's martyrdom.[111] The dates of these events were inscribed on the inside walls of the border gate in 1870 when it was constructed. The gate, with the dates inscribed on its walls, is now still standing at Guangzhou as an historical relic (see Figures 2.6a and 2.6b). The Guangdong government executed Shen Zhiliang and returned the remains of Amaral to the Portuguese (see chapter 4 for a poem commemorating Shen). The increased domination by the Portuguese continued.[112]

This domination finally led to the signing of the Luso-Chinese Treaty of Friendship and Trade in 1887, which stipulated the perpetual occupation and government (永居管理) of Macau and its dependencies by Portugal. But it also stipulated that the Portuguese could not cede Macau to other countries without the approval of the Chinese government. This seems to say that the Chinese did not give the full sovereignty away to Portugal. The treaty was first negotiated over

Figure 2.6a
The Border Gate, at Love Food blog at http://hk.lovefood.cc/2015/11/blog-post_6.html, accessed August 11, 2019.

Figure 2.6b
The dates inscribed on the inside and front of the walls, at Memory Macau blog at http://memorymacau.blogspot.com/2012/03/blog-post_14.html, accessed August 11, 2019.

20 years earlier, and Robert Hart 赫德 and his assistant, James Duncan Campbell 金登幹, played a key role for the last version of the treaty. The colonial control of Macau was formalized. But the treaty left unresolved the border delineation. The Portuguese wanted not only Taipa but also Coloane, Hengqin islands, and the surrounding waters (see Figure 1.5).[113] But the Chinese government refused their request. When the Portuguese later reached out to these other areas, with land-filling around Qingzhou for example, they would receive serious protests from the Chinese government.[114]

In 1888 the Portuguese government in Macau claimed that the smaller Hengqin Island was Portuguese territory and the Chinese should not build houses there. That set off another round of arguments between the two sides, but the Qing government did not budge. In 1889, the Portuguese Macau put up a street lamp north of the border, but had to take it away after the Chinese protested. In 1908, a Chinese merchant in Macau hired a Japanese boat (二辰丸) to smuggle weapons to China, and the boat was intercepted by the Chinese naval forces off the waters of Coloane. The Japanese claimed that the Chinese had no right to do so since it was Portuguese territory. The Portuguese agreed. Arguments went nowhere, and the Japanese threatened the Chinese with war. The latter gave in, apologized, bought the weapons themselves, released the boat, and paid for the damages. In 1910, the Portuguese answered the call for help from Chinese families whose children were kidnapped by bandits in Coloane. They sent troops in, put torch to the houses, arrested 450 bandits, and an unknown number of villagers died in the process. Thirty-eight of them alone died while escaping the ordeal in boats.[115] (See Plate 4.5 for the Portuguese monument commemorating the war on Coloane, and chapter 4 for a Chinese poem criticizing the Chinese government.)

After the founding of the Republic of China in 1911, the Chinese even thought about abolishing the 1887 treaty. Meanwhile, conflicts continued.[116] One of the most serious occurred on May 29, 1922, when the Portuguese soldiers shot 70 Chinese to death. People had been protesting a black soldier's disorderly conduct towards a Chinese woman and matters had gotten out of hand. Chinese workers and shopkeepers then went on strike in the following days. They received support from workers in Guangdong and the Guangdong government, who threatened to cut off supplies again. But because of the chaos in the mainland itself, the event went unresolved in spite of the ensuing five months' turmoil.[117]

Declining Portuguese Domination since 1945

If Amaral's rule in the 1840s, the treaty in 1887, and the 5-29 massacre in 1922 symbolized an ascending colonial rule, three other events symbolized its decline: 1) the continued intention and discussion to take back Macau by the new Chinese governments, first the Republic of China (ROC) and then the People's Republic of China (PRC) since the end of World War II; 2) the armed conflicts at the border in 1952; and 3), the 12-3 incident in 1966.

With the end of World War II, a movement to recover Macau began in Macau and Guangdong. In 1945, the European Bureau of the Foreign Affairs Office of the ROC suggested ways to take back Macau, including a referendum by the residents in Macau and negotiations with Lisbon. On February 5, 1946, Liu Shaowu 劉紹武, one of the KMT army officers stationed in Zhongshan, Guangdong, even led his troops into Macau to protest the Portuguese occupation, and received support from over 10,000 Chinese in Macau.[118] This signaled the beginning of the decline of the Portuguese dominance in the colonial period.

Then on July 25, 1952, the PLA troops clashed with the Portuguese troops at the border with casualties on both sides, called the Guanzha Incident (see Figure 2.7). There were two deaths on each side, seven wounded on the Portuguese side and thirty on the Chinese side. Another report said that there was only one dead on the Portuguese side.[119] The Chinese government again cut off supplies of food and vegetables to Macau. The latter then apologized and compensated the Chinese monetarily for their loss.[120] Apparently the Portuguese no longer had the power they used to regarding the relationship with mainland China.

In November 1966 a clash between the Chinese and Portuguese policemen over the construction of a new addition to a Chinese school in Taipa led to an uprising in December (see Figure 2.8). The uprising and riots culminated in December 3, 4, and 5, with Chinese people attacking government officials and battling policemen. They were encouraged by the Cultural Revolution that was happening on the mainland. Indeed, the Guangdong government also sent their protests to the Portuguese government in Macau, and Chinese gunboats cruised at the waters close by. The incident led to 8 Chinese deaths and the injury of 212 people by December 5. Some Portuguese and Macanese were badly beaten.[121] Under enormous pressure,

Figure 2.7
The border gate. Lei Kun Min and Lam Fat Lam, *Macao in Postcards*, Macau: Macao Association for Historical Education, 2008, p. 33.

Figure 2.8
Confrontation between the police and union members that led to the 12-3 Incident. Li Hongjiang, *Danzai Qinghuai* (Taipa remembrance) (Macau: The Civic and Municipal Affairs Bureau, 2001), p. 188, cited in Ruan Zirong and Li Jinglin, "Aomen koushu shi: 'huo huashi' de huiyi" (Macau oral history: "the live fossil" remembers), September 23, 2018 at Pengpai News, https://www.thepaper.cn/newsDetail_forward_2463790, accessed October 9, 2018.

Figure 2.9
The Portuguese Macau government accepted all the conditions raised by the Chinese community. Chief among the Chinese community leaders receiving the agreement and apology were Ho Yin (何賢, Edmund Ho's father, second from left) and Ma Man Kei (馬萬祺, sixth from left). Chen Shurong, *Yishiting Qiandi* (The Lea Senado Plaza) (Macau: Jun Liang Tang Press, 2013), p. 59.

the Portuguese government finally yielded to all the Chinese requests, including the compensation of the loss of lives, punishment of those responsible, and permission to build the school annex. This is known as the 12-3 Incident.[122]

The results of the 12-3 Incident indicate the further decline of the Portuguese power in Macau. As Shipp comments, from the moment when the Macau governor, Brigadier Nobre de Carvalho, agreed to the demands of demonstrators supported by the mainland Chinese government, "it was clear to all sides that China was in full control of activities in Macau, despite any Portuguese efforts to claim otherwise."[123] The Mao portrait on the wall of the room where the agreement was presented is symbolic of that control (see Figure 2.9). There was what Lo Shiu Hing calls a "dual rule,"[124] reminiscent of the dual jurisdiction in the early days of the Macau's politics.

Moving towards a Democracy?

But China might not be in full control of activities in Macau, unlike what Shipp claims above. Macau was in fact moving toward a democracy and has gone farther along that road than mainland China has.

In the first 300 years, Macau practiced dual jurisdiction between the Chinese *xian cheng* and Tongzhi on the one hand and the Portuguese Senate on the other, with the captain-general oftentimes playing a major role. In the colonial period, although the governor-general at first amassed much more power, he later began to share power with a number of other newly established organizations. The Provincial Organization Charter of Macau in 1917 stipulated that there would be an Administrative Council composed of not only government officials but also senators. Two representatives of Chinese in Macau would also be included in the

Council. The Council would administer everyday affairs as well as make law. In 1920, the legislative part was separated from the Administrative Council and a Legislative Council was established. But it was mainly an advisory council, and most of the legislative power still lay with the governor, although there were some beginning checks and balances.[125] (See Plate 2.5 for the Governor's Mansion, and later the Government House in Macau.)

In 1976, the Organic Statute of Macau was put into practice.[126] The Legislative Council became fully independent of the governor, who was appointed by the president of Portugal. There were 17 legislators, 6 of whom were popularly elected, i.e., "by direct suffrage," 6 elected by functional constituencies, i.e., "by indirect suffrage," and 5 appointed by the governor. By 1990 the total number increased to 23, with 8 popularly elected, 8 elected by social organizations, and 7 appointed by the governor. By 1984 the Chinese Macau basically had already dominated the first two parts of the legislature. The Macanese (those with mixed blood of Portuguese, Chinese, or other Asians) had to negotiate with the Chinese societies to have representatives in the legislature. The Portuguese Macau would have to be represented by the appointees of the governor. In addition, Macau now had its own independent legal system. The courts were subject only to the law. It would enjoy self-autonomy.[127]

But as Wu Zhiliang points out, although there might be a structure that resembled a division of power among the three branches of the government, democratic representation and checks and balances were still lacking.[128] In 1996, for example, only about a quarter of the residents in Macau registered to vote for the allocated number of legislators, and only 64.49% of those actually voted. Most people in Macau were not in those social organizations, so they were not represented by functional constituencies either. The administrative and judicial branches of the government were also overly represented by the Portuguese. There were indeed hundreds of social organizations, but their political participation was very much limited.[129] The governor simply had too much power: he had both legislative and executive powers, formulating the general policy of the territory, coordinating the entire public administration, executing the law, administering the finances, and defining the structures of the monetary and financial markets.[130] Nonetheless, Macau was moving toward democracy. A similar political structure has remained after the handover of Macau to China in 1999.

The True Chinese Macau Period (1999–2010)

The Basic Law of the Macau Special Administrative Region (MSAR) of the People's Republic of China (1993) stipulates a basic division of power among the chief executive, the Legislative Council, and the Courts. There are some differences and similarities compared with the political structure under the colonial rule.

In 2012, most likely under instructions of the Central Government, Macau set out to do some political reform. Two positions are added to the directly elected category of legislators, two to the indirectly elected category, no change in the number of appointed positions, and 100 more to the election committee for the Chief Executive. This changed some numbers but not the power structure itself. The chief executive is now elected by an Election Committee composed of 400 members: 120 from the industrial, commercial, and financial sectors; 115 from cultural and educational sectors and other professions; 115 from labor, social services, religious, and other sections; and 50 from representatives of the Macau legislature, Macau municipal government organizations, Macau deputies to the National People's Congress (NPC), and Macau representatives to the National Committee of the Chinese People's Political Consultative Conference (CPPCC). The selected chief executive will then be appointed by the Central People's Government in Beijing. The process seems to be more democratic than in the colonial era, since there are at least a group of people who will serve as representatives of the populace to elect the chief executive.

The problem is, however, whether this group of 400 people can truly present a populace of 660,000. The practice has been viewed by some as "election by a small circle of people" (小圈子選舉), and there is plenty of truth in this view. According to the Basic Law, the Election Committee members need to be elected themselves by the groups in different categories. But few people actually join these groups and only few established groups can participate in the category to select the Election Committee members. Even if the group is in the category, there are hardly any elections going on among the groups. In fact, the prominent group leaders will consult one another and come up with the candidates for the category. The First Election Committee for 1999's first Chinese chief executive was more or less democratically selected, since there were more candidates for the committee than the exact number required. In the third election committee in 2009, the number of candidates they came up with was the exact number of representatives to the Election Committee. No elections were needed. And the representatives and deputies to the NPC and CPPCC were not popularly elected, either.

Furthermore, once the Election Committee is formed, they may find that they do not need elections for the chief executive, either. There is only one candidate, as in the case in 2004, 2009, and 2014. Edmund Ho was re-elected by 99% of the vote. And Fernando Chui Sai On was elected as the third and fourth chief executive with over 95% of the vote. The same happened in 2019.

Theoretically, if there is no competition of candidates and participation of the populace, there is almost no democracy. As a result, even if the selection of the chief executive is indeed an improvement over the colonial times, the actual practice in Macau now does not make a real difference. One might even be able to say that the probability of yielding a good chief executive is about the same between the election by the Election Committee and the direct appointment by the central government.

The selection of the Legislative Assembly members is similar to the past except that the number of legislators has increased to 33 since 2014 with 14 directly elected, 12 indirectly elected, and 7 appointed by the chief executive. Although the way to select the members is quite the same as before the handover, the number of directly elected members has increased, from 8 in 1990.

The problems that plagued the legislators still largely exist, though.[131] Most of them are still part-time legislators, with other private occupations to busy themselves with.[132] More importantly, the representation of the legislature has always been a problem. The set-up is such that businesses are overly represented, while the lower classes are underrepresented. The number of each category may go up and down in each Assembly, but the fifth one in 2013 is probably most telling. In 2013, of all the legislators, 60.6% of them were from business groups, 24.2% from professional and managerial groups, and 15.2 % from the working class and social service groups.[133] The problem is the same with the composition of the Administrative Council, which assists the chief executive of the Macau SAR in making important policy decisions, proposing new legislation, making new regulations, and even dismissing the Legislative Assembly. This is a very important body next to the chief executive but above the Legislative Assembly. It is also overly represented by business people: out of the 11 members of the third Council (2009–2014), 64% were from businesses, 18% from professional and public administration groups, and 18% from representatives of labor and social services.[134] Such composition of the two most powerful bodies of the government effectively guarantees that the businesses will be able to maximize their interests sometimes at the expense of the middle and lower classes. Rather than "Macau governed by Macau people," it is more like "Macau governed by business people."

Most importantly, the ability of the Legislature to introduce bills is severely restricted. According to Article 75 of the Basic Law, "Bills which do not relate to public expenditure or political structure or the operation of the government may be introduced individually or jointly by members of the Council. The written consent of the chief executive shall be required before bills relating to government policies are introduced."[135] As a result of this constraint, the Legislature is almost crippled. There is probably no law that does not have to do with "the operation of the government." And if they do introduce a law, the chief executive has to agree to it first anyway. What actually has happened is that the Legislative branch rarely, if ever, introduces bills. If they want to introduce bills, they have difficulty getting through the Executive branch.

For example, legislators had been pressing for three years about a law that would set a waiting period for the high level retiring government officials to go into private business (過冷河制度), and it did not pass until the last few remaining days of the

Third Council. Apparently the Executive branch did not like the idea. Some in the government even said that since they were appointed by the central government, they did not have to be subject to such Macau laws.[136] The same fate had befallen the legislation regarding imported labor. The law would set more restrictions and place more responsibilities on employers. Some legislators wanted it, but some business representatives and the Executive branch apparently did not. So the law was lingering in the political process for many years before it was finally passed in 2009.

In contrast, if the Executive branch likes something, it can get it done in almost no time. On October 22, 2008 the Executive branch introduced a draft bill to enact Article 23 of the Macau Basic Law regarding national security. The consultation period given was only 40 days. On January 6, 2009 the bill was passed in principle in the Assembly. Then the final draft of the bill was passed by the Legislature on February 26, signed into law by the chief executive, and went into effect on March 3. Compared with other bills that take years and years, the lightning speed this bill took to pass is very impressive. The power of the Executive branch is in sharp contrast with the power of the Legislature.

Indeed, the Legislature does not provide much balancing power. Rather, the Executive is making all the important policy decisions. This is the so-called "executive-led" principle (行政主導), and apparently the system has more disadvantages than advantages. The chief executive has amassed as much power as the Portuguese governor in the colonial time, if not more.[137]

In addition, the presidents and judges of the courts at all levels as well as prosecutors are appointed or removed by the chief executive. The appointments are based on the advice of a committee composed of judges, lawyers, and other dignitaries of society. The Courts have independent judicial power, including that of final adjudication. How the judicial branch may or may not balance the power of the other two branches of power is, however, yet to be studied. For example, in 2018, Sulu Sou Ka Hou, the newly elected legislator and a democracy advocate, was fined by the court for supposedly violating demonstration laws rather than being sentenced to jail terms which would lead to his expulsion from the legislature. But we do not know the original intention of the chief executive so we cannot judge whether the court's decision was in line with the chief executive's intention or against it. And we do not know to what extent the Central Government was involved in the Sou case.

So the political system in Macau now is more authoritarian, if not plutocractic, than democratic, although there are more democratic elements than in the colonial times.[138] As we mentioned at the beginning of the chapter, when Edmund Ho was re-elected as the chief executive on August 29, 2004, he was contemplating on how he could do differently than the Portuguese governor before him. But that contemplation apparently did not include democratization, which is why almost nothing happened in his second term in that regard. In 2008 when the government was working on three new laws on elections, some raised the issue of increasing the number of electors of the Election Committee for the chief executive and the number of directly elected legislators. More citizens should be able to participate in the election of indirectly elected legislators as well. These seem to be moderate requests, and they did not even ask for universal suffrage. But those requests went nowhere.[139] The government's argument is that democratization has to go slowly. Unlike the Hong Kong Basic Law, the Macau Basic Law does not mention that eventually both the chief executive and the Legislature will be selected by universal suffrage, so they do not want to consider it now.

But even if universal suffrage is mentioned in the Hong Kong Basic Law, we know that it is not going to happen in the near future after the Umbrella Movement failed in 2014. Seeing what happened in Hong Kong, almost no one in Macau is talking about universal suffrage now.

In fact, the government officials' constant mentioning of the Basic Law in defending their positions makes one think more about the sovereignty issue. The extent to which Macau can pursue its own course depends on the level of Macau's sovereignty. The dominant discourse is that the sovereignty of Macau now belongs to the People's Republic of China (PRC), and Macau is part of the PRC.[140] Therefore, there is nothing much people in Macau can do because the Basic Law is governed by the Chinese constitution, and the chief executive and the major officials of the government are appointed by the central government. But the way the government operates actually suggests that sovereignty is shared between the Macau government (indirectly by the people in Macau) and the central government, just like before.

It is the MSAR government that largely manages the people in Macau. A border exists between Macau and the mainland, and travel documents are processed when border-crossing. The MSAR government has its own monetary system, and does not pay taxes to the central government. But the latter does have troops stationed in Macau and formally appoints the chief executive and the major government officials immediately below him. Even though the diplomatic issues are largely handled by the central government, the MSAR is part of some international organizations and is party to 60 international treaties.[141] While gambling is illegal in China, it is the main industry in Macau. It is true that the Basic Law does not mention universal suffrage, but it does not rule it out either. Rather, it stipulates that the Macau government propose changes to the political system to the NPR, which will then prove or disapprove the proposal. The Macau government is not totally powerless. All these points indicate that Macau has some sovereignty. If that is the case, then the MSAR government and the people in Macau do have more leeway in running the region politically than people would think.

Just like the political elites in mainland China, the elites in Macau think that their political system is the best. It does seem the best for them since they are benefiting the most from it as we have analyzed earlier. But they might also agree that better checks and balances would more likely prevent corruption cases like that of Ao Man

Figure 2.10
The protests against the possible legislation of Article 23 in Hong Kong in 2003. Fu Hualing, Carole J. Petersen, and Simon N. M. Yong, *National Security and Fundamental Freedoms*, Hong Kong: Hong Kong University Press, 2005, cover page.

Long, the first secretary for transport and public works of the MSAR. Ao embezzled and took bribes in the amount of hundreds of millions of MOPs (Macau patacas or dollars, eight of which equal one US dollar) while in office, and was arrested at the end of 2006 and sentenced in 2008 to 27 years of prison. The elites in Macau need to understand that by holding back democratization, they are virtually encouraging more unfairness, inefficiency, inequality, and corruption in the government.

The debate about a fuller democracy for Macau and how it can be achieved based on the local circumstances here will continue. Is there a possibility of universal suffrage for both the chief executive and the Legislative Council in the near future? What does the legislation of Article 23 of the Basic Law mean for Macau concerning the crime of subverting the Central People's Government, stealing state secrets, and relating to political organizations outside Macau?[142] (See Figure 2.10.) Will it have an effect on freedom of speech in Macau? Social problems cannot be addressed to people's satisfaction if the citizens are not directly related to their representatives in the government. One still wonders in what way the Chinese chief executive can be different from the Portuguese governor.

Conclusions

No matter the political form or the stage of history in international politics, much of the conflict discussed in this chapter concerns sovereignty. If sovereignty means the supreme authority of a state to make rules to govern the people in a certain territory regarding its own political, economic, and social activities, and it is the power of the state to maintain international relations with other countries in the world,[143] then the sovereignty of Macau has almost always been shared, between China and Portugal first, and between Macau and the Chinese central government later.[144] Even after the "permanent occupation and government" arrangement in 1887, the Portuguese did not have full control over the land. In contemporary times, the central government of China does not have full sovereignty of Macau either. This sharing of sovereignty is an interesting phenomenon and has many implications for the future relationships between mainland China and Macau, Hong Kong, as well as Taiwan.

The other interesting issue is the development of democracy, which is related to sovereignty. One can argue that since the Senado period, there have been more and more democratic elements in Macau. At first, there was not a clear division of power between the captain-general, the Senate, and the Judiciary. But since the 1970s, the Senate became independent of the governor, and some of the senators were elected by the populace, most of whom were Chinese. After the handover in 1999, the chief executive was elected by a committee, and then appointed by the central government, rather than only appointed by the latter, as the Portuguese governor used to be by the Portuguese authorities. Even though this is still not a full democracy, we already see more democratization than before. Both the sovereignty and democracy arrangements in Macau, administered under the principle of the "one country, two systems" formula, reflect flexible thinking on social organization on the part of China.

But more democratization is still badly needed. The Chinese Macau has to make an effort to show that it is really different from the Portuguese Macau. The "one country, two systems" formula, "Macau governed by the Macau people," and the "high level of autonomy" will have no real meaning if the form of government does not really bring benefits to the majority of the people in Macau, and if it is still the elites that control all the powers of the city. The current practice has implications for the democratic development in China as well as for the development of future relations among mainland China, Hong Kong, and Taiwan. Political development in Greater China needs to reflect that the Chinese have learned from the lessons of the two Opium Wars.

Macau has existed amid Western capitalist expansion, and its political status fluctuated along with that of China. Now that China is becoming one of the world powers, it faces the question of what kind of world leader it wants to be. And Macau faces the question of what kind of polity it wants to build.

3 Macau's Economy
Making a Living

Cheng Ah-po (鄭阿婆), age 78, was the last remaining daughter of an old and once-wealthy Macau Chinese family whose other members have all emigrated overseas.... [S]he stopped me in front of the enormous old mansion on Rua do Campo ... and told me that every time she passes that building she thinks of the time when it was still inhabited by the man who built it—a businessman by the name of Gou (高), who made his fortune by obtaining the monopoly rights to run gambling establishments in the territory in the first half of the twentieth century.... [On the other hand,] unlicensed opium dealers would disguise themselves as itinerant musicians, she recalled, concealing their merchandise in the pipes of their instruments. It was a kind of tradition they had—they'd travel from wealthy house to wealthy house, playing their instruments and plying their trade, until one day they earned enough money to obtain a license and open a shop. That kind of "*pin mun saang yi*" (偏門生意), or illicit trade, she told me with a certain degree of mirth, is what Macau was built on.

Cathryn Hope Clayton describing her ethnographic studies in Macau[1]

Cheng Ah-po mentioned two *pin mun saang yi*, gambling and opium dealing, that have historically played prominent roles in Macau's economy. Some argue that if fewer people come to Macau to gamble, which happened during the SARS epidemic in 2003, the government will lose most of its income, and Macau will be bankrupt. The restrictions the mainland government occasionally places on the number of times individuals can travel to Macau often lead to a temporary decrease in Macau's gaming incomes. Although overall the income is on the rise, the threat exists. Another possibility is that mainland China and Hong Kong may also establish their own casinos. Singapore has built its own casinos now and Taiwan is likely to build one as well. That is probably why Edmund Ho, then chief executive, said in his press conference on August 29, 2004 that Macau has to be concerned about its future while in prosperity (居安思危).

Macau's Economy

Macau's economic history can be divided into two periods, before the First Opium War, mostly non–*pin mun* business, and after the First Opium War, mostly *pin mun* business (except the cases like fishing and craft industries), when Hong Kong took over Macau's trading role, leading to Macau's search for alternative ways to make a living.[2] We will discuss the gun foundry, or the weapons industry, trade in the 16th and 17th centuries, trade in opium and coolies in the 18th and 19th centuries, as well as various other occupations especially engaged in by the Chinese working and lower classes, including fishing. We will also discuss the rise of the Chinese capitalist class and of the gaming industry, and its problems and prospects in contemporary times.

Cannon Building

Macau's gun foundry probably started between 1557 and 1623. It was controlled by a Spaniard from Manila, who was replaced by Manuel Tavares Bocarro in 1626.[3] The cannon were made of either copper or iron, and the workers were both Chinese and Portuguese. The raw materials, including gun powder, were from China, although Boxer thinks that much of the copper was from Japan.[4] The consumers included both Macau (126 cannon), mainland China, Vietnam, Japan, and the Philippines. (See Figure 3.1.) The Ming dynastic government bought cannon from the Portuguese to fend off both the peasant uprisings of Li Zicheng and the Nuzhen aggression in the Northeast. In fact, they came not only to buy cannon, but to hire Portuguese soldiers to help with the operation of the cannon (購炮募兵).[5] They came to Macau at least three times for the purpose.[6] The gun foundry and the cannon trade ended in 1672 when Bocarro died.[7]

Figure 3.1
Mount Fortress (大炮臺) in Macau with its cannon. Photo by Wang Xin and Zhang Kai.

Trade in the 16th and 17th Centuries

Other trade lasted longer. In the late 16th century and early 17th century, still in the Ming dynasty, there were at least four sea routes, with Macau as their base. They were 1) between Macau and Lisbon via Goa; 2) between Macau and Nagasaki, Japan; 3) between Macau and Mexico via Manila; and 4) between Macau and Timor. The major trading items were silk and textile products from China, and silver to China.[8] For example, concerning the first route between Macau, Goa, and Lisbon, ships would depart from Macau, go through Siam (Thailand now), Burma, Timor, Malacca, Ceylon (Sri Lanka today), and reach Goa. Then they went to Portugal from there. Traders exported silk, jewelry, porcelains, and other textile products from China, and then from Lisbon via Goa, they would take to China pepper, ivory, sandal wood, and silver. Most of the goods were silver, which they originally obtained from Mexico and Peru in exchange of African slaves. This was the time when the Portuguese skirmishes with the Dutch occurred.[9]

One can imagine Portuguese traders sailing in a ship like the one in Figure 3.2. There were big and small ships. It is said that the great ships could hold 600–1,600 tons of goods and could take 500–600 people. Other times they would enjoy Praia

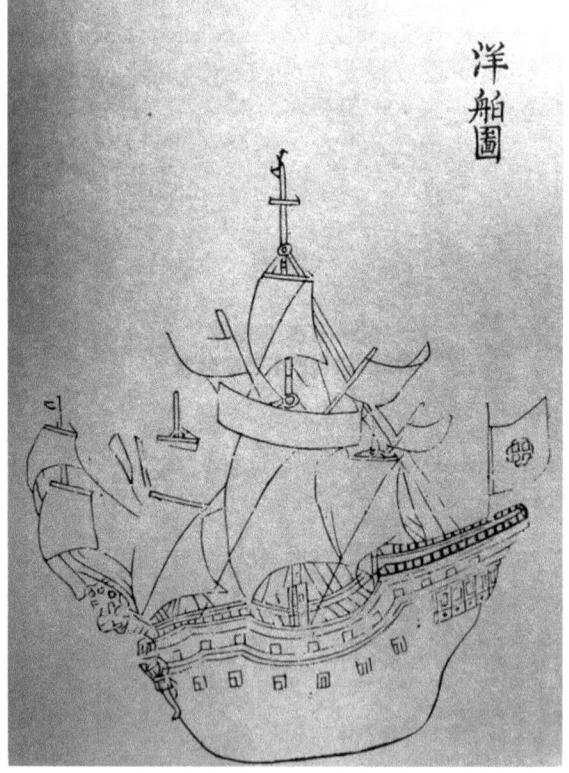

Figure 3.2
A Portuguese ship. Yin Guangren and Zhang Rulin, *Aomen Jilue Jiaozhu*, p. 233.

Figure 3.3
The view of Praia Grande, or Grand Beach. Lei Kun Min and Lam Fat Lam, *Macao in Postcards*, Macau: Macao Association for Historical Education, 2008, p. 105.

Grande (Figure 3.3) while staying in Macau waiting for the proper wind to blow so that they could set off.[10]

Between the founding of the Qing dynasty (1644) and the beginning of the First Opium War (1839), Macau's trade already went through some ups and downs. But trade was in general declining, because, first of all, the Qing government policy in 1655–84 forbade trade and even fishing on the sea as a way to constrain Zheng Chenggong (Koxinga) in Taiwan. When the ban was lifted, the impetus was already gone because other ports like Guangzhou, Ningbo, Quanzhou, and Songjiang were open to foreign trade. In addition, the Japanese expelled the Portuguese from Japan in 1636, so trade there was stopped. The Spanish, the Dutch, and the English all joined the Asian trade and became competitors to the Portuguese. Furthermore, Macau's shallow waters were not helpful at all.[11] After the First Opium War (1839–42), Hong Kong was ceded to the British and became a trading center and Macau's role in trade declined even more.[12]

The Trade in Opium

In the face of declining normal trade, the Portuguese resorted to the trade of opium and coolies. Although it was not clear exactly when opium came to China, one source says that it was brought to China by Buddhist priests and doctors from Tibet around the first century C.E., and used to cure pain. After the Tang dynasty, there were more records of its use, but only after the Ming dynasty did people actually smoke it. Then it became popular, and large quantities of it were smuggled from Taiwan to the mainland. From 1685 on, "most ships coming from India and the South Seas carried opium among their other cargos."[13]

In 1729 the Portuguese were also exporting opium to China through Macau. By the First Opium War, the trade was flourishing, and Macau had become the collection and distribution center. Thousands of chests of opium were exported to China each year. This can be seen by one estimate of the number of Chinese smoking opium: 20% of peasants, 30% of workers, 60% of merchants, 80% of soldiers, 50% of literati, and 80% to 90% of officials (農之食煙者十之二，工之食煙者十之三，買之食煙者十之六，兵之食煙者十之八，士之食煙者十之五。上至督撫僕隸之私，下及縣門與台之賤，其食煙者又十之八九).[14] (See Figure 3.4.) Although those numbers might have been exaggerated, the actual numbers would still be very high. Another estimate puts the number of opium addicts in China in 1835 at 2 million.[15] It became a major social and financial problem.[16]

This problem prompted the Qing government to issue orders in 1756, 1809, and 1821 to forbid the use and import of opium. But the Chinese officials also profited in the opium trade and were part of the smuggling network. Coates observes that if the Chinese officials really wanted to stop opium from coming into China, they could have done it easily in the 1700s[17] and there would not have been any opium wars. But China lost the wars, and the opium trade continued. Although the British now became the number one trader and the Americans the second,[18] the Portuguese in Macau still played a big role.

Opium was Macau's major money maker, just like the gaming industry is today. *Chinese Repository*, an English monthly published in Canton between 1832 and 1851, summarized in one issue that between August 1841 and January 1843, out of the 250 ships recorded, 37 were selling opium. (See Figure 3.5.) Three quarters of the opium to China was from Macau.[19] Macau warehoused opium in its "opium hulks," waiting to be transported to China.[20] In 1918 Macau still made 667,600 dollars from the opium trade, although it declined to 181,900 dollars in 1925.[21]

Figure 3.4

Opium smoking. Geoffrey Gunn, *Aomen Shi* (Encountering Macau), Beijing: Central Compilation and Translation Press, 2009, p. 128.

Figure 3.5
An opium smuggling ship off the coast of Macau in the late 19th century. 孔繁壯, 陳伯良, 劉雅煌, *Macau*, Macau: 澳門出版社, 2002, p. 47.

The Trade in Coolies

The Portuguese began their human trafficking as early as 1443, when they bought and sold African slaves to Europe. When they came to China in the early 1500s, they also bought and sold the Chinese to India. The Chinese did not know what the Portuguese did with those people, so word spread that the Portuguese ate them.[22] By the 1670s, the Portuguese had traded 7,500 negroes to Brazil, mostly from Angola, a colony of Portugal.[23] In the years of the declining normal trade in the late 1800s, they stepped up their trade of "slaves" in China, or what was called the "coolie trade." A formal government office was set up in 1860 to regulate the agencies in Macau to do the business. Such agencies were called *zhuzai guan* (豬仔館, a place that sell pigs) by the Chinese. The Portuguese called them barracões (barracoons), which were also referred to as "holding cells." By 1866 there were already 35 to 40 such agencies/holding cells, owned by either the Portuguese, the Spanish, or the Dutch. There were 800 coolie brokers by the 1870s.[24]

According to some Portuguese government documents, from 1856 to 1873, there were 180,061 coolies exported to Cuba and Peru.[25] Many of them were said to be either misled, kidnapped, or lured to gambling in Macau. To pay for their gambling debts, they sold themselves as coolies. But Coates writes that the Chinese came to Macau because they wanted to emigrate to other countries and wanted a place on the ships. Pina-Cabral also mentions that the coolie trade was "largely due to the fact that there was a large increase in the number of people wishing to emigrate from southern China in the decades that followed the social disorder and devastation caused by the Taiping revolution and its suppression (1850–64)."[26] That was probably true, and there might have been voluntary emigrants. But these other situations probably happened as well. When they were in Macau, they were put into holding cells by the employment agencies until they were shipped overseas. The conditions of those cells were so harsh that about 10 of them would commit suicide each day. On their way to South America, they were housed in close quarters, with often only sitting space, and were fed simple food. As a result the average death rate was 35.3%. Other times, uprisings led to the destruction of both the ships and the people on it

Figure 3.6
Coolies in rebellion. Edgar Holden, *Harper's New Monthly Magazine*: A Chapter on the Coolie Trade 29 Vol. Harper & Brothers, 06/01/1864. Web. November 20, 2015. 1–10, at http://scalar.usc.edu/works/the-voyages-of-the-clarence/norway-2, accessed October 9, 2018.

(see Figure 3.6). The accounts in Box 3.1 by the coolies themselves are most illuminating.[27] The coolie trade was officially forbidden in 1873 after protests and outcries from the Chinese as well as international communities, but it continued secretly. Then the British took over the trade through Hong Kong.[28] Since people could no longer engage openly in the coolie trade, gambling made bigger strides in Macau.

Box 3.1 Accounts by Coolies

> Of the more than 140,000 Chinese who sailed for Cuba, more than 16,000 died during the voyage . . . the petition of Li Chao-chun (李肇春) and 165 others states, "when, quitting Macao, we proceeded to sea, we were confined in the hold below; some were even shut up in bamboo cages, or chained to iron posts, and a few were indiscriminately selected and flogged as a means of intimidating all others; whilst we cannot estimate the deaths that, in all, took place, from sickness, blows, hunger, thirst, or from suicide by leaping into the sea."
>
> The petition of Hsieh Shuang-chiu (謝雙就) and 11 others states, "on landing, four or five foreigners on horseback, armed with whips, led us like a herd of cattle to the barracoon to be sold." The petition of Chiu Pi-shan (邱碧山) and 34 others states, "Chinese (in the Havana baraccons) are treated like pigs and dogs, all the movements, even their meals, being watched, until, after the lapse of a few days, they are sold away."

The petition of Yeh Fu-chun (葉福君) and 52 others states, "when offered for sale in the men-market we were divided into three classes—1st, 2nd, and 3rd, and were forced to remove all our clothes, so that our persons might be examined and the price fixed. This covered us with shame."

Wu A-chiang (伍阿祥) deposes also, "I myself have seen men flogged until they vomited blood, and death ensued a few days afterwards." Li A-wu (李阿伍) deposes, "if on the sugar plantations the task assigned is executed at all slowly, the overseers at once inflicted several tens of blows, drawing blood, lacerating the skin, and causing inflamed swellings." Chen te-cheng (陳得正) deposes, "if the work is not performed to the satisfaction of the administrator, imprisonment and working in chains are resorted to, or 20, 25, 50 or an indefinite number of blows are inflicted, causing the blood and flesh to trickle down." Chu Chia-hsien (朱甲先) deposes, "the overseer said it did not matter if we died, as others could be bought to take our places."

Pilots, Compradors, Servants, Slaves, Coolies, Prostitutes, and Pirates

The following are some different supporting roles to the traders. Some had higher social status, while others lower.

Pilots and Compradors[29]

The ships coming up the Pearl River numbered 20 in the 1760s, 50 in the 1790s, 70 in the 1810s, and over 180 in the 1830s.[30] Traversing the Pearl River from Macau to Humen (Bocca Tigris) and Huangpu (Whampoa) was no small undertaking in the early 18th century: there were strong currents, frequent storms, and many perils lying beneath the river, especially for deep-running vessels. So pilots were needed, of which there were two kinds: licensed and outside pilots. There were 14 licensed pilots in the early 1830s,[31] and they would pilot the ships from Macau to Whampoa. Outside pilots would direct the ships from the outer waters to Macau. Both kinds were Chinese, because foreigners were not allowed to pilot ships to Canton, and they were frequently fishermen by trade. They could speak a few words of Portuguese or English or at least knew how to use gestures regarding the job. They were hard bargainers, too; the following description by an Englishman gives us an idea of their everyday interaction among themselves and with foreigners:

> At one in the afternoon, a Chinese pilot came on board; and very soon after, another arrived, and insisted upon conducting the ship, and without any ceremony began to order the sails to be trimmed. The first however would not give up the point, and a long altercation ensued, but at length they settled it, having agreed to divide the money which has to be paid and which amounted to twenty-five dollars.[32]

These pilots would also sell provisions to foreigners, and they might also be closely involved in the contraband trade and assist ships that smuggled contraband to China. The outside pilots, for example, would direct the foreign ships to bypass the Chinese authorities in Macau and Canton. Macau pilots were found to use their connections with the foreigners to smuggle opium into China.[33] Nonetheless, piloting was a way of life for some Chinese.

Van Dyke's description of compradors in Canton might also help us understand the compradors in Macau. The word "comprador" is Portuguese, meaning "buyer," but compradors tended to both buy and sell between the Chinese and the foreigners. There were ship-compradors, house-compradors, and factory-compradors that serve foreigners' trading needs, especially their provision needs. They would deliver baskets of fruit and vegetables, huge quantities of coal, charcoal, and firewood, as well as fresh water. They would even take care of the foreign sailors' burials when the latter died of illnesses or accidents while staying in Canton.[34]

Compradors were many, since the foreigners needed them to help in their interaction with the Chinese in their trade and provisions. Harriett Low, a young American woman who had come to Macau with her uncle's family, which conducted business in China, wrote about her encounter with a Chinese comprador in her diary in 1829:

> Our servant or Compradore is [a] very shrewd fellow, speaks pretty good English; he wanted to know to day if Mr. Cleveland was not 30 years older than I am. [He was 32 years older.—Comments like this should be the editors'.] I asked how he knew how old I was. O, he says, "I can see; I can *sava* (know)." He inquired if I had father, mother, brothers, and sisters, and if they "liky have me catchy" this country. He made many inquires which amused me much. His name is Apew. The boy's name is Apun. The others I know nothing about.[35]

Slaves, Servants, Coolies, and Prostitutes

There were also slaves, servants, coolies, and prostitutes, at the bottom of the social ladder. In 1749, for example, 70 woodworkers and bricklayers, 10 butchers, 4 blacksmiths, and 100 coolies were permitted to live in the Portuguese city. Most people worked in the city during the day and left at the day's end. There were personal servants, laundrymen, hawkers, as well as laborers.[36] The following descriptions give an idea of these groups of the working class.[37] According to a description of Macau in 1635 by Antonio Bocarro, chronicler-in-chief of the State of India,

> The families in this city number 850 Portuguese with their children, who are much stronger and lustier than any others in this East. These all have on the average about six slaves capable of bearing arms, amongst whom the majority and the best are Negroes and such like. When it is considered that these latter row small skiffs (balloes) in which their masters amuse themselves by cruising amongst those

islands, they might very well have larger yachts (manchuas) which would be very useful for their own welfare as well as for the service of His Majesty.[38]

The description tells us that there were many African slaves living in Macau. This is a time when there were most African slaves, about 5,100. In comparison there were about 1,000 to 2,000 during the later Portuguese rule in Macau.[39]

Harriett Low wrote in her journal on Saturday, December 6, 1829, about a woman friend's household:

> She lives in a perfect palace. She has 18 Caffres live with her and is obligated to keep 12 sepoys to take care of them beside China servants, Bengalies and every thing else. She has an immense household.[40]

Based on Yin Guangren's and Zhang Rulin's description, here the word "Caffres" refers to slaves from Africa and from some other South Sea Island. The sepoys were natives of India employed by Europeans as guards or soldiers.

> Below the main floor of the typical house and its verandas was the dark, arched ground floor, to which the slaves and servants were relegated and where merchandise and supplies were stored. "Leftover food [was] thrown into a dish like a horse trough for the black male and female slaves to eat as they please."[41]

They could be treated cruelly, as Harriett Low describes:

> My chair was stopped on its way home with old Golatti beating his slaves. They misbehaved and he took his stick to them and gave them some awful thwacks, and I was made an unwilling witness of it, for my bearers would not go on, thinking I suppose they might come in for a *share* in passing. These streets are so narrow.[42]

But other times, especially on the New Year's Day, slaves could be happy, as Low observes, although her own racism is again in display:

> The Caffres were all dressed in most fantastic dresses parading the streets, singing and enjoying themselves—seem the happiest creatures in existence. Animal pleasures alone constitute their happiness, however.[43]

Because the Africans were often soldiers in Macau, they tended to get into direct conflict with the Chinese. For example, the 5-29 Incident in 1922 began with an African-Portuguese soldier's harassment of a Chinese woman.[44] The Guanzha Incident at the border in 1952 with the mainland soldiers occurred when an African Portuguese soldier crossed the demarcation line.[45]

Coolies would include people who carried the sedan chairs or pulled rickshaws. Here is what Low wrote about at least one of them and about some Chinese men, whose jobs we do not know (see Figure 3.7):

> I forgot to tell you of the walk we had Saturday afternoon. We went out with the coolly, and he carried us all around the Prio [Praya] Grande, over the great hill and

Figure 3.7
A sedan chair for women. Yin Guangren and Zhang Rulin, *Aomen Jilue Jiaozhu*, p. 232.

back through the town, a monstrous walk. And for the first walk it was terrible. It is so long since we have walked that it overcome us all. The streets here are intolerable, hilly, irregular and horribly paved. You meet no one but Portuguese and Chinese men, and they annoyed us very much by their intent gaze.[46]

Although we do not know exactly how this Chinese carried the women, it is clear he was their servant.

Apparently many Chinese served the foreigners in Macau. For an idea of the specific interactions between the Chinese and foreigners, I will again cite a quote in Van Dyke, originally from a 1787 foreign trader's description of Chinese serving foreigners in Huangpu (Whampoa):

> Soon as we cast anchor [at Whampoa] the vessel was surrounded with sampans. Every one had some request to make. Tartar [Chinese] girls requested our clothes to wash, barbers to shave the crews, others with fowls to sell; indeed, every necessary we could want. The first we made bargain with was a barber, Tommy Linn. He agreed to shave the crew for the six months we were to be there for half a dollar from each man, and he would shave every morning, if we chose, on board the ship, coming off in this sampan.
>
> The Tartar girls washed our clothes for the broken meat or what rice we left at mess. They came every day in their sampans and took away the men's shirts, bringing them back the next, and never mixed the clothes. They all spoke less or more English and would jaw with the crew as any women of their rank in England. They

had a cage-like box fixed to the stern of their sampan in which was a pig who fed and fattened there at his ease.⁴⁷

In chapter 4, we cite a quote from Harriett Low where she discusses her encounter with an old Chinese lady asking her for housework to do. Chinese served not only foreigners, but also the Macanese and Chinese wealthy families. We see that, for example, in memoirs of Jorge Rangel, Arnaldo de Oliveira Sales, José Chui, and David Chow Kam-fai.⁴⁸

A sex market also existed in Huangpu (Whampoa). Those involved in the business were either small entrepreneurs or working for brothels. There were also floating brothels, known as "flower boats," which serviced foreign ships. Although no Chinese was allowed to contact the foreigners directly, those rules were ignored if the Chinese officials got a payment in exchange.⁴⁹ Harriett Low writes:

> near Whampoa, was a whole class of water-borne prostitutes, whose services presumably helped to calm restless sailors during their "lay-days" at the anchorage.⁵⁰

In Macau, a class of prostitutes existed and they were more or less regulated by the state since 1851 and confined in certain areas or sanctioned houses of prostitution. Some of them were orphans that had been taken care of by the Santa Casa da Misericordia. In the 1930s the government sought to eliminate exploitation and abuses of prostitutes, but it did not aim at the elimination of prostitution.⁵¹ (See Plate 3.1, Fulong Xin Jie or Rua da Felicidade, where many brothels were located.)

Pirates

One of the reasons the Chinese government allowed the Portuguese to stay in Macau was the latter's help in fending against foreigners and pirates (see Figure 3.8 for a pirate ship). The first excerpt below is about pirates attacking opium ships after the First Opium War. Jules Itier, a French businessman and traveler, was visiting a French opium ship anchored in Taipa, Macau in 1842. He was asking the captain why they had their cannon aiming to sink and whether they intended to fight off Chinese government inspectors. No, the captain said, their aim was the pirates. He went on to say,

Figure 3.8
A pirate ship. Courtesy of Oxford University Press.

The Chinese pirates who infest this neighborhood are very fond of our cargo, and because it is necessary to beware of such people. They gather together in large numbers in their boats, and during the night, encircle anchored ships that have no artillery to fight them off. Then they mount a resolute attack, cutting the throats of the crew and pillaging the cargo. Such events are common.[52]

The second excerpt is from Aleko E. Lilius, an American journalist. He was commissioned by a group of magazines in the United States to do a report on pirates in the Pearl River Delta, in which he writes about what is described as "a female Chinese version of Robin Hood," "the Queen of the Macao pirates" (see Figure 3.9). Her name was Lai Choi San, and she inherited the businesses and ships from her father. She now had 12 junks, and like her father, also helped the government in protecting Macao's enormous fishing fleets and doing general police duty. But pirates "harass and plunder any ship or village they can lay their hands upon. They kidnap men, women and children, hold them for ransom, ransack their homes, and burn their junks and sampans … Lai Choi San is supposed to be the worst of them all; she is said to be both ruthless and cruel."[53]

What a woman she was! Rather slender and short, her hair jet black with jade pins gleaming in the knot at the neck, her earrings and bracelets of the same precious apple-green stone. She was exquisitely dressed in a white satin robe fastened with green jade buttons, and green silk slippers. She wore a few plain gold rings on her left hand; her right hand was unadorned. Her face and dark eyes were intelligent—not too Chinese, although purely Mongolian, of course—and rather hard. She was probably not yet forty.

Every move she made and every word she spoke told plainly that she expected to be obeyed, and as I had occasion to learn later, she *was* obeyed.[54]

Figure 3.9
Queen of Pirates. Courtesy of Oxford University Press.

The third excerpt is an eyewitness account by Richard Glasspoole, an Englishman, whose boat had been lost in a storm about six to seven miles from Macau, and he and his crew of seven men were captured by Chinese pirates. His boat had been separated from his East India Company's ship, *Marquis of Ely*. They now sailed with the pirates while waiting for the ransom money from his company. This is what he saw:

> I must not omit to mention a most horrid (though ludicrous) circumstance which happened at this place. The Ladrones [Portuguese word for thieves] were paid by their chief ten dollars for every Chinaman's head they produced [in their raids to a town named Little Whompoa, and the Englishmen also agreed to join the raid and would be paid 20 dollars for every head they would produce]. One of my men turning a corner of a street was met by a Ladrone running furiously after a Chinese; he had a drawn sword in his hand, and two Chinaman's heads which he had cut off, tied by their tails, and slung round his neck. I was witness myself to some of them producing five or six to obtain payments!!![55]

This happened around 1801, a time around which Macau's pirate activities peaked. Of course, the above accounts were written by a Frenchman, an American, and an Englishman, and they might look at Chinese pirates from an Orientalist point of view. Nonetheless, they still provide a rough idea of what pirates were like at the time. It was at least a way of making a living.

In the conflicts between the Portuguese and the Dutch, both parties would also sometimes behave like pirates, especially the latter. There was indeed a group of Portuguese who became pirates, called "Macau ruffians," or policemen who turned bad, along with "Manila-men" from the Philippines and escaped African slaves. Their fleet attacked "the Cantonese ships when they could get them at an advantage, and murdered their crews with circumstances of great atrocity."[56] They were destroyed in Ningbo by a fleet of Chinese pirates with the support of the local Chinese government and other Europeans.[57]

Fishermen and Fisherwomen

The people of *Dan*, fishermen and fisherwomen, are the aborigines in Macau. Fishing as an occupation continues today, albeit in decline. George Chinnery, a British artist, for example, lived in Macau for more than 20 years and painted many Macau scenes, including the life of fishermen and fisherwomen. Plate 3.2 is one of them.[58]

Rebecca Kinsman, an American woman living in Macau at the time, like Harriett Low, wrote in her diary about fishermen and fisherwomen, especially a fisherwoman and her child, which gives us a fuller view of the lives of the fishing families. Here is what she wrote on August 3, 1844:

> ... as I raise my eyes from my paper, and see this beautiful roadstead with the numberless boats, so near us, that the voices of the boatmen are distinctly heard, and could we understand the language, we might know (were it worth knowing) what they say. At this moment, a little tankah-boat is before the window, looking almost like an egg-shell upon the waters, from its smallness and frailty of appearance. Here lives a family—here probably they were born, and will perhaps die. The mother has her baby fastened to her back, and as she pulls the oar, the motion rocks the little one, who seems to enjoy it. I cannot see how many this boat contains, as it is covered or roofed over one end, but frequently a mother, with one or two grown-up daughters, and two or more little children, live on the boat, and sometimes two women join their means and take a boat together. They are managed entirely by women, whose husbands are either coolies on shore, or more probably fishermen of larger boats. But it is really interesting to watch with what skill they manage these little cockleshells.[59]

Peter Mundy, an English traveler, also depicts a fisherman's home in his travelogue in 1637. Here is an excerpt:

> A poore mans boate by which he getteth his living either by Fishing or transporting or carrying goodes, where hee keepeth house with his Family, soe thatt not only himselffe, but his weife with a Child att her backe (which is as good as rocking For it), with the rest of the Children, alle putt hand to the Oare. This representts a watcheboate with a Portugall sitting in her, hired; of these Many aboutt and in Macao.[60]

These two depictions, though 200 years apart, are very similar. There was, however, a trend for fishermen and women gradually moving to live on land.

But life on a boat was not really as easy and calm as one would think. Here is Mrs. Fong Gamho's description of her life on the sea. She was born on a junk on the sea south of Macau in 1934. She first describes how difficult it was to raise children on the sea.

> It isn't easy coping with young children on a working boat. When they were very little, we tied them onto the boat with a rope harness for their own safety. When they got a bit bigger, we'd tell them to stay lying down. Otherwise they could get hurt with everything going on around them. Then, from the age of about four, they started working with us, helping out with the catch. We might still tie them up to something on the boat for a while so they wouldn't get swept overboard.[61]

Following is a long quote that depicts how Mrs. Fong Gamho coped with cooking for the family on the boat. If the sea was too rough, they had to go without eating at all.

> I did all the cooking for the family. I had to keep both hands on the stove when it was lit and hold down everything else as well or things would all spill. We had a small wood burning stove, and carried enough split wood for about ten day's cooking.

> Our diet was fish. That was it. No chicken, or pork, or any other kind of meat. We didn't have any fresh vegetables either. So we ate fish with rice, sometimes with a kind of pickled vegetable, and I cooked with oil and sugar. That was the lot. No milk, nothing. Sometimes I'd make congee [rice porridge]. Other times, we bought some beans and I cooked them with sugar and rice to make a sort of sweet congee. If there wasn't any sugar, we'd put fish in it instead and make it a salty congee.
>
> If the weather was bad and the boat was pitching and tossing, I couldn't cook at all. It was too dangerous. So either we'd have to go without food all day or we'd have to head off to somewhere calmer, like the nearest typhoon shelter, and I'd start cooking when we go there. We didn't get ill very often. In fact, I think we get ill more now, since we came to live on the land![62]

Indeed, not only did she get ill more often on land, she found that she would have to spend "a lot of" money to buy fish, whereas in the olden days they could get as much fish as they wanted, free of charge! Nonetheless, she was much happier when they sold their boat and began to live on dry land. Life was more secure, and there were no pirates or storms to deal with. Their four sons were all working on land.

It is no wonder then that in Macau there are only about 500 fishermen and women now.[63] In contrast, in 1920, there were 1,800 boats and 40,000 people, or 28% of the population were engaged in the fishing industry, either out on the sea or doing trading on land.[64] There are many reasons why they moved on shore. In the 1960s and 1970s there used to be plenty of fish around, but not any more now due to land reclamation and water pollution. The fishermen have to go farther away from the land to deeper waters, and stay longer on the sea. But that would require better and larger vessels, and more money to buy them, and they did not really get much help from the government. Fong Gamho's husband, Sin Dohan, reported that he bought a motorized boat in 1978 and it cost him 200,000 patacas, which was a lot of money.[65] So by the 1980s, many fishermen and women moved ashore and found new jobs, most likely in the construction business. The fishing industry is thus in danger of virtual extinction. There are no longer fishing families in boat dwellings. The fishing crews are more likely to be composed of male relatives with hired hands from the mainland.[66]

In sum, other than the traders, Portuguese or otherwise, there were also compradors, African slaves and soldiers, Chinese servants and workers of various kinds, as well as fishermen and fisherwomen. They played a supporting role for the traders in Macau. Apart from the compradors, most people in these groups belonged to the lower class in the Macau society. There seemed to be a dual track of the foreign traders on the one hand and Chinese/African/Indian servants on the other. In addition, there was a group of wealthy Chinese who would play a leading role in Macau's economy just as the Portuguese traders did before. A dual track of the Portuguese political elite vis-à-vis the Chinese economic elite might have developed, as had a dual track of the working class and the capitalist class.

The Development of the Modern Chinese Working and Capitalist Classes

If the fishermen and fisherwomen, coolies (cargo coolies, waterfront coolies, rickshaw coolies), prostitutes, and other servants were one kind of working class, there was another kind: the craft workers and a smaller number of other industrial workers.

While the Portuguese trade declined in importance in Macau's economy, Chinese industry began to develop in the late 1800s and early 1900s. According to one estimate, by 1896 there were already 1,075 commercial and industrial enterprises owned by the Chinese, with 6,803 workers, while there were only 11 Portuguese enterprises with 35 workers engaged in trade concerning tea, construction materials, and textiles.[67] In 1920, commercial and industrial development grew so fast that there were 7,154 people engaged in commerce, stocks, and exchange, while over 26,000 engaged in industrial production, including incense (神香), firecrackers (爆竹), matches (火柴), tobacco, Chinese liquor, etc.[68]

In 1930, incense products constituted 6% of Macau's total exports, and there were 20 such factories, employing over 3,000 workers. Firecrackers constituted 15.9% of the exports, with 10 such factories, each employing over 1,000 workers. Matches also constituted 15.9% of Macau's total exports, with 3 major factories, each employing around 700. At the same time, there are other factories such as boat building (20), tobacco (10 of them), canneries (8), cooking oil (6), liquor (54), flour (18), glass (10), copper (12), etc. They might have hired fewer workers than the three major craft industries above, but together the number hired could still be great. A textile factory alone, for example, hired 300 workers.[69]

The development of such industries helped the growth of a working class. The working class, as usual, while having a job to do so as to make a living, often had to suffer from the consequences of industrialization and for the wealth accumulation on the part of the capitalists. For example, in the 20 years in the early 20th century, ten serious accidents happened in firecracker factories, leading to the deaths of 20 workers. In addition, workers were subject to various professional diseases caused by powder dust. The unions were not able to help them much. (In the 1960s about 2,000 workers joined trade unions.) There were more women workers than men workers, and their children often went to work with them, as we can see in Figure 3.10.[70]

Along with the growth of a working class, an industrial capitalist class had arisen among the Chinese. In the early years of the Portuguese trade, and by the beginning of the 20th century, a commercial capitalist class was also already in the making. If the Portuguese were doing business with China in the 300 years after they came here, they needed not only compradors, but also a corresponding Chinese commercial class at the same time. According to Yang Renfei, there were two kinds of traders on the Chinese part: the government traders and the private traders.[71] Both made money in their trade with the Portuguese, either in silk and tea at first

Figure 3.10
A firecracker workshop, a traditional handicraft in Macau. Ruan Zirong, "Aomen Koushu Shi: Huo Huashi de Huiyi" (Macau oral history: The memory of a "living fossil"), at https://www.thepaper.cn/newsDetail_forward_2463790, accessed October 9, 2018.

or opium and coolies later. So a commercial capitalist class, or comprador class, was already in the making in the first 300 years of the Portuguese trade in Macau. By 1930s and 1940s, commerce and trade flourished. Between 1937 and 1941, for example, there were 2,804 shops in Macau of various kinds.[72] One could see the further growth of a bourgeois class. Figures 3.11, 3.12, and 3.13 show the prosperity of businesses in the street.

Some of the famous industrialists and commercial capitalists in the early 20th century include Wang Fu 王福, who came to Macau before the First Opium War and worked in a foreign company engaged in tea trade. He and his son Wang Lu 王祿 accumulated enough capital and invested in real estate business in Macau. Chen Fang 陳芳, Chen Jiageng 陳嘉庚, Liang Chang 梁昌, and He Xian 何賢 (Ho Yin) also did business in Macau and made their fortunes.[73] He Xian ran a business empire composed of banks, hotels, restaurants, and transport companies, and also served as

Figure 3.11
Street vendors. Photo by Ou Ping. *A Voyage in Time*, Macau: Museu de Arte de Macau, 2005, p. 47.

Figure 3.12
Chinese grocery stores. Photo by Raymond Wong.

Figure 3.13
Market-place in front of Largo do Pagode do Bazar. Ho Weng Hong, *The Past of Macau*, Macau: Macao Foundation, 1994, p. 164.

a bridge among the Chinese community in Macau, mainland Chinese government, and the Portuguese Macau government.[74] Edmund Ho Hau-wah, his son and the chief executive of Macau for the first two terms, also served the same functions later.

In 1880 there were 400 gambling parlors and many made their fortunes in that field and became *du wang* (賭王), or "gambling tycoons" since the 19th century, including Lu Jiu 盧九, Lu Lianruo 盧廉若, Xiao Yingzhou 蕭瀛洲, Gao Kening 高可甯, Fu Laorong 傅老榕, and Fan Jiepeng 范潔鵬. Lu Jiu, born in 1837, was engaged in opium and gambling businesses, and also functioned as the bridge between the Chinese in Macau and the Portuguese government. Lu Lianruo was his son, and he did real estate in addition.[75] The most famous of all the *du wang*, of course, is Stanley Ho 何鴻燊.[76]

But the traditional craft industries gradually declined and a manufacturing industry arose, which produced toys, electronic goods, artificial flowers, as well as textiles and garments. In the 1980s, textiles and garments dominated the sector and employed 64% of the total labor force. (The population in Macau at that time was about 170,000 to 180,000.) They accounted for 73% of Macau's total exports.[77] With the opening up of mainland China, however, manufacturing in Macau declined. It constituted 36% of the total industrial output in 1984, but by 1990, its share already decreased to 26%.[78]

On the other hand, there has been an increase in the number of construction companies. In the early 1990s, there were 170 construction companies that hired over 10,000 workers. Among the companies, some were local, and others were from mainland China.[79]

While the conventional businesses like the industrial factories declined toward the latter part of the 20th century, the gambling business thrived.

The Rise of the Gambling Industry

There were many reasons why gambling flourished in Macau. First, there was the urgent need for a source of revenue for the Macau government, as the opium and coolie trade declined in Macau in the latter half of the 19th century. The situation in Macau was dire, as can be seen from a description by one of the Qing officials in his memorial to the emperor:

澳門居住葡人，官無善政，商無善賈，工無善藝，惟藉賭館娼寮，包私庇匪，收受漏規，為自然之力。……葡國既無商船來往，澳門別無地利可圖，市面蕭條，人情渙散，其坐困情形，可立而待。[80]

The report says that without the foreign trade as before, neither the government nor the people in Macau knew what to do except rely on gambling and prostitution as well as other non-conventional businesses. This dismal situation was also depicted by Montalto de Jesus.⁸¹ This provided the needs to find a source of income for the government.

Second, gambling may be in the nature of all human beings, and the *vaeseng* lottery (闈姓) was already popular in Guangdong in the latter half of the 19th century. The participants in the lottery gambled on the names of the successful candidates in the imperial examinations. Other forms of gambling like *fantan* (番攤) (see Box 3.2), *baigepiao* (白鴿票), *mahjong* (麻雀, or 麻將) also flourished.⁸² One newspaper reports specifically picked out Guangdong people as the number one in China (or in the world) who enjoyed gambling: 粵賭風之盛甲於天下.⁸³

Box 3.2 Fantan, the oldest way of gambling

> **Fantan, a Way of Gambling**
>
> 所謂"番攤"，是由莊家從一堆銅錢或鈕扣、蠶豆之中取出一小攤，用一個盅子將這小"攤子"蓋住，然後由賭客在1、2、3、4這四個數字上投注。隨後由莊家揭開盅子，當眾將銅錢或鈕扣以4個一組予以清點，最後如果剩1枚銅錢或一粒鈕扣，即以押"1"數者為中彩，如剩2枚（粒），即以押"2"數者為中彩，餘類推。中彩者可得賠所押之注款2.8倍的彩金，而押其餘數字者均為輸家。⁸⁴
>
> Fantan is a game usually played upon a mat-covered table, with a [randomly selected] quantity of Chinese coins or other small objects [like buttons] which are covered with a cup. The players guess what remainder will be left when the pile is divided by four [or one, or two, or three], and bet upon the result. The name means "repeatedly spreading out," and refers to the manner in which the coins or other objects are spread out upon the table.⁸⁵

Third, although it is not clear how important this factor is, the rise of the gambling industry in the middle of the 19th century might have to do with the coolie trade. One of the ways for the businessmen to find people willing to be sold overseas in servitude is to get them to Macau and in debt through gambling. Then they would have to sell themselves to pay off their debts.⁸⁶

Fourth, and maybe most importantly, both Hong Kong and mainland China banned gambling. Although the ban was not very effective, it nonetheless gave Macau an opportunity to develop gambling and attract businesses. In 1872, the British government prohibited gambling in Hong Kong, so gamblers had to travel to Macau. At the same time, gambling was banned on the mainland. The Chinese businessmen moved to Macau to set up shop. This combined ban outside of Macau certainly helped the gambling business grow. The city then was seen as the Monte Carlo of the East.

With all these factors, gambling flourished. In fact, the Portuguese had already formally licensed the gambling houses, like the *fantan* saloon in 1847 (see Figures 3.14 and 3.15).⁸⁷ Gambling was therefore legalized. Gambling facilities numbered

Figure 3.14
A *fantan* saloon in old Macau. Macau Data website: http://www.macaudata.com/macauweb/book114/, accessed February 16, 2005.

Figure 3.15
Playing *fantan* in a gambling den in Macau. Benjamim Videira Pires, "The Chinese Quarter One Hundred Years Ago," Macau Cultural Affairs Bureau at http://www.icm.gov.mo/rc/viewer/20007/867, accessed October 9, 2018.

Figure 3.16
Casino Lisboa. Photo by Wang Xin and Zhang Kai.

up to 26 in the 1870s, especially *fantan*.[88] In 1910, according to government statistics, 70% of the administration's income came from gambling and opium.[89]

There were many other ways of gambling, including playing dice (*tou zi* 骰子 or *shai zi* 色子), or lotteries like *pupiao* (鋪票), *shanpiao* (山票). Horse racing was introduced in 1842, suspended in 1846, but resumed in 1924. In the 1940s, dog racing and cricket fighting were also introduced.

With the growth of gambling, the government granted exclusive rights to the Taixing Company for casino-style gambling in 1937. When Taixing's contract expired in 1962, Stanley Ho's Macau Tourism and Entertainment Company (Sociedade de Turismo e Diversões de Macau, or STDM) won the monopoly (see Figure 3.16).[90] Stanley Ho's business interests have extended also to transportation, real estate, electronics, hotels, air cargo, and restaurants. His Shun Tak Holdings, for example, owns the largest fleet of jetfoils in the world, which accounted for 70% of the Hong Kong–Macau passenger traffic.[91]

In 2001, two years after Macau was returned to China, the MSAR government decided to open the industry to competition rather than keep the STDM monopoly. In 2002 it granted new licenses to three gaming companies: STDM, now called SJM, or Sociedade de Jogos de Macao, i.e., Macao gaming company; Wynn Resorts; and the Galaxy Group of Hong Kong. Then the Galaxy Group offered a large concession to Las Vegas Sands (LVS), a former partner, which immediately built one of the largest casinos in Macau, Sands Macao, opened in 2004, and then the Venetian Macao in 2007, The Plaza Macao in 2008, Sands Cotai Central in 2012, and The Parisian Macao in 2016.

Meanwhile, Wynn Resorts offered a sub-concession to Melco PBL, which opened Crown Casino in Taipa in 2007. Then it opened another casino on the Cotai Strip in 2009, named it Crown, and renamed the other hotel in Taipa as Altira. Melco is the Melco International Development Limited 新濠國際發展有

限公司, a conglomerate in leisure, gaming, and entertainment, located in Hong Kong and with Yau Lung Ho, a son of Stanley Ho, as the chairman of the board and chief executive officer. PBL is a broadcasting and entertainment industry based in Australia. But PBL (Crown) sold its stake in 2016 and 2017 and Melco has then become the single largest shareholder of the company now called Melco Resorts (Macau) Limited. Melco's properties include City of Dreams, Studio City, Altira Macao, and various Mocha clubs. It has become a transnational corporation with a casino in the Philippines, another being built in Cyprus, and ambitions to build one in Japan.[92]

SJM offered a concession to MGM Grand Macao, which opened in late 2007. MGM Grand Macao is a partnership between MGM Mirage of Las Vegas and Pansy Ho Chiu-king, one of Stanley Ho's daughters, the chairwoman of Macao Tower Convention & Entertainment Centre, and executive director of Air Macao Company Limited. Now it has two properties: MGM Macao and MGM Taipa. Now there are six casino operators in the industry.

At the same time, SJM has built a number of new casinos, including Grand Lisboa, Casino Ponte 16, Casino L'Arc Macau, etc., and it now has altogether 20 casinos. Wynn Resorts opened Wynn Macau in 2006 and Wynn Palace in Taipa in 2016. In addition to building a number of other casino hotels, the Galaxy Group opened its first flagship casino StarWorld in 2006 and then Galaxy Macau and Broadway Macau in Taipa in 2015. According to government statistics, by the second quarter of 2018, Macau had altogether 41 casinos.[93]

Several issues about the gambling industry need to be discussed. I will focus only on some political, economic, ethical, and even legal issues and problems in this chapter, and will discuss various casino-related social problems in chapter 7. First, it is still not clear whether it was legal for the original three concessions to each offer a sub-concession to a different company, especially when the offerings were not free. While the split between Galaxy and Sands did not involve a payment, MGM Grand paid US$300 million to SJM, and Melco-PBL paid US$900 to Wynn Resorts for their sub-concessions.[94] If there had been a need for sub-concessions, should not the licensing power have been in the hands of the government? If money had needed to be paid, should not the government have been the payee? This should say much about the nature of politics in Macau we discussed in chapter 2. Does it favor the rich and powerful?

Second, gambling is the leading industry in Macau and the major money maker for the government. Macau has already become the world's gambling mecca, having logged over MOP$360.7 billion, or US$45.1 billion, in 2014 (with MOP$8 equals US$1), surpassing Las Vegas's US$ 7.0 billion in the same year.[95] There was a major decline in revenue in 2015 and 2016 to about US$27.9 billion. But revenue increased again in 2017 to US$33.2 billion and it is continuing to grow sometimes by double digits. The increased casino revenue also means increased government tax dollars. The six concessionaires each have to pay 35% taxes on their gross gaming revenues in addition to 1.6% of them to the Macao Foundation for social, economic, and cultural development, and 2.4% for urban development and construction. This means that in 2013 alone, the Macao government collected MOP$140.7 billion in gambling taxes. Over 80% of government revenue comes from gambling. According to the World Bank, with a GDP per capita of US$80,892.8, Macau became the second richest territory in the world in 2017, trailing only Luxembourg.[96]

Third, we have mentioned the problem of granting sub-concessionaire licenses. But along with such economic successes are more political, ethical, and legal problems. For example, an interim gambling industry review commissioned by the Macau government found that the number of non-compliance, i.e., failing to exercise minimum internal control required for their operations, is fairly high.[97] The review report does not give specific examples of non-compliance, but it does give the official numbers of violations. From 2010 to 2014, the respective numbers of non-compliance instances with each casino operator are: Galaxy 16, Melco-PBL 12, MGM 12, SJM 23, Sands (the Venetian) 21, and Wynn 14.

We can have a glimpse of what some of those violations may be like in the litigation against Sands by its former executive Steve Jacobs and related fines imposed on Sands by two U.S. government agencies. Sands admitted that its executives knowingly failed to set up controls to ensure payments were legitimate and did not properly record the payments in its records.[98]

The company is controlled by U.S. billionaire and prominent Republican donor Sheldon Adelson. In 2016 its parent company Las Vegas Sands Corp paid Sands China's former chief executive, Steve Jacobs, US$75 million to settle a wrongful termination lawsuit. Jacobs contended that the termination was to cover up a host of improper activities in China and Macau, including paying US$62 million to a Chinese consultant to help it do business in China and Macau. This settlement comes immediately after the company paid US$9 million (less than two days' profit for the company) fine to end a U.S. Securities and Exchange Commission's probe into the company's possible violation of U.S. federal anti-bribery laws. Other problematic business dealings in China and Macau involved buying a Chinese basketball team, planning for a business center in Beijing, obtaining a ferry contract in Macau, etc. In 2017, the company agreed to pay US$7 million criminal penalty to end a probe by the U.S. Department of Justice into whether the company violated anti-bribery laws when obtaining its license in Macau.

Were there people from Macau involved in these dealings? Sands internal email and company documents indicate that there were, according to a report by investigative journalists from ProPublic and PBS Frontline.[99]

We are going to call this person L. He has been one of the eleven members of the powerful Macau Executive Council since 2004. This is a body that the chief executive is legally required to consult when making important policy decisions, proposing new legislation, formulating new regulations, and dismissing the Legislative Assembly, as we discussed in chapter 2. In addition, he was a member of the Legislative Assembly from 1984 to 2017, and a member of the Chinese People's Political Consultative Conference from 2008 to now. So he has been a government official and was a legislator for many years.

In 2009, L served as a middleman between "someone high-ranking in Beijing" and Sands China's top executives in resolving two vexing issues: a lawsuit by a Taiwanese businessman and a government permission to sell luxury apartments at the Four Seasons Hotel that Sands built in Macau.[100] This would need a payment of US$300 million, according to L's emails. Meanwhile, he said he would apply "pressure" on local planning officials. He positioned himself as someone uniquely situated both as counsel and legislator although in fact he was also an official involved in decision-making.

In 2009, Sands paid L's law firm US$700,000, about three times the previously agreed amount. His law firm billed Sands for "meetings and contacts with Macau government," including successful lobbying of the chief executive to award a ferry contract to Sands without competitive bidding. In 2010, L pushed to provide Sands with full legal service for a fee of MOP$1 million or US$125,000 per month with no obligation to providing billing details. But his offer was rejected by Sands executives as being "outrageous." They were afraid that such dealings might violate the U.S. Foreign Corrupt Practices Act. But Adelson had his own ways of doing things. The events led to the resignation of general counsel of Las Vegas Sands and firing of Jacobs in 2010. L was retained as outside counsel for an unknown amount of money. Hence the lawsuits and consequences we discussed above.

The questions for Macau are: With so much evidence of wrongdoing on the part of a Macau politician and legislator, why did the Macau government not do anything? Where were the police, the prosecutor, and the Commissioner Against Corruption? Are there similar political, ethical, and legal problems with other casino operators and government officials? What are the specifics of non-compliance found in the interim report? How serious are those violations? Are they as serious as the Sands' case we discussed above? To what extent are government officials involved in those violations? Again this speaks much about the nature of politics in Macau.

It also says much about Macau's civil society. There are 8,000 social organizations in Macau and many media outlets, which we will discuss further in chapter 7. Why did not anybody, at least nobody this author knows of, raise the issue since what we discussed above regarding Sands is open information that can be found online? Indeed, according to the interim report, one casino operator did complain that the government treated Sands favorably when granting its ferry contract (p. 129). It must have complained at the time when the contract was granted, but it went nowhere. Did it have to do with the help Sands received from its friend(s) within the government? We will come back to these issues later in the book.

Fourth, when such political, ethical, and legal problems occur, it means that a company is not fulfilling its corporate social responsibility (CSR), at least not fully. CSR in this regard means that casino operators should take care of their obligations and responsibilities to the stakeholders in the industry, including the shareholders, employees, customers, suppliers, the government, and the community. In addition to making money for the shareholders, there are other areas of concern: treating their employees with fair pay and decent working conditions; adequate measures preventing the dealers and customers from getting addicted to gambling; warning customers about problem gambling; holding the agencies that supply them with imported labor accountable so they are not exploiting these employees by charging them excessive fees. Regarding their relationship with the government, are they influencing the workings of the government towards more fairness in businesses, more democracy in political management, and more protection of human rights, or do they actually work with the government in unfair and even illegal practices, as we have shown above? Regarding the community, in addition to their philanthropic work, do the casino operators care about connecting with the community concerning ways, for example, to deal with such problems as traffic jams, some of which are caused by the increased number of the casinos' own buses transporting customers from the entry points of Macau to the gaming venues? Since casinos are the major industry in Macau, they have a special responsibility to the city. However, they have a long way to go towards responsible gaming. How they handle this issue may influence the willingness of the central government to loosen or tighten the individual travel schemes, which in turn affects whether the casinos can make money and whether Macau can survive. We will come back to these problems in chapters 7 and 8.

The interim report has given the gaming industry more than a passing grade in CSR saying that the casino operators have taken on a substantial amount of social responsibility (pp. xiii, 174). And it focuses only on issues such as casino employee housing, customer transportation, support for small and medium-sized enterprises, non-gaming elements, customer satisfaction, responsible gambling, and casino companies' involvement in community development. But a more comprehensive look at their CSR would find that a lot is still lacking. We will come back to this issue in chapter 7 on more social problems related to gambling-related crime and deviance and what casinos and the government need to do.

Fifth, the development of the gaming industry is a double-edged sword. On the one hand, economy seems booming in general, with gambling income constituting 87% of Macau government's total income in 2014 according to the interim report (p. 78), despite the temporary setbacks from 2008 to 2009 and 2015 to 2016 due to financial or other problems. The interim report also finds that all the six gaming operators have fulfilled the capital commitment in their contracts, and the gaming industry has a positive impact on the economy. It is also true that the proportion of local employees of managerial grade or above increased from around 60% in 2008 to 80% in 2014."[101] But on the other hand, casino-related political, ethical, legal, and social problems abound.[102] In addition to the problems we have discussed, the interim report recognizes that the gaming industry is pushing up the inflation rate, housing prices, and business operation costs, creating crowding-out effects on SMEs and affecting social values. The non-compliance problems the report recognizes are internal control and reporting deficiencies in prevention of money laundering and terrorist financing and the execution of Minimum Internal Control Requirements and Guidelines on Responsible Gambling. But we do not know the specifics. The interim report also points out problem gambling as an issue. But it has avoided the political, legal, and ethical problems we mentioned above. Again we will come back to these and other social problems in chapter 7. We will see more of the other side of the industry.

Conclusions

In the last 450 years, Macau's economy has undergone ups and downs, just like its politics. When the military industry and conventional trade declined, the opium and coolie trade thrived. When the latter trade again declined, the gambling industry thrived. While a Chinese commercial class had always worked alongside the Portuguese traders, there was also a class of Chinese and other foreigners who worked as their servants and as soldiers. In the 20th century, there was a rise of the Chinese (mostly craft) industrial capitalist class and the accompanying working class. There was indeed an economic dual track, and a class dual track, as the wealthy people, Chinese or Portuguese, followed one track, and the poor followed another.

The economic dual track compares interestingly with the political track in the colonial period: the Portuguese political elite vis-à-vis the Chinese economic elite, a track characterized by ethnicity. The development of the gambling industry and a Chinese commercial class as well as an industrial capitalist class in Macau in the 20th century indicates the culmination of the Chinese businesses and almost an end of the Portuguese trade. The Portuguese, however, retained their political power and mostly stayed in that track until the 1999 handover. We will discuss what it is like after the handover in chapter 7.

So it seems that the Chinese and the Portuguese followed two different tracks in the colonial period after the Opium War, one economic and the other political. This is different from the dual jurisdiction we discussed in chapter 2. It resembles an ethnic division of labor and power, economic and political.

The rise of the gaming industry causes questions like whether Macau's society can afford to allow only one major industry to dominate its economic life and impels us to examine other ways of making a living. When discussing modernization, people often use the proportions of the three sectors in a country's economy to describe its development. Macau's primary sector has little agriculture and a bit of fishing. Its secondary sector (manufacturing industry) is small and shrinking still. The sector that used to produce textile and electronic products and toys has been decreasing in its proportions in industrial output and in the number of workers employed.[103] By 2002, the total industrial output decreased to only 12.6%, even though the government has built a cross-border industrial zone between Zhuhai and Macau.

The tertiary sector is the service industry, which dominates Macau, especially the gaming business. In more developed countries, the last two sectors are of roughly equal proportions, and the first sector employs less than 5% of the total labor force. In Macau, the service sector is bound to be the dominant sector with gambling as its leading industry. The economic structure will remain the same for a long time to come.

Given the current economic development and Macau's historical vulnerability in relation to its environment, it seems that Macau's best chance is to build a strong tourism industry. This industry will still prioritize gaming as its leading sector, as the government is already doing, but it will also make use of the various historical resources unique to the city. Macau can offer something that others cannot, in terms of culture and history as well as Las Vegas–style recreation. In this way Macau can soften its image as a city based on only *pin mun saang yi*, and seize the opportunity to develop its cultural image. We will discuss more on Macau's economic identity in chapter 8.

4 Social Interaction
The Clash of Civilizations and Cultures in Macau

[D]ifferences among civilizations are not only real; they are basic. Civilizations are differentiated from each other by history, language, culture, tradition and, most important, religion. The people of different civilizations have different views on the relations between God and man, the individual and the group, the citizen and the state, parents and children, husband and wife, as well as differing views of the relative importance of rights and responsibilities, liberty and authority, equality and hierarchy. These differences are the product of centuries. They will not soon disappear. They are far more fundamental than differences among political ideologies and political regimes. Differences do not necessarily mean conflict, and conflict does not necessarily mean violence. Over the centuries, however, differences among civilizations have generated the most prolonged and the most violent conflicts.

Samuel P. Huntington explaining one of the reasons why civilizations clash[1]

Beyond the Barrier there appears to be a piece of neutral ground. The distinction between occidentalism and orientalism; between civilisation and barbarianism; between the European and the Asiatic is noticeable at once …

A European visitor to Macau in the 17th century, cited in Porter[2]

In this chapter, we will focus on social interactions among people from different cultures and civilizations when the East met the West. (See Plate 4.1 which depicts a harmonious scene.) The concept of the clash of civilizations and even of subcultures within one civilization could very well apply to Macau. We will discuss how the Chinese and the Westerners viewed each other, the emergence of the Macanese, "the tale of one city and two cities," and examine the implications of a Macau model for the clash of civilizations and for the future of Greater China.

The Clash of Civilizations

The clash of civilizations, a concept raised by Huntington, is a framework he uses to understand the world politics today. He wrote in his 1993 article that the world is characterized by a clash of civilizations especially between the Christian/Judaic West, and the Confucian and the Islamic East. He elaborated his points in his 1996 book, which was translated into Chinese and published in 2002. In 2004, he published another work discussing the clash of cultures in the United States, following the same arguments he made in 1993.[3] The current global conflicts in the Middle East, the conflicts in Greater China (within and between mainland China, Taiwan, Hong Kong, and Macau), and the continuing ethnic conflicts within the United States all seem to validate Huntington's analysis.

Huntington in the above quote gives us one of the reasons why civilizations clash: they are essentially different. The other reasons are, according to Huntington: 1) increasing interactions intensifying civilization consciousness and awareness of differences; 2) the revival of religion further dividing people into groups; 3) a de-Westernization and indigenization of elites occurring at the same time as non-Western countries accept popular culture of the West; 4) the very nature of culture whose "characteristics and differences are less mutable and hence less easily compromised and resolved than political and economic ones"; and 5) an economic regionalism reinforcing civilization consciousness.[4]

Huntington makes a distinction between cultural and political differences, and believes that the former is more fundamental than the latter in leading to the clash of civilizations. Some would say that there are multiple causes of conflict, and intra-civilizational differences and domestic conflict may even be more conspicuous. Edward Said would even say that rather than a clash of civilizations, there are closer ties between apparently warring civilizations than most of us would like to believe.[5]

Nonetheless, Huntington finds it hard to reconcile between different values from different cultures, with each culture needing a rival to define its own identity. Indeed, ethnically or culturally human beings are organized into groups and people in one group tend to be suspicious of people in other groups.

In addition to Huntington's reasons for the clash of civilizations, one also wonders whether the inevitable conflict may be partly due to human beings' limited ability to understand each other.[6] Usually the perception is that the "other" is somehow inferior,[7] which sociologically, we call *ethnocentrism* (judging other people's culture according to the standards of one's own), which may lead to *racism* (the belief that one's own racial or ethnic group is superior to people from other groups), and then *discrimination* (the practice of offering more life chances to people of our own group).[8] These three concepts developed only after the clash of civilizations since the 16th century, although the terms were not used to describe such phenomena until probably the 20th century.

In other words, we need to look at the interactions at more *social as well as sociopsychological levels*.[9] The assumptions about one another and the negotiations of their identities are underlying political and economic conflicts and cooperation among cultural and ethnic groups. Our analysis of the clash of civilizations in Macau and China may serve as an empirical study to see the extent to which the Huntingtonian argument holds.

How the Chinese Viewed Europeans

In the early 1600s, the population in Macau was: 437 Portuguese and Eurasians; 403 native Christians, exclusive of women, children, and Chinese; and 10,000 Chinese. If we add the large numbers of slaves, the total population at the time was between 15,000 and 20,000. Macau was "the most populous city in the Portuguese colonial empire after Goa."[10] Although there had been ups and downs in the population flow, by 1849 about 4,000 Portuguese and 34,000 Chinese lived in Macau.[11] In addition, there were other foreign traders from the United States, Britain, France, etc. as well as African slaves. In 1844, for example, there were 1,300 black slaves, mostly from Africa. Our discussion of social interaction is based on such a demographic background.[12]

The Chinese view of the West was ambivalent. On the one hand, most admired the Western cultural achievements, especially the technology;[13] on the other hand many had a profound distrust for foreigners. There was undoubtedly xenophobia, unhelped by the looting and killing of the Chinese by British sailors during the Opium Wars. There were voices that advocated rational and fair dealings with the foreigners, but those voices were weak.

The Chinese Admiration of the West

Yin Guangren and Zhang Rulin described with admiration the astronomical devices, weapons, musical instruments, clocks and watches, magnifiers, telescopes, as well as Portuguese costumes, calendar, and language.[14] For example, they described various kinds of "automatic sounding clocks" or "the chime clock" (自鳴鐘), including hanging clocks, table clocks, and small handholding ones. They would chime once if it was one o'clock, twice if it was two o'clock, and so on. There was also the hourglass, which they called 鵝卵沙漏, or "goose egg shaped sand glass."[15]

Their detailed and enthusiastic description of Portuguese customs includes the colors and texture of their clothes, the marriage that was not arranged by the parents (unlike that of the Chinese), the funeral events that lasted less than seven days, the Portuguese wines, etc.[16] They also described their church and religion, for example, St. Paul's Cathedral.[17] Lin Zexu was so impressed with the guns and ships of the British during the First Opium War that he wanted to see the same for China. Better guns and ships did happen in the later self-strengthening movement, although it was too little and too late.

The Chinese Dislike of Westerners

On the other hand, the words the Chinese used to describe foreigners were still derogatory. For example, Yin and Zhang referred to them with *yi* (夷) or *fan* (蕃). But that seemed much milder than *gui* (鬼), whose direct translation would be "devil," or "ghost." In fact, they did use *gui* to refer to African slaves, although they said that "they were called *gui nu*,"[18] meaning others called them "*gui nu*," not necessarily the term they would use. Still, they said that the African slaves "looked like humans" (略似人者).[19]

If Yin Guangren and Zhang Rulin's reference to foreigners was somewhat mildly derogatory, others' references to them were much more disparaging. In his description of the Portuguese, Pang Shangpeng said they looked weird, wore strange clothes, armed with daggers and cannons, and they were humans when happy and animals when angry. He thought that was their nature (詭形異服，劍芒火炮，彌漫山海，喜則人而怒則獸，其素性然也).[20]

Qu Dajun 屈大均 (1630–96), another man of letters at the time, described African slaves as with extremely dark skin, fluffy hair, and a strange odor. "They look like devils (or ghosts), and only their lips and teeth somewhat resemble that of humans" (通體如漆精，鬚髮蓬然，氣甚腥，狀正如鬼，特紅唇白齒略似人耳).[21]

This difference in outward appearance, compared with the Chinese themselves, led some Chinese to think that Westerners must have a different nature and would do outrageous things. As Pang Shangpeng pointed out, "they are not of our kind and they must think differently than we" (非我族類，其心必異).[22] The implication is that they could not be trusted. Zhang Zhentao 張甄陶 said that Westerners were by nature crafty and arrogant (黠而傲) and the African slaves were not so smart and were greedy (愚而貪).[23] He thought that the Portuguese were insidious and cunning, that they would lure the Chinese into their religion, take their eyes out, add drops of a certain liquid, and they would get silver that way.[24] There were also rumors that the Portuguese ate Chinese children (掠取童男童女，烹而食之).[25] Chen Xichang 陳熙昌 commented that the Portuguese often killed the Chinese in dozens (殺民動以十數),[26] and that they had insidious motives (虎狼之心叵測).[27] Some Chinese children were indeed kidnapped and sold as slaves and domestic servants to Macau or Goa, for 12 to 15 taels per person. This would not have happened, though, without the help of the native pimps and corrupt and venal local and provincial government officials.[28]

Zheng Guanying 鄭觀應 (1842–1921) was a comprador-official who studied in Macau when young, and wrote his famous *Sheng Shi Wei Yan* (盛世危言,

Warnings to the seemingly prosperous age) in Macau in the last days of his life. In his career, he worked in foreign firms for about 30 years and later served as manager in several Chinese enterprises, including Hanyan Iron Foundry, in Li Hongzhang's Self-Strengthening Movement. He was an advocate of China's modernization, especially in the areas of businesses. His observation of foreigners helps us understand the Chinese view of the Westerners:

> The Westerners frequently take advantage of the differences in language and in law to profit themselves at the cost of others, and do as they please without regard for reason … When a foreign ship collides with and destroys a Chinese boat, the latter, contrarily, is blamed for being slow in avoiding the collision or is falsely charged with having a dim light on its mast … When a foreign stagecoach hurts a Chinese, the latter is, contrarily, charged with not knowing how to yield the right of way, so that he incurred the disaster himself. Even if the driver is taken to court, he only pays a small fine. Furthermore, Chinese employed by foreign companies or as sailors on foreign ships frequently have their wages cut on some pretext or are even beaten to death. Cunning Westerners ally themselves with local rascals to kidnap and sell the foolish country fellows, whose grievances and miserable lives are like those of the dark ages. Again, for example, when a Chinese merchant owes money to a foreign merchant, as soon as he is accused his property is confiscated and his relatives and friends are disturbed; whereas when a Westerner is in debt to a Chinese, even though he has abundant private savings, by following the regulations for declaring bankruptcy, he is entirely free from obligation.[29]

Zheng questions whether there was justice and humanity, but he does not seem to blame the Chinese government, neither did he mention that "local rascals" probably included local officials. Nonetheless, Zheng's description of injustices and humiliations suffered by the Chinese in the hands of Westerners explains partly why the former disliked the latter.

This lack of trust had already lasted several hundred years and culminated in the Sanyuanli peasant uprisings in the First Opium War, about the time when Zheng was born, and in the Boxers rebellion in the end of the 19th century. Some of their proclamations below, the first two from Sanyuanli, and the third from the Boxers, might give us a better idea of their thinking, although as Teng and Fairbank point out, these words were probably written by the local literati.[30]

> The thoroughly loyal and patriotic people of the whole province of Kwangtung instruct the rebellious barbarian dogs and sheep for their information. We note that you English barbarians have formed the habits and developed the nature of wolves, plundering and seizing things by force…. In trade relations, you come to our country merely to covet profit. What knowledge do you have? Your seeking profit resembles the animal's greed for food. You are ignorant of our laws and institutions, ignorant of right principles…. You have no gratitude for the great favor of our Celestial Court; on the contrary you treat us like enemies and do us harm. You use opium to injure our common people, cheating us of our silver

and cash…. Although you have penetrated our inland rivers and enticed fellows who renounce their fathers and their ruler to become Chinese traitors and stir up trouble among us, you are only using money to buy up their services—what good points have you?…. Except for your ships being solid, your gunfire fierce, and your rockets powerful, what other abilities have you?[31]

We patriots have received the favor of the Celestial Dynasty in nourishing us for two centuries. Today, if we do not exterminate you English barbarians, we will not be human beings. You have killed and injured our common people in many villages, and seriously hurt the universal harmony. You also completely destroyed the coffins in several places, and you disastrously damaged the Buddhist statues in several monasteries. This is properly a time when Heaven is angered and mankind is resentful; even the ghosts and spirits will not tolerate you beasts… [32]

Attention: all people in markets and villages of all provinces in China—now, owing to the fact that Catholics and Protestants have vilified our gods and sages, have deceived our emperors and ministers above, and oppressed the Chinese people below, both our gods and our people are angry at them, yet we have to keep silent. This forces us to practice the I-ho magic boxing so as to protect our country, expel the foreign bandits and kill Christian converts, in order to save our people from miserable suffering. After this notice is issued to instruct you villagers, no matter which village you are living in, if there are Christian converts, you ought to get rid of them quickly. The churches which belong to them should be unreservedly burned down. Everyone who intends to spare someone, or to disobey our order by concealing Christian converts, will be punished according to the regulation when we come to his place, and he will be burned to death to prevent his impeding our program. We especially do not want to punish anyone by death without warning him first. We cannot bear to see you suffer innocently. Don't disobey this special notice![33]

Several points can be deduced from these proclamations as well as the derogatory descriptions previously related. First, like Yin Guangren, Zhang Rulin, Lin Zexu, and others, the villagers at Sanyuanli and the Boxers were impressed with Western guns and ships, and thought that these weapons did make a difference. Second, despite that fact, they still despised the Westerners, describing them as "barbarians," "dogs and sheep," or other kinds of "beasts." Third, there was xenophobia, partly based on the Chinese lack of understanding of the Westerners. There was also a hatred for foreigners, which was partly based on what they saw Westerners do in China, as in the Opium Wars,[34] which reflected badly on them. Their daily interactions with them, as seen in Zheng Guanying's observations above, were not complimentary to foreigners either.

Fourth, it was also true that the Boxers were instigated by the Empress Dowager. She issued a series of denunciation edicts, marked with bitterness and hate, which helped stir up the anti-foreign feelings among the common people who then organized the campaign to eliminate the foreigners and support the Qing dynasty (see Plate 4.2 for a scene of the Boxers fighting the Eight-Nation Alliance).[35] She capitalized on the cultural differences between the East and the West for her own political purposes.

Fifth, if "a life for a life" was the Chinese law at the time, and some killing could be somehow justified by the Chinese custom, since the British did kill Chinese (although the Chinese also killed Westerners), then killing Christian converts was certainly a violent clash of civilizations. But even the age-old "life for a life" law was challenged by the Westerners, since different civilizations approached the issue differently. This may not be a good example, but in 1784, an English country ship,[36] *Lady Hughes*, fired a customary salute upon arriving at Huangpu (Whampoa) and accidentally killed two Chinese and wounded a third one. The governor of Guangdong ordered the surrender of the gunner. But the English authorities at the East India Company replied that the person was missing. Finally upon repeated requests, they "selected the oldest and most decrepit sailor on board" and sent him up to the governor.[37] The sailor was executed several weeks later. Apparently both the English and the Chinese botched on this one.

One may question whether that was a clash of civilizations—it was more like a clash of ignorance, to use Edward Said's words—but the *Lady Hughes* incident certainly intensified the mistrust and dislike of one another. It was also interpreted as a clash of legal codes. As Fay points out, the very nature of Chinese justice bothered the English: killing by accident, as in this case, was considered murder, rather than manslaughter, which would carry a different penalty under English law. And there was no jury, no pleading. It seemed that a man in China had no rights, only duties.[38] The *Lady Hughes* incident was the precursor to further clashes between the two sides, including the Opium War.

The Chinese Views on and Efforts at Reconciliation and Appeasement

On the other hand, there were efforts by Chinese scholars to understand Westerners. In contrast to the hostile feelings among some Chinese towards the Westerners, there was a feeling towards understanding and appreciation, echoing the admiration of foreign technology. Lin Xiyuan 林希元 of the Ming dynasty, for example, wrote that the Portuguese did not kill or loot Chinese; rather, they did fair business with them, and paid more than or even double the market prices for grain, pork, poultry, etc. The Chinese were happy to do business with them. In addition, they helped to expel pirates, and the latter were thus constrained in their harassing and plundering of the common people. Here are his words:

> 佛朗機之來⋯⋯與邊民交易，其價尤平，其日用飲食之資於吾民者，如米麵豬雞之數，其價皆倍于常，故邊民樂與為市。未嘗侵暴我邊疆，殺戮我人民，劫掠我財物。且其初來，慮群盜剽掠累已，為我驅逐，故群盜畏憚不敢肆。[39]

It was therefore good to have them.⁴⁰ Ye Quan 葉權, also of the Ming dynasty, and Wang Zhi 王植 of the Qing dynasty, said that the Westerners were here only for commercial purposes, and the interaction between the Chinese and the Portuguese was largely peaceful: 夷利貨物，無他志，or 夷志在貿易，曆皆安靜，無桀鶩事。⁴¹

Reflected in international relations, one would see a more conciliatory tone, or a policy of appeasement. Pan Siju, the Guangdong surveillance commissioner, wrote in a memorial to the emperor in the early 1700s:

> The benevolence of the sacred Son of Heaven extends the generosity of his government to those from outside. Because of this, in my humble opinion, I think it possible to completely suspend the prohibition against the barbarian foreigners entering the interior of the country, since they only stay there with the aim of encouraging commerce and conducting business so as to take an annual profit.⁴²

Of course he did not forget to remind the emperor that there should be rules and regulations for the foreigners to follow, since there were indeed those who would "insult and maltreat the residents and mock the laws," "seduce the stupid people to join their religion, auction off their sons and daughters as slaves, and clandestinely export prohibited goods overseas."⁴³

Qishan, the Manchu official succeeding Lin Zexu in 1840–41, and Qiying, another Manchu official succeeding Qishan in 1842–48, were in charge of the negotiations with the British after Lin Zexu in the First Opium War. They were examples of conciliation and appeasement. Qiying said in one of his memorials to the emperor:

> [T]he barbarians are born and grown up outside the frontiers of China, so that there are many things in the institutional system of the Celestial Dynasty with which they are not fully acquainted. Moreover, they are constantly making arbitrary interpretations of things, and it is difficult to enlighten them by means of reason.⁴⁴

There is no doubt that Qiying was ethnocentric as well, but he was already trying to understand why Westerners thought differently than the Chinese. Meanwhile, he was also trying to educate the emperor about foreign customs:

> Moreover, the barbarians commonly lay great stress on their women. Whenever they have a distinguished guest, the wife is certain to come out to meet him. For example, the American chief Parker and the French chief Lagrene both brought their foreign wives along with them, and on occasions when your slave [referring to himself] has gone to the barbarians' storied residences to discuss business, these foreign wives have rushed out and saluted him. Your slave was confounded and ill at ease, while they on the other hand were deeply honored and delighted. Thus in actual fact the customs of the various Western countries cannot be regulated according to the ceremonies of the Middle Kingdom. If we should abruptly rebuke

them, it would be no way of shattering their stupidity and might give rise to their suspicion and dislike.

Furthermore, the various barbarians have come to live at peace and in harmony with us. We must give them some sort of entertainment and cordial reception; but we are on guard against an intimate relationship in intercourse with them.[45]

The Western customs regarding women apparently impressed Qiying. Although he was on guard against them, he nonetheless thought that they came to live harmoniously with the Chinese. Later on in the same memorial, he discussed the political systems in the West: Britain was ruled by a female, and the Americans and the French by males. And the Americans changed their president once every four years. Upon leaving office, the president was of equal rank with the common people. Feng Guifen and Guo Songtao, in the latter part of the 19th century, advocated learning from the West and treating Westerners with sincerity and reason, as we discussed in chapter 2.

But as history developed later, these opinions on learning from the West became 中學為體，西學為用, meaning, Chinese learning as the foundation, and Western learning for practical purposes only. So the Chinese were not going to adopt the Western political and social organizations but were only going to adopt their ships and guns. Those who advocated reconciliations and appeasement with foreigners were often treated as traitors, even if they might have also emphasized pacifying the barbarians or bringing them under control through the imperial "compassion for strangers coming from afar."[46] This principle is still true to a great extent in today's China.

Lin Xiyuan's, Ye Quan's, and Wang Zhi's descriptions of Westerners might be too optimistic, while Pang Shangpeng's, Chen Xichang's, and Zheng Guanying's observations might be too pessimistic. The truth probably lies in between, as in Pan Siju's descriptions.

Conclusion

In sum, the Chinese felt somewhat ambivalent towards Europeans. On the one hand, they admired the latter's cultural materials like clocks, ships, and weapons; on the other hand, they felt that the Westerners were unfathomable, killed the Chinese, and therefore could not be trusted. If many Chinese were xenophobic at the time, "The English raised that xenophobia to its most intense level."[47] This dislike led to what Teng and Fairbank call a proto-nationalism, or "one of the first stirrings of Chinese nationalism," as demonstrated in Sanyuanli.[48] But on the other hand, not all Westerners came for the purpose of conquering China; some Chinese scholars noted that many Westerners came for commercial purposes and were good traders. They wanted to live in peace with the Chinese. These scholars, as well as the Chinese officials like Qishan and Qiying, urged the Chinese to understand the Westerners and craft a policy in dealing with them.

But the admiration for foreign things was largely limited to technology only, and the voice of treating foreigners with reason was weak. The advocates could be viewed as betraying one's own country. This is evidence to substantiate the theme of the clash of civilizations: that in addition to political and ideological difficulties, the differences between cultures are also, if not more, formidable to overcome. But on the other hand, it is possible to negotiate those differences. People like Lin Xiyuan, Ye Quan, Wang Zhi, Qiying, Feng Guifen, and Guo Songtao were trying. When these differences could not be negotiated, a violent clash might occur, as it did in China's recent history.

How Westerners Viewed the Chinese

In general, the Western views of the Chinese were comparable to the Chinese views of the West. While there was no lack of admiration of the way the Chinese did some things, there was also intense dislike of the way they did other things. The pendulum theory describes the alternating of Westerners' positive and negative images of China in the past several hundred years in the East-West exchange.[49] There were also voices of reconciliation, but again those voices were weak, just as the corresponding Chinese voices were.

Westerners' Admiration of China

The Jesuits were one of the earliest groups of Westerners in the 16th century who wrote much about China. Although there were things they disliked about China, many of them discussed the Chinese people as being more civilized than the Europeans with better political and educational systems. They admired Confucius for developing a system of rites for the Chinese civilization, and thought that the emperor Kangxi was an intelligent and benevolent monarch. They found the Chinese people mild and modest. Some earlier travelers to China also praised the Chinese practice of taking care of the aged and the lonely. They thought that even the roads and sanitation conditions were better than those of Europe.[50] The following is how Voltaire (1694–1778), the French writer, philosopher, and historian, describes Yongzheng (r. 1723–35), the son of Kangxi, who inherited the throne:

> this emperor was one of the wisest and most generous princes who has ever reigned. He was always concerned with alleviating the plight of the poor and putting them to work. He observed the law carefully, he curbed the ambitions and deceits of the bonzes, maintaining peace and prosperity, encouraging all useful skills and arts, and above all the cultivation of the land. From his time public buildings, large-scale highways, canals joining all the rivers of this great empire,

were maintained with a splendour and thrift which has no equal other than among the ancient Romans.[51]

The 17th-century Russian travelers and traders to China described the impressive palace where the emperor lived and worked. The 18th-century English travelers, traders, and soldiers, such as Aeneas Anderson, also admired the pastoral scenes in China's countryside, the agricultural skills of the farmers, and the prosperous cities.[52]

Miss Harriett Low was an American. She came to Macau with her uncle who was engaged in China trade in the 1830s and 1840s, as we mentioned in chapter 3. Her views on the Chinese in Macau may give us a good idea of what in general Westerners thought about the Chinese. (See a portrait of Harriett Low in Plate 4.3.) The overriding theme of that encounter is ambivalent, but her admiration, just like her dislike, was obvious.

Here is her description in her 1831 journal of people using shoulder poles to carry things when they were helping her move house (see Figure 4.1):

> Everything is carried upon men's *shoulders*. It is astonishing to see what burdens they carry with apparent ease, great heavy trunks, sideboards. Now, they do not shoulder them, as a man in America would shoulder an axe, but have poles, ropes, etc. You never see a China man carry anything in his hands, but always in baskets, jars, etc.[53]

In another journal in 1831, she wrote about the Chinese being more civilized than the Americans. Apparently many people in Canton had never seen foreigners, so they all gathered around the house where some of her friends lived to see them.

> They gathered in crowds round the house when they were expecting them out, but filed off on both sides at their approach and made no noise. Nothing but a little buzz of admiration was heard. Mrs. Baynes says when she first arrived, the people had boats stationed upon the water, and they paid 3 cash to see the *Fanqui* [foreign devil] women, but none made the least disturbance. Mrs. B. says she thinks they

Figure 4.1
Shoe-mender (approx. 1890) with his shoulder pole and baskets. Ho Weng Hong, *The Past of Macau*, Macau: Macao Foundation, 1994, p. 160.

must have made their fortunes. Now I think the Chinese are much more civilized than either American or English people would have been if a China woman had have [sic] appeared in our streets dressed in the costume of her country with little feet. Why she would be robbed and hooted at immediately.[54]

A British aristocratic couple, Reverend Lord William Gascoyne-Cecil and his wife, visited China in the first decade of the 20th century after the suppression of the Boxers. They had extremely positive views about China. Here is what they say about Confucianism:

> Confucius advocates the reform of society by the action of the State. Thus the sanitary laws, the education laws, the temperance laws of the West are thoroughly consistent with the teaching of Confucius. Where that teaching differs from the West is that it disbelieves in democracy. Yet Confucianism cares nothing for a man's birth: all men are born equal to the Confucianist as to the Christian; and so Confucianism has, for many centuries, welcomed people of the lowest birth as Governors, if they could pass the requisite examinations, and, having given every opportunity to men of all classes to become official, it entrusts them and not the people with the government of the country.[55]

The description is fairly accurate, though not as critical as it should be.

Westerners' Dislike of the Chinese

In their earlier encounters with China, the Jesuits in the 16th century were already critical of the Chinese emphasis on an educational system that neglected the building of a military force. They also believed that China's mathematics and astrology were lagging far behind Europe. They criticized the Chinese for being arrogant and blindly worshiping ancient things. They did not like Chinese music, either, thinking it was too loud. The *Book of Changes* (易經) was full of superstition, and was not worth the attention the Chinese gave it. The Chinese worship of their emperor was too much for them: it resembled the worship of a god and was simply unnecessary.[56] In a book written in the 16th century, Frei Gaspar da Cruz described how he appreciated the Chinese artifacts, but he was critical of the Chinese businessmen's cunning and deceitfulness. He thought women were beautiful and he liked the design of Chinese clothing, but he did not like the way Chinese men looked. He thought most of them were ugly.[57] An early Portuguese document describes the Chinese they encountered in Malacca as low and weak, who used two sticks to push food into their mouths with their bowls close to their lips.[58]

A 17th-century work on China by Jean Mocquet published in Paris also described the Chinese as greedy and good at playing little tricks. The way they ate was not pretty either. Another book by a Dutch said that the Chinese were wicked and dangerous, not worthy of their respect. Like the French, the Dutch did not like the way the Chinese ate. Neither did the Russians, who also disliked the Chinese music. Maybe the typical reaction was from Captain George Anson, whom we met in chapter 2. He led his warships to China in 1742 on his voyage across the Atlantic, Pacific, and Indian Oceans. His book on this voyage, with the last few chapters on his experience in Macau and China, was very popular in the 18th century, and was also published in French, Dutch, German, and Italian. He thought that the Chinese were cheaters in their businesses who would feed small stones and sands into ducks or force water into pork to increase their weight when selling them to foreigners. The local officials were corrupt and they used various methods to embezzle public money and obtain bribery. Being greedy, selfish, and tricky were characteristics of the Chinese.[59]

About 100 years later in the mid-19th century, Harriett Low made similar comments on the Chinese, alongside some of her admirations. She thought that the Chinese were not really a refined people:

> A lovely morning. Went on deck. A smuggling boat alongside. Such a sight you never saw. They contain generally about a 100 men, when *alongside* they generally take this opportunity to eat or "*catchy chow chow*" and they form in little groups of 4 or 5 each round 5 or 6 little messes of fish and oysters cooked in divers ways. Each has his bowl of rice in his hand chop sticks in the other which each one dips into the *public* bowl and from these into their mouths. Having none of the delicate ideas of more refined people, they then shovel as much rice into their mouths as they can possibly *crowd* in. They appear to eat with *glorious appetites* I assure you. They sit on their feet, and are *dirty* and *ugly*. They are generally the lowest class of people and as to morals, I will not say. If they have a moment's leisure, they commence gambling and I see them generally as soon as they have crammed down their food either have cards or dominos, each playing with all the interest possible. It is a curious sight to watch the expressions of their faces and if by chance they have any expression at all, it is an expression of avarice and love of gain. You see one laying on the side of the boat smoking his long pipe with apparent indifference to every thing in this world and the next. I often wish to ask what they *do think*, or if they think at all.[60]

Low was not only very curious about what the Chinese men thought but distained for the way they ate, their avarice and love of gain, and their apparent indifference. There is an effort to understand things foreign, but there is also ethnocentrism and racism. This process of social interaction between people from different cultures tends to be a common phenomenon.

On another occasion, when her uncle told her about saving some Chinese crew from a sinking boat and about five other Chinese having been drowned, she caught her indifference on this issue and was trying to understand it:

> I can hardly account for the indifference we feel regarding these creatures. We hear of their being killed and drowned and misfortunes of divers kinds of occurring but

not with the feelings that we should have in parallel cases in our own country or Europe. It must be that we have no sympathy with them, they appear to me to be a connecting link between man and beast, but certainly not equal with civilized man. And you see the different grade and links in all the rest of nature's works is it not reasonable to suppose there are higher and lower orders of men? They certainly do not possess the sensibility and feelings of other nations. And when we hear of these accidents, our imaginations never picture distressed and bereaved families, and happy families destroyed—for knowing their brutal customs we cannot think such distresses exist.[61]

At first she thought it was difficult to account for her indifference towards these Chinese men, dead or near perishing. Then she explained to herself, well, after all the Chinese were not as human as we were. Although she was struggling to understand the Chinese, her racial superiority took over. Another quote from Harriett can further illustrate this point:

The China men are jabbering below. I should admire to have you hear their jargon. There is no words to be made of it to my ears, it seems to consist of low guttural sounds. They are a stupid set of people. They spend most of their time in sleeping. That is the servants. They will do only just such work as belongs to each one, and when that is done, you hear them snoring.[62]

Another 100 years passed, and here is another description of the Chinese living in the Chinese part of Macau. Father Benjamim Antonio Videira Pires liked the beautiful Chinese furniture made of quality wood and expensive marble with exquisite artistic carving. But he also described how the Chinese lived together with animals, and how their greed made them turn all the ground floors into stores so as to make money. "The basic nature of the Chinese laziness and dirtiness causes the huge living area to smell all day of musk, opium, paint, cooking smoke. Especially, the strange smell of fish and animal feces makes one sick."[63] He felt that even at the time of his writing, people had to hold their nose when passing the area. (See Plate 4.4 for a possible place he might have been describing.)

What did more well-known philosophers, historians, and writers think about China? Montesquieu (1689–1755), the French political philosopher, was not complimentary about the Chinese:

It is strange that the Chinese, whose life is entirely directed by rites, are nonetheless the most unscrupulous people on earth. This appears chiefly in commerce, which has never been able to inspire in them the good faith natural to it. The buyer should carry his own scale as each merchant has three of them, a heavy one for buying, a light one for selling, and accurate one for those who are on their guard.[64]

Some things that Westerners particularly disliked included penalty afflicted on the offender's whole family, not just on the offender himself; polygamy that caused suffering especially on the part of women; foot-binding; infanticide; the flogging of suspects to force a confession; a self-serving political system that was corrupt to the core where the mandarins made an effort to get as much out of the people within his jurisdiction as he possibly could in his tenure.[65] Speaking of the political system, A. F. Legendre's comments may be illuminating:

> where there is no collective effort, there is no community of soul or sentiment. The general interest is ignored. The mandarin who has paid for his right to enrich himself is never sure of the morrow. He is then in a hurry to heap up money for his old age, and is concerned with himself and not with his district. Thus it is from top to bottom of the mandarin ladder.[66]

Legendre, a Frenchman, lived in China for most of the first quarter of the 20th century. This critique of the Chinese officials was in fact quite common among the Westerners. W. A. P. Martin, an American who lived in China in most of the second half of the 19th century, commented, "Had the mandarins acted in concert, they might have suppressed the vice [opium] even after the legalization of the import; but they never pull together for any public purpose whatever."[67]

Even after the Republican Revolution, when the officialdom was supposed to think about the needs of the people, they simply "used" people for their own purposes rather than "served" them. Arnold Toynbee (1889–1975), the British historian, talked with a KMT official when he visited China in the end of 1929 and the beginning of 1930. He suggested that "the ultimate victory would fall not to those who sought to impose unity by force but to those who sought to give the people the things that the people wanted deep down in their hearts." The reply of the KMT Party man was: "You are quite right. We certainly ought to learn how to use the people. If we don't, we shall find our opponents using them against us." Toynbee was shocked at how the Party man thought about "using" the "too sorely tired, too tamely long-suffering people, whose miseries touch the heart even of the casual passing foreign traveler!"[68]

The Communists did not really value the peasants and used people that way too. Pearl Buck (1892–1973), an American writer and Nobel Laureate in literature who lived in China three months after she was born until the mid-1930s, wrote in her autobiography:

> my continuing regret concerning Asian leaders is that so few of them have understood the quality of their own peasants, and therefore few have valued this mighty and common man of the earth.
>
> And among them the Communists are the most guilty, for with all their talk, I do not see that they have valued this man, either, and their condescension to him makes my soul sick. Yesterday in New York a young Chinese woman sat in my small living room and told me breathlessly of the great and marvelous changes that the Communists are making in China. And in her words, too, I caught the old stink of condescension.[69]

The following quotes summarize fairly well how Westerners viewed the Chinese at the time:

> John Chinaman was industrious. John Chinaman respected his elders. John Chinaman, being largely free from that "sullen notion of honor" that so easily drove Europeans like Innes to violence, would stand and reason with a man (as the elder Morrison once put it) "when an Englishman would knock him down or an Italian stab him." But here John Chinaman's virtue ceased. He was frivolous. He was avaricious. He bullied, stole, and fornicated. Above all he lied—Protestant missionaries did not encounter John Chinaman in his commercial capacity and so did not see him as a Hunter or a Jardine did—continuously, systematically, and on purpose. How contrary he was too, seeing that he mourned in white instead of in black and wrote from top to bottom of the page instead of across it. And how barbarously he lived! He ate dogs and cats; you came across the poor creatures being poked and examined in the markets just like rabbits or fowl. To public charity he seemed an utter stranger. Morrison had noticed how, after the disastrous Canton fire of 1822 when the factories and most of the waterfront went up in flames, suspected incendiaries were beheaded, wretches caught plundering the ruins flogged, but then for the homeless (whom one Chinese informant estimated at fifty thousand) nothing at all was arranged, not even a public subscription. As for John Chinaman's religious life, it appeared to consist of theatrical performances, colored-paper images with movable heads and goggle eyes, fireworks, temples, gongs, roast pig, the continual burning of joss sticks—these and the most extravagant idolatry. "Will not like sins produce like punishments?" Morrison had asked.[70]

And the civil servants:

> When ... something occurred to break the even surface of public life, the high civil servant tried not to see it. He pushed it out of sight, or he reported just enough of it so that the news, when it reached Peking from another source, would not infuriate the emperor. Barbarian affairs fitted naturally into this last category. They were always disagreeable. They were usually difficult to hide. As a consequence the dreadful things the *fan kuei* did—the riot at Chien-sha-tsui, the affray off Kowloon, the battle at Chuenpi, the blockade of the Canton River, the assault on Tinghai—became known at Peking promptly enough, but became known in the form that largely concealed their seriousness, big matters being reduced to small matters and small matters to nothing at all. The truth was that the English intruders were resolute and dangerous. That ought to have been apparent. To Peking, looking darkly through a glass held backwards, it was not.[71]

The Westerners' thoughts about the Chinese may be exemplified by a Frenchman's comment: "I think that in all things the Chinese are decidedly inferior to the Europeans."[72] Many of the things that were said here were true at the time, but they were not the full picture.

This dislike of the Chinese ways often led to discriminatory practices. Some scholars believe that one of the reasons why no Chinese held any high positions like as an instructor at the St. Paul's College (1594–1762) in Macau was the Western priests' lack of trust in them just because they were Chinese.[73] Indeed, the Chinese Christians in Macau at the time did write letters to the Portuguese king in Lisbon complaining that they were not allowed to sail and invest overseas, or to attend events in Guangzhou. But when there was war, they had to help to fight the enemies of Portugal. The Portuguese attitudes and words were humiliating to the Chinese. Boxer reports that the Portuguese social, political, and legal discriminatory practices against the Chinese Christians did not change much later.[74]

The same happened in the Portuguese treatment of Chinese customs. In early 17th century, Francisco da Rosa, the acting bishop of Macau, ordered to tear down the Chinese opera performance stage. In 1758, Father José Gonçalves Pereira, the Macau representative of the Inquisition of the Roman Catholic Church, asked the Senate to restrict the parade of Ma Zu to designated areas. Up until the early 19th century the Chinese Christians were not even allowed to view the parade.[75]

There were indeed some efforts to change prejudicial and discriminatory attitudes and make compromises. In 1883, the city government regulated the time when the Chinese could set off firecrackers on festivals. For example, they were not allowed to do this after 11:00 p.m. and before 7:00 a.m. But on the other hand, the compromise sometimes could go so far as to allow the Chinese practices of male polygamy and discrimination against females in their rights to inherit family properties, as in the 1909 law on Chinese customs (華人風俗習慣法典). The law was not abolished until 1948.[76]

Racial dislike can lead to more serious discrimination practices like killings.[77] Although killings happened on a smaller scale in Asia than in the Americas, they nonetheless happened fairly often. The various wars we discussed so far are outstanding examples of such killings. Prejudice and racism on both sides were probably the basis of such actions. Even in the modern world, either in the killing fields of Europe, Asia, the Middle East, and Iraq in the 20th and 21st centuries, or in racial discrimination practices in multiethnic societies, we can see the same kind of reasoning. In chapter 2, we mentioned the Portuguese attack of the pirates in Coloane, when they torched houses and killed both the guilty and innocent Chinese. This was often referred to as the "massacre of Luhuan,"[78] and there is a small monument in Luhuan that commemorates the event (see Plate 4.5 for the monument).

If a biologically based racism picked up momentum in the latter part of the 19th century,[79] ethnocentrism and racism in general must have already developed when the West began to meet the non-West, including Asia, Africa, and Americas in the 16th century. For the colonists needed a theory to justify their conquering the non-white peoples and establishing colonies in these other places. In the 19th century the racist thinking developed further, assisted by science.[80]

However, most of the criticism above is accurate about the problems China was and is still facing now, although this criticism is also typical of the problems of

Orientalism as described in Edward Said, viewing the West as civilized while the East as uncivilized.[81] It only becomes racism when it assumes the inferiority of the entire Chinese nation. After all, the colonial discourse is not unified—it is fractured.

Westerners' Efforts to Understand the Chinese

In the examples above, we could already see how Harriett Low was struggling in her understanding of the Chinese people and things. On another occasion, she was sitting on the deck meditating when a Chinese woman came up to her, as a woman in Figure 4.2 might have approached her:

> Here I was sitting contemplating the different objects around me, moralizing and etc., when I heard at my side the words *How do, do,* and turned around to answer my *friend*, and who should it be but an old ugly China woman. I knew her not, but I was very ready to hold a conversation with her, if we could make ourselves understood. Her knowledge of English & Portuguese was, however, very limited, and I found much to my amusement after she had gone, that I had made some ludicrous mistakes—such a jargon as it was *you* never heard. Her object was however to know if I wanted a servant. She chatted some time in great good humour and left me.[82]

She just did not like the way the old Chinese woman looked, but she enjoyed the conversation with her. Again we see a mixture of ethnocentrism and a desire to understand Chinese things. She was not amused by the bound feet of Chinese women, either, but she was beginning to understand that the constraints put on women were not just a Chinese phenomenon. "They commence swathing the feet at the age of two and for years they suffer excessively. The poor child does nothing but scream from pain and all to gratify the pride of the mother who thinks her child will not be beautiful without."[83] She talked about this with "a very intelligent compradore," and the latter thought that to pinch the feet was no more barbarous than nipping in the waist. In this conversation, Low was beginning to understand that it was not just a problem of the Chinese, but one of Europeans, too.

Lord Macartney was the first British ambassador sent to the Chinese court in 1792, although he failed to establish an embassy in China. He was open, honest,

Figure 4.2
Along the docks of the Inner Harbour (approx. 1920). Ho Weng Hong, *The Past of Macau*, Macau: Macao Foundation, 1994, p. 119.

and willing to criticize both China and his own country based on his observations from the trip. He criticized foot-binding in China in his diary, but he also criticized the British customs of putting similar restrictions on women:

> Perhaps we are not quite free from a little folly of the same kind ourselves. We have not yet indeed pushed it to the extreme the Chinese have done, yet are we such admirers of it, that what with tight shoes, high heels and ponderous buckles, if our ladies' feet are not crippled they are certainly very much contracted, and it is impossible to say where the abridgement will stop. It is not a great many years ago that in English thread-paper waists, steel stays, and tight lacing were in high fashion, and the ladies' shapes were so tapered down from the bosom to the hips that there was some danger of breaking off in the middle upon any exertion. No woman was thought worth having who measured above eighteen inches round at the girdle.[84]

Although one might question the Jesuits' motives for trying to understand and accommodate the Chinese customs, the end result was that they donned Chinese clothes (see Figure 4.3), and believed that the Chinese Christians could worship Confucius and their ancestors at the same time they worshiped God. Indeed in 1659, the Propaganda Fide (傳信部) of the Roman Catholic Church, the department that was overseeing the missionary work in the Far East, even issued an order to the three new vicars-apostolic in Tonkin and Cochinchina, instructing them to be flexible with Chinese customs:[85]

> Do not try to persuade the Chinese to change their rites, their customs, their ways, as long as these are not openly opposed to religion and good moral; what would be sillier than to import France, Spain, Italy, or any other country of Europe into China? Don't import these, but build faith. The faith does not reject or crush the rites and customs of any race, as long as these are not evil. Rather, it wants to preserve them.

Figure 4.3
Portuguese missionaries clad in Chinese costume in Macao in the early 1900s. 林明德, 澳門的匯聯文化, Taipei: Chinese Folk-Arts Foundation, 1997, p. 21.

Generally speaking, men prize and love their own ways, and especially their own nation more than others. That is the way they are built. There is no more effective cause of hatred and estrangement than to change a country's customs, especially those people have been used to them from time immemorial. This is particularly true if, in place of the customs that have been suppressed, you substitute the practice of your own country. Do not disdain Chinese ways because they are different from European ways. Rather, do everything you can to get used to them.

These words are progressive even today, even though they did not carry the order of the day and they did not distinguish between good and bad ways of doing things according to universal values. Theirs was a merge of civilizations rather than a clash of them as the later Controversy of Rites was. In the colonial times, the Senate in Macau disagreed with Amaral for his colonial efforts and tried to accommodate the Chinese in Macau, just like the Chinese were accommodating the Portuguese.

Conclusion

Where different cultures are concerned, ethnocentrism and often racism become unavoidable. Rodney Gilbert thinks that the Chinese are just like children: they are "each a bundle of likable, amusing but perplexing and often irritating contradictions."[86] But there were some, like the Jesuits, who made efforts to reconcile the Christian/Western and Chinese ways of thinking.

But just as the voice of Chinese scholar-officials advocated understanding and accommodation, the Western voices along the same lines did not go very far. The Jesuits were expelled from China, because other orders of the Roman Catholic Church wanted to pursue a non-conciliatory line. Also the St. Paul's College was closed. The Senate had to yield to Governor Amaral. Conflicts intensified.

There were indeed violent clashes, but the emergence of the Macanese community seems to indicate that people did get along. Most of the time, life was peaceful among the different cultures, but it also seems that this cultural and ethnic integration only becomes another way to set people apart. There was still a tale of two cities in one city. The walls between ethnic groups have continued to exist.

The Macanese

In the case of America, the Europeans conquered the American Indians and established their colonies. The locals were at first enslaved but later more or less segregated from the dominant white groups (see Plate 4.6 for the famous picture of The Trail of Tears, where some native Americans were forced to relocate far away from their homes).[87] In the United States, after many years of conflict among different race and ethnic groups, all groups are legally guaranteed equal status. But in today's reality, whites in general still occupy a more advantageous position, and conflict has continued, though to a much lesser extent than 50 years ago.[88] In contemporary times, assimilation has been gradually replaced with diversity, pluralism, and multiculturalism. That does not mean that people will lose their commonalities but it has nonetheless caused much resentment among the dominant white community, especially the Trumpian followers. The future of race and ethnic relations in the U.S. is still uncertain.

In Macau, race and ethnic relations have not developed as conflictually as they have in America. The Chinese were not enslaved. In fact, the Chinese government was stationed in Macau for most of its 450 years of history, its influence keenly felt even during the more colonial era. Equally important, the Portuguese intermarried with the Asians, first Malaccans and Indians, and then the Chinese, on a much larger scale proportionally than the British marrying Chinese in Hong Kong or Europeans marrying native and African Americans in the United States. The result is the emergence of the Macanese in Macau, like the mestizos in north, but especially south, Americas.[89]

When the Portuguese went around in the world establishing colonies, few women went with them, probably because of at first a ban on women going with men and then later the extreme difficulties of life on the sea.[90] Largely as a result, the Portuguese first married women in Goa and Malacca in the early 1500s. Many such interracial families, sometimes with three to six wives for one man in one family, later moved to Macau. Under such circumstances, the early Macanese were results of interracial marriages between the Portuguese men on the one hand and Malaysian, Indonesian, and Japanese women on the other.[91]

By 1625, one report by Jesuits at the time claimed that many wives of Portuguese men were already Chinese or had Chinese blood. At the same time, there were also interracial marriages between Portuguese men and Filipino and Vietnamese women.[92] The tradition of interracial marriage continued after the "perpetual occupation and management of Macau" in 1887, when Portuguese military officers and soldiers married either Macanese or Chinese women. That stopped only after 1975 when the military retreated from Macau.[93] After that the tradition was continued by Portuguese professionals who came to Macau to serve in the government or in other professional jobs.

In contemporary Macau, there are fewer than 10,000 Macanese. Bruning estimates that about 20,000 Macanese live outside Macau in Hong Kong, the United States (California), Canada, Brazil, Australia, and Portugal.[94] So altogether there are about 30,000 Macanese in the world.

Jia Yuan 賈淵 (João de Pina Cabral) and Lu Lingsuo 陸淩梭 (Nelson Lourenço) believe that there are three indicators of Macanese:[95] the mixture of blood between European and Asian ancestries, language, and religion. Macanese did have their own language, or Macau Creole, for an estimated 300 years until the 19th century. It peaked in the 17th to 19th centuries. But even then only about several thousand Macanese spoke the language. Now only several dozen people can speak it.[96] Linguistically it is a language composed of elements from several other languages, mainly Portuguese. According to Bai Dali 白妲麗, cited by Xu Jieshun and Tang Kaijian (see note 96), out of the 426 non-Portuguese words, 17.5% comes from Chinese, 20% from Indo-Portuguese and Malaysian-Portuguese, 7.5% from English, 35.4% from Malaysian, and 19.2% from others. Its grammar contains the elements of both European and Asian languages, according to Bruning.[97]

Along with the declining Portuguese domination in the 1970s, more and more Macanese, especially their children, began to speak Cantonese. As a result, the younger generations are able to speak both Portuguese and Cantonese, although they may not be able to write the latter.[98] They are moving toward bilingualism, or even multilingualism. Berlie reports of a marriage ceremony in a Catholic church in English. The bride was Chinese and the groom Macanese, but at home they spoke Cantonese and English.[99] At another marriage ceremony between again a Macanese groom and Chinese bride, reported by Jia Yuan and Lu Lingsuo, Portuguese was the language used, even though most of the guests were Chinese.[100] Or they may conduct two ceremonies and have two meals, one Chinese and the other Portuguese.[101]

Belief in Catholicism is yet another characteristic of the Macanese, as Luís de Sales Marques comments in Box 4.1. The Macanese or their families tend to identify with Catholicism to a certain degree, going to church on Sunday and/or conducting their marriage ceremonies in a Catholic church.[102] I do not yet have the specific figures for the number of Macanese who believe in Catholicism, but research indicates that the younger generations are less religious than the older ones and their beliefs are more diverse.[103]

Although interracial marriage does reduce racial prejudice, ethnic groups still largely live their own lives. As Cabral and Lourenço point out, historically Macau was "in a state of constant unstable equilibrium" between the Chinese and Portuguese or some "deep rooted instability."[104] This structural characteristic would make the Macanese privileged sometimes but put them in a conflictual and precarious situation at other times. The imminent return of Macau to China made them feel especially so: the article in Box 4.1 describes this in more detail.[105]

Jia Yuan and Lu Lingsuo observe that the Macanese have changed their negative attitudes towards the Chinese,[106] and this may have to do with the interracial marriage that has been going on for some centuries. They have also quoted others' observations on the more open attitude of Portuguese towards people of color. Interracial children were treasured rather than discarded, as in many other societies.[107]

But on the other hand, the formation of this ethnic group also sets an additional boundary. The Portuguese, for example, did not think much of the Macanese culture. At the end of the 19th century, the government began to teach them standard Portuguese, and their effort to eliminate the Macanese language was largely successful.[108] Some identify with Macau more than with Portugal; they say they "go

Box 4.1 The Macanese Dilemma: Three Personal Stories

Henrique de Senna Fernandes [see Figure 6.5] plods slowly up the narrow stairs that lead to his law office in a bustling neighborhood along Avenida de Almeida Ribeiro, his slow pace betraying his 76 years. Fernandes's office is lined with books, some of which are novels he wrote about the Macanese people. Regrettably, none has been translated from Portuguese into English, though the Chinese made a popular movie, The Bewitching Braid, from one of them. Many of the stories are set in the 1920s and 1930s, which Fernandes considers the golden period for the Macanese people. "All the traditional families were intact then," he remembers. Many left after World War II, and it is estimated that about five out of six Macanese now live abroad—in Portugal, Brazil, the U.S. or Canada. Fernandes says: "My purpose [in writing the stories] was to explain the two cultures, Portuguese and Chinese. They are so different from each other, but we can live together and create one mixed culture. Look at me—I'm a product of many cultures."

Fernandes's family has lived in Macau for at least 250 years. Various ethnic strains—Indian (Goan), Chinese, French and Portuguese—flow in his veins. But, above all, he says, he is Portuguese. "We consider ourselves different from European Portuguese, but we love the [national] flag." The ways of the Portuguese in Macau were different from those of the British in Hong Kong, he says. "The Portuguese never put us aside; they married our girls." In Hong Kong, the offspring of the British and locals were termed half-castes and later Eurasians. "We Macanese never considered ourselves Eurasian," he says.

Fernandes was invited to Beijing in 1987 to witness the signing of the Sino-Portuguese Joint Declaration, which set out Macau's return to China. For him, it was a sad occasion. "I consoled myself with the excellent food they served." Now comes an even more poignant moment, when the flag he loves so much is hauled down for good. But he will be staying on. "I have homes in Portugal that I could go to any time," he says. "But I want to see the passing of the millennium in my birthplace."

When Isabel Eusebio was 16, her family sent her to live with an uncle in Brazil. That was in 1975, a year after the "Carnation Revolution" in Portugal overthrew the right-wing Salazar dictatorship. Democracy followed, but there were fears that Portugal—and its overseas territories—might descend into Marxism. "We lost a lot of our community back then," says Eusebio. "I was one of them." But she returned, and in 1990 she and her mother opened the Balichão restaurant in the middle of a public park on Coloane Island.

Macanese cuisine is basically Portuguese, but with local ingredients and embellishments. The concept springs from the days when Chinese wives tried to reproduce Portuguese dishes for their husbands, but often lacked the right ingredients. So they began to improvise: cloves from the Spice Islands, saffron from India, Chinese sausage instead of Portuguese, crabs and prawns from the local market, and, of course, rice. All with a smidgen of Thai, Vietnamese or Philippine food. "Time did the job," Eusebio says.

Hundreds of Macanese recipes have probably been lost to history, either because they were never written down or because some families kept them a secret. The difficulty for restaurants serving this food is that dishes were usually prepared in large portions for family sittings, and so many do not lend themselves well to smaller servings. Still, some are relatively economical to prepare and will undoubtedly survive even as the Macanese community fades away.

Eusebio, 40, has little doubt that fading away is the ultimate fate for her people. "We'll become totally diluted," she says. "We're only a few thousand, the leftovers." The military garrison, which used to provide many eligible bachelors, was withdrawn in 1976. "I can count on my fingers the number of marriages involving Portuguese," Eusebio says.

A grand Portuguese heritage party is planned for the evening of the handover, but nothing special will be happening at the Balichão. It is not that Eusebio fears the loss of the freedoms enjoyed under Portuguese administration—"We've had two years of the Hong Kong experience to digest and to choose [whether to emigrate to Portugal]," she says—it is just that something precious is disappearing. There is nothing to celebrate.

From his elegant office on the second floor of the gleaming white Leal Senado (Loyal Senate) building, Jose Luis de Sales Marques [see Figure 4.4] looks out over the picturesque town plaza, lovingly restored with tiles imported from Portugal. As chairman of the Macau Municipal Council, Marques is, in effect, Macau's mayor (the islands of Taipa and Coloane are administered separately). Like many others in the Macanese community, Marques, 43, comes from a long line of civil servants. His father worked for the post office; his mother was a city administrator. Playing the role of middlemen has come easy to the Macanese. On the one side were the senior Portuguese officials, who spoke no Cantonese. On the other were the Chinese, who until the late 1970s found government work unattractive and preferred to start businesses. Between the two are the Macanese, who can speak both languages.

However, many have left in recent years to take up civil-service jobs in Portugal. What used to be their trump card—language ability—has, in their view, now become a liability. While fluent in spoken Chinese, most Macanese cannot read or write the language. Government reports will increasingly be written in Chinese after the handover, leading Marques and others to worry that Macanese civil servants will be sidelined. Marques believes that in the long run the differences between Macanese and local Chinese will probably disappear, unless the Macanese find a way to preserve their culture. "We have our religion—we're all Catholic—our food and our language," he says. And there are the intangibles. "We feel and believe that we are not Chinese. Not superior—just that we are different." Marques hopes, however, that the Macanese may find a new role in helping build a multicultural Macau. "In a way, being Macanese is like being a citizen of the world," he says.

to" rather than "come back to" Portugal.[109] On the other hand, others do identify with Portugal more than with the Macanese, like Henrique de Senna Fernandes (see Box 4.1). Their identities may be conflicting, but the Macanese are indeed more likely to identify with the Portuguese.

For another example, Dona Aida's Macanese restaurant used to be frequented by many Portuguese and Macanese. But later on both have left Macau in large numbers, and now there are more Chinese. She also operates a friendship club, which has only Macanese as its members, about 50 of them.[110] The Macanese tend to know each other very well. Jia Yuan and Lu Lingsuo found in their research that everybody they interviewed knew everybody else: they were either classmates, colleagues, or neighbors. The rate of finding a relative or former lover was fairly high among the Macanese.[111] But their interaction with different groups is more rare.[112]

Their other social and political characteristics also set them apart from the Chinese. They enjoyed many privileges before the return of Macau to China. For example, the majority of the civil servants were Macanese, who enjoyed much higher salaries than the average Chinese in Macau. One survey indicates that 70% of the public servants in 1993 were Macanese.[113] Besides, they tended to be professionals like lawyers, engineers, architects, and engaged in high income jobs such as banking or insurance. They had their own organizations, such as the Macau Club, Macau Macanese Educational Association, and the Holy House of Mercy.[114] As the middleman between the Portuguese and Chinese, they enjoyed much social power, prestige, and many other indirect interests.[115]

Many policemen were also Macanese, who tended to treat the Chinese rudely if not brutally. It was not uncommon for the regulatory forces of the police to take bribes or beat Chinese merchants before the 12-3 Incident in 1966. Police brutality was one of the factors that led to the riots.[116]

In sum, the interracial marriage in Macau is the most meaningful social interaction between different groups but it is no guarantee for interracial harmony, for the resultant Macanese have then become a more or less distinct group, with its own political, social, and economic interests to protect. That sets them apart from both the Portuguese and the Chinese. They have largely lived separate lives.

Figure 4.4
José Luis de Sales Marques, the then chairman of the Macau Municipal Council before the handover. Leal Senado de Macau, *Relatorio de Actividades de 1997*, Macau: Leal Senado de Macau, 1997, p. 5.

A Tale of One City and a Tale of Two Cities: A General Examination of the Interaction between the Chinese and the Portuguese/Macanese in Macau

One City

From the Macau experience, it seems that interracial harmony or intercultural integration can be defined by mutual respect for and safe distance from one another. This in fact corresponds to Huntington's solution to the clash of civilizations problem.

We have already mentioned that the Macanese language does have an element of Chinese. Most Macanese speak Cantonese, although they do not write it. On the other hand, some Portuguese words have also slipped into the Cantonese language spoken in Macau. "*Folga*," a Portuguese word that means having some time off work, has become a Cantonese word, although it does sound like 放假, the Cantonese word for the same meaning. Other Portuguese words that have come into Cantonese include "*tudo*" (all), "*falar*" (speak Portuguese), "*nao tem*" (not having any), etc. Cantonese also borrows many English words, such as stamp, tyre, stick, jam, bus, tie, pan, fuse, steam, shopping, tips, show, cash, lunch, toilet, copy, interview, etc.[117] Although such linguistic integration is limited in scale, it is integration or diffusion nonetheless.

People also pick up each other's habits. It is common for the Chinese to drink coffee and have Macanese food and for the Portuguese and Macanese to drink tea and have Chinese food. Some Portuguese and Macanese would consult a Chinese doctor when sick.[118] Not many believe in Buddhism, but more Chinese believe in Christianity, even if they are still a small number. Two Macanese architects, Carlos Marreiros 馬若龍 and José Maneiras 馬斯華, report that when they designed buildings in Macau, they purposefully combined both Portuguese and Chinese elements, including Chinese symmetry, *fengshui*, use of furniture, etc.[119] The political system has some integration—the Chinese system now follows the Portuguese system of limited division of power, although there is a bit more democracy than before. This is in some contrast with the mainland China system of the one-party rule. The building of democratic institutions, including a habit of democratic practice, is still lacking. In other words, there is no doubt that integration of civilizations happens, but it remains mainly on a superficial level.

In sum, the Chinese and Portuguese live and work alongside one another and there is some cultural integration and diffusion. In that sense, one might say that there is one city.

Two Cities

Most of the time, however, there seem to be two cities, each living its own life. At the worst of time, the two cities would get into violent clashes, as in the assassination of Amaral in 1849 or the killing and wounding of the Chinese and the Chinese beating of the Portuguese and Macanese in the 12-3 incident in 1966. But mostly, if there was a clash between the two cities, it was not violent. People just kept their respectful distances from each other.

In a physical sense, during the 16th and 17th centuries there used to be two cities with a physical wall between the Portuguese/Macanese side and the Chinese side in Macau to keep the two peoples apart.[120] Here is a fuller quote by the European traveler who saw the wall (see Figure 4.5 for a section of the original city wall) and the two societies that were separated by it:

> Beyond the Barrier there appears to be a piece of neutral ground. The distinction between occidentalism and orientalism; between civilisation and barbarianism; between the European and the Asiatic is noticeable at once; for the well-made Portuguese road is at once changed for the wretched little foot-path, meandering hither and thither, ragged and uneven, never properly made, unkept and uncared for, running through a perfect necropolis of poorer graves.[121]

The city wall, which was first built in 1568 and went through several constructions and reconstructions, was meant as a defense construct against the Dutch and Chinese pirates. It was probably also meant to fend off possible Chinese attacks from the north.[122] It was frequently torn down by the Chinese officials because of its sensitive nature. Finally it was totally abolished by Amaral who included the Chinese city into the colonial territory in the 19th century, except for some short remaining sections we may still see today as in Figure 4.5 (see Plate 4.7 for a depiction of the original complete wall). For some time, however, it separated the Christian city,

Figure 4.5
A section of the old European city wall that still remains today. Photo by Vincent Ho.

where there were fortifications, churches, and commercial houses, from the Chinese countryside, where there were farm lands and graves, as the quote above shows.¹²³ In the Christian city were mostly Europeans, their slaves, and some Chinese converts to Catholicism. The Chinese who worked in the city during the day, that is, the farmers, traders, fishermen, coolies, and others, would leave the city after work when the city gates closed at night.¹²⁴

Even long after the wall was torn down, the two cities still existed. Henrique de Senna Fernandes recalled that when he was young, he noticed the two cities with striking contrasts. The houses in the Chinese city were pressed in tightly against each other, and there were no trees. The Christian city, however, was full of private houses, with traditional cobbled streets and secluded avenues and gardens.¹²⁵ There are more mixed neighborhoods now, but as late as the 1960s, the Portuguese, Macanese, and Chinese lived in relatively distinct neighborhoods reflecting the basic division of the population.¹²⁶

Even when neighborhoods are more mixed, there are other virtual barriers. One of them is reflected in the use of street names. As Clayton explains in her ethnographic work on Macau's streets, "an enormous number of streets are named for colonial administrators, governors, generals, bishops, traders and other important personages and events from the history of the city."¹²⁷ These names are then transliterated into Chinese, but when they are, they become utterly meaningless collections of syllables. For the Chinese people to remember these syllables is quite difficult. So when referring to a place in the city, the Chinese either simply use the name of a landmark there to signify the place or give them a new name in Chinese. Rather than using street names, they use such expressions as "at the fountain," "across the street from the phone company," "next to McDonalds," etc. The *Rotunda Carlos de Maia* becomes *San Zhan Deng* (Three lamps, or 三盞燈), which refers to the lamppost that stands at the center of the plaza that has three lamps. *Avenida do Conselheiro Ferreira de Almeida* becomes Helanyuan Da Malu (Hoh Laan Yuhn Daaih Ma Lou, or 荷蘭園大馬路), connoting the presence of the Dutch in the past.¹²⁸ In this way, the Chinese and Portuguese residents in Macau "inhabit two different cities in the same place."¹²⁹

The Portuguese, Macanese, and Chinese had a separate existence, which affected their daily lives. One Macanese man experienced extreme discomfort once he got on the wrong bus and landed in the northern district populated by recent Chinese immigrants. The bus stop signs were in Chinese, which he could not read. He was lost, and angry. He felt like "a foreigner in what he considers to be his own city."¹³⁰ Some Macanese, like Sir Roger Lobo, thought that the Portuguese did try to integrate, but he supposed that the Chinese did not want to integrate too much either and stuck to their own districts, clubs, and restaurants. Business people might mix, but only for business purposes. "It was almost like two separate worlds." There was very little social contact between the Portuguese and Chinese, Lobo observed.¹³¹

At least one more Portuguese thought the same: that the Chinese and Portuguese/Macanese had never been friendly towards each other.[132]

The Chinese thought likewise, although they also emphasized the Portuguese discrimination of the Chinese in Macau. José Chui thought that it was a shame that the Chinese and Portuguese and Macanese did not mix well together. "They were brought up in their culture and we were brought up in ours.... We had a different lifestyle, and different traditions, but we both belonged to Macao."[133]

Some thought that the Portuguese treated them well. Stanley Ho recounts how the Portuguese helped him in World War II. Some new immigrants related how the Portuguese government helped them in their settling down in Macau.[134]

Others felt that they were discriminated against by the Portuguese and Macanese. Gary Ngai said that the Portuguese, especially the police force, had always discriminated against the Chinese. He himself saw how they used to beat the Chinese. Father Peter Chung thought that it was unfair that the Church had to use Portuguese rather than Chinese in their liturgy. He said, "The Church in Macao is still very colonial. It still uses Portuguese as the official language. My assignments from Bishop Lam are written in Portuguese. Even now! I am Chinese and so is he, but his instructions come in Portuguese. The Church hasn't been localized." George Smith complained that the Portuguese were renovating all the beautiful Western colonial buildings but were leaving the beautiful old Chinese buildings to deteriorate.[135] Police officers also complained that they were required to write reports in Portuguese.[136] One of Clayton's interviewees said that one's name would even make a difference in one's pay.

> In the olden days, if your name was Wingsit Cheung, or Cheung Chi Lok, like my name, your salary would be 80 dollars per month. But if your name was Louis Cheung [meaning you are baptized], you'd get 100 dollars, even for the same position. It was discrimination. Absolutely, racial discrimination. Now if your name was Louis Clayton, you'd get 120.[137]

A Chinese complained about the way Macanese civil servants treated the Chinese customers. One of them criticized the Chinese for failing to understand simple Portuguese. Another said that if they did not understand Portuguese and yet had dignity, they should not come there. If they wanted to use Chinese, they should wait after 1999. One of them even raised a mirror, showed it to the Chinese, and said, "Take a look at your face, [it is] like a batch of barking dogs."[138]

No wonder Henrique de Senna Fernandes thought that Macau was a strange place: the Chinese and Portuguese have cohabited for over 400 years, yet their interaction was always problematic. Some did not even interact with the other their whole lives.[139]

But maybe it is what Ng Kuok Cheong (吳國昌) terms as a "you don't bother me, I don't bother you" kind of attitude that defines Macau.[140] In Coates's words:

Culturally there has never been anything like Macao, where so much of China and so much of Europe are enshrined in one small place. Goa, for all the magnificence of its buildings, never achieved this. Goa is European; the Indian element is missing. Only in Macao can one experience the extraordinary sensation of being one moment in the Lin Fong Temple, and ten minutes later in the Teatre Dom Pedro V, each an emphatic expression of a disparate civilization, yet producing no sense of cultural clash. Everything of distinction in Macao tones into the mellowness of the place, the whole creating a peculiar cultural unity, which is unique.[141]

Coates's description of Macau might be too romantic. "Ambivalence" might be a better way to describe Macau. That may be the best civilizations can get: beauty in ambivalence.

Conclusions: The Macau Model of the Interaction of Civilizations

What we see in Macau is what Pina-Cabral calls "a mutual agreement to disagree than, properly speaking, a cross-cultural dialogue."[142] In chapter 2, we discussed the Macau formula, which was a strategy the Ming dynasty adopted for both coastal defense and commercial profits. We might now be able to develop a Macau model, which describes a set of processes and characteristics of the clash of civilizations and cultures that is typical of Macau but has implications for other cases. We will examine three characteristics of the Macau model: conflicts, cooperation, and the "you don't bother me and I don't bother you" attitude. We will also see why this is the case, how we can improve this model, and the implications of an improved Macau model.[143]

Conflicts and Clashes of Civilizations and Cultures

Ethnocentrism and racism contributed greatly to the discrimination and killings that happened in the first few centuries of China-West interaction. The Opium Wars, the Boxers' uprising and riots, the assassination of Amaral, the 5-29 and the 12-3 incidents were some of the violent examples of the clash of civilizations. Other non-violent clash of civilizations would include discriminatory practices, especially by those in power. In contemporary Macau, one might not expect those violent clashes but one wonders to what extent ethnocentrism, racism, and discrimination still exist. Civilizational clashes are, of course, intertwined with political clashes.

In chapter 2, we mentioned the conflict between the Portuguese and the Dutch partly as one between Catholicism and Protestantism. To a British Protestant, "the facade of St. Paul's—elegant, imposing, and with nothing behind it—seemed a perfect symbol for the hollowness of Catholic religious life."[144] Harriett Low also concluded that "there was no more religion in Josepha 'than there is in a bamboo'."[145] Conflicts also occurred between the Portuguese and Macanese, when, for example, the former forced the latter to speak standard Portuguese, and when they recruited more Portuguese than Macanese in important government positions.[146]

In the 21st century, there is no longer a physical barrier, like the one in Macau 400 years ago. But other kinds of walls have continued to exist. In the Macau model, conflicts will continue to characterize the clash of civilizations and cultures, although they may not necessarily be violent (see chapter 7 on ethnic and class stratification and politics). Cultural differences will be enhanced to protect one's political and economic interests, and the deepening of the political and economic conflicts will further highlight and solidify the cultural differences. As we cited Huntington at the beginning of the chapter, globalization might bring people together, but it may also serve to enhance their differences.

Cooperation among Cultures and Civilizations

Seeing the violence that one group might do to the other, both the Chinese and Westerners sought to understand each other's cultures and civilizations more fully. Some Portuguese and Macanese reported receiving help from their Chinese friends during the difficult days of the 12-3 Incident. When they were afraid of going out, their Chinese friends brought baskets of daily necessities to them.[147]

Macanese, a new ethnic group, came into existence. Because of their multicultural background, they are more able to identify with both the Portuguese and Chinese cultures. Interracial marriage requires looking for commonalities, negotiating cultural differences, and working out a way to accommodate one another. That success symbolizes cooperation between civilizations and cultures. In chapter 7 on ethnic and class politics, we will see more to what extent that is possible.

The "I Don't Bother You and You Don't Bother Me" Attitude and Way of Life

But neither conflict nor cooperation has dominated Macau people's social interaction in the past 450 years. Most of the time, they seemed to be preoccupied with ambivalent feelings. This Chinese saying can describe the interethnic relations in Macau: people can hear each other's roosters and dogs, but in their whole lives they do not interact with each other (雞犬之聲相聞，老死不相往來).

Little amalgamation has taken place between the Portuguese, Macanese, and Chinese cultures, as Zepp points out.[148] Liu Denghan describes Macau culture as a cocktail that mixes different elements but these elements remain relatively independent.[149] To quote Zepp again, "these two cultures have met and have played to a draw."[150] Or as many say, it is *he er bu tong*, i.e., "differences in harmony" (和而不同) or *rong er bu rong*, i.e., "tolerance in disintegration" (容而不融).[151] It is "I don't bother you and you don't bother me." One wonders whether that is the solution to

Huntington's clash of civilizations, although Huntington himself would likely think so.

Jorge Rangel's words are a good summary of the future of the Macanese community in Macau.

> Our future may depend on how many Macanese stay here, and how far they'll be united in defending our interests. We already have our own associations here and we've decided to establish a school that will continue to use Portuguese as medium of instruction, supported by the ministry of education. There will be other clubs and associations that will help the Macanese community to have a voice. We hope the new government will understand that it is important for Macao to keep this community here. It's an issue of continuity.[152]

The Chinese community is doing similarly, having their own clubs and associations, and making sure that their tradition is carried on from generation to generation.

When discussing the encounters between the Chinese and the British, Coates comments on the "total void in understanding" between the Chinese and the foreigners, a mental no-man's-land. The Chinese lacked the knowledge of the outside world, and continued to think that they were the only civilized country in the world with the rest being just barbarians.[153]

If that was the case 150 years ago, there is no lack of knowledge of the outside world now, but people still have a limited capacity to understand each other. In response to Martha Nussbaum's advocacy of cosmopolitanism, Elaine Scarry observes,

> The difficulty of imagining [and understanding] others is shown by the fact that one can be in the presence of another person who is in pain and not know that the person is in pain. The ease of remaining ignorant of another person's pain even permits one to inflict it and amplify it in the body of the other person while remaining immune oneself. Sustained and repeated instances of this are visible in political regimes that torture.[154]

Our imagination is far from accurate and vivid compared with the real thing. Scarry cites Jean-Paul Sartre's study of the imagination to underscore the limits of it.[155] If we imagine the face of a person that we know in intricate detail and then look at the real person, the real face is more vital and vivacious while the imagined face is thin, dry, two-dimensional, and inert. Scarry therefore concludes, "*the human capacity to injure other people is very great precisely because our capacity to imagine other people is very small.*"[156] Because of this human limitation, we rely on stereotypes and generalizations, which tend to develop a life of their own. The end result, then, in most cases of social interaction, is "I don't bother you, and you don't bother me."

An Improved Macau Model and Its Implications

The Macau model is problematic. It recognizes the desire and difficulties to form ties with others, and it has a strategy for the clash of civilizations. But it is still a passive and weak strategy and calls for improvement.

Lack of understanding is the major source of prejudice, racism, discrimination, wars, and other conflicts, and breeds fear and distrust of the "other."[157] The current mainland China/Taiwan and mainland China/Hong Kong situations are at least partly due to a lack of understanding and trust. If a society does not constantly address these issues, it runs the risk of expanding conflicts and increasing dissatisfaction among its population because of the real or perceived unfairness and injustices.

Interaction does not necessarily work either, as Huntington would say. The more interaction we have with others, the more differences will be surfaced.[158] Huntington suggests that in order to get along, civilizations should learn to negotiate their differences and avoid getting into conflicts. He would love the Macau model. For example, he cautions against the United States getting involved in a conflict with the Muslim world, which is what we see today. One might argue that the U.S. invasion of Iraq and the resultant quagmire is a classic example of the clash of civilizations Huntington was trying to avoid. How can an improved Macau model enlighten us, then?

The Macau experience shows us that *the negotiation of differences means, first of all, that different groups of people have to focus on their commonalities.* The "one country, two systems" formula is the majority's biggest political interest. But as we see in chapter 7 on ethnic and class stratification and politics, Macau is increasingly becoming "one country, one system" with the momentum of mainlandization in the past 20 years. That political consensus is now being eroded. What still remains may be an agreement on a diversified economy, a sharing of a rich multi-culture in Macau, some limited checks and balances of government, and some limited freedom of speech. But the operationalization of that agreement is increasingly difficult. We will further discuss this in chapter 8. Nonetheless, focusing on their commonalities is still key to mitigating clashes of civilizations and cultures.

Second, the negotiation of differences means that the interacting parties have to acknowledge one's own weaknesses and learn from other people's strengths. Chinese culture can learn from the Western culture its respect for individual rights and democracy, and the latter can learn from the former the traditional respect for the collectivity and for the elderly. A new culture can be built on each other's strengths. Again, that remains a challenge.

Third, it is important to preserve one's own cultural differences. To use Clayton's words, "if we are not different, we will cease to exist" (her dissertation title). This applies to the differences not only between ethnic groups, but also within a group. In the Chinese community, for example, there are differences between the Cantonese,

Fujianese, and the mainlanders. Different people have different political points of view. More conflicts will only arise if society moves towards a unified, mainland Chinese culture (i.e., mainlandization). The Macanese fear of being homogenized by the Chinese after the return of Macau to China is not without reason or implications.[159]

Fourth, the challenge is, though, how one can preserve one's own ways of doing things while at the same time being integrated into a common culture. In Britain, as in other parts of Europe, the Muslim women's wearing of full-face veils, the *niqab*, has been criticized as their unwillingness to integrate into the local culture.[160] Wearing a veil is a way of showing one's own identity. Chinese, Portuguese and Macanese also have their own ways of showing their identities. The real challenge is in what ways, politically, economically, and culturally, people can show their respect for each other and *sometimes* compromise their differences for the purpose of integration, without losing one's own identity. This requires political will and cultural creativity.

So *finding commonalities, learning from each other, preserving one's own identities while still being integrated into a new common culture* may be the only way to negotiate boundaries and deal with differences and conflicts. This would be an improved Macau model.[161] It will take the collective efforts of both the government and community organizations to make this happen. We will come back to this issue in chapter 8.

In sum, the Macau story has given us food for thought concerning the clash of civilizations and cultures. If Huntington's views on the clash of civilizations reflect some of his own ethnocentrism, when he says, for example, that the West is unique and not universal and when he lays too much emphasis on the separation of civilizations rather than their integration, an improved Macau model would correct that. It has important implications for the future of Macau as well as for national and international relations, including the relationship between mainland China, Hong Kong, and Taiwan. What is needed may be some of the hardworking spirit of the missionaries to bridge the cultural gaps without losing one's own identities.

Plate 1.1
India, Malacca, and South China. Maria do Carmo Maia Cadete, *Museu de Macau*, Macau: Pro-Jardim, 1999, p. 40.

Plate 1.2
Temple of Goddess A-Ma in 1842. 霍啟昌, 蘇慶彬, 鄭德華, 澳門歷史實驗教材, Macau: 澳門大學實驗教材編寫組, 1998, p. 6.

Plate 1.3
The memorial rock in A-Ma Temple commemorating the arrival of Portuguese ships. Photo by Jerry Wu.

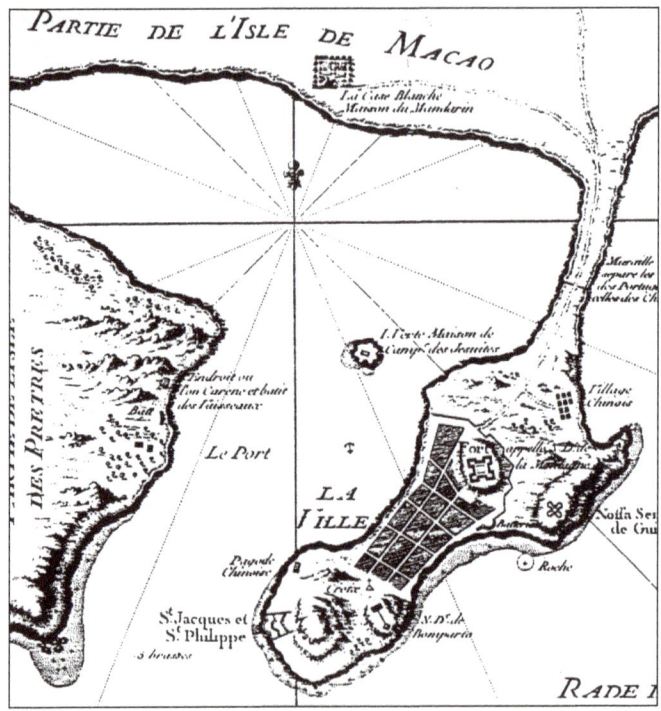

Plate 1.4
A historic map of Macau in the 18th century. Isabel Leonor da Silva Diaz de Seabra, *Relacoes entre Macau e o Siao*, Macau: University of Macau, 1999, p. 24.

Plate 2.1
Statue of Amaral. Photo by Raymond Wong.

Plate 2.2
The First Opium War. 孔繁壯, 陳伯良, 劉雅煌, *Macau*, Macau: 澳門出版社, 2002, p. 47.

Plate 2.3
The Senate building. Photo by Jerry Wu.

Plate 2.4
Mesquita, and his statue standing opposite the Leal Senado and being pulled down in 1966. Lei Pang Chu, *Macao China*, Macau: Macao Daily News, 1999, p. 65.

Plate 2.5
The Governor's Mansion, and now part of the Chief Executive's Office. Photo by Jerry Wu.

Plate 3.1
Fulong Xin Jie where brothels were located. Photo by Jerry Wu.

Plate 3.2
A fisherwoman, painting by George Chinnery (1774–1852). Rosmarie W. N. Lamas, *Everything in Style: Harriett Low's Macau*, Hong Kong University Press, 2006, Fig. 12.

Plate 4.1
Chinese and Westerners in Macau. Macau Data website: http://www.macaudata.com/Macau/draw/pic/02_17.html, accessed on February 19, 2005.

Plate 4.2
Chinese Boxers fighting the Eight-Nation Alliance (English and Japanese soldiers depicted), http://en.wikipedia.org/wiki/Boxer_Rebellion, accessed on October 8, 2009.

Plate 4.3

A portrait of Harriett Low. Chen Jichun, 錢納利與澳門 *Qian Nali yu Aomen*, Macau Foundation, 1995, p. 197.

Plate 4.5

Monument commemorating the war on Luhuan (Coloane). Photo by Wang Xin and Zhang Kai.

Plate 4.4

Rua da Guimarães 海邊新街, approx. 1890. Ho Weng Hong, *The Past of Macau*, Macau: Macao Foundation, 1994, p. 163.

Plate 4.6
The Trail of Tears. Robert Lindneux (1942), The Granger Collection, New York.

Plate 4.7
A picture of the city in 1635 with the city wall seen, Liu Yuelian, Zhang Tingmao, and Huang Xiaofeng, *Aomen Lishi: Chuzhong buchong jiaocai* (Macau history: A supplementary textbook for middle school students) (Macau: Macau Education and Youth Bureau, 2006), p. 18.

5 Religion and Social Development in Macau and China

> A religion is a unified system of beliefs and practices relative to sacred things, that is to say, things set apart and forbidden—beliefs and practices which unite into one single moral community called a Church, all those who adhere to them.
>
> It is through religion that we are able to trace the structure of a society, the stage of unity it has reached and the degree of cohesion of its parts, besides the expanse of the area it inhabits, the nature of the cosmic forces that play a vital role in it, etc.
>
> Emile Durkheim[1]

A sociology of religion would deal with the various expressions of religious beliefs and practices and their social influence on individuals and society. This chapter is not a full-fledged discussion on the sociology of religion in Macau and China. We will focus on how people in Macau have expressed their religious beliefs and how religion may influence the future of Macau.

Specifically, we will first discuss the Chinese religions of Daoism and Buddhism. Second, we will discuss the establishment of Christian churches in Macau. Third, we will examine the influence of religion, including the general influence of beliefs, the relationship between church and state, the Controversy of Rites, and the contribution of the Christian church to the exchange between Chinese and Western civilizations. Finally, we will ask what roles religion may play in Macau's future. What we discuss here will have an implication for a Macauan identity which we will focus on in chapter 8.

The Chinese Religions in Macau

The two major Chinese beliefs in Macau are Daoism and Buddhism. One may also add Confucianism, although it is not always viewed as a religion.

Daoist Beliefs

The belief in Mazu, as embodied by A-Ma Temple, or Ma Kok Miu (see Plate 1.2), is often viewed as a kind of Daoism as opposed to Confucianism or Buddhism. Confucianism believes in actively engaging in world affairs, political or social. So college students are supposed to study hard now so that they can train themselves into a role, say an official, through which they will change the world. By implication and modern application, they may also want to make money and enjoy luxuries in the world. Daoism, on the other hand, believes that all of those human endeavors are empty. What people should enjoy is what they have available to them. They should return to what is natural rather than try to achieve what is artificial.[2] Lao Zi and Zhuang Zi from 2,000 years ago are viewed as the founders of the Daoist philosophy.

But in what way is the Mazu belief a kind of Daoism, then? Confucianism has been the dominant ideology in the Chinese culture for over 2,000 years, but it has not been able to help people with what they do not often understand. For example, what about the natural and supernatural things? Are we governed by them as well? Confucianism does not address these questions, which leaves room for Daoism. So Daoism develops from the natural to the supernatural. After Lao Zi and Zhuang Zi (about the time of Confucius, i.e., 2,500 years ago), dozens of other Daoist priests joined in developing the religion, and many schools have arisen. Hundreds of temples have been established all over China, books have been written, various practices of the *qi* and *gongfu* or other ways of keeping fit have been developed, and gods and goddesses were created to take care of various things in this world, including the land, the sea, happiness, wealth, the wind, rain, and thunder, etc.

Among the goddesses created was Mazu.[3] The story goes that Mazu was born in the year of 960 C.E. of the Song dynasty into a family of an official named Lin Yuan 林願. Her name was Lin Moniang 林默娘. She had the ability to save lives. She died when she was 28 years old. When she died, she was made a goddess, whom one would pray to for safety, especially when on the sea. She received many honors and titles in the succeeding dynasties such as *Tianfei* 天妃, *Tianhou* 天後, *Tianfei Niangniang* 天妃娘娘, *Tianshang Shengmu* 天上聖母, etc. and was made the goddess of sea. When fishermen encountered dangers on the sea, she would rush to their rescue. (See Plate 5.1 for a depiction of Mazu's deeds.) She is the most famous goddess for Fujian and Guangdong fishermen. In Taiwan alone there are 74 Mazu temples. The temple in Putian county, Fujian, is viewed as the earliest and the head temple, because Mazu was born there.

A-Ma Temple, or Ma'ge Miao in *pinyin*, as seen in Plate 1.2, is the oldest temple in Macau. Although it is not clear exactly when it was built, we mentioned in chapter 1 that when the Portuguese came to Macau in 1553, the temple was probably already there. It has been believed that Fujian and Guangdong (Chaozhou)

Religion and Social Development in Macau and China

merchants established the temple in the Chenghua (成化) years of the Ming dynasty's Xianzong 憲宗 emperor, i.e., between 1465 and 1487.⁴ When it was first built, there were only a few thatched cottages. It has gone through many renovations and expansions to become what we see today.⁵ Given the importance of fishing in Macau since the early days, it is understandable that Mazu was worshiped as the most important goddess by the Chinese in Macau.

In addition to A-Ma Temple, there are many other temples in Macau that relate to the Daoist tradition, including Nezha Temple (哪吒廟) (see Figure 5.1), Lu Zuxian Yuan (呂祖仙院), Huang Daxian Temple (黃大仙廟), Mong Ha Kang Zhenjun Temple (望廈康真君廟), San Jie Huiguan Guandi Temple (三街會館關帝古廟), Taipa Guandi Tianhou Temple (氹仔島關帝天後古廟), Coloane San Sheng Temple (路環九澳三聖廟), Coloane San Shenggong (路環三聖宮), Nu Wa Temple (女媧廟), Ling Yan Xian Guan (靈岩仙觀), Bao Gong Temple (包公廟), Taipa Beidi Temple (氹仔北帝廟), etc. These temples worship other gods or goddess such as the above mentioned Lu, Huang, Guandi, Nu Wa, etc.⁶

According to Berlie, 49% of Chinese people in their research on Macau worshiped various divinities (拜神), 37% had no religion, 11% were Buddhist, and 3% Christian. More than two thirds of the Chinese population went to temples occasionally.⁷ Another research found that 16.8% of people in Macau in 1991 declared themselves as Buddhist, while 6.7% declared themselves as Catholic. Meanwhile, 61% declared no religious affiliation.⁸ Although there are some discrepancies between

Figure 5.1
Nezha Temple. Photo by Jerry Wu.

the two sets of statistics, and they may not talk about the same concepts (practice vs. affiliation), we can safely assume that most people's lives are only marginally influenced by religion in Macau, in spite of the many temples. But compared with other places in China, Macau is probably still more religious than most. Further research, however, has to be done on how many people in Macau actually visit these temples as part of their religious practice, and how specifically all these beliefs in Macau have affected people's lives.[9]

Buddhist Beliefs

In addition to Daoism, another major Chinese religion in Macau is Buddhism. Like Daoism, this religion also provides people with knowledge of the unknown. If Daoism advocates disengaging with the political and social world and returning to a natural state of affairs, Buddhism advocates aggressively getting rid of one's desires such as wine, women (or men), avarice, and pride. One should not have any desires at all, because the whole world is empty and is not worthy of our desiring. So one should not kill, steal, lie, (mis)use sex, and consume alcohol, things that result from man's desires. If one can forget about these desires, one is able to face old age, sickness, and death with calmness. Failures in achieving these desired objects are the real success.[10] Not having any desire makes one strong (無欲則剛). One then enters nirvana, a state of complete freedom from suffering.

Buddhism was created by the Buddha, or Siddhartha Gautama, a prince of the Sakya tribe of Nepal, 2,500 years ago, about the time of Confucius and Lao Zi. Although he was born into a rich family, he wanted to know why people would age, get sick, and die. He wanted to know the meaning of life. After many years of meditation and reflections, he came up with the principles of Buddhism and began to teach others about them. Finally a religion was born.

About 2,000 years ago, shortly after the creation of the religion, Buddhism spread to China. In the following years, classics were translated into Chinese, and just like Daoism, new schools of thoughts were developed, and hundreds of temples were built in China. The religion became one that would compete with Daoism and Confucianism.

Buddhism in Macau began with the establishment of Puji Chanyuan (see Plate 5.2), which was built in 1632, with a history of 368 years now. (This is where the Sino-American treaty was signed on July 3, 1844 after the First Opium War.) "Chan" 禪 here refers to the branch of Buddhism that has been Sinocized. Shortly after, another temple, Lianfeng Miao (蓮峰廟), was built about 340 years ago. Other temples were built in more recent times, including Puti Yuan (菩提園), Yaowang Chanyuan (藥王禪院) (1933), Gongde Lin (功德林), Zhulin Si (竹林寺), Puti Tang (菩提堂), Xiyun Si (西雲寺), etc. There are now various Buddhist organizations, including Macau Buddhist society (澳門佛學社), Macau Buddhist

Youth Center (澳門佛教青年中心), Yong Shan Lianyuan (永善蓮苑), Buddhist Pumen Hui (佛教普門會), and branches of international Buddhist societies.[11]

Given the basic teachings of Buddhism, one could imagine the role it played in the past several hundred years during the dual jurisdiction period, the colonial period, and the Chinese period, in mitigating people's needs and wants and pacifying their minds. More studies should be done in this regard. The case with Christianity, however, is somewhat different.

Christianity in Macau

If Daoism and Buddhism, especially the branch of Chan, were Chinese or Asian religions, Christianity is European. But like Buddhism, it spread to China. Christianity has three main branches: Catholicism, Eastern Orthodox Church, and Protestantism. The chief belief of Christianity is that individuals are sinful. Jesus Christ, who is God's son, sacrificed himself for the redemption of men and women (see Plate 5.3). By believing in the faith, Christians will be forgiven of their sins and reconciled with God. They will be saved and reunited with God in heaven in an everlasting life.

Many ideas of Christianity have entered the Western political institutions, including the idea of limited government, of the inviolable rights of the individual, the claims to international jurisdiction, the recurrent attempts to forbid or control usury and speculation, and the ideas of the just war and the just practice of war.[12] One would assume then that the European Christians who came to Macau and the Chinese who were baptized would also embody these qualities. Much research, however, has to be done in that respect, but let us now see what we do know regarding the history of Christianity in Macau and its social effect.

Catholicism

Christianity first spread to China in 635 C.E. in the Tang dynasty through what is now Xinjiang, but it disappeared in about 200 years. Then in about 1294, the religion again came to China, and churches were established in Beijing and Quanzhou. But it again disappeared in about 100 years. Then in the 16th century, Christianity again came and it stayed first in Macau and then spread to China as well as to other parts of Asia in spite of the many difficulties it had gone through in previous years.[13]

In 1563, there were about eight Jesuits from the Society of Jesus (耶穌會), who baptized about 600 Chinese believers either from Macau or from other parts of Guangdong. Then they built Santa Casa da Misericórdia (仁慈堂; see Figure 5.2), Hospital de Lázaro (痲瘋院), and Hospital de Rafael, which raised orphans and treated sick persons while teaching Christianity. Other churches have also been built since then, including St. Lazarus Church (望德聖母堂, 1569; see Figure 5.3);[14]

Figure 5.2
Santa Casa da Misericórdia (仁慈堂). Photo by Jerry Wu.

Figure 5.3
Igreja de Sao Lazaro (聖望得堂, also called 望德聖母堂). Photo by Wang Xin and Zhang Kai.

Figure 5.4
St. Lawrence Church (風順堂街聖老楞佐堂). Photo by Jerry Wu.

St. Lawrence Church (風順堂街聖老楞佐堂, 1569; see Figure 5.4); St. Francisco Chapel (聖方濟各堂, built in 1579, but became an army quarter in 1841); and St. Francis Xavier (another 聖方濟各堂 in Coloane, 1928; see the background of Plate 4.5); St. Paul's (1582, burned in 1595, rebuilt soon after; burned again in 1601, rebuilt again in 1602 with money from Japanese Christians and with craftsmanship of both Chinese and Japanese, but burned the third time in 1835);[15] St. Dominic's Church (板樟堂, 1587, the headquarters of the Dominicans who preached in Fujian, China; see Figure 5.5); St. Augustine's Church (崗頂聖奧斯定堂, 1589; see Figure 5.6); and the Church of St. Anthony (聖安多尼堂, 1608, burned in 1609, rebuilt in 1610; burned again and rebuilt again in 1638; burned yet again in 1809 and 1847, rebuilt again in 1875; see Figure 5.7). Other churches include the Cathedral of Macau (主教堂, 1850) (see Figure 5.8) and Chapel of Our Lady of

Figure 5.5
St. Dominic's Church 板樟堂 (又名玫瑰聖母堂). Photo by Wang Xin and Zhang Kai.

Figure 5.6
The outside of St. Augustine's Church (聖奧古斯丁教堂). Photo by Jerry Wu.

Figure 5.7
The inside of the Church of St. Anthony (聖安多尼堂). Photo by Jerry Wu.

Figure 5.8
The Cathedral of Macau (主教堂). Photo by Jerry Wu.

Figure 5.9
Chapel of Our Lady of Penha (主教山小堂). Photo by Jerry Wu.

Figure 5.10
Chapel of Our Lady of Guia
(聖母雪地殿堂). Photo by
Jerry Wu.

Penha (主教山小堂, 1622) (see Figure 5.9), Church of Our Lady of Fatima (1968), the Church of the Seminary of St. Joseph (1758), the Chapel of St. James (1740), the Chapel of St. Michael (1875), the Chapel of Our Lady of Guia (聖母雪地殿堂, 17th century) (see Figure 5.10), the Church of St. Joseph of Iao Hon (1998), the Church of Our Lady of Carmel in Taipa (1885), and the Chapel of Our Lady of Sorrows (1966).[16]

The large number of churches indicates the success of Christianity in Macau. Indeed, by 1644, according to one estimate, there were already 40,000 Christians in Macau, mostly Chinese.[17] Despite the periodic bans of Christianity in China, Christianity has persisted, though with less success now than in the middle of the 17th century. In 1999 there were still about 24,000 Catholics in Macau, or about 6.7% of the population, and about 60% of them were Chinese. The bishop was Lin Jiajun, the first Chinese in this position.[18]

Protestantism

Protestantism is another branch of Christianity, and it came to Macau in 1805 with a British missionary named Robert Morrison 馬禮遜 (1782–1834).[19] (See Figures 5.11 and 5.12.) Morrison baptized Cai Gao 蔡高, a young worker who helped him print biblical pamphlets in Macau, and who became the first Protestant in Macau, and in China, in 1814. Liang Fa 梁發, the second Chinese worker who helped Morrison in his printing work, became the second Chinese Protestant and the first Chinese Christian pastor in 1823. Liang's wife became the first woman in China who believed in Protestantism. Liang baptized his wife, and Morrison later baptized Liang's son. They were the first Chinese Protestant Christians.[20]

Protestantism in Macau developed quite slowly, and by the 1830s, there were about 10 Protestants. By 1985 there were 33 church organizations, most of which had fewer than 50 parishioners. By 1999 there were about 6,205 Protestant

Figure 5.11
The Morrison Protestant Chapel (馬禮遜基督教堂). Photo by Wang Xin and Zhang Kai.

Christians, accounting for about 1.8% of Macau's population. These church groups did not have much coordination of activities other than the yearly memorial activity to commemorate Robert Morrison on the day of his death.[21]

The Social, Cultural, and Political Influence of Christianity

Religion has played major roles in Chinese history. The influence of Confucianism is obvious. Daoism was considered as the national religion for some time in the Tang dynasty (618–907) and influenced not only the Huang Jin peasant uprising (184 C.E.) at the end of the Eastern Han dynasty, but the Boxers Rebellion in the Qing dynasty in the early 20th century as well. Buddhism was often the favorite religion of many emperors, and state leaders have befriended Buddhist priests throughout history. One of the most wide-scale peasant uprisings, the Taiping Uprising (1851–1864), was based on Hong Xiuquan's own interpretation of Christianity. So one cannot underestimate the influence of religion in Chinese people's lives, although other than Confucianism, other religions have never had as much influence as Christianity in the West and, in Macau as well.[22]

The General Influence of Beliefs and Use of Temples

In addition to the beliefs Christianity embodies, legends also have it that the saints have helped believers in various ways. St. Anthony, for example, "is a 'military' saint and a 'Captain' in the Portuguese army. Each year on his feast day (June 13) a ceremony takes place in which the president of the Senate presents him with his 'wages' and his image is taken in a procession to inspect what is left of the old city battlements."[23] Just like A-Ma Temple, the Chapel of Our Lady of Penha "served a point of pilgrimage for sailors embarking on a hazardous voyage."[24] St. James of the Chapel of St. James "is the military protector of Macau, and legend has it that he frequently goes on patrol around the city, and, at times, his boots are found to be muddy. A soldier used to be given the duty of cleaning the boots of the statue. On one occasion the man forgot his duty and received a crack on the head from the saint's sword."[25] The story of the Chapel of Our Lady of Guia says: "During the Dutch invasion of 1622, legend has it that the image of the Virgin left the chapel and held out her robe to deflect the enemies' bullets."[26] (See Plate 5.1 for what Mazu does.)

Religion also gives people a concrete place to come together to talk about public issues. The Chinese temples, for example, have always been a place for such gatherings. A-Ma Temple and Lianfeng Temple were where businessmen used to gather. They also set up schools there for poor children in the late Qing and early Republic of China eras. Puji Chanyuan and Lianfeng Temple organized relief work. The latter used to be the guest house for Chinese officials when they were in Macau: that was where Lin Zexu stayed when he was in Macau to deal with the opium issue.[27]

The Relationship between Church and State

Here we will examine the political, military, and social aspects of the relationship between the Church and the State in Macau. In 1575, shortly after the Portuguese settled in Macau, Pope Gregory XIII founded the Episcopal See of Macau with jurisdiction over China, Korea, and Japan. The church in Macau thus became not only "the focal point of intense missionary activity from China to Japan," but also "a power in its own right alongside the state."[28] The Jesuits founded their branch in 1563–65, Franciscans in 1579–80, Augustinians in 1586–89, and Dominicans in 1558.[29] In 1586, with different religious orders established in Macau, it was designated as the "City of the Name of God of Macau in China."[30] Macau was co-governed by both the Senate and the Society of Jesus.[31] Catholicism was the religion of the state.

Given the importance of Catholicism in the city, it is understandable that the bishop played a major role along with the governor in the politics of Macau, and the Senate members had to be Catholics as well, as we mentioned in chapter 2.[32] The bishop was opposed to the Senate's inclination to accept the Yongzheng emperor's suggestion to make Macau the place where all foreigners had to go through first before they came to mainland China. He won.[33] The political deference to religion can also be seen in the following example. In 1849, a British teacher, James Summers, from Hong Kong was arrested by Amaral, the governor, because he did not take off his hat while watching a Catholic procession. This was the feast of Corpus Christi, and as the Host in the procession approached, everybody was supposed to take off his hat. Summers was arrested on the charge that he offered insult to the religion of the State.[34]

In addition to the political role of the Church, the Catholics also played a military role. In fact, it was the Church which wanted to build the city wall as a defense mechanism against possible attackers, first the pirates, then the Dutch, in 1568. Both the Portuguese priests and Chinese Christians took part in building the wall.[35] As we mentioned in chapters 1 and 4, the Christians in Macau also participated in defending the city against the Dutch. Father Rho, whose cannon hit the main Dutch powder magazine, played a crucial role in that battle.[36]

The Jesuits also played a very important role in social development in Macau. They introduced the printing press to Macau, and indeed, to the Far East, using movable type in 1588, and St. Paul's College pioneered education in Macau.[37] Although it had fallen to 50% in the 1990s, the Catholic Church used to run two-thirds of Macau's schools.[38] The Catholic schools still teach about half of Macau's students as we discuss in chapter 7 on middle school education. "Most social welfare programs are still run by religious institutions."[39] From Stanley Ho's point of view, the Catholic schools also weathered the storms of the 12-3 Incident in 1966 beautifully. They were asked to teach Mao's Little Red Book, but the Church refused, and closed all the churches and the schools. They did not reopen the schools until the Chinese community agreed to clean off all the slogans on the church and school walls.[40]

Pina-Cabral points out that the privileged relationship between the Administration and the Church did not change even after the 1911 Portuguese Republican Law of Separation between the Church and the State. In the 1990s, the Administration still subsidized annually the activities of the Church, and "Catholic priests continued to have the status of civil servants."[41] Bishop Lam (Lin) also played a very important role in drafting the Basic Law of the Special Administrative Region of Macau.

Currently Macau has about 20,000 Catholic believers and 50 priests. According to Liang Jiefen 梁潔芬 (Beatrice Leong), the Church has kept a low profile after the handover of Macau to China, unlike the Church in Hong Kong.[42] While the Church in Hong Kong has taken an active role in the democratization movement there, the Church in Macau is largely silent on such issues. It has maintained a harmonious relationship with the government. Our comparative study on the Catholic church's civic engagement in Shanghai, Hong Kong, Macau, and Taipei analyzed three factors that made a difference in the church's civic engagement: structural in terms of state rules and regulation; cultural, both state and local cultures; and individual, especially the role of the bishops.[43] On the other hand, the Society of Jesus has founded the Ricci Institute, which has taken an active role in cultural exchange and China scholarship. It is not clear whether the Church will be able to play a more active role in Macau's political and social development, as it did in the past. It publishes a weekly newspaper in Chinese, *Aomen Guancha Bao* (the observer of Macau), which is fairly critical of the government. But it is only four pages long and does not seem to have much political influence.

The Controversy of Rites

The Controversy of Rites, or the Rites Controversy, is one of the most fascinating and arguably most unfortunate events in the cultural exchange between China and the West. It lends support to Huntington's theme of the clash of civilizations, but also shows clearly the possibility of negotiating and integrating cultural differences. When they first came to China, the Jesuits adopted a conciliatory attitude towards the Chinese culture. Michel Ruggieri 羅明堅 (1543–1607), an Italian Jesuit, came to Macau in 1579. He believed that if you wanted the Chinese to understand and believe in Christianity, you had to study the language first and learn the Chinese ways of doing things, such as kowtowing, praising others, and being humble.[44] He set up a school in Macau to teach Christianity to the Chinese and teach Chinese to the missionaries who were getting ready to go to the mainland. Matteo Ricci 利瑪竇 (1552–1610), another Italian Jesuit, came to Macau in 1582, studied Chinese at this school with Ruggieri and later went with him to Zhaoqing, Shaozhou (called Shaoguan now), Nanchang, Nanjing, Beijing, etc. to preach the religion.

They also helped the poor and the sick. In 1569, the Jesuits founded the ancient charitable organization in Macau, the Santa Casa da Misericórdia (Holy House of Mercy). It was to assist "fellow men, whose means of subsistence are too small and inadequate for the maintenance of a numerous family, to relieve bedridden, respectable people, and those who reluctantly go abroad asking for alms, and to bring up orphans and foundlings."[45] Dom Belchior Carneiro, the first bishop of Macau and founder of the Holy House of Mercy, said that he would like the Church to help the hungry, the crying, the wounded, the thirsty, the bounded, and the weak (饑者能得飽，哭者能止淚，傷者得敷藥，渴者能得水，束縛者得解放，衰弱貧乏者能得救助).[46] This way, they not only helped the disadvantaged, but attracted Chinese to Christianity as well.

Their early success led to the establishment of the St. Paul's College in Macau in 1594, one of the first few Western-style colleges in Asia. It taught not only Christianity but also mathematics, astronomy, physics, medicine, philosophy, theology, Chinese, Latin, music, and rhetoric. This became a place that trained missionaries from various branches of the Catholic Church, including the Jesuits (耶穌會士) of the Society of Jesus, the Franciscans (方濟各會士) of the Franciscan Order, the Dominicans (多明我會士) of the Order of Preachers, and the Vincentians (遣使會士) of the Congregation of the Mission.[47] Of all the Jesuit missionaries in China during the Ming and Qing dynasties, about 200, or 50% graduated from the College. About 30 Chinese also graduated from the College, including Wu Li 吳曆,

a man of letters whom we will talk more about in the next chapter, Li Ande 李安德 (or Andreas Ly), and Lu Xiyan 陸希言. These Chinese also became missionaries in China.[48]

There indeed appeared to be a merge of cultures and civilization. The Jesuits donned Chinese clothes (儒冠儒服), and Chinese Catholics donned Western clothes.[49] As a result of their missionary work, the number of Christians in China increased to 150,000 by 1644, including not only ordinary people but also officials. Xu Guangqi, a minister of the Ming government (禮部尚書), was one of them (see the picture of Ricci and Xu in Plate 5.4). There were also other scholar-officials like Li Zhizao 李之藻 (1565–1630) and Yang Tingyun 楊廷筠 (1557–1627) at the time. Zheng Zhilong 鄭芝龍, Zheng Chenggong's father, a business tycoon and pirate, was also baptized.[50] By the end of the Ming dynasty, there were churches in 13 of the provinces, and by 1667, the Jesuits alone had 159 churches all over China, with additional 21 Dominican and 13 Fransciscan churches.[51] By 1735, there were already 300,000 Chinese Christians.[52]

Part of the missionary success was based on their understanding that cultures had to integrate with one another rather than exclude each other. But things changed soon in the 1600s. As we observed above, both Ruggieri and Ricci believed that the Chinese worship of ancestors and Confucius was only showing thankfulness and respect for these people. It was not superstition and it was compatible with Christianity. However, Niccolò Longobardi 龍華民 (1559–1654), another graduate of St. Paul's College, took over as the chief executive officer of the Society of Jesus after Ricci died in 1610, and he thought that this kind of worship was superstition and it was against the principles of Christianity. He disallowed the Chinese to worship their ancestors and Confucius, although most Jesuits did not agree with him. This intensified the conflict that existed already between the Chinese and the Westerners over Christianity.

A movement against Christianity was already in the making before Longobardi came to power. By 1610, there had already been 54 incidents related to the conflict between the Chinese and Catholic missionaries, mostly in Guangdong and of small scale.[53] But it picked up momentum after Ricci died and Longobardi came to power. A more serious clash of civilizations between the Chinese and the Westerners then followed. Many Chinese scholars had already been writing articles attacking the missionaries, accusing them of sabotaging Chinese culture.[54] Then in 1610, the government in Nanjing arrested the missionaries and the Chinese Christians there, and with the emperor's approval, sent the Catholic priests to Macau, including Álvaro de Semedo 謝務祿 (later named 曾德昭).[55] Finally the Ming dynasty emperor decided to expel all the Jesuits from the mainland to Macau in 1616.[56]

But the Controversy of Rites did not stop there. Although most Jesuits still followed Ricci's footsteps, they did not recover their lost ground in the mainland until the latter half of the 17th century. But only a few years later did they meet another setback, when they were attacked by Dominicans for allowing their Chinese believers to worship their ancestors and Confucius. Now this is a clash of religious cultures within the Western civilization. The Chinese emperor Kangxi supported the Jesuits, sent envoys to the pope, and tried his best to arbitrate rationally in the Rites Controversy.[57] But the Vatican supported the Dominicans against the Jesuits. Indeed some in the Roman Catholic Church would agree with Kangxi. As discussed in chapter 4, the Propaganda Fide of the Church even issued an order to ask the missionaries in the Far East to be flexible in regard to Chinese customs. But apparently this brand of thought did not become the order of the day.

Emperor Kangxi had been friendly toward Christianity, having issued an Edict to Tolerance (容教令) in 1692 to allow Christianity in China, and hired several Jesuits he liked, who worked as scientists or artists in the imperial court. But he decided in 1723 to ban Christianity. The ban was in effect for 130 years.[58] Chinese Christians were viewed as betraying their ancestors (亡宗滅祖). Zhang Rulin, the Chinese official in Macau, made a point in prohibiting the Portuguese from enticing the Chinese into their religion. It was under these circumstances that the Chinese Christian Church in Macau (唐人廟) was closed by the Chinese government.[59]

In 1784, Emperor Qianlong continued his grandfather's anti-Christian policy and issued orders to disallow missionaries in China. The Chinese who believed in Christianity or taught foreigners the Chinese language would also be executed.[60] All kinds of anti-Christian incidents happened, and the Jesuits were expelled to Macau again. The Society of Jesus was subsequently disbanded by the pope in 1773 under the pressures of the Portuguese, French, and Spanish governments. They were not able to come back and to be in full function until the middle of the 19th century after the Opium Wars.[61]

Although one may still debate about who was responsible for this development in the process of the East meeting the West,[62] it is clear that cultural integration and diffusion are difficult problems. The Controversy of Rites had caused serious interruption in the East-West exchange and affected negatively the understanding and integration of Chinese and Western civilizations. It created difficulties between civilizations and affected the direction of modern Chinese history.[63] As Spence says, "Had either side been more flexible, then later in the eighteenth century, when the Catholic Church accepted the findings of Galileo and the missionaries started to introduce up-to-date Western astronomy to the Chinese, the new knowledge and techniques might have led to significant changes in Chinese attitudes about thought and nature."[64] Nonetheless, despite the great vicissitudes of the missionaries in China in the 16th, 17th, and 18th centuries, much cultural exchange was done and the achievements were impressive.

Christian Church's Contribution to the Exchange between Chinese and Western Civilizations

On the one hand, Chinese culture was introduced to the West. Matteo Ricci translated the Four Books (四書) into Latin in 1593: *The Great Learning*, *The Doctrine of the Mean*, *The Analects of Confucius*, and *Mencius*. Nicolas Trigault 金尼閣 translated the Five Classics (五經) into Latin: *The Book of Songs*, *The Books of History*, *The Books of Changes*, *The Book of Rites*, and *The Spring and Autumn Annals*.[65] Philippe Couplet 柏應理, a Belgian Jesuit and a graduate of St. Paul's College, wrote a book in 1681 on Confucianism. When he went back to Rome in 1682, he took 400 Chinese books with him. Álvaro de Semedo 曾德昭 wrote an encyclopedic volume on China.[66] Forian Joseph Bahr 魏繼晉, a German Jesuit and another graduate of St. Paul's College, compiled a *German Chinese Dictionary* in the middle of the 18th century. Huang and Zha listed 25 Jesuits' 77 books of writings and translations on Chinese philosophy, history, literary works, as well as dictionaries in the 16th, 17th, and 18th centuries. Meanwhile, Chinese medicine, mathematics, and arts and crafts were also introduced to the West.[67]

Likewise, Western culture was introduced to China by the missionaries. Ricci and Ruggieri compiled a Portuguese Chinese dictionary in 1584. Ricci, a mathematician and astronomer, and Xu Guangqi translated mathematics works into Chinese, which started a wave of studies in the field: Huang noted 112 Chinese scholars who had written works on Western mathematics in the beginning of the Qing dynasty.[68] When Ricci came to China, he brought books and astronomical instruments with him and also helped the Chinese make more once there. One estimate puts the number of books brought to China by Jesuits at 7,000.[69] While Father Francisco Cardoso drew the first map of China,[70] Ricci drew the first Chinese map of the world. He also wrote medical books in Chinese. The titles of some of his books in Chinese include *Treatise on the Celestial Bodies*, *Work on Trigonometry*, *Treatise on Geometry*, and *Elements of Geometry of Euclides*. He was considered as the pioneer of European science in China.[71] Books on physics were also written by Jesuits in Macau. Johann Adam Schall von Bell wrote a book in 1626 on microscopes which he brought to Macau in 1620.

Jesuits were also pioneers of European humanities in China. Here are more of their works. Alfonso Vagnoni 高一志 (1566–1640, Italian Jesuit), introduced Greek philosophy to China when he was expelled from Nanjing to Macau in the beginning of the 1600s. Giulio Aleni 艾儒略 (1582–1649) and Francisco Furtado 傅汎際 both wrote on Western philosophy for the Chinese readers. They were both Jesuits graduated from St. Paul's College. These were earliest Western philosophical works available to the Chinese. Another St. Paul's College graduate, Thomas Pereira 徐日昇 (1645–1708) introduced the theories and practices of Western music to China and became a music teacher at the imperial court in the Kangxi era. (The University of Macau used to locate at Av. Padre Tomas Pereira, a road named after the missionary musician graduated from St. Paul's College.) Altogether, Liang Qichao counted 320 works translated and written by 67 Jesuits, in both sciences and humanities.[72] Ricci was dubbed as a Western Confucian (西儒), and Aleni was even dubbed as the Western Confucius (西來孔子). Xu Guangqi praised the Western missionaries as righteous, disciplined, knowledgeable, refined, sincere, and resolute (其道甚正，其守甚嚴，其學甚博，其識甚精，其心甚真，其見甚定).[73]

Among the Western technology introduced to China was also various other glassware, for example, glass lamp, glass cups, glass screen. There were, of course, the chime clocks and other Western gadgets we mentioned in chapter 4. Western architecture was also introduced to China, first in Macau with the church buildings we mentioned earlier.[74] Then Western medicine was introduced first in Macau with the hospital run by the Holy House of Mercy, and the first Western medical hospital in China was established in Macau in 1569, which introduced smallpox vaccine first in Macau and later to the mainland in 1805. East India Company's surgeon, Alexander Pearson, vaccinated a number of mainland Chinese against smallpox in 1805, and wrote a pamphlet on vaccination for Chinese readers. George Staunton translated it into Chinese and printed at the Company's Canton press. But before that, it was the Portuguese doctor named Domingo sjost Comes who introduced it in Macau.[75] Many agricultural crops and technology were also introduced to Macau and China, including corn, peanuts, sweet potatoes, etc.[76]

Father Schall, Ferdinand Verbiest, Grimaldi, and Antonio Tomas even served as presidents of the Tribunal or Board of Astronomy and mathematics in Beijing. Father Gabriel de Magalhaes, a mechanical artist, was said to have improved the observatory in Beijing with the help of 150 to 200 Chinese. It was through Father Tome Pereira, the vice-president of the Board of Astronomy that Kangxi the emperor issued the Edict to Tolerance in 1692.[77] As Pina-Cabral points out, the Jesuits in Beijing "played a decisive role in protecting Macau's situation before the Emperor, particularly during the long rein of Kangxi" (which lasted until 1721).[78] Other Europeans even thought that the Jesuits in Beijing were "scheming against them in the commercial interests of Catholic Macao."[79]

If the Catholic missionaries made enormous contribution to the exchange between the Chinese and Western civilizations,[80] Protestant missionaries, too, did their part, although not on such a large scale. Reverend Robert Morrison published the first Anglo-Chinese dictionary, *Dictionary of the Chinese Language* in Macau in 1815.[81] He translated the New Testament into Chinese in 1814, and then both the Old and New Testaments in 1823 (see Figure 5.12). This was the first time the complete texts of the Bible were translated for the Chinese audience.[82]

Robert Morrison was the first Protestant missionary in China, and the East India Company's Chinese interpreter. In June 1821, his wife died while giving birth

Figure 5.12
Robert Morrison translating the Bible with his Chinese helpers; painting by Chinnery. *Review of Culture* N°58, Macau: Instituto Cultural de Macau, 2006, p. 28.

to a child. Being a Protestant, he could not find a burial place for her in Macau. Neither the "Papists" (Morrison's own word) nor the Chinese allowed him their burying ground to Protestants. The East India Company finally decided to buy a piece of land in Macau. They bought it from Manuel Pereira, a wealthy Portuguese merchant and financier. But the Portuguese law prevented foreign ownership of land in Macau, so if allowed, both the governor, Castro Cabral, and the bishop would face the consequences of breaking the rule, the former two with Goa and the latter with Rome. They took the risk, and the Protestant Cemetery has remained there since then.[83] But before the Protestant Cemetery came into being, Morrison's wife had been buried in a "no man's land," with the risk of the tomb being spoiled or desecrated.[84] In fact, even before the death of his wife, Morrison had already had a difficult time in Macau since they disapproved of Catholicism and had almost no friends in this Catholic city. His wife, Mary, spoke Portuguese but was friendly with only one family.[85] The Protestant missionary's life in Macau was a difficult one indeed. Morrison died in 1834 at the age of 51.

John Robert Morrison, the son of Mary and Robert, was also a brilliant Sinologue, like his father. He served as interpreter and adviser to Charles Elliot in the Opium War and played an important role in the negotiations between the Chinese and the British. He later became the Chinese secretary of Hong Kong but died soon thereafter of the Hong Kong fever in 1843. His body was buried near the graves of his father and mother in the Protestant Cemetery.[86]

Robert Morrison taught Christianity to his assistants. He had two assistants who helped him in the work of the Chinese-English dictionary. They read Chinese books to him and helped him translate words, learning English at the same time. He wrote on April 24, 1808,

> Learning with my two assistants the word "hope," we made two sentences to exemplify it—"I hope you are well," and "the hope of a future life." The former, when rendered into English, they learned with all eagerness, but discovered an aversion to the latter. I asked them how it came to pass that the affairs of the present life were esteemed so important, whilst those of a future and eternal state were neglected. Without returning an answer, and merely to gratify me, it was with a sneer that they desired me to teach them the English of the sentence in question.[87]

This reminds us of the principle of Chinese learning as the essence and foreign learning for practical purposes. Rather than learning the idea in the sentence, they wanted to study the skills to speak it. In fact, it was also Emperor Kangxi's position. Although he was very fond of the Jesuits, befriended them and hired them in his court for astronomical and mathematical issues, Kangxi was not that interested in their religion, even if the latter did try to teach the emperor some Christianity.[88] It was amid this clash of cultures and civilizations that the cultural diffusion happened, paradoxically—Morrison did work out a Chinese-English dictionary and the Chinese version of the complete Bible.

After Morrison's death, an educational foundation was set up in his name. In 1839, the foundation set up the first Protestant elementary school, the Morrison School (馬禮遜學堂).[89] Yung Wing 容閎 (Rong Hong, 1828–1912), who later became one of the famous Qing government officials, was a student there. The school taught English, Chinese, mathematics, algebra, geometry, physics, chemistry, health, geography, music, and arts. Yung Wing later went to Yale University in 1846 along with Huang Kuan 黃寬 and Huang Sheng 黃勝, and was among the first Chinese to graduate from an American university in 1854.[90] As a government official, he was an advocate and was in charge of sending children to the United States to study Western culture.[91] (See Figures 5.13 and 5.14.) Huang Kuan, a classmate of his at the Morrison School, later studied in Britain and became the first well-known medical doctor in Western medicine.

In 1827, Thomas R. Colledge, a British missionary in Macau whom Harriett Low mentioned many times in her diary (he married one of her friends, an American), established an eye hospital in Macau. He saw large numbers of Chinese walking about with physical complaints that could be remedied with the simplest surgery rather than always relying on traditional Chinese medicine. He was determined to treat them and he did. He also operated for cataract, lanced abscesses, and excised tumors (see Plate 6.10).[92]

Finally, we must mention that the first newspaper was published in Macau in 1822, "a small sheet printed on Chinese paper at the Government printery under

Figure 5.13
Yung Wing. 錢鋼 胡勁草, *Chinese Educational Mission Students* (大清留美幼童記), Beijing: Contemporary China Publishing House, p. 2.

Figure 5.14
Students sent to the U.S. 錢鋼 胡勁草, *Chinese Educational Mission Students* (大清留美幼童記), Beijing: Contemporary China Publishing House, p. 47.

the Municipal Senate edited by a Dominican friar named Fr. Antonio de S. Gonzalo de Amarante."[93] In 1832, the first lithograph press was introduced to Macau, and "exploited by British and American missionary enterprise in the publication in Macau of *The Canton Register* (1827–44), *The Chinese Repository*, a monthly published between 1832–52, *The Evangelist and Miscellanie* (1833), and *The Canton Press* (1839–1844)."[94] These must be the newspapers that Lin Zexue studied avidly when he was working on the opium issue here.

Although compared with that of the Catholics, the Protestant contribution came later and of a lesser scale, it was important nonetheless. With both their efforts, extensive cultural exchange took place in the first 300 years of Macau's history in China. The works introducing Western culture to China by missionaries numbered 187 and by Chinese scholars numbered 104 during the Ming and Qing dynasties.[95] All of these happened amid the Controversy of Rites. As Jonathan Spence comments, which we quoted earlier, had there not been those difficulties, the entire Chinese history might have been rewritten in the later years of the Qing dynasty.[96]

Conclusions

There have been other religious orders in Macau: there used to be Zoroastrianism (瑣羅亞斯德教), which no longer exists; there are also Bahaí (巴哈伊教), Islam (伊斯蘭教), Shen Ci Xiu Ming Hui (神慈秀明會), and the Mormons (摩門教). But they are all relatively small in size,[97] and have been exerting less influence in Macau in particular and China in general compared with the other religions.

In conclusion, first, it is striking that in such a small place as Macau, so many religious orders have existed. Even with the dual tracks in religion, they seemed to have lived alongside each other largely in harmony, but separately, most of the time.[98] Second, the Controversy of Rites tore apart not only the Chinese society but the European missionaries as well. In Macau, the Chinese Catholic Church, or the Church of Our Lady of Defense (唐人廟), was closed by the Chinese authorities in 1749. The Controversy of Rites indicates the incompatibility between Chinese and Western beliefs, with one wanting to overpower the other.

Another example of cultural and civilizational clash may be the description of "The Holy Mother tramples on the dragon's head," or 聖母踏龍頭, as the Chinese words say next to the picture (see Figure 5.15). It is one of the sculptures on the St. Paul's façade. It is a reference to the Book of Genesis,[99] but it may be a symbol of Western beliefs overpowering Chinese beliefs in this case in the form of dragon. Notwithstanding that this dragon looks very different from the usual Chinese

Figure 5.15
St. Mary stepping on the head of the dragon. Photo by Wang Xin and Zhang Kai.

Figure 5.16
The Temple of Nu Wa. Photo by Wang Xin and Zhang Kai.

dragon—this one has seven heads and it is like a big and fat bird—in the Chinese belief, a dragon is not only a symbol of the emperor, but it is also the embodiment of the earliest Han Chinese: Nu Wa and Fu Xi, as Eve and Adam in the West. Both Nu Wa and Fu Xi had snake-like bodies, and a snake and a dragon are oftentimes interchangeable in meaning in the Chinese belief. A snake is simply a small dragon. Interestingly, just opposite the St. Paul's ruins and down the street there is a temple of Nu Wa (see Figure 5.16).[100]

Within the Catholic Church itself, the Dominicans had conflicts with the Jesuits because the former sided with the pope against Macau's bishop in the said controversy.[101] At times, the Jesuits even banned communication with the Protestants.[102] Harriett Low, a Protestant, did not like Catholics. Her comments on the Catholic religion are worth quoting in full here. She was describing what seemed to her the "shocking" manners of Catholic burial and the way they treated a woman who had said good things about Protestants. Here are her comments:

> I wonder if the time will come when this Catholic religion (if we can call it so) will be done away. Yes by degrees I think it will; think of the time when all Europe was in the same state, but as the world becomes enlightened, this bigotry and superstition will be done away. The might fabric is gradually decaying—the foundation will soon be undermined and a new one will be erected. The religion of Jesus Christ is growing in *America* and it cannot fail of spreading itself. I should like to look upon this little planet 2000 years hence and see what *mind* will be then. See if people will not think for themselves and consider themselves the keepers of their

own consciences and God their only master, their best judge. How different the world is now or the state of society from what it was in the 15th century and shall it not go on towards perfection? We certainly have not retrograded since then,—I prophecy it will! We shall, or others will see these Chinese exalted in the scale, their turn must come I think—the barriers must be broken down, ignorance must give place to knowledge, and slavery to freedom. Females will then be exalted; what a state they are in now, poor degraded beings, mere toys for the idle hours of their oppressive masters—crippled, tortured, merely to please them.[103]

Harriett Low raised many interesting and still challenging questions for us today. We need again to emphasize that the clash of civilizations and cultures occurred at the same time an enormous amount of cultural exchange took place.

What roles can religion play in China's development in the future?[104] What is the relationship between church and state? At the time of writing, religion is suppressed in mainland China and the practices similar to those of the Cultural Revolution, such as closing down churches and removing crosses, are spreading from one province to another. It appears that China is experiencing another round of Rites Controversy. It is not clear how long this anti-religious movement is going to last. It certainly does not bode well for China's integration into the world.[105] Meanwhile, it remains to be seen whether the contemporaries of Macau will learn from their predecessors and found a better society in which everybody is treated with respect and people learn from and appreciate each other. We will continue to discuss these issues in the following chapters.

6 Literature and the Arts in and about Macau

> It is the task of the sociologist of literature to relate the experience of the imaginary characters to the specific historical climate from which they stem and, thus, to make literary hermeneutics a part of the sociology of knowledge. That sociologist has to transform the private equation of themes and stylistic means into social equations.
>
> Adorno once said, "Works of art . . . have their greatness only insofar as they let speak what ideology conceals. They transcend, whether they want to or not, false consciousness."
>
> Leo Lowenthal[1]

The sociology of literature and the arts can be defined as the study of those who have created works of reflection on our society, how these works help us understand societies, and how they have impacted social change. We will examine those who created the poems, essays, stories, plays, paintings, architecture, etc., how and to what extent they help us understand the various historical developments in Macau society, including the clash and cooperation of civilizations and cultures, the Macau model, and the transformation of the Macau society. We will discuss the following topics: 1) the traditional Chinese literature on Macau during the Ming and Qing dynasties; 2) the continuation of the Chinese literary tradition in the modern times; 3) traditional operas and modern plays; 4) Chinese arts in Macau; 5) Macanese arts, literature, and plays; and 6) Portuguese, English, German, and French poems and paintings in and about Macau.

As is the case with our analysis of religion in Macau, we are not doing a full-fledged study of the sociology of literature and the arts in Macau, but our examination will nonetheless help us better understand Macau society. As Pittis and Henders point out,[2]

> It was in Macao that the Chinese and Western worlds first came face to face on a permanent basis, sometimes with violence, at others with admiration, often with

misunderstanding. Writers from both civilizations have recorded their impressions of one another's curious customs, incredible inventions, peculiar foods, and presumptuous claims to control the tiny piece of the South China coast.

We will discuss how writers from both civilizations saw each other in the form of literature and the arts, and see how the themes we have discussed in the previous chapters are reflected in various literary forms.

The Traditional Chinese Literature on Macau during the Ming and Qing Dynasties

Since the Portuguese began to settle in Macau to do business in the 1550s, a dual system of politics, economy, and culture began to develop, and the Chinese and Western cultures began to interact. Chinese scholar-officials frequently visited Macau, and there were also scholars who fled the Qing government on the mainland or who came to study religion in Macau. These scholars created a large amount of poetry reflecting on what they experienced and thought about while in Macau. Zhang Wenqin colleted 544 poems by 129 poets in the two volumes of poetry covering a period of over 300 years.[3]

Commerce in Macau

Tang Xianzu 湯顯祖 (1550–1616), a renowned Chinese poet and playwright, arguably the Shakespeare of China, wrote about his admiration of the jewels the Portuguese traders brought to China in the following poem entitled 香嶴逢賈胡 (or "Meeting Foreign Traders in Macau").

> 不住田園不樹桑，珴珂衣錦下雲牆。明珠海上傳星氣，白玉河邊看月光。

He is saying that these Portuguese traders do trade rather than agriculture like the Chinese. Wearing colorful clothes and in big ships with tall masts, they bring to China the jewels as bright as the stars and as brilliant as the moon. One of the scenes in his famous work *Peony Pavilion* is based on what he saw in Macau.[4] This admiration of foreign cultural products reminds us of what Yin Guangran and Zhang Rulin say about the chime clock and magnifiers. It also reminds us of the Ming scholars who spoke of foreign traders as being here for businesses only.

Feng Gongliang 馮公亮, another poet, sings the praise of prosperous business in Macau:

> 濠鏡由來荒僻濱，今成戎蠻貿易津。十字門中擁異貨，蓮花座裏堆奇珍。

What used be a barren area has now become a business center with many exquisite commodities and treasures.[5]

Wu Li 吳曆 (1632–1718), another famous poet and painter, describes Chinese people busy doing business between Macau and what is now Zhuhai at the time when the Qing government forbade trade on the sea:

小西船到客先聞，就買胡椒鬧夕曛。十日縱橫擁沙路，擔夫黑白一群群。

The poem says that when the foreign ships arrive in Macau, the Chinese come to buy pepper till dusk. On the dusty road, you see many people, old and young, carrying their goods on shoulder poles across the border.[6] This is indeed a picture of peace and prosperity. Recall that in chapter 2 we related some Chinese scholars' assessment of foreigners as peaceful and interested only in business. There are still many people crossing the border every day now, but they are mostly people from Macau who are going to Zhuhai for shopping or eating, or tourists from the mainland coming to Macau gambling. Very few are engaged in small businesses of trade, like those middle-aged or elderly Macau people who cross the border back and forth several times a day transporting a small amount of groceries from Zhuhai to Macau with their luggage carts and making very little money. Large-scale transactions are done by other means, using trucks, ships and airplanes.

Cultural Exchange and Social Interaction in Macau

Like Kangxi the emperor, Chinese scholars also appreciated Western music very much. Here is Liang Di's (梁迪) description (1718) of a Western musical instrument, the organ:

奏之三巴層樓上，百里內外閒聞聲。……幽如剪刀裁繡閣，清如鸛鶴唳青冥。和如鶯燕啼紅樹，哀如猿猱吟翠屏。……或如寒淙瀉三疊，水廉洞口流瑽琤。或如江濤奔萬馬，石鍾山下聞噌[口+宏]。……或如龍吟水晶闕，老魚瘦[蟲+交]舞縱橫。……或如蒲牢敲百八，振盪心魂群動醒。[7]

The sound of music from St. Paul's Cathedral is described as being heard many miles away. Sometimes it is like a bird singing, or monkeys calling. Other times it is like a waterfall rushing down several layers of rock, like 10,000 horses running. The sound touches one's heart deeply.[8]

Wu Li came to Macau to study religion. Here is his poetry regarding that experience:

關頭粵盡下平沙，濠境山形可類花。居客不驚非誤入，遠從學道到三巴。

It means: Passing the border, I come to the end of Guangdong to the sands of Macau. The mountains look like flowers. People in Macau need not be surprised: It is not a mistake that I am here. I have come from afar to St. Paul's to study your religion.[9]

Wu Li also discusses his life at St. Paul's, especially the cultural differences. He says that while in China one knows it is time to get up when the rooster cries in the morning, in Macau, it is the chime clock that will tell you the time:[10]

紅荔枝頭月又西，起看風露眼猶迷。燈前此地非書館，但聽鐘聲不聽雞。

In the following poem, he discusses the difficulties of learning a foreign religion from a Westerner and of having to communicate with each other in one's own language. Chinese is written from top to bottom and right to left, but Portuguese is written from left to right. However it is written, it is difficult for them to understand each other.[11]

燈前鄉語各西東，未解還教筆可通。我寫蠅頭君寫爪，橫看直視更難窮。

It means: People speak different languages and cannot really understand each other. So they use their pens. While I use a brush to write Chinese characters, they use a pen to scratch down something like the claws of a bird. We still have difficulty understanding each other however we look at the words.

In a long poem Li Xialing 李遐齡 (1766–1823) describes an encounter with a pretty little girl of eight years old (most likely Portuguese). He describes how cute and smart this child is. He even carries on a conversation with her, asking her what she plans to do in the future, etc.[12]

The above literary descriptions tell us much about the life in Macau and the social interaction between the Chinese and the Portuguese in the old days. We see a prosperous Macau where people from different ethnic groups seem to enjoy each other. This indeed is a counter-argument against the clash of civilizations theme.

But, of course, that is not the full picture. It reflects on a time during the late Ming and early Qing dynasties when China was fairly strong and could accommodate foreign cultures to a great extent. The Chinese government was largely able to control the political, economic, and social matters regarding Macau. Things changed especially after the Opium Wars in the 1840s and 1850s, when the Portuguese government gradually obtained almost full control over Macau. Later literary figures' description of Macau also changed.

Political Concerns about Macau and China

Chen Zhengwen 陳徵文, a scholar-official in Xiangshan between 1875 and 1889, wrote the following poem reflecting on the perpetual occupation and management of Macau by Portugal after the Luso-Chinese Treaty in 1887.

竟許西夷受一廛，遂令聲教阻南天。可憐臥榻旁餘地，酣睡他人四百年。

He resents the occupation of Macau by the Portuguese in the past 400 years, lamenting that the orders of the emperor and teachings of Confucius could not reach Macau.¹³

Qiu Fengjia 邱逢甲 (1864–1912), another poet and scholar-official, after witnessing the loss of Taiwan to Japan and fighting for its survival but failing, also wrote about his unhappiness of the Portuguese occupation of Macau, and contemplating on whose fault that was.¹⁴ It is he who wrote 宰相有權能割地，孤臣無力可回天 (while the ministers have the power to cede our land to others, we lonely lower-level officials have no power to turn the tide). He was talking about Taiwan. The Qing government ceded Taiwan to Japan after losing the war in 1895. In one of the battles involving the battleship *Zhiyuan*, all the crew members died in the battle. Deng Shichang from Panyu, Guangdong, was the captain of the ship. He was making a suicidal attack with his ship when she was hit by a torpedo. From the eyes of these scholars, just like the full colonization of Macau a few years earlier, the Taiwan cession is another indication of the government's inability to protect its own land and people. That is what the poets were lamenting about, and it feeds into the development of Chinese nationalism.

While they are talking about the loss of Macau, they are also concerned about the life of the Chinese in Macau. Yang Yinglin 楊應麟 felt sorry and angry when in 1907, in order to expand the roads, the Portuguese government in Macau forced over 30 Chinese families to move out of their houses. When they refused, they were beaten. Their houses were later burned and they were only given token compensation. Many did not have a place to go. The poem describes elderly persons weeping for their lost houses and is critical of the Chinese government which abandoned its people.¹⁵ This appears very much like what has happened in the urbanization movement in mainland China in the past several dozen years, although it is the Chinese government, not foreigners, that is demolishing Chinese people's homes.

禾黍龍田恨故閭，楚人一炬竟燒秦。白頭野老吞聲哭，一樣中原有棄民。

Another scholar-official criticizes the Chinese government for allowing the Portuguese soldiers to massacre the Chinese in the name of eliminating "bandits" or "pirates" in Luhuan, or Coloane, in 1910:

我有兒女我不哺，我有盜賊我不捕。任教異類戕同胞，更是喧賓來奪主。¹⁶

Cai Qiu 蔡球 discusses the Portuguese government's taxes on the Chinese and wonders whether there would be somebody who would save the Chinese:

鬼市抽人稅，民脂奉虜糧。誰為班定遠，生縛左賢王。¹⁷

In the poem, Ban Dingyuan was Ban Chao (32–102) of the Eastern Han dynasty, and Dingyuan was his official title, meaning "pacifying the remote areas." Ban Chao led Han troops in fighting the Xiongnu in the northern and western borders of

Literature and the Arts in and about Macau 143

China, killing hundreds of thousands of them. Zuo Xianwang was the official title next to the paramount leader of the Xiongnu. The poet asks who would be the Ban Dingyuan now to take alive Zuo Xianwang (in the form of the Portuguese). So when Shen Zhiliang assassinated Amaral, the Portuguese governor-general, in 1849, he was praised by these scholars. Liu Sufen 劉燏芬 praised him as a "just hero":[18]

> 香山有義士，沈姓志亮名。少小抱至性，弱歲飛英聲。……

The poet says that there was a hero from Xiangshan, whose name was Shen Zhiliang. He was very determined from very young, and was already famous from his early age.

Social Life in Macau in the Late 19th Century

There are also descriptions of social and religious life in Macau. I am quoting six of them by Liang Qiaohan 梁喬漢 (1851–?).[19]

> 賃車一月費金多，辛苦生涯力自任。度日有餘租不足，得償枵 (xiāo) 腹稅難禁。

This poem is about the life of rickshaw men. It says that one has to pay to rent a rickshaw, and the money one earns can cover neither food nor the rent. Add on the taxes to pay, and one often has to go hungry. (See Plate 6.1 of rickshaw men in Macau.)

The following is a poem about prostitutes:

> 妓館迷離客棧旁，沿門倚笑競時妝。年來衣飾翻新樣，錯認歌場即戲場。

It says that brothels are located near the hotels, and prostitutes are leaning on the door, in fashionable clothes and smiling. They change their costumes (often) and you may mistake a brothel as a theater.

The following poem is about gambling in Macau:

> 賭餉承充累萬千，番攤、圍姓數淵連。草堆街畔人如蟻，燈火家家不夜天。

It means that the gambling industry has to pay lots of taxes to the government, and the various kinds of gambling businesses abound. People on the street of Caodui are as many as ants, and lights are on in every house the whole night.

The next poem talks about the prosperous businesses of gambling, prostitution, and hotels.

> 往來嫖賭最豪奢，客棧租錢不慣賒。地段無多生事少，竟然消費十餘家。

It says that people coming for prostitution and gambling tend to spend lavishly, and hotels do not let them stay on credit, either. In such a small place where there is not much to depend on for a living, there are a dozen hotels around. (See Plate 3.1 of

福隆新街 or Rua da felicidade, now. This was where the brothels, gambling houses, and hotels were concentrated.)

The following two poems describe the Catholic religious practices in Macau. (Plate 6.2 depicts a contemporary scene of the religious procession.)

> 一年兩度出觀音，大廟迎來旅若林。扈從十分虔謹事，沿途經咒誦沉吟。

It means that every year the church people parade on the street twice with the portrait of Mary, whom the poet uses the word Guanyin, the Chinese goddess, to describe. Many people come to the church (which the poem uses the word "temple" to refer to) and they are all piously praying and singing along the way. The following poem talks about the Catholic tradition:

> 風信名垂廟祀華，年年禮拜勤清茄。洋人數典難忘祖，姓字猶談嗎喇呀。

The poet speaks about St. Lawrence Church (see Figure 5.4), where people come and worship with music. The foreigners do not forget their ancestors (while in China), since they still use their names such as Maria (Mary).

So despite all the political problems in Macau, especially beginning in the late 19th century, life went on. These poems paint pictures of the life of the working people, the prostitutes, the gamblers as well as the religious believers in Macau. They describe the political, economic, and social transformations we discussed in the earlier chapters. In the era of the Republic of China in the mainland (1911–49), literary figures continued to describe life in Macau and their concern with China. Zhang Wenqin collected in the two volumes of Macau poetry 84 poets and 656 poems from this period.[20]

The Continuation of Chinese Literary Tradition in the Modern Times

We define the modern times as from 1911, when the Republic of China was founded, until now, or about 100 years in the most recent past. Modern literature has continued the tradition of concern with life of ordinary people and political concerns, although the more contemporary literature seems to move more towards aesthetic appreciation and self enjoyment of the artists themselves in their own times.

Xian Yuqing 冼玉清 (1895–1965), a native of Macau, describes how gambling, prostitution, and illnesses have led to the destruction of a family. The poem is written from the point of view of the mother about her son and grandson:

> ……阿兒日夜縱遊冶，毫呼一擲傾錙銖。敗亡已分溝中脊，無端疫鬼更相圖。阿兒死去媳婦嫁，小孫念母常號呼。……

The poem says that the son is out day and night having fun, and spends whatever money he has. While being bankrupt, he is caught in an epidemic. He dies and his wife remarries. Now their son is missing his mother, crying often.[21] The grandmother came to Macau from the suburb of Guangzhou (Canton) to avoid the domestic wars that occurred often in the years of the Republic of China in the mainland. But they did not seem to be able to escape the pitfalls here in Macau. She is now left alone, waiting to die with nobody to take care of her. Such tragedies repeat themselves throughout Macau's gambling history. This concern with ordinary people's lives is often accompanied with a political concern with the life of the country. Here is a poem by Chen Haiying 陳海瀛 (1883–?) entitled 至澳門觀白鴿巢花園 (Visiting the Camões Garden in Macau):

> 世外桃源且莫誇，珠崖早已屬他家。強收一掬傷心淚，來坐濃陰看物華。²²

It says that the garden is like a paradise, but it now belongs to someone else. Holding his tears, the poet sits down to enjoy the beautiful and exuberant gardens. This poem describes both the landscape and the poet's feelings at the same time.

Many other poems about Macau describe beautiful scenes they see in the city, which we have not quoted, because our major concern here is the poets' sociological reflections on the people and the place. But for aesthetic purposes, those poems are nonetheless worth reading. See Figure 6.1.

Later poets like Wen Yiduo 聞一多 are more passionate about the fact that Macau became a colony. He wrote in 1925 the following poem, in the modern style.

> 你可知"媽港"不是我的真姓名？／我離開你的襁褓太久了，母親！／但是他們擄去的是我的肉體，／你仍然保管著我的內心的靈魂。／三百年來夢寐不忘的生母啊！／請叫兒的乳名，叫我一聲"澳門"！／母親！我要回來，母親！

Figures 6.1a, 6.1b, 6.1c
The Camões Garden (白鴿巢花園) today. Photo by Jerry Wu.

The poem says that Macau is not my real name. And I have left my mother for too long. But although they have captured my body, my mother still has kept my soul. For 300 years I cannot forget my mother and dream about her all the time. Please call me "Aomen, my pet name." Mother, I want to go home, Mother. As Tao Li and Zhuang Wenyong point out, even though Wen was not in Macau and not from Macau when he wrote the poem, the poem nonetheless expresses very strongly the nationalist feelings of many Chinese in Macau. It was also the beginning of Macau's new poetry.[23]

Another poem of the new style describes a corner in Macau that has been left behind by the modernization efforts:

破落的陋巷／瑟縮在陰暗的角落／被都市的繁榮遺忘／遍地的果皮、空罐、狗糞／還有蒼蠅吸吮著腐爛的肉片／窮家的孩子在追逐嬉戲／在臭氣四溢的公廁旁邊／在濺灑著污水的管道下麵[24]

The poem is written by Jiang Siyang 江思揚 in 1976. It says that the place is littered with fruit skin, empty cans, and dog droppings. Flies are sucking slices of rotten meat, and children from poor families are running around playing, beside the smelly public lavatory, and under a ditch that splashes with dirty water. This picture not only describes a residential area populated by poor people, but also implies the discrepancy between the rich and the poor.

But is modern life necessarily good? Gao Ge 高戈 says that it is not so.

在摩登時代的陰影下 ／ 幸福的含義就是豬玀 ／ 難道還有什麼雜牌貨 ／ 比得上豬們那麼好運

The poet says that happiness under the shadow of modern times is to live like a pig. No other lives are better than those of the pigs. The poem is entitled 豬在澳門偷笑 (the pig is secretly smiling in Macau).[25]

Other than the poems, these men and women of letters also write essays about social issues and problems in Macau, including safety, telephone fees, and parks, and some complained about the Macanese and Portuguese attitudes toward the Chinese especially before the 1980s.[26] Ding Bing 丁兵 charges that prostitution, gambling, and drugs were the works of some people with ulterior intentions in the colonial period. Other essayists write about Macau's history, geography, customs, scenery spots, famous buildings, etc., such as Li Pengzhu 李鵬翥 and Xu Min 徐敏.[27]

Story writing in the form of short stories and novels emerged in the 20th century. Lu Mao 魯茂, for example, wrote over 20 novels between 1968 and 1995, describing love, youths, as well as the life of Macanese in Macau. Zhou Tong 周桐, a woman novelist, wrote 13 novels between the 1970s and 1990s. Lin Zhongying 林中英, Liang Liling 梁荔玲, Tao Li 陶裏, Zhou Tong 周桐, Lu Mao 魯茂, Liang Shuqi 梁淑琪 etc. are among the best short story writers. Lu Mao's *Bai Lang* (白

狼, or The White Wolf) tells the story of a Portuguese man who became a gangster but later reformed himself. It describes corrupt government officials working with gangsters and committing crimes.[28] Modern life seems as complex as life in the earlier times.

Traditional Operas and Modern Plays

The Yue opera is the local opera that has been popular in Guangdong, although it is hardly so now with young people, a fate other traditional forms like the Peking opera face. Although I have not found the earliest date when the Yue opera was played in Macau, there is one newspaper report about an opera event in 1895. At that time, a local group invited an opera troupe to perform Yue opera. It was scheduled on the tenth of the month, but since they were already here on the ninth, the local people responsible thought that they could begin their performance a day earlier than scheduled. But the Portuguese government officials thought the locals violated their contract. So they intervened when the opera was about to begin. They stopped the performance, and the local managers had to return the money to the audience.[29] Figure 6.2 is one of those scenes where the opera was played and Plate 6.3 portrays some Yue opera singers. These operas are usually historical stories and legends about Chinese emperors and their struggles with their enemies or the struggles of ordinary people in their daily lives.

Figure 6.2
Going to watch Guangdong Yue opera. *Review of Culture* N°10, Macau: Instituto Cultural de Macau, 1992, p. 73.

Modern plays began in the 1930s along with the development of the resistance movement against the Japanese occupation of Chinese territories. The plays with the movement theme began in 1937. Many refugee players came to Macau when Hong Kong was occupied by the Japanese in 1941. An opera troupe was formed, and they played such titles as *Wu Zetian* (武則天, the title character is the empress in the Tang dynasty), *Sheng Si Lian* (生死戀, Love of life and death), *Lei Yu* (雷雨, Thunderstorm), *Richu* (日出, Sunrise), *Cha Hua Nu* (茶花女, The camellias girl), etc.[30]

A short play performed on the street, for example, depicts the conflict between a poor Chinese and some Macanese.[31] Still other playwrights followed the Chinese Cultural Revolution on the mainland in the 1960s, and rewrote revolutionary operas like *Hong Deng Ji* (紅燈記, The Red Lantern), *Shajiabang* (沙家浜), *Zhi Qu Weihu Shan* (智取威虎山, Taking the Tiger Mountain by Strategy), etc.[32] Although they do not really describe life in Macau, they do indicate how closely connected some people were to mainland China and its revolutions.

A play by Li Yuliang 李宇梁 depicts the life of an elderly couple who, neglected by their grown-up children, have to rely on each other for their daily lives. This is a sharp criticism of modern society, and the play won awards for the best script in both Hong Kong and Macau in 1993.[33] Many of these plays are written and played in Cantonese, and do have a function in social criticism. But we do not know the number of people who actually watch operas and plays, or the extent to which the plays influence social change.

A more recent production of art works is the ballet *Macau Bride*. Written by Choi San 徐新, it tells the love story between a Portuguese girl, Maria do Mar, and a Chinese sailor, Chon Kou. They meet in Portugal and fall in love with each other. She hides in the ship Santiago when the sailor is going back to Macau. On the way, she is captured by some natives on an island when the ship anchors to avoid a storm, and she is saved by her lover-hero. The two come to Macau and get married in a splendid ceremony.[34] In 2009, *Diago*, a novel by Liu Chi-Hing 廖子馨, was made into a movie. It describes the Macanese dilemma before the return of Macau to China. But the description is far from the real thing as we will discuss in this chapter. In 2015, Mu Xinxin (穆欣欣, the current director of the Cultural Affairs Bureau of the MSAR in 2018), made the story of Shen Zhiliang, one of Amaral's assassins, into a Peking opera, *Jinghai Hun* or the *Soul of Macau*, in cooperation with Jiangshu Peking Opera Theater. It was played in Beijing, Shanghai, and Macau. It was a good effort in tackling history but it is more of a presentation of nationalist feelings than of a play that would exhibit historical complexities.

Western operas were performed as early as 1832, if not earlier. Harriett Low writes in her diary about an Italian opera she went to see to celebrate her birthday. D. Pedro V Theatre (Teatro D. Pedro V), named after the then sovereign, was built in 1858. Since then many Italian, French, and other Western opera and music groups have traveled to Macau to play there.[35]

In 1994, Giuseppe Verdi's *Falstaff* was played in the Eighth Macau International Music festival, using a Beijing orchestra, a Shanghai chorus, and soloists from Italy, Portugal, Spain, and America.[36] The play was adapted by Arrigo Boito from Shakespeare's *The Merry Wives of Windsor* and scenes from *Henry IV*. Among the operas played since the Sixth Macau International Music Festival are *Il Barbiere di Siviglia, Turandot, Falstaff, Il Trovatore, Tosca, Carmen, Un Ballo in Maschera, Aida and Otello*, and *La Traviata*. The social needs the opera serve are probably no more than to lift the image of the city and satisfy the desire of the middle and upper middle class citizens.

The exchange of artistic skills is limited, and the exchange of Eastern and Western themes would not happen until the emergence of Macanese plays, which we are going to discuss in a moment, although it is still minimal.

Chinese Arts in Macau

Other than the poets we mentioned above, the earliest Chinese artists were those who left their calligraphy on the hundreds of stones in the various temples in Macau. In A-Ma Temple alone, there are over 30 stone inscriptions like those in Plate 6.4, which were mostly made in the past 200 years.[37] These Chinese sculptors and calligraphy writers and those who worked on the ancient city hall have left with us some of the earliest art works in Macau.[38]

Then there is St. Paul's Cathedral, the façade of which is the only part we can see today. It is said to be built by both Japanese and Chinese Christian craftsmen.[39] Although it is not clear what roles the Chinese artists played in building the cathedral, judging from the styles and contents of the sculptures, including the Chinese words, Chinese craftsmen were apparently involved (see Figure 6.3), notwithstanding the content of the sculpture.[40] They were among the first artists in Macau.

The paintings and poems of Wu Li (1632–1718) followed, although with a different style. Scholars do not agree whether his paintings are influenced by Western styles, since he was quite familiar with the latter.[41] But the fact that he was related to Macau in some significant ways makes us want to treat him as one of the first artists in Macau. (See Plate 6.5 for one of Wu Li's paintings.)

Lin Gua 啉呱 (Lamqua, or 關喬昌 or 關作霖, 1801–?), a Guangdong painter based in Guangzhou (Canton) first and Hong Kong later would be among the first painters who had some relations with Macau. He had some working or teacher-student relationship with George Chinnery, the painter who lived and worked in Macau for about 20 years. In addition to his own paintings, Lamqua was also famous for imitating others. Some of his portraits and street scenes of Macau were probably done in his shop in Canton.[42] He was one of the first Chinese painters to introduce

Figure 6.3
Part of the façade of St. Paul's College and cathedral built in 1620. Photo by Wang Xin and Zhang Kai.

Western-style paintings.⁴³ (See Plate 6.6 for Lin Gua's painting of himself.) You might notice the difference between the Western and Chinese styles in the picture and that of Wu Li's above.

Many contemporary Macau Chinese artists' works may describe the physical beauty of the place, but some works may be political and social critiques, as we can see in some of the cartoons by Chou Cheong Hong 曹長雄 in Figure 6.4, commenting on corruption in Macau.

Macanese Literature, Arts, and Plays

For a long time, Macanese literature was viewed as part of Portuguese literature because most Macanese authors write in Portuguese, and not many Chinese can read Portuguese. There have not been as many Macanese writers as Chinese or Portuguese writers, understandably, so the study of Macanese literature is a fairly new endeavor.⁴⁴

Nonetheless, from what we can see in the poetry, short stories, and novels since the 19th century, many important writers have emerged, and have dealt with issues

Figure 6.4
Corruption in Macau. Courtesy of Chou Cheong Hong.

that are related to their lives, especially the Macanese as a social group. One of the most representative authors is Henrique de Senna Fernandes 飛歷奇 (Fei Li Qi, see Figure 6.5), mentioned in chapter 4. His description of Macanese life paints one picture after another of Chinese girls, Portuguese sailors, Spanish doctors, Catholic fathers, open-minded rich people, humane pirates, and various places in Macau.[45] One of his most famous works is *The Bewitching Braid*, which tells the love story between a rich Macanese man and a poor Chinese girl. The story has been made into a movie, which has won both Chinese and Portuguese awards (see Plate 6.7 for a scene from the movie). The theme of the story seems to defy the idea of the clash of civilizations.[46] One could, however, argue just the opposite based on the contents of the story.

The tendency of Portuguese (Macanese) men (rich) marrying Chinese women (poor) as described in this and other works of literature seems to reflect also what often happens in reality.[47] In a work by Deolinda da Conceição 江蓮達 (Jiang Lian Da), the son given birth to by an unmarried Portuguese father and Chinese mother finds it so difficult to reconcile his identities that he decides to leave Macau. He refuses to recognize his weeping mother who comes to see him off.

Figure 6.5
Henrique de Senna Fernandes. Goodreads at https://www.goodreads.com/author/show/781735.Henrique_de_Senna_Fernandes, accessed November 6, 2018.

> He had asked his mother not to come to the pier. He had said goodbye with a broken heart, as he knew he would never see her again. But, at the same time, he had agonized over her ample gestures, all that crying and snorting—all those theatrics of emotion that were so characteristic of her position. He watched her as she cleaned her eyes with her *cheong-sam*. Once again he observed how grotesque and ungainly her posture was. Half grieving, half relieved—he just ran away.[48]

But her mother still comes to the pier to see him off. And while crying aloud, she is trying to get through the crowd. She finally reaches him, with disheveled clothing and loud laments, characteristic of a lower class. Feeling ashamed and not wanting to recognize her, he treats her as if she were a beggar and gives her a coin. Trembling nervously, he runs away to the boat.

> On the pier, with her eyes wide open with craziness, the woman repeated amidst her convulsive crying: "He gave me alms, he gave me alms in exchange for the life I gave him!"[49]

Another of her stories portrays a Chinese girl falling in love with a Portuguese architect, but her family was vehemently against it. She decides to end her life. Deolinda da Conceição herself was born into an interracial marriage, with a Portuguese father and Chinese mother.[50]

Understandably, the Macanese are preoccupied with the identity issue, their relationship with others, their future, and the significance of their interracial background.

In 1993 Edith Jorge Demartini 愛蒂斯・喬治・瑪爾丁妮 published *The Wind amongst the Ruins*, remembrances of her childhood years in Macau. She portrays the integration of cultures: Western coffee and churches amidst Chinese tea, porridge, silk, and mahjong. Her father's friendship with a Chinese entrepreneur in the firecracker business lasted several dozen years.

In other works of Macanese writers, we see themes like "the conflict (often seen as a conflict of loyalty) between the aspirations of western educated women and the expectations placed upon them within traditional Chinese marriage," Chinese female placing her misguided trust in a foreigner, the promise of love as an antidote to poverty and neglect, the Macanese diaspora, and Macau as a refuge place and therefore the problem of exile and displacement.[51] Interestingly, as another kind of exile and displacement because of limited job opportunities and various other crises afflicting the city over the years, two thirds of Macanese have lived since the late nineteenth century either in Portugal, Brazil, Shanghai, Hong Kong, Australia, Canada, or California, and many literary works evoke the vulnerability of the Macanese in the diaspora. Just like in Chinese literature where we see Chinese writers writing from China, we also see Portuguese writers writing from Portugal. One constant theme is again, of course, the negotiations of identity. Here are more examples.

The late poet Leonel Alves 李安樂 (Li Anle) writes in his poem,

> Your souls meet here,
> And the mysterious fate attracts each other.
> This fate gives birth to me.
> 你倆的靈魂在此相遇,
> 神秘的命運把它們吸引一起,
> 這命運也使我在此誕生。

In a poem entitled "Know Who I Am," he writes,

> I have inherited the excellence of Camões,
> As well as the shortcomings of the Portuguese,
> But at other times I am filled with Confucius in my mind.
> 我繼承了些許賈梅士的優秀
> 以及一個葡國人的瑕疵,
> 但在某些場合,
> 卻又滿腦的儒家孔子。[52]

The Macanese feelings of conflict in their identities might be a result of the clash of civilizations and cultures. This is also reflected in the Macanese plays, especially those by the group "The Sweet Language of Macau," formed by Julie de Senna Fernandes and her friends.[53] (Miguel de Senna Fernandes 飛文基, the son of Henrique de Senna Fernandos 飛歷奇, is the playwright and director of this group.) One play describes the difficulty of applying for a Portuguese passport at a Portuguese consulate in America. The protagonist asks, "We are not Portuguese, we are not Chinese, who are we after all?"

Another play portrays a retired government worker who decides to move to Portugal and finds that the Chinese food he takes with him, which he likes, invites disgust and criticism from the Portuguese customs officers. After he comes out of the airport, he sees no Chinese and wonders, "How come there are no Chinese? Why do people all look alike?" He finds that he has left a place he is familiar with and comes to a country full of strangers. Conflicted they may be, the Macanese do have a special feeling toward the Chinese and the Chinese culture. Many of them also worship Guan Gong, take Chinese medicine, observe the Chinese New Year, and eat Chinese dim sum.[54]

Their multiple identities made them wonder what it was going to be like after 1999 when Macau would be transferred to China. Teresa, one of Watts's interviewees, believed that the traumatic experiences she had during the 12-3 Incident in 1966 would never happen again in Macau.[55] Nonetheless, it is still not yet clear how they can keep their Macanese identity. As José dos Santos Ferreira (better known as Adé, in Chinese 若瑟・多斯・聖托斯・費雷拉, see Figure 6.6 with Adé sitting in front of a casino though across the street) writes in his poem, 澳門的未來……將會怎樣？／中國人的未來？／葡國人的未來？／那些生長在澳門／葡萄牙的兒子們的未來？... (What is Macau's future? Chinese people's future? Portuguese people's future? Those children of Portuguese ancestors who were born here?) In another

Figure 6.6
Adé. Christina Miu Bing Cheng, "The Son of Macao and the Mandarin's House" at the website of the Cultural Affairs Bureau, MSAR, http://www.icm.gov.mo/rc/viewer/40052/2215, accessed November 6, 2018.

poem, he portrays Macau as a son of Portugal, just as Wen Yiduo does about the relationship of Macau (son) with China (mother). He (Macau) does not want to leave his mother (Portugal).

> 親愛的母親
> 我甜美的愛
> 我不離開你
> 不願另認一個娘

The mother nonetheless wants him to accept reality. The son then

> 帶著憂傷的神色
> 雙膝跪地
> 仰起頭
> 淚滿眼框 …

With sadness and eyes filled with tears, he knelt on the ground, looking up in the sky, and hoping that God will take care of him. The future is ambiguous, uncertain, and insecure.[56]

Other literary and art figures we need to mention include Carlos Marreiros 馬若龍, the architect, painter, and poet who makes an effort in integrating the Chinese and Portuguese cultures;[57] Victor Hugo Marreiros 馬偉達, graphic designer and artist; Fernanda Dias, painter, poet, and writer of poems and short stories;[58] Alberto Estima de Oliveira (1934–2008), a poet and artist who lived in Macau since 1982 and whose photography works had won a number of awards; and João Aguiar, a writer. For the preservation and propagation of Macanese culture and its people, in addition to the contributions made by the Macau Foundation, the Cultural Institute of Macau, and the Institute of Municipal and Civic Affairs, we should also mention the publishing house "Livros do Oriente" of Portuguese Rogério Beltrao Coelho and his Macanese wife, Cecilia Jorge.[59]

In sum, Macanese literature, arts, and plays portray the social interactions with other ethnic groups. The dilemma of the Macanese is something that the Chinese men and women of letters do not generally talk about in their literary creations, so it seems that a dual track exists even in the literary tradition. But the Macanese identity is part of a Macauan identity, and their story provides much food for thought when we consider the future of Macau in chapter 8.

Portuguese, English, German, and French Poems and Paintings in and about Macau

Macau also hosted a number of other famous poets and artists. Some lived here longer than twenty years, as in the case of George Chinnery. Their creative works touch on a broad range of themes, many of which have to do with Macau. Rather than going into details of each one of them, we will mention a few well-known figures and briefly introduce them, especially if their works relate to Macau. Thus this section will only give the reader a glimpse of this part of Macau's rich creative history.

Fernão Mendes Pinto, whom we mentioned in chapter 1, is a famous name in Portuguese literature related to Macau, but the most well-known poet is Luís de Camões (1524–80), who wrote the epic poem *The Lusiads* (Port. *Os Lusíadas* [sons of Lusus], i.e., the Portuguese), or 《葡國魂》 (1572). "The beauty of its poetry is enlivened by a vigorous and realistic narrative that embraces not only the voyage of Vasco da Gama but also much of Portuguese history."[60] He is said to have composed his poem in what is now the Camões Garden (see Plate 6.8 and Figure 6.1).[61]

Camilo Pessanha (1867–1926), another Portuguese poet, arrived in Macau in 1894 and died there in 1926. He is famous for his symbolism and modernism. He was a lawyer, judge, teacher, keeper of the colonial government's estate registry, journalist, and opium addict. He had three Chinese mistresses and fathered several children.[62] Pessanha was one of those who thought that they were wandering and wasting away in distant regions. So one of his purposes of writing was to "sing of the absent homeland," voicing the "incurable sorrow of all exiles."[63] This falls into the genre of exiled literature and also reminds one of the Chinese scholars who visited Macau and wrote about their "lost homeland." Sebastião da Costa, a friend of Pessanha's, describes him this way on the occasion of the poet's death:

> The city [Macau] lacked bread for the soul … The crass materialism that today is Chinese life [as if he is talking about China and Macau today], the cheap oriental commercialism, the obstinate preoccupation with gain, the unbridled and voracious graft, the overflowing sensuality, are reflected and perfected in our colonial people. One needed two lamps and considerable careful selection to find a pure and stainless soul in that desert. Pessanha was at least a beautiful spirit.

Pessanha's ambiguous thoughts on Chinese culture, history, and contemporary affairs are also worth noticing, as they reinforce the clash and cooperation of civilizations and cultures. He fathered interracial children, but he used insulting terms to describe his son. He liked Chinese literature, but his language used to describe China was filled with the presuppositions of European superiority.[64] Here is one example:

> … and if it is perhaps true that no Chinese work equals in the grandeur of its conception the great works of Western literature [he said substantially the same thing about Chinese art, described as essentially decorative—comment by Brookshaw],—what no one who has begun to study the Chinese language can doubt is that that language is the most beautiful and the most suggestive of all the literary languages, alive or dead.[65]

Literature and the Arts in and about Macau

Rodrigo Leal de Carvalho, a Portuguese novelist, was born in 1932 and moved to Macau in 1976. He lived in Macau for most of the 40 years between 1959 and 1999. He served as the prosecutor and later the president of the Court of Audit in Macau. As if to complement Pessanha who wanted to give a voice to the exiles, Carvalho describes the lives of refugees in the First and Second World Wars. The reasons why refugees came to Macau are various, but they tend to be because of politics, poverty, or war, and the refugees tended to close themselves from the outside world, alienated and distant.[66] Carvalho also defines the Macanese community:

> The Macanese community, predominantly Portuguese in culture, enriched with oriental elements—Chinese, Malay, Indian—combined a genuine tradition of hospitality, a capacity for living life to the full inherited from better days, and a cosmopolitan air that came from centuries of international trade.
>
> It was a class with its own peculiar sophistication, having as its basis the open and frank hospitality of the Portuguese, polished by contact with the British in Hong Kong and by the moral flexibility learned through contact with the majority Chinese community.[67]

One hopes that this "moral flexibility" does not include corruptive characteristics such as bribery, graft, and embezzlement. At any rate, his description of a cosmopolitan class has significant meanings for the future of the Macanese group.

Carvalho discusses refugees. Indeed, the number of Chinese refugees to Macau throughout history is also huge. To complement both Pessanha and Carvalho, the novels by Maria Ondina Braga 瑪麗亞·翁迪娜·布拉加 (1932–2003) depict life of the lower classes in Macau as well as the problems of exile and displacement.[68] Here is a description of the Chinese refugees:

> They were refugees from all corners of China, who arrived in large numbers day after day, and used false names. They knew nothing of each other, spoke different dialects, crowded together and hated one another, all living under the most tragic of possible fates: the lack of a piece of land.[69]

Wenceslau de Moraes (1854–1929), Pessanha's colleague in Macau's secondary school and yet another Portuguese poet and writer, arrived in Macau at the age of 34. He began to write *Traços do Extremo Oriente* while in Macau. He lived with an Anglo-Chinese girl and had two sons. Ten years later he moved to Japan and lived there until his death.[70]

There are also some famous painters whose works we have frequently cited in this book. The most well-known of them is George Chinnery (1774–1852, see Plate 6.9). Some of the portraits and sketches we have used in this book include Morrison translating the Bible with his Chinese helpers, the portrait of Harriett Low, and A-Ma Temple. Plate 6.10 is a painting of Dr. Thomas R. Colledge, who established an eye hospital in Macau.

Chinnery was born in London and arrived in Macau in 1835 after spending 23 years in India. He came to Macau to escape from his wife, as he said, and his debts. He received commissions for portraits from wealthy Europeans and Chinese from Canton, Macau, and later Hong Kong. But he also left us with endless numbers of sketches of life of local fishermen and village folk.[71] He had good humor although he was "the ugliest fellow imaginable, with shaggy eye-brows, a high forehead with hair all over the place, a rock of a jaw and a lower lip so big that when he closed his mouth it almost hid the upper one."[72] People rumored several times that his wife was coming to Macau, and for several times he escaped to Canton. His wife could not go there since the Chinese government would not allow women to go to Canton. He said, "What a kind providence is this Chinese Government that it forbids the softer sex from coming and bothering us here. What an admirable arrangement, is it not?"[73] Lin Gua, the Chinese painter, studied and worked with him, as we mentioned earlier. Chinnery died in Macau in 1852 and was buried in the Protestant cemetery here.

Another painter, M. A. Baptista, was a student of Chinnery's. He was born in 1826 in Macau, and later became an accomplished painter.[74] Other painters include Thomas Allom (1804–72), British; James Wathen (1751–1828, also known as Jemmy Sketch), a celebrated traveler, writer, and sketcher; Thomas Daniell (1749–1848) and William Daniell (1769–1837; see Plate 6.8 of the Camões Garden); William Heine (1827–85), a German artist (see Plate 6.11 and 6.12 for two of his paintings—see how different these places are now than they were before); and Barthelemy Lauvergne (1805–75), a French artist.

Conclusions

Macau has a long and rich history of literature and the arts. Contributing to this history are various poets, writers, painters, and sculptors who have left an abundance of works. We can appreciate not only their artistic skills, but also the meanings and feelings they are trying to convey. Each of their works is a story of the past, and of themselves, often representing social interaction and social conflicts. We see this from the examples of those who were involved in the building of St. Paul's Cathedral, the poet and painter Wu Li, to the examples of the Macanese and the multinational painters and writers. Their efforts in trying to live a culture and to understand it, Chinese, Western, or a mixture of them, have been impressive. We have not used many examples of photographs. So here is one more in Plate 6.13, depicting passengers going to Taipa in a boat. There were no bridges then, and Taipa is so different now.

However, from what we can see in these works of literature and the arts, by and large Chinese and Westerners still lived separate lives. Race, gender, and class inequalities were the order of the day, as they still largely are today. Even the literary tradition seems to have followed a dual track system, with the Chinese on one hand, and the Macanese and various foreigners on the other. One has to try hard to find a literary integration of some kind with the few exceptions like the examples of the ancient city hall (see Figure 2.2), St. Paul's Cathedral, and the export painters in Guangzhou.

The literary dual tracks prompt us to think more about the future of our society: the creation of a Macauan culture based on an improved Macau model, needed for a "city of culture." Life should only get better if people can appreciate literature and the arts and the meanings they convey.

7 Social Issues and Problems in Macau

> Nowadays men often feel that their private lives are a series of traps. They sense that within their everyday worlds, they cannot overcome their troubles, and in this feeling, they are often quite correct: What ordinary men are directly aware of and what they try to do are bounded by the private orbits in which they live; their visions and their powers are limited to the close-up scenes of job, family, neighborhood; in other milieus, they move vicariously and remain spectators. And the more aware they become, however vaguely, of ambitions and of threats which transcend their immediate locales, the more trapped they seem to feel.
>
> C. Wright Mills[1]

In this chapter, we will explore some specific contemporary social problems, or "traps" in Mills's term, and their connections with the past. In his classic work on the sociological imagination, where the quote above comes from, Mills talks about public issues and individual troubles.[2] His usage of the terms "social issues" and "social problems" may give us some insight to the differences between them. Mills is saying that what seem to be individual troubles, or problems, like unemployment, divorce, crime, ethnic conflicts, etc. may have social reasons that relate to the political, economic, cultural and social structures in that society.

For example, a woman who wanted to jump off Casino Lisboa because of gambling addiction might have some serious psychological problems, which may be individual in nature. But she was not alone in taking such a drastic action. So if enough people do it, this so-called individual problem reflects a social problem, a public and social issue, because apparently these people have been affected by a number of similar political, economic, and social structural factors. (Recall that in chapter 2, we discussed cultural and structural factors affecting the outcome of the Opium Wars. Lin Zexu himself was constrained by those factors.) When we talk about "social problems," we refer to "individual" problems that have a "social and structural" base. Since we are only talking about individual problems with a social nature, we will use these two terms, social issues and social problems, interchangeably.

If they are "social problems," then the government, social organizations, industrial corporations, as well as individuals themselves all have a responsibility to tackle them. In this chapter I intend to give a bird's eye view of several social problems in Macau.[3] These include ethnic and class stratification and politics, gambling-related crime and deviance, education issues in middle and postsecondary schools, and civil society and public sphere. These problems often interact with and influence one another. Further development in a democratic political polity and a much stronger civil society and public sphere are crucial in handling Macau's social problems.

Ethnic Stratification and Politics[4]

Ethnic stratification can be seen in Macau's population change before and after 1999 and the changes in political position of different ethnic groups, especially the transfer of power to the Chinese from the Portuguese and Macanese. This part delves into demographic change first and ethnic politics second.

Demographic Change after the Handover: Ethnic Population and Political Positions

In 1997, two years before the handover, there were 452,000 people in Macau. Of this total, 96% were Chinese. Most of the remaining population, about 4% or 18,000 persons, were either Portuguese or Macanese, with the Portuguese constituting 1.8% of the total population or about 8,000 people and the Macanese, about 2.2% of the total population or about 10,000 people. By contrast, according to the 2011 census data, there were 552,503 people in Macau, 92.4% of whom were Chinese, 0.6% (3,485 persons) Portuguese and 0.7% (4,019 persons) Macanese. Thus, between 1997 and 2011, the number of Portuguese and Macanese declined by 56% and 60% respectively. As a percentage of the total population, the Portuguese population declined by about 1.2% (from 1.8 to 0.6%) and the Macanese by 1.5% (from 2.2 to 0.7%) after the handover (Table 7.1).

The huge decline in the Portuguese and Macanese population by 56% to 60%, respectively, reflects the change in their political positions. Table 7.2 presents the change in the number and percentage of government officials by ethnicity. The percentage of Portuguese government officials at the secretary level (one level below that of the governor or chief executive) plummeted from 83% to 11% for the Portuguese and Macanese combined, while the percentage of Chinese government officials at the same level increased from 17% to 89%. As shown here, the Portuguese/Macanese and Chinese make-up of government officials at this level has

Table 7.1 Population change around the handover between 1997 and 2011

	1997		2011		% change in the total population	% change within one's own ethnic population
	Population	% of total population	Population	% of total population		
Chinese	434,000	96.0	510,383	92.4	−3.6	+18.0
Portuguese	8,000	1.8	3,485	0.6	−1.2	−56.0
Macanese	10,000	2.2	4,019	0.7	−1.5	−60.0
Other				6.4	+6.4*	
Total	452,000	100.0	552,503	100.1**		

Notes:
* These are mainly people from the Philippines, Vietnam, Indonesia, etc., many of whom are domestic workers. But they may also include professional and managerial staff from different countries who come to work in higher education, casinos, and other enterprises.
** Error due to rounding up.
Sources: Data based on Wu Zhiliang and Yang Yunzhong, eds., *Aomen baike quanshu* (*Macao Encyclopedia*) (Beijing: Zhongguo da baike quanshu chubanshe [China Encyclopedia Press], 1999), p. 393; and Government of Macao Special Administrative Region (MSAR), Statistics and Census Service website, at http://www.dsec.gov.mo/default.aspx, accessed October 21, 2013.

more or less reversed. Similarly, the percentage of Portuguese/Macanese officials at the deputy secretary level dropped from 46 to 15%, while the proportion of Chinese rose from 54 to 85%.

The statistics in Table 7.2 can shed some light on the ethnic make-up of government officials in general. More than 85% of the major officials in Macau today are Chinese, whereas in the past, 83% of all secretaries were Portuguese or Macanese, although Chinese seem to have constituted 54% of all deputy secretary-level government officials. That indeed signals a shift of political power from Portuguese to Chinese.[5]

Ethnic Politics after 1999: Marginalization of the Macanese

Nonetheless, there is still a fairly sizeable presence of officials of Portuguese and Macanese origins in the government, ranging from 11 to 15%, even though the ethnic population had dropped by 50 to 60%. This falls in line with the Macau Basic Law, which states in Article 42 that the interests of the offspring of Portuguese will be protected. Apparently, Portuguese representation in some form in the government

Table 7.2 Number and percentage of government officials in 1997 and 2013 by ethnicity

	1997			2013			
	Total Number	% of Portuguese	% of Chinese**	Total Number	% of Portuguese	% of Chinese	% change
Secretaries*	59	83	17	9	11 (1 person)	89	+72
Deputy secretaries in 1997 but known as bureau chiefs etc. since 1999†	50	46	54	300	15 (44 persons)‡	85	+31

Notes:
* In 1997, there were deputy appointments to the secretaries. However, since 1999, the deputy appointments have been removed and there is only one hierarchical level for secretaries. Therefore, the author has presented only the number and percentage of secretaries, including also the secretary-level officials.
** Chinese, in this context, means "mostly" are Chinese. There is an unspecified "other" category subsumed under the "Chinese" group, although it always constitutes a very small number, ranging from two at the secretary level to six at the deputy secretary level.
† This refers to officials at the level of bureau chief and deputy bureau chief, including public university presidents and vice presidents and chiefs of government foundations.
‡ The number was derived by visually counting the officeholders with Portuguese names and this would also include Macanese. However, there may also be cases of Macanese names created from Portuguese spelling of Chinese names. In the latter case, the person would be counted as Chinese, though cases like this should be rare.
Sources: The statistics for 1997 are based on Wu Zhiliang and Chen Xinxin, *Aomen zhengzhi shehui yanjiu* (Studies of Macao politics and society) (Macao: Aomen chengren jiaoyu xuehui, 2000), p. 126. The statistics for 2013 are based on the MSAR Court's website regarding major government officials' declarations of their assets, at http://www.court.gov.mo/zh/subpage/property-search, accessed October 21, 2013.

guarantees that someone will speak on their behalf officially. That, however, does not preclude Macanese claims of discrimination against them by the Chinese as, apparently, the tide of discrimination had reversed at least in some cases.

For example, in 2009, José Maria Pereira Coutinho (Kou Tin Chi 高天賜), a directly elected legislator born in Portugal but who identified himself as Macanese, raised the issue of discrimination against Macanese concerning promotion in government agencies. But other prominent Macanese like Leonel Alberto Alves (Ao On Lei 歐安利), an indirectly elected legislator and a member of the government's powerful Executive Council, António José de Freitas (Fei An Da 飛安達) and Jorge Fao (Fang Yong Qiang 方永強), Chinese born but who identified himself as

Macanese, quickly came to the defense of the government, countering that there was no discrimination; rather, it was the policy of the Macau government to make the best use of the Macanese and employ them in important positions. Fao even accused Coutinho of instigating racial conflict.[6]

It is true that prominent Macanese occupy important positions. Alves was an indirectly elected legislator for five terms (1999–2017) since the return of Macau to China. One cannot help but believe that it is the result of affirmative action. However, the fall in the percentage of Macanese legislators from 39% (nine out of 23 in 1999) to 6% (two out of 33 in 2013) leads to the deduction that Macanese are by and large marginalized, at least politically.

Traces of marginalization of Macanese are also noticeable in Macanese media, which has been sidelined in Chinese Macau politics. TDM, Macau's public television, offers both English and Portuguese programs. There is no interaction between TDM's Portuguese and Chinese programs. Since the Portuguese and English programs appeal to an audience that are mainly Portuguese- and English-speaking Portuguese, Macanese and other foreigners, TV programming has little influence over the politics of Macau. The power elite can always ignore whatever the non-Chinese media say, and this also applies to the Portuguese and English media in general. *Macao Business*, run by Portuguese and Macanese, for example, frequently criticizes the Macau government. But then again, very few Chinese people read this monthly magazine or other English-language newspapers which also tend to be critical.

The Portuguese and Macanese do still have a stronghold, albeit seemingly their last one, in law. But that stronghold is being eroded on the eve of the 20th anniversary of the handover. Article 8 of the Macau Basic Law stipulates that the original law of Macau would remain intact except for any law that contradicts the Basic Law or any laws and regulations revised later by the new Macau government. Article 9 of the Macau Basic Law stipulates that in all government agencies, Portuguese can be used in addition to Chinese and remains an official language. These two articles say that the new Macau government can modify the old law if it wants to; otherwise, it can follow the original law. Also, the new government can use Chinese in its government agencies if it wants to; otherwise, it can use Portuguese. The original law was written in Portuguese, and its Chinese version is hard to understand due to poor translation. So if the government does not want to commit great effort to translate and modify the current Portuguese-based law, Portuguese will remain the dominant language, and Portuguese and Macanese the key players in Macau's legal realm. That is exactly what has happened during the 20 years since the handover. The Portuguese and Macanese have had an advantage as we discuss below at least until recently.

First, the domination of the Portuguese language required that there be more Portuguese-speaking judges and lawyers. Indeed, out of Macau's 52 judges by 2017, 25% or 13 of them were Portuguese or Macanese, a much higher percentage than that found in other government agencies.[7] The percentage of Portuguese and Macanese lawyers was even higher: 76.4% of Macau's 272 registered lawyers were Portuguese or Macanese around 2010 although there seemed to be more Chinese lawyers on the eve of the 20th anniversary of the handover. By October 2017, according to Li Huanjiang, a registered lawyer in Macau, there were 356 registered lawyers, out of which 150 were Chinese, or less than 50%. About 60 of those 150 can speak both Chinese and Portuguese.[8] But in an interview in October 2018 with *Platforma*, a Portuguese/Macanese news organization in Macau, Jorge Neto Valente (華年達), the president of the Macau Lawyers' Association (AAM), said that there were 300 Chinese lawyers.[9] In other words, only 100 out of 400 were Portuguese/Macanese. All of Macau's lawyers have to register with and be approved by the AAM in order to become a lawyer and Jorge Neto Valente himself is Portuguese/Macanese. According to the above numbers, the increase in the number of Chinese lawyers is incredible, and even if those reports are inaccurate, the trend is still there.

It used to be difficult for a Chinese to become a registered lawyer in Macau as proven in a lawsuit initiated by a Chinese with a law degree. This person sued AAM for twice refusing to allow him to become an apprentice lawyer, in 2004 and 2009. AAM argued that the courses the plaintiff took, at both the Macau University of Science and Technology and the University of Macau, did not meet the association's standards. In 2013, the Administrative Court decided that AAM must admit him as an apprentice lawyer, because all of the courses taught at the universities were approved by the MSAR government and therefore should be recognized by any institution in Macau. AAM planned an appeal to the government's Intermediate Court. Apparently, AAM has made deliberate efforts to protect its job market by enforcing its rules and regulations that are less friendly to applicants whose native language is not Portuguese and who are not trained under its supervision. But they may be fighting a losing battle.

Second, for some years after the handover, the domination of Portuguese language was reinforced by the requirement that legal documents must be written in Portuguese, even if the people involved in lawsuits were mostly Chinese. In this case, many people had to learn Portuguese so that they could translate legal documents into Chinese for Chinese people to understand. Thus, other than protecting the job market for lawyers, Portuguese and Macanese also tried to protect their own culture by effectively forcing more people to study Portuguese and using Portuguese at the expense of Chinese involved in lawsuits. The legal domination of Portuguese and Macanese in a predominantly Chinese society that does not understand Portuguese apparently had created convenience for the former two groups but inconvenienced the latter one. But that is changing fast, too, as we will discuss below.

Third, this Portuguese/Macanese domination of legal affairs in Macau had contributed to a slowdown in the city's legal processes. Indeed, as of August 31, 2013, there were 8,052 cases waiting for trial decisions in the various courts of Macau, with a decrease of 12% in the decision rate compared with the previous year.[10] Susana

Chou Kei Jan (Cao Qizhen 曹其真), the chairperson of the Legislative Assembly between 1999 and 2008, pointed out when she retired from her position that it became simply unacceptable when "it would take two years to put a case on agenda, wait for another three years to have a trial, and then yet another three years to hear the result."[11] She commented that the government was being irresponsible in its passivity regarding legal reforms including, for example, the training and hiring of more judges and the timely presentation of bills for the Legislative Assembly to consider.[12]

The reform of the legal system should also allow a form of bilingualism that allows some cases to be tried in Chinese and others in Portuguese, depending on the needs of each case. Chan Wa Keong (Chen Huaqiang 陳華強), president of the Association for Macao Legal Studies, emphasized that not every judge has to be well-versed in both Chinese and Portuguese, as it is mandatory today.[13] Chan Chak Mo (Chen Zewu 陳澤武), a legislator, also highlighted that the mandatory requirement for judges to be perfectly fluent in both Chinese and Portuguese is not justified when most of the lawsuits involved Chinese people. It is also unnecessary for lawyer candidates to procure someone to translate their exam papers, originally written in Chinese, into Portuguese so that Portuguese lawyers can read them.[14] This infers that only Portuguese lawyers have the right to read.

Fourth, however, things are turning in a more complex direction politically on the eve of the 20th anniversary of the handover. The localization of Macau law is done more to serve political purposes than practical ones as part of a larger picture of mainlandization. Paulo Taipa and Paulo Cardinal, two renowned legal advisors to the legislature who served in the government for 26 and 17 years respectively and who used to train local judges and prosecutors, were abruptly dismissed in August 2017 for no good reason other than "restructuring" according to the head of Macau's legislature, Ho Iat Seng (賀一誠). The real reason may be that they were critical of some government's bills in the past few years for breaching the Basic Law, according to the Macanese legislator Jose Coutinho. Furthermore, legislation was proposed in 2018 to remove Portuguese judges from sensitive cases altogether.[15]

Chinese is now prioritized in the government although Portuguese is also an official language. Sulu Sou, a leader of New Macau Society and Macau's youngest lawmaker, was charged with aggravated disobedience in a protest demonstration of what they believed to be an administrative abuse of power. His lawyers, Jorge Menezes and Pedro Leal, were denied translation of a 66-page Chinese ruling. The judge thought that it was the defendant's own fault for not hiring a Chinese lawyer. According to Master's report, courts have largely stopped providing Portuguese translations. This would effectively squeeze out Portuguese lawyers.

This new development has raised many concerns among the Portuguese/Macanese legal practitioners, even among those who were otherwise very pro-government. Jorge Neto Valente, the AAM president, who claims that the Chinese government considered him as one of their own,[16] said that freezing out Portuguese judges violated the Basic Law. Indeed, both this and the squeezing out of the two lawyers from the legislative advisory body are creating a patriotism test based on their feelings towards China. Valente says also that a Chinese-only policy would be a bad development. Bilingualism is still needed and Macau law will not be replaced by mainland Chinese law. He hopes that what happens to the Uyghurs in Xinjiang will not happen here. He believes that there is freedom of speech and human rights in Macau.[17] Leonel Alberto Alves, the Executive Council member and former legislator, also said that he could not understand why the two legal advisors were let go. Their role would be very important if the legislature wanted to make fewer mistakes. Interestingly, three democracy-prone legislators, Sulu Sou, Ng Kuok Cheong and Jose Coutinho also requested an explanation from Ho Iat Seng for dismissing the two advisors. It is fairly clear that the decision is political as well as ethnic.[18]

At the very least, this new development is to mitigate the influence of the Portuguese and Macanese in the legal field for political reasons. They can stay in the field if they toe the Party line and if they can restrict their roles to helping China build Macau into a trade and business center for Portuguese-speaking countries including Portugal, Brazil, Angola, etc. The Chinese lawyers have already learned to avoid politically sensitive cases. Now the Portuguese and Macanese lawyers are learning to do the same. Bill Chou, an associate professor of the University of Macau, who sued the University for wrongful termination, already had difficulty finding a lawyer in 2014. The case went nowhere. It is now difficult to find a lawyer who is willing to take on a case of political nature. But that may be the strategic plan of the central government, which is in line with the current larger legal environment in mainland China.

In sum, ethnic stratification and politics in Macau has continued after the handover albeit in a very different fashion. Reversing the pattern before the handover, ethnic politics in Macau today is characterized by the political domination of the Chinese and marginalization of the Portuguese and Macanese. This happens despite the fact that some Portuguese and Macanese like Alves and Coutinho remain in the political structure, while others, like Raimundo Arrais do Rosário (羅立文), Secretary of Transportation and Public Works, and Maria Helena de Senna Fernandes (文綺華), director of the Macao Government Tourism Office, occupy important government positions. Portuguese and Macanese used to dominate legal affairs, but this is changing fast. While the Portuguese domination in law should be corrected, it is now done in a way that is more for mainlandization purposes than for fairness and justice.

The situation is exacerbated by the government's passivity towards political and legal reforms. However, this may suit the government's interests. Greater incorporation of Portuguese and Macanese in politics may unite Portuguese and Macanese democratic advocates with their Chinese counterparts and entice more criticism of the government, which MSAR officials would not like. More efforts at legal reform would invite greater controversy and may even be beyond their abilities. So it might suit their own purposes to do as little as possible. Or if they want to do anything, it will always have to be politically and ethnically correct, as they did in dismissing the two Portuguese lawyers and barring Portuguese judges from politically sensitive cases.

Will social stratification and class politics push the government to change its course, anyway? That is indeed the next question to examine.

Class Stratification and Politics

Social Class before and after the Handover: Well-established and Organized

There is not much study done on this issue, but researchers largely agree that there are at least three classes: upper, middle, and lower.[19] In the colonial era, the upper class comprised the Portuguese Macau government officials and prominent Chinese industrialists and merchants or capitalists. The middle class were composed of professionals and small entrepreneurs and merchants. The lower or working class comprised workers, servants, and fishermen. The class structure has not changed after the handover except that more Chinese are government officials as we discussed above.

In tandem with the formation and growth of these classes, representative organizations have also developed. This section focuses on associations that represent these classes in order to give readers a glimpse of class stratification and representation. According to its website, the Macao Chinese Chamber of Commerce (MCCC) was formally established and registered with the Portuguese Macau government in 1912. A century later, at the end of 2012, it had a membership of 3,000, including both individual and group members (i.e., other associations of commerce). Its objectives are:

> To support the principle of "one country, two systems," to be persistently devoted to the country and Macao, to unite different entities and individuals in the industrial and commercial sectors in Macao, to serve them and safeguard their legitimate rights and interests, to promote the commercial links with other countries and regions, and to strive for the social stability and economic prosperity of the Macao Special Administrative Region.[20]

The "one country, two systems" wording is new; however, the protection of members' rights and interests has probably been the organization's core objective since it was first established. This includes protecting the interests of small industrialists and merchants who were in the middle class. However, since the MCCC's leaders were often big capitalists, they represent first and foremost the interests of the upper class. Shiu Ying-chau (蕭瀛洲), a gambling tycoon, was the organization's first president, followed by Lo Chak Sun (盧焯孫), Fan Kit Pan (范潔朋), Ko Hor

Ning (高可寧), Lau Pak Ying (劉柏盈), Ho Yin (何賢), Ma Man Kei (馬萬祺), and Ma Iao Lai (馬有禮, the current president), all of them business tycoons and members of the upper class.

Likewise, Macau workers' unions are supposed to serve workers' interests. According to the Macao Federation of Trade Unions' website, the unions were established sometime around the 1840s. By 1922, there were already three major federations of trade unions, with a total of 30,000 members in a city with only 100,000 inhabitants. However, they were disbanded after a clash with the Portuguese Macau government in the aforementioned 1922 protest movement. The Macao Federation of Trade Unions (MFTU) was formally established in 1950, after World War II and the founding of the People's Republic of China. According to its charter, the MFTU must:

> Promote love of the country and love of Macao, unite the broad masses of the workers in Macao, develop and strengthen workers unions; strive for and protect workers' legal rights and interests, protect their social and cultural rights, engage in activities regarding workers' culture, education, health and other benefits and services; support "one country, two systems," protect the Basic Law, participate in the construction of the MSAR, and promote social stability and economic development.[21]

Similar to the MCCC, the MFTU's core objective is to protect and promote its members' interests and benefits.

If the MCCC and MFTU are regarded as largely representing the upper class and the lower class, respectively, then professionals' organizations can be considered representative of the middle class. There are indeed a number of professional organizations, including those for doctors, engineers, accountants, lawyers, translators, journalists, public servants, and others, in addition to associations of educators and artists. Most of these organizations are newer than the MCCC and MFTU. According to Lou Shenghua, of Macau's 62 professional organizations, 59 were established after 1980.[22]

For example, the Association for Civil Servants in Macao (ATFPM) was established in 1987. Now headed by the Macanese legislator José Coutinho, the association's objectives include the representation of its members and protection of their professional interests—especially whenever they experience unfairness in joining a profession or getting promotion at work—and provision of legal aid to its members.[23] Rights and interests protection of members has been the core objective of ATFPM since its inception and also a common objective of other professional associations.

As analyzed, different classes have existed throughout Macau's history and are fairly well organized. The pertinent issue is the situation of social stratification today, about 20 years after the handover. The following are the findings based on a

2012 survey, of which I was a coinvestigator, that studied three important indicators of class, namely occupation, income, and education.[24] The findings reveal that, on average, 1.2 to 3.6% of Macau's population belong to the upper class, 16.2 to 33.2% belong to the middle class, and 53.6 to 70% belong to the lower class, depending upon which parameter is used—occupation, income or education (see Figures 7.1, 7.2, and 7.3).

In terms of occupation, high-level government officials at or above the *chu* (chief of division) level (0.7%)[25] can be categorized with entrepreneurs and managers of large enterprises (2.9%) as the upper class that constitutes 3.6% of Macau's total population (Figure 7.1). The middle class comprises the professionals (16.7%) together with ordinary civil servants (9.1%), managers of social organizations (1.6%), and entrepreneurs and managers of medium- and small-sized enterprises (5.8%), thereby accounting for 33.2% of the total population. The lower class constitutes the office clerks and sales persons (39.9%, including casino dealers), workers (11.2%), independent workers (2.2%), and agricultural and fishermen (0.3%), making up to 53.6% of the total population.

In terms of income, those who earn a monthly income of MOP100,000 or more constitute 1.2% and are considered to belong to the upper class (Figure 7.2). Note that income is only one indicator of class. Government officials at the *ju*

Figure 7.1
Class identification by occupation.

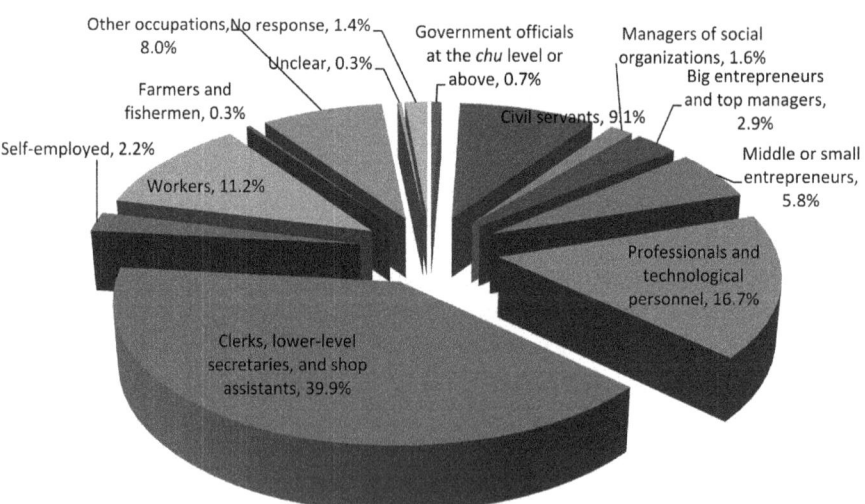

Source: 2012 research report by the Institute of Social and Cultural Studies, Macau University of Science and Technology.

Social Issues and Problems in Macau 171

Figure 7.2

Class identification by monthly income (MOP).

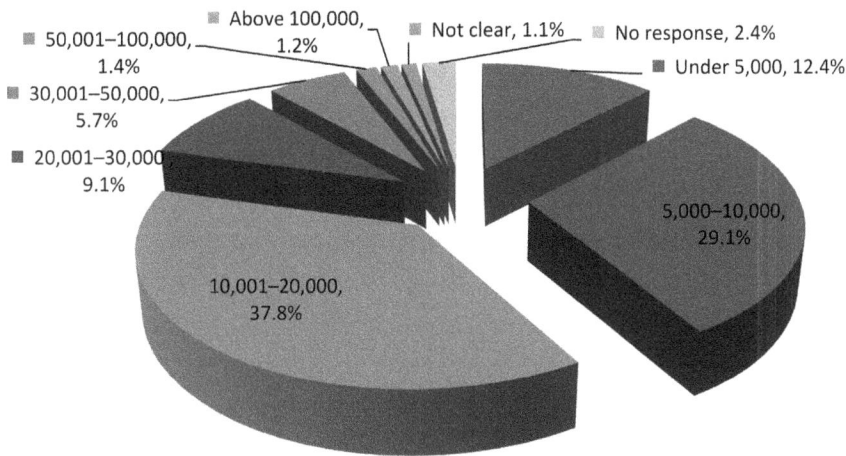

Source: 2012 research report by the Institute of Social and Cultural Studies, Macau University of Science and Technology.

(bureau) level may not earn as high as MOP100,000; however, they wield a lot of power, which therefore places them in the upper class. Thus, the actual number of people in the upper class is higher than 1.2% if a combined index is used. If those earning between MOP20,000 and MOP100,000 are considered the middle class, the group will constitute 16.2% of Macau's population, much lower than that defined by occupation. If those who earn MOP20,000 or less per month are considered the working class and the lower class, that will account for 79.3% of the total population, much higher than the 53.6% measured by occupation.

In terms of education (Figure 7.3), it is difficult to deduce that there is a strong association between education and the upper class. Therefore, those who have a postsecondary degree, including college, master's and PhD degrees, are considered to belong to the middle class, accounting for 25.6% of Macau's population. Those with a secondary school diploma or less, including primary school and no schooling, are grouped as the lower class, making up to 73.9% of total population.

The findings are as follows, taking the average of the two or three measures of occupation, income and education calculated earlier: the upper class constitutes 2.4% of Macau's population (3.6% by occupation and 1.2% by income); the middle class, including the upper middle class, accounts for 25.0% (33.2% by occupation, 16.2% by income and 25.6% by education); and the lower class makes up 68.9% (53.6% by occupation, 79.3% by income and 73.9% by education).

Figure 7.3
Class identification by education.

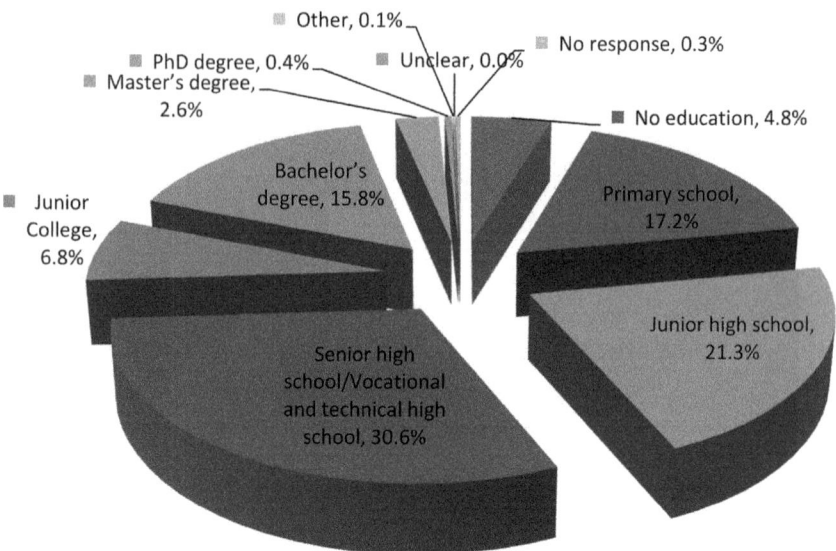

Source: 2012 research report by the Institute of Social and Cultural Studies, Macau University of Science and Technology.

The 2012 survey data showed similar trend as the 2006 census data and another representative survey published in 2007 (Table 7.3). Still, however we look at it, the capitalist or upper class including higher-grade government officials constitutes 2.4% to 3.8% of the population, the middle class 20.9% to 29%, and the lower class 68.9% to 75.3%. There is no doubt, then, that Macau society is sociopolitically and socioeconomically stratified, with a very small upper class, a relatively small middle class and a very large lower class.

Class Politics before and after the Handover: Persistent and Occasionally Intense

In addition to ethnic politics, class politics has also changed since the return of Macau to China. As analysis of the objectives of the various associations of the upper, middle, and lower class has indicated, traditional sociopolitical organizations, like the MCCC and MFTU, claim to love the country and Macau, support "one country, two systems" and promote stability and harmony in Macau. Importantly, they also support the MSAR government. This is contrary to the colonial times,

Table 7.3 Class distribution in Macau in 2006, 2007, and 2012 (%)

	2006 census	2007 survey	2012 survey of the upper, middle, and lower classes		Notes
Capitalist/upper class	3.8	0.0	Upper class	2.4	Employers hiring 20 or more employees and higher-level government officials
Old middle class	4.6	1.3	Middle class	25.0	Small proprietors with or without employees
New middle class (of higher rank)	7.0	8.0			High-level administrators, corporate managers, and professionals
New middle class (of lower rank)	9.3	19.7			Small business managers and associate professionals
Marginal middle class	40.3	40.7	Lower class	68.9	Clerks, service workers, shop sales workers, and foremen
Working class	35.0	30.2			Workers and those in elementary occupations, and agricultural and fishery workers
(N = total population for census and sample size otherwise)	290,316	1,491	1,200		

Sources: The 2006 census data and 2007 survey data are based on Timothy Ka-ying Wong and Wan Po-san, "The Emerging Middle Class in Post-Colonial Macao: Structure, Profile, and Mobility," *Issues and Studies* 45, no. 2 (June 2009): 227–8. The definitions are slightly modified for the upper class. The 2012 data originated from a 2012 report on a project on social stratification in Macao, produced by the Institute of Social and Cultural Studies, Macau University of Science and Technology.

when the Chinese upper, middle, and lower classes largely united against the Portuguese Macau government. In the May 29 Incident of 1922, workers and businessmen went on strike against the Portuguese Macau government. In the 12-3 Incident, Ho Yin, president of the MCCC, represented the Chinese in Macau in their negotiation with the Portuguese Macau government as we discussed in chapter 2. Both incidents, which seemed to be more about ethnic politics than class politics, are evidences of opposition to the colonial government.

From opposing the Portuguese government to supporting the Chinese government, Macau politics experienced sea of changes but it does not actually constitute class politics, since there are no differences envisaged between the upper and lower classes. This is, however, only one layer of the picture. It is hard to believe that class conflicts do not exist with such sharp class stratification, i.e., a very small upper class in contrast with the vast majority of the lower class. There are indeed newer sociopolitical organizations, such as the ATFPM, that hold different attitudes from those of the traditional ones. Such class conflict is demonstrated in three areas: (i) the composition of the Legislative Assembly and the Executive Council, the decision-making body of the chief executive; (ii) the legislative behavior of legislators representing different classes; and (iii) social protest movements.

Class Politics as Seen from the Composition of the Legislative Assembly and the Executive Council

Table 7.4 shows the percentage of legislators from different categories of occupational background. The first category comprises businessmen and businesswomen, the second category professional and public administration personnel, and the third category labor and social service personnel. It is true that not every businessman and businesswoman legislators would represent only his or her fellows, especially if the legislator is directly elected by the populace or if the legislator needs support from people from all walks of life and would therefore likely represent people beyond his or her own ranks. Directly elected former legislators like Chan Meng Kam and Chan Mei Yi were known for their social service work and often called upon for the protection of the interests of less advantaged groups. Although indirectly elected members by occupational groups and members appointed by the chief executive would also claim to represent all people in Macau, it is not incorrect to assume that businesspeople tend to represent the upper class, professional and public administration personnel tend to speak for the middle class, and those from labor and social service sectors tend to represent the working class.[26]

Table 7.4 shows that legislators with a business background have maintained a dominant presence and a steady increase from 41.4 to 60.6% in the five terms since the handover in 1999. However, there was only one instance in the pre-handover terms when businessmen had a presence of more than 40%. Meanwhile, there is a

Table 7.4 Percentage of legislators in different categories of occupational background, 1976–2013

Year/occupational background	Businesses	Professional and managerial	Labor and social services
1976	35.3%	64.70%	0.0%
1980	29.4%	70.50%	0.0%
1984	47.1%	47.00%	5.9%
1988	26.1%	60.80%	13.0%
1992	26.1%	56.50%	17.4%
1996	39.1%	43.50%	17.4%
1999	47.8%	34.70%	17.4%
2001	44.4%	33.30%	18.5%
2005	41.4%	41.30%	17.2%
2009	48.3%	31.00%	20.7%
2013	60.6%	24.2%	15.2%

Notes:
1. The data for the years before 2013 are based on Cai Yongjun, "Cong Aomen lifahui de liyi daibiao kan huigui hou de shehui yundong" (Social movements after the handover as seen from legislators representing different interests in Macau), in *Yiguo liangzhi yanjiu* (Academic Journal of One country, Two Systems), no. 2 (2013): 4. However, I have combined professional and public administration personnel into one category in order to indicate a representation of the middle class and then added data from 2013.
2. For data covering 2013, Si Ka Lon and Song Pek Kei were grouped in the business category, because they were on the same ballot ticket led by Chan Meng Kam and would most likely vote with him.
3. Leonel Alberto Alves, in the indirectly elected category, has a business of his own, but he is not counted as a businessman because he is supposed to represent the professional category. However, Cheung Lup Kwan and Chan Chak Mo are categorized as businessmen because they seem to own various businesses even though they are representing cultural and sports groups.

steady decrease in the number of professionals and public administration personnel and a plummet in the percentage labor and service representatives in 2013 defying its seeming steady increase over the years. As a majority of the members of the Legislative Assembly are appointed and indirectly elected, the upper class ensures that it has a larger presence. The upper class has strong representation from businessmen and businesswomen both pre- and post-handover as well as support from the governor before 1999 and the chief executive after 1999.[27]

The composition of the MSAR's 11-member Executive Council, whose job is to assist the chief executive in policymaking, is similar to that of the Legislative Assembly. According to Article 58 of the Basic Law, the chief executive must consult the Executive Council when making important decisions, proposing new legislation, making new regulations, and dismissing the Legislative Assembly. Apparently, this is an important body that ranks just below the level of chief executive but above that of the Legislative Assembly, as we mentioned in chapter 2.

The make-up of the third Executive Council (2009–2014) was as follows: 64% of the body were people with business background (Liu Chak Wan, Ma Iao Lai, Cheang Chi Keong, Leong Vai Tac, Chan Meng Kam, Eddie Wong Yue Kai, and Lam Kam Seng); 18% were professional and public administration personnel (Florinda da Rosa Silva Chan, also one of the five secretaries in the MSAR government, and Leonel Alberto Alves); and the remaining 18% were from the labor and social services (Ho Sut Heng and Leong Heng Teng). That people with business backgrounds make a dominant presence in both the Legislative Assembly and Executive Council implies that rules and regulations made by the MSAR government will most likely be pro-business and pro-upper class.

A pro-business and pro-upper-class attitude is often equated with a disinterest in democratization, which would concern mainly middle-class professionals and social activists. Thus, if the government does not care much about democracy, it seems rational to maintain a high percentage of legislators with a business background through indirect elections and appointments, and a low percentage of legislators with professional, youth, and social movements backgrounds, while controlling the percentage of legislators with labor and social service backgrounds. That is the reality in Macau's class politics, as evidenced in the election and selection of legislators. The same holds true with the selection of Executive Council members.

Legislative Behavior of Different Classes Represented at the Legislative Assembly

To determine if legislative decisions are pro-business and pro-upper class, I examine the laws passed before and after the handover, focusing on two kinds of laws: one deals with labor relations and the other democratization, i.e., election and composition of legislators and the legislation of Article 23 of the Basic Law. The former concerns the relationship between labor and capital, and the latter is most likely a middle-class concern. The circumstances under which these laws were passed pre- and post-handover were studied to see how much they exhibit traits of class politics.

In August 1984, the Macau colonial government issued its first labor law. Information about the circumstances in which the law was made is scarce. However, Macau Chinese were not really involved in politics at this time in their history. There were a few Chinese in the Legislative Assembly; however, the governor dismissed the assembly, and the new Legislative Assembly would not return to session until October 25, 1984, when Macau Chinese began to participate in politics on a larger scale.[28] Nevertheless, the passage of labor law of any kind was better than no law at all. It is thus understandable that the legislation stirred little controversy if any at the time. In contrast, the controversy over the new labor law in 2008 indeed reflects the presence of class politics.

In 2008, nine years after the handover, the Labor Law, or the Labor Relations Law, was revised and passed. Major debates about the law focused on the type of power entitlement employers have to make contracts with employees, and whether employers who delay paying wages to workers should be punished.[29] At first, the draft law stated that employers had the power to make contracts notwithstanding the labor law. This is typical of a government and legislature that largely represented the interests of the capital and the upper class. This move sparked a protest movement by labor, i.e., the lower or working class. After this, the draft law was revised, stipulating that an employer might negotiate contracts with employees, but the terms in the contract could not fall below the standards of the Labor Law. This seems to reflect a compromise.

The labor class had also requested to penalize employers who delayed in paying wages to their employees. However, the draft law, which represented the interests of the capital and upper class, did not allow this. Some employers argued that they owed wage arrears due to financial difficulties and should therefore be excused. However, Kwan Tsui Hang, a legislator representing labor, argued that non-payment of wages is tantamount to stealing goods from a shop without being punished; likewise, without legal protection of the laborer, employers could steal money from the laborer without punishment. Legislators eventually reached a compromise by setting up a complex procedure of punishment in order to appease both labor and capital, rendering the new law almost toothless.[30]

The minimum wage law has been a hotly debated topic since the 1980s, but the government had dragged its feet on this issue until 2013 when law was drafted. One would think that the outcome would have been different if labor had greater representation in the government and legislature. The labor law case and the minimum wage law case have presented an interesting study of class politics beyond the patriotic propaganda. We see and understand the importance that capital enjoys and the position labor has adopted as well as the battlefield in the executive and legislative branches of the government.

If the two cases signify conflicts between labor and capital, then the issues regarding the legislation of the composition of the Legislative Assembly in 1980, raised again in the late 1980s and early 1990s, and the legislation of Article 23 in 2008 and political developments in 2012 are evidence of conflicts between the upper and middle classes, with the former class supported by "patriotic" labor and social service organizations. In 1980, four Macanese legislators—who were lawyers and personnel from public service sectors like the late Dr. Carlos d'Assumpção, chairman of the colonial government's Legislative Assembly, and Jorge Rangel, a civil servant—proposed an amendment to the Organic Law that would change the current rules of selection for the Legislative Assembly from a mix of direct election, indirect election, and appointment of legislators to the direct election of all legislators. Moreover, the proposed law would grant the Legislative Assembly the power to remove the governor from office. This represented a drastic change towards full democracy, although it was mainly a middle-class Macanese movement. Both the Portuguese governor and mainland Chinese government opposed the move for fear of losing control of Macau. Five pro-Beijing Chinese legislators, led by Ho Yin, the father of the first chief executive after the handover in 1999, aligned with the Beijing government against the proposal. Xi Zhongxun, the governor of Guangdong province, stated that the move might jeopardize Sino-Portuguese interests. The Macanese rebellion failed.[31]

The struggle for democratization carried on into the late 1980s and early 1990s, when the Macau Basic Law was being drafted. Middle-class representatives like Ng Kuok Cheong and Wong Cheong Nam criticized the proposal's small representation of directly elected legislators and lack of a timetable for universal suffrage, unlike Hong Kong's. But their efforts did not go very far.[32]

In 2012, the government proposed a law to revise the methodology of direct and indirect legislative elections and of selecting the election committee for the chief executive. This provided an opportunity to make big strides in democratization with something like a timetable and roadmap for universal suffrage. But that was not what the government had in mind. It pushed to add two directly elected legislators and two indirectly elected legislators and to also add 100 members to the election committee of the chief executive. The law was passed and it did not change the structure of power distribution.[33] The upper class certainly made an effort to keep power in its own hands with the support of the lower class in the name of patriotism. The middle class's efforts to push for greater change have failed, and full democracy therefore does not appear likely in the foreseeable future. Again, the upper class has won.

Another concern of the middle class is the legislation of Article 23 of the Basic Law in 2008. Article 23 addresses the prevention of subversion of the state and is related to how much power the state has in curtailing regular citizens' behavior and even thoughts, particularly critical behavior and thoughts. This has always been a concern by the Chinese Party-state.[34] Critics were especially concerned about the definition of crimes considered as subversion of the state and the implementation of the law. Might it mean that democrats could no longer hold June Fourth vigils? What type of criticism directed at the mainland government would amount to a violation of the law? Would Macau police be able to define and implement the law with due justice? Professionals and democracy movement advocates, who are mainly of the middle class, were naturally concerned. Still, the bill sailed through the Legislative Assembly without much of a challenge.

From the above discussion about the legislation of the labor law, a concern of the working class, and the legislation of the election laws and Article 23, more of a concern of the middle class, it is obvious that the smooth passage of bills in favor of the upper class is attributed to the composition of "who's who" sitting at the Legislative Assembly. Of course, as mentioned earlier, the executive-led system, which gives the chief executive almost full power, makes it next to impossible for the Legislative Assembly to even propose laws for discussion. Therefore, the upper and business classes enjoy the double guarantee that they will win in class politics: both by default in the system and through control of legislation processes. But will middle and working-class social protest movements make a difference?

Social Protests

Politics among Macau's upper, middle, and lower classes can also be discerned in social protest movements before and after the handover in 1999. Table 7.5 lists out the major social protests between 1989 and 2014. There are incidences of both middle-class movements and working-class movements. Middle-class movements are often about demand for democracy and also benefits-related issues. The working or lower class has organized many more protests than the middle class, focusing on issues such as illegal workers, imported labor, and unemployment. The two classes often join hands to protest against corruption, inflation, labor issues, and even the denial of democracy, especially in 1989, in response to the crackdown on the June Fourth Movement in Beijing and massacre of students and workers, and in 2014, against the legislation of benefits for high-level government officials.

Thus, in terms of social protest movements, the middle and working (lower) classes of Macau are fairly active in asserting their interests, although the latter seems to have been more active than the former. Also, their targets are often the upper class, in particular, either government officials or employers. Have their protest movements made a difference? The answer is mixed. Democratization has not made much progress, as Ng Kwok Cheong and Wong Chang Nam predicted in the late 1980s when the Basic Law was being drafted. However, the lower class's interests have been enhanced in terms of public housing, labor practices, and restricted labor imports, to name a few, although progress has been very slow. The 2014 movement,

Table 7.5 Major social protest movements between 1989 and 2013

Date	Class identity of major participants	Number of participants	Type of appeals
February 18, 1989	Middle class: civil servants	Several hundreds	Demand for pay raise
May 20, 1989 to July 2, 1989	Middle and working classes: teachers, students, journalists, engineers, workers	200,000 (on June 4, 1989)	Protest against Beijing's crackdown on student movements
July 31, 1989	Working class: taxi drivers	500	Protest against on-call taxi drivers to pick up customers on streets
August 5, 1989	Working class: unionized workers	50,000-signature gathering	Protest against imported labor
August 15, 1989	Working class: cleaning workers	At the Leal Senado	Request for pay raise and regular work status
January 8, 1990	Middle class: small entrepreneurs	100-signature gathering	Protest against imported workers quota system
March 27, 1990	Middle class: college students from the East Asian University (EAU)	On strike	Request for recognition of diploma from EAU
March 30, 1990	Working class: police	1,000	Request for pay raise
January 3, 1991	Working class: employees at the weather station	On strike	Protest against the layoff of a woman employee
December 6, 1991	Middle class: employers from the tourist industry	Press conference	Protest against government tax on tourists of MOP 20 per person
August 18, 1992	Working class: cleaning workers	200	Protest against employers' change of benefits
June 8, 1993	Working class: cleaning workers	All on strike	Request for pay raise
March 6, 1996	Working class: parents of students with no legal documents	200	Request for legal identity
March 19, 1996	Working class: imported workers	200	Protest against a factory for laying off workers before contract ends

(continued on page 181)

Social Issues and Problems in Macau 181

Table 7.5 (continued)

Date	Class identity of major participants	Number of participants	Type of appeals
March 14, 1997	Working class: parents of students with no legal documents	3,000	Request for legal status
October 20, 1998	Lower class: prisoners	On hunger strike	Protest against new measures of prison visits
July 5–7, 2000	Working class: workers	A number of demonstrations involving 1,000 people at one time; a hunger strike involving 10 workers	Protest against illegal workers, unemployment
May 1, 2001	Working class	300–500	Protest against unemployment, imported labor; demand for minimum wage and eight-hour work day
May 1, 2006	Middle and working classes and other disadvantaged groups, especially new labor groups	5,000	Protest against imported labor and illegal workers
December 21, 2006	Working class: various union groups	700	Protest against corruption and imported labor; demand for family reunion
May 1, 2007	Working class: various union groups	2,400–10,000	Protest against corruption and imported labor; demand for family reunion
October 1, 2007	Working class: non-traditional groups	2,000–6,000	Protest against corruption and imported labor, traffic law
December 18, 2007	Working class	150	Protest against corruption, imported labor, traffic law
December 20, 2007	Middle and working classes	2,000–7,000	Protest against corruption, imported labor, inflation, the widening rich-poor gap and legislation of Article 23, and demand for universal suffrage
April 14, 2008	Working class	Not clear	Protest against imported labor, traffic law, inflation

(continued on page 182)

Table 7.5 (continued)

Date	Class identity of major participants	Number of participants	Type of appeals
May 1, 2008	Middle and working class	800–1,000	Protest against imported labor and illegal workers, corruption and inflation, demonstration for the Beijing Olympics
September 6, 2008	Middle class: New Macao Society	Not clear	Protest against imported labor
September 28, 2008	Middle class: civil servants	450–1,000	Demand for pay raise and protest against firing of teachers
November 23, 2008	Middle-class social movement organization	60–100	Protest against the legislation of Article 23
December 20, 2008	Middle class	1,000	Protest against corruption and the legislation of Article 23; demand for democracy
May 1, 2009	Working class: new labor groups	500	Protest against government by the businessmen (not by the people) and illegal and imported labor; demand for more public housing
December 20, 2009	Middle class, including students	1,500	Protest against corruption; demand for more public housing, democracy and universal suffrage by 2019
May 1, 2010	Middle class	1,500	Protest against imported labor; demand for more public housing, youth employment and family reunion
December 20, 2010	Middle and working classes	1,200	Demand for justice and universal suffrage; protest against skyrocketing housing prices
May 1, 2011	Middle and working classes	2,300	Protest against corruption and illegal workers; demand for teachers' benefits, release of dissidents in China, universal suffrage, etc.

(continued on page 183)

Table 7.5 (continued)

Date	Class identity of major participants	Number of participants	Type of appeals
June 30, 2013	Middle class	100	Demand for Florinda Chan, secretary of the government's Department of Administration and Law, to step down
August 11, 2013	Working class	400	Protest against non-Macau students who stay to work in Macao after graduation
October 10, 2013	Working class	3,000	Protest against hiring non-Macau residents to work as casino dealers or non-Macau students to stay and work in Macau after graduation, and demand for a total ban of smoking in casinos
May 25, 2014 May 27, 2014	Middle and working class	10,000 to 20,000	Protest against the legislation of benefits for higher-level government officials before and after retirement

Sources: Compiled from *Macao Daily*; *Va Kio Daily*; *Citizen Daily*; *Tai Chung Daily*; Bryan Ho, "Political Culture, Social Movements, and Governability in Macao," *Asian Affairs: An American Review* 38 (2011): 59–87; Cai Yongjun, "Cong Aomen lifahui de liyi daibiao kan huigui hou de shehui yundong" (Social Movements after the Handover as Seen from Legislators Representing Different Interests in Macau); Lin Yuan, "Tantao Aomen shimin de shehui zhengzhi canyu" (A Study of Macao Citizens' Social and Political Participation), paper presented at a conference on Macao in the 10 years after its return to China, 21–2 April 2009; Lou Shenghua, Pan Guanjin and Lin Yuan, *Xin zhixu: Aomen shehui zhili yanjiu* (New Order: A Study of Macao Social Management) (Beijing: Social Science Academic Press, 2009); Zhuang Jinfeng, "Cong Aomen shetuan de teshu xing kan 'yiguo liangzhi' de Aomen moshi" (The Macao Model of "One Country, Two Systems" as Seen from the Particularities of Macao's Social Organizations), *Yiguo liangzhi yanjiu* (Journal on the Study of "One Country, Two Systems"), no. 6 (2010); and *Aomen baike quanshu* (Macao Encyclopaedia), at http://www.macaudata.com/macaubook/encyclopedia/index.html, accessed November 11, 2013.

the largest since 1989, forced the government to retract its proposed legislation. The minimum wage law was finally passed but only in a restricted version. Moreover, the government's attitude often seems to be one that avoids offending anyone. It has made a great effort in accommodating contradictory requests regarding imported labor: capital wants more, while labor wants less. In the end, the government has done little to change the status quo. So, will Macau democratize at all? That is still the question. We will discuss this further in chapter 8.

Gambling-Related Crime and Deviance and What Casinos and the Government Need to Do

Before the return of Macau to China, crime was a serious issue. Violence proliferated: in 1996 there were 21 murders, then in 1997 there were 29, 1998, 30, and 1999, 42. Even government officials were shot dead. Triads were running the day-to-day business of protection, loan-sharking, debt collection, money laundering, prostitution, drug-running, other racketeering activities as well as the management of the VIP rooms in casinos. Triad turf wars regularly broke out.[35]

After the handover, the situation has vastly improved but it still fluctuates in some areas and the overall number of crimes has risen: in 1998 it was 8,487, but in 2008, it was 13,864 and in 2017, 14,293.[36] This has to do with the population increase from 452,000 in 1997 to 525,000 in 2011 and 650,000 in 2017, and the expansion of the gambling industry. Many crimes are gambling-related. According to the above cited report, there were 12,629 cases of crime filed in 2017, and out of which 4,714 cases were related to gambling, including 428 serious cases of loan-sharking and 464 cases of serious illegal detention or kidnappings (p. 1). Four of the illegal detention cases caused deaths of the kidnapped persons either by suicide or falling upon escape. The situation has become so dire that "Macau casino operators are taking out insurance policies to protect themselves against the kidnapping of wealthy guests over unpaid gambling debts."[37]

In 2014 there were 1,812 cases of money laundering according to the government released interim report in 2016 (p. 75). In 2016, the Judiciary Police reported that 1,341 loan-sharking suspects were sent to the prosecutor's office. In 2017, a total of 2,171 gambling-related crime suspects were sent to the prosecutor and charged (pp. 2, 7).[38] The government's interim report finds that between 2007 and 2014, there was an increase of gambling-related crimes from 1,279 to 3,023, a rate of 12.8% to 28.2% increase from the previous year (p. 76). But it seems that what we see here represents only a small percentage of actually existing crime cases. For example, there are many more loan-sharking cases as we were told in our own research interviews.

We will now summarize what we find in the government data, our own research, and various media sources regarding loan-sharking, VIP room gambling, and problem gambling. Between 2012 and 2013, two professors and I researched responsible gambling practices in Macau, Las Vegas, and Melbourne, focusing on the casinos that did business in at least two of these places, i.e., Sands, Wynn, MGM, and Melco-Crown.[39] We must emphasize that all these problems, along with money laundering, kidnappings, etc. highlight the risks to the integrity of the industry and the credibility of the Macau government.

Loan-sharking

The Macau government's own 2016 interim review of the gambling industry reported that there were 208 cases of loan-sharking in 2014, an annual increase of 29% (p. 74). In 2015 when there was a downturn in gambling revenue, the Judiciary Police handled 318 cases of loan-sharking, an increase of 55% from the previous year, and sent to the prosecutor's office 966 suspects.[40] But the problem may be more widespread. As one of our industry interviewees points out,

> loan sharks are those who prey on people. We kick out about 200 such people each eight-hour shift. The loan sharks are well-organized, having their own publicity brochure and customer services, etc. They prey on people who are vulnerable. But the police don't prosecute them unless they kidnapped someone. There should be zero tolerance.[41]

If what this interviewee says is credible, in over 40 casinos in Macau, loan sharks may run up to thousands. Loan sharks prey on not only the high rollers in the VIP rooms, but also the gamblers on the mass gaming floor. It seems that "business in Macau is conducted with one eye open and one eye closed," as another interviewee points out.[42] Some casinos actually allow loan sharks to roam around their facilities. To maintain the integrity of the industry and the credibility of the government, both sides have to do much more such as mandatory reporting on the part of the former of loan-sharking activities and strict law enforcement in finding and prosecuting loan sharks on the part of the latter.

VIP Room Gambling[43]

The government's 2016 interim review reports that over the years about 60% to 70% of the casino's income comes from VIP room gambling. In Las Vegas, slot machine revenue accounts for 51% of total gaming revenue and VIP or high roller gambling represents a very small percentage.[44] Our interviewees estimate that about 80% of casino revenues come from these rooms. Apparently there are fluctuations in VIP room gambling revenues and it is also true that VIP gambling may decrease in importance and mass floor gambling is on the rise. In the third quarter of 2018, for example, VIP gambling accounted for 54% of the total casino income.[45]

Nonetheless, it looks that VIP gambling will continue to generate the most income for Macau's gambling industry for a long time to come.

The biggest contributors to this income are mainland Chinese high rollers: one-fourth of them are government officials, one-fourth executives of state-owned enterprises, and one-third owners of private companies according to the interim report (p. 74). One well-known example is Yang Kun, a deputy director of Agricultural Bank of China, who owed RMB 3 billion in gambling debt in 2013. There are many cases of high rollers owing millions upon millions of dollars. According to one study of 82 highly publicized cases of high rollers, the amount of money bet by a private entrepreneur from mainland China in his gambling career was RMB 29 million, by a corrupt government official, RMB 22 million, and by a corrupt manager of state-owned enterprises, RMB 16 million (US$1 equals RMB 6.8).[46] The money was often embezzled public funds. As a result of such problem gambling, many lost their official positions, businesses, and families, and were sent to prison.

In addition to the tragedies causing those individuals involved, there are several problems with VIP room operators or junket operators (over 10,000 of them, out of which only about 260 are legal according to our interviewees). First, the rate of bad loans usually runs up to 10% to 20% according to the government-released interim report in 2016. Because gambling is illegal in mainland China, the junket operators cannot sue the debtors in court and will have to use other, sometimes illegal, means to get their money back (pp. 242–43).

Second, people use the casino facility to gamble illegally. Some may gamble "under the table," meaning, for example, that if they win or lose, say, HK$100,000 at the casino, the actual money involved in win or lose will be multiple times that amount. As a result, the government loses the tax and the casino loses its cut in profit (pp. 243–44). Because of the large amount of money involved, it can also quickly lead to bankruptcy of either the VIP rooms or the gambler. Others use the internet or phone to direct someone else to gamble on their behalf from a distance, which is also against the law. They are able then to hide their identities.

Third, partly because lawmaking is lagging far behind development, rogue junket operators can easily embezzle money up to hundreds of millions of dollars (p. 246). The two embezzlement and abscondment cases in 2014 and 2015 were thought to be part of the reasons for the decline of casino income in 2015 and 2016 since too many investors and players lost huge amounts of money and the VIP rooms were losing credibility. (Another reason for the decline was thought to be the corruption crackdown in mainland China.)

The industry relies on the junkets to make most of its revenue. It is indeed difficult to ask the junkets to bear solely the responsibility of problem gambling prevention. But they are the key link in the industry, and both the government and the casinos have an obligation to regulate their activities and enforce regulation. As is the case now, much more is needed on both parts. Again it is a matter of industry integrity and government credibility. One direction of the reform is to make both the junkets and the casinos pay a price if problem gambling under their watch has led to the loss of individual lives and public funds. The U.S. Department of State's suggestion to Macau in its 2016 annual report on anti-money laundering (AML), financial crimes and drugs still applies and may help the casinos deal with other VIP room-related gambling problems:[47]

> While Macau's AML law does not require currency transaction reporting, gaming entities are subject to threshold reporting for transactions over MOP 500,000 (US$62,640) under the supplementary guidelines of the Gaming Inspection and Coordination Bureau. Macau should lower the large transaction report threshold for casinos to $3,000 to bring it in line with international standards. The government also should continue to strengthen interagency coordination to prevent money laundering in the gaming industry, especially by introducing robust oversight of junket operators, mandating due diligence for non-regulated gaming collaborators, and implementing cross-border currency reporting.

Problem Gambling

The government's 2016 interim review of the gambling industry acknowledges that the rate of problem gambling was 6% in 2007, the highest ever (p. 71). Although there has been some decline over the years, there are still about 14,000 problem gamblers in Macau. Another research in 2010 found that 55.9% of residents in Macau participated in gambling and 2.8% of them were problem gamblers.[48] Whatever the case, the number of problem gamblers is very high. But official figures in the government's interim report indicate that in 2011, 2012, 2013, and 2014, the number of problem gamblers who sought help was only 144, 149, 134, and 141 respectively and about a third of them were casino employees (pp. 72, 73). Our own research also finds that employee gambling is prevalent. Cumulatively since 2011 when the government began to tabulate the number of problem gamblers seeking help, there have been altogether only 947 cases until the first half of 2017, dwarfing the total number of addicted gamblers.[49]

Numbers may not give us a feeling of the problem, so here are some specific cases reported in *Macao Daily* in March and April 2013. They show us what happens to individuals:[50]

- A casino employee committed suicide by jumping off his apartment building because he could not pay his gambling debts (March 7, p. A7).
- A mainland woman attempted suicide by drowning herself in the sea when her husband refused to lend her money to gamble (March 25, p. A3).
- A Guangdong woman hung herself when she could not find money to pay her debts to the loan sharks (March 27, p. A1).

- A case was reported in which two mainlanders were killed in a Macau hotel because of gambling debts (April 9, p. A1).
- A mother stole her son's watch worth HK$120,000 and pawned it for HK$100,000 to gamble, losing HK$10,000.
- A 24-year-old young man, addicted to gambling, cheated an acquaintance of MOP600,000, saying that he was going to help her buy an apartment (April 11, p. A7).
- A woman junket operator stole her patron's HK$ 2 million and disappeared (April 23, p. B11).

Here are three more detailed stories of problem gambling:[51]

CASE 1: A young man began to gamble when he was in high school. He liked playing football very much. He began sports gambling on the internet and lost a lot of money. Then he stole money from his family-owned restaurant and went to gamble at casinos with the hope that he could win more money. He came to our center when he was 25 years old. Now he has got rid of gambling for about one year. He used to be a very shy boy and was not good at study in high school. He has a younger brother who did pretty well in school, which made him disappointed with himself. He could not find his position either in school or in the family. Only when he won in the casino could he feel a sense of fulfillment. That is why he became an addicted gambler.

CASE 2: A young and hardworking chef was enticed by his colleagues to gamble when he was 20 years old. As a chef, he had nothing to do in the afternoon. So his colleagues asked him to hang out with them. At first, he only lost a little money, but the more he played the more he lost. He always thought he would win a lot next time until he was in heavy debt. He had no choice but to escape to Taiwan. He thought he would stop gambling in Taiwan since there is no casino there. But when he came back to Macau, he continued to gamble. His mother was in great distress and became seriously ill because of his gambling addiction. His whole family was deeply affected by his problem gambling. So he decided to undertake rehab in the SKH center.

CASE 3: This is a woman who gambled because of family relationship problems. Gambling gave her a feeling that she could escape from the unhappy family environment. She made more money than her husband; however, the husband took charge of everything at home, which she didn't feel good about. She worked at a casino, and many of her colleagues liked to go gambling after they finished work. At the beginning she was not interested at all. Later on she could not help trying the game a couple of times. She found she could forget all those unhappy things when she won money. But when she lost money, she wanted to play again to get her money back, which caused her to lose even more.

The government and casinos have a responsible gambling publicity week every year. Casinos also have brochures in their facilities reminding people to gamble responsibly. Macau government has initiated a self-exclusion program since 2012 but very few people are enrolled in it and besides they are not excluded from all the casinos. Apparently the government and casinos have to do much more. Rather than relying on the gamblers themselves to be responsible, as they define responsible gambling, the government and casinos have to take their responsibilities by establishing more active, well monitored and enforced intervention programs, professionally staffed in-house counselling centers that are open 24/7, and an effective self-exclusion program that would ban the problem gamblers from entering all casinos, not just particular casinos.

The broader issue is that of casino duty of care to patrons and whether there are adequate policies and practices in place to not just intervene when people hit crisis point with their gambling but to prevent it from getting to that point. One of our interviewees says, "You don't ignore the person with problems at a supermarket. So you take care of people at your venue."[52] As another interviewee points out, casinos should fund support programs just as ski operators have to fund emergency personnel just in case someone breaks a leg. It's the same thing. With the entertainment of gambling will come consequences and so casinos should prepare their business models to address these consequences.[53]

In a nutshell, casinos have a duty of care to their employees and customers, and the government has a responsibility for regulation and law enforcement. They cannot just take the money without taking their responsibilities. There are many things they can do; the question is whether they are willing to do them.[54] As one of our interviewees observes, to ask an addicted gambler to take responsibility, as the current concept of responsible gambling means, is to ask people with disordered frontal lobe to function and make right decisions.[55] Casinos will change if there are lawsuits, or if the government requires them to change. They are concerned about civil litigations.[56] With the current political and social systems that we have discussed earlier, however, one cannot be very optimistic. But industry integrity and government credibility and legitimacy are on the line.

In the long run, casinos and the government should follow the Las Vegas model where a great portion of visitors flocks to the city's non-gambling facilities rather than coming mainly for gambling offerings as in Macau.[57] In 2017, Macau's gross gambling revenue was US$33.217 billion while Las Vegas's was only US$7.092 billion. But the latter had more visitors in the same year than the former: 42.2 million vs. 32.6 million.[58] Las Vegas is a healthier model. In chapter 8 we will discuss how Macau may be able to transform a "city of sin" into a "city of culture" so that it can attract more non-gamblers. It is not going to be easy, but it is the right thing to do.[59]

Middle School Education

Education in Macau has a very long history, and sometimes even a glorious one, with St. Paul's College as its highest point. After the Rites Controversy and towards the end of the 18th century, however, schools in Macau ceased to function. And neither the Macanese nor the Chinese public education became a movement again until the middle of the 19th century. Yet towards the end of the 20th century, education was still one of the most publicly criticized problems in Macau. The city-state could not control the curriculum of the schools. Prior to the mid-1980s, the territory was notorious for high rates of illiteracy, and the work force had, on average, less than five years of education. There were no standards for teacher training, and in 1987, 34% of the entire teaching staff had only a secondary education. Almost none of the 98.5% of the non-Portuguese residents of a Portuguese-run city spoke Portuguese.[60] In 1994, the government-run schools accommodated less than 7% of the student population but received about two-thirds of the total government funding for education.[61] This had to do with the government's "non-interventionalist" policy, derived from both the Chinese ambivalence towards the Portuguese state and the Portuguese colonial state's ambivalence regarding its responsibilities in Macau.[62]

After the handover in 1999, progress has been made, but problems still abound. The question is whether education in Macau can produce the professionals and skilled workers who are able to handle Macau's problems. In the following pages, I will first discuss Macau's middle school education, and then higher education, using the findings in two of my research projects in the past few years.

There are 62 middle schools in Macau including their branches: 32 private religious schools, 22 private non-religious schools, and 8 public schools (see Table 7.6). Religious middle schools teach about 45.8% of students, non-religious schools,

Table 7.6 The number of religious and non-religious middle schools and their students 2015/2016

	Number of schools not including their branches	Number of schools including their branches	Number of students	% of students
Private religious schools	18	32	13,997	45.8%
Private non-religious schools	20	22	15,245	49.8%
Public schools	6	8	1,353	4.4%
Total	44	62	30,595	100%

Source: Zhidong Hao, "Aomen de jiaohui xuexiao zai aomen shehui fazhan zhong de zuoyong," based on the website of Education and Youth Affairs Bureau of Macau government.

49.8%, and public schools, 4.4%. There are three main differences between the religious and non-religious schools: the mission of the school, contents and methods of teaching, and the extent to which they are influenced or influencing politics. I am now going to discuss these three issues respectively.[63]

The Mission Statements of Different Schools

There are some very important differences in mission statements between religious schools and non-religious schools. Those in the latter category are often referred to as schools with "red background" or 紅底學校. Such "red" schools emphasize well-rounded development in morality, intellect, physical fitness, aesthetics, and social abilities. But they also emphasize fostering students who will "love the country and love Macau." Such schools include Hou Kong Middle School, Keang Peng School, The Workers' Children High School, Kao Yip Middle School, Macau Fong Chong School, Macau Kwong Tai Middle School, Macau Tong Nam School, Seong Fan Evening School, etc.

Religious schools, however, often emphasize loyalty, love, serving the poor, Christian world views, individuality, etc. in their mission statements. If they mention China or Macau, it is that the students should learn to be somebody who is based in Macau of China but who can also face the world. Unlike the "red" schools, they do not mention "love the country and love Macau." These schools include Santa Rosa de Lima (a girls' school), Santissimo Rosario, Macao Sam Yuk Middle school, Yuet Wah College, Instituto Salesiano (慈幼中學), Escola Católica Estrela do Mar (海星中學), Colégio Diocesano de São José (5ª) (聖約瑟教區中學第五校), Sacred Heart Canossian College, Chan Sui Ki Perpetual Help College, etc. There are also religious schools that do not mention patriotism or religion, but emphasize spirituality and universal values, such as devotion, enthusiasm, excellence, critical ability, and ethics, which are somehow related to religion. These schools include Colégio Mateus Ricci and Sheng Kung Hui Choi Kou School.

Other religious schools are even more specific in what characters they are fostering in students. Macau Anglican College emphasizes that "the truth shall set you free," and both teachers and students will learn to be "articulate, confident, creative, cheerful, inquisitive, well-motivated and work hard together to become lifelong independent learners." Saint John de Brito School requires students to be self-confident, considerate, accommodating, and doing things. The School of the Nations (Bahá'í) wants to "nurture the highest standards of intellect, character, and physical development."

Religious schools usually do not emphasize patriotism towards China and Macau, but there is also an exception. One of the most reputable schools, Pui Ching Middle School, emphasizes both patriotism and Christian education such as love, responsibility, critical ability, competitiveness, and comprehensive development.

Differences in Textbooks Used, Contents Taught, and Teaching Methods

Mission statements do not always tell what schools actually do, so we need to look at the textbooks they use and how they teach them. "Red" schools usually use textbooks on Chinese and English languages produced in Hong Kong but their math, politics, history, geography, chemistry, and biology books are from the mainland. Their use of mainland Chinese history and political books explains their being "red." Our interviews also find that teachers usually teach by the book. They do not actively guide their students in certain directions or express their own points of view. They avoid sensitive issues.

Religious schools, however, use mainly textbooks produced in Hong Kong, such as those on math, Chinese, English, and history. They may use mainland-produced textbooks on natural sciences such as physics and chemistry. In teaching methods, they may occasionally touch on politically sensitive issues, but not in details. But their teachers do tend to be more balanced in teaching different points of view on Chinese history according to an interviewee in another project.[64] They have classes on religion, but not that many.

Neither religious nor non-religious schools teach Macau history. A teacher interviewed in another research project commented that the reasons are the lack of time and textbooks and there is not much to teach since Macau's history is very short.[65] Those are, of course, excuses. Lacking consensus on Macau's colonial history is probably the main reason why it is not being taught.

Political Engagement

Both religious and non-religious schools organize student field trips to mainland China to learn Chinese revolutionary history and culture and participate in military exercises and raising the national flag, etc. But the "red" schools get more favorable treatment from the state. The then CCP chairman Jiang Zemin visited Hou Kiang Middle School in 2000; Hu Jintao visited the Workers' Children School in 2004; and Premier Li Keqiang visited Keang Peng Middle School in 2016. Religious schools never get visited by such VIPs. The principal of Keang Peng Middle School wrote in *Macao Daily* (October 17, 2016) after Li Keqiang's visit that they will inherit several decades' tradition of patriotic education and strive to establish a Chinese national identity with "love the country and love Macau" being the core of that identity. They will make concrete steps to help realize the Chinese dream. This is very typical of "red" schools.

In Hong Kong's 2014 Umbrella Movement for democracy, Macau's "red" schools were required by the Chinese Educators' Association of Macau, to which most of these schools and their teachers belong, to carefully guide their students in opposing the movement. They were supposed to teach their students that the movement disturbed social order and caused division in society and losses in the economy in Hong Kong. And one should not violate the law in pursuit of justice. Religious schools tended to adopt a more open attitude; or if their teachers had a point of view, they did not advocate it. Some schools did stop their students from tying yellow ribbons as a symbol of their support for the movement, but they did not explain why.

As far as their graduates are concerned, there does not seem much difference in their becoming legislators and government officials between these two different schools. Of the two most well-known and long-term democracy advocates and legislators, Ng Kuok-chang is from a religious school but Ou Gan Xin is from a "red" school. But it does seem that many more leaders of influential and "patriotic" social organizations are from "red" schools rather than from religious schools. For example, Chio Ngan Ieng (women's association), Leong Heng Teng (neighborhood association), Ma Iao Lai (association of commerce), Lei Pui Lam (educators' association, and Lau Cheok Vá (workers' union) all come from Hou Kiang Middle School. Their leadership positions in "patriotic" organizations often lead to political positions in the government. But Sulu Sou Ka Ho, Scott Chiang Meng Hin, and Jason Chao Teng Hei, the current and former main leaders of New Macau Society, a democracy advocacy organization, are all from religious schools except that Kam Sut Leng who is from a "red" school. They tend to be in the opposition.

So it does seem that different educational background may have an influence on their political attitude and engagement although their later life experience and higher education will also be important.[66] And their tradition may be continued in higher education: high school students from "red" schools tend to choose universities in Macau and mainland China while those from religious schools tend to choose universities in Taiwan. A 2010 survey found that 77.9% of Macau students in Taiwan universities were from religious schools.[67]

A Possible Future

Just because of the implications of middle school education for the current students' future political inclinations, the mainland Chinese government is making an effort to entice Macau students to attend universities in politically safe mainland China rather than in Taiwan or even in Macau. In 2017, mainland Chinese government decided to expand the quota of school-recommended Macau students from 580 to 930, and Jinan and Huaqiao Universities in Guangzhou would expand their quota of Macau students to 1,000. That will be 1,930 graduating high school students out of 4,511, or 43% of the total graduating students (see Table 7.7). But as Table 7.7 shows, the quota was far from filled: only 1,063 students ended up in mainland universities. Still, it was a 7.5% increase from the previous year for mainland China

Table 7.7 The distribution of countries and regions where graduating high school students enrolled in colleges and universities from 2012/2013 to 2016/2017 academic year[68]

Regions	Number of Students					Percentage of Students Enrolled in a Region or Country				
	12/13	13/14	14/15	15/16	16/17	12/13	13/14	14/15	15/16	16/17
Macau	2,844	2703	2,455	2,306	2,154	57.2%	54.6%	50.8%	49.4%	47.7%
Taiwan	1,030	1105	1,218	1,195	822	20.7%	22.3%	25.2%	25.6%	18.2%
Mainland	739	669	699	749	1,063	14.9%	13.5%	14.5%	16.1%	23.6%
Other	361	473	456	416	473	7.2%	9.6%	9.5%	8.9%	10.5%
Total	4974	4950	4,828	4,666	4,511	100%	100%	100%	100%	100%

(from 16.1% to 23.6%), and a 7.4% decrease for Taiwan (from 25.6% to 18.2%). That may be the exact strategic thinking of the mainland Chinese government.

Just as Chan Hong, the director of the Chinese Educators Association of Macau, a legislator, and vice principal of Hou Kong Middle School, points out, this measure by the mainland government is a demonstration of the nation's care and support of Macau and its love and value placed on Macau's youths. Indeed, the quota for Macau is eating into the quota for students from other provinces in mainland China: one more Macau student to go to these colleges and universities would mean one fewer mainland Chinese student can go to these usually elite schools.[69] The principal of Pui Ching Middle School also says that to attend mainland universities will foster students' deep feelings toward the nation and the state.[70] Three representatives to the National People's Congress made suggestions to the central government that students from Hong Kong, Macau, and Taiwan should be given specific courses on national education and they should be encouraged to do military training just as other mainland students are required to do.[71] To get them to love the Party-state is exactly the point, and the state is successful to a certain extent. Apparently mainlandization of both middle school and higher education is likely to be the future although it will not happen too fast. After all, the "one country, two systems" principle is still in effect, even if it is more and more likely a principle mainly on paper. "Red" schools are becoming "redder" and religious schools risk losing their characteristics. It remains to be seen what the future is going to be like.

But many social problems still remain that do have to do with education. Three years after the handover of Macau to China in 1999, Yu Zhen and his colleague, Michael DeGoyla at Hong Kong Baptist University, did a survey on Hong Kong and Macau citizens' political attitude and participation. When asked whether people with different, even radical, opinions like people who believe in Falun Gong, should be allowed to speak in public, 71.00% of people in Hong Kong but only 48.95% of the respondents in Macau thought so.[72] If this is any indication of tolerance, the score for Macau was over 20% lower than it is for Hong Kong, which contradicts Macau's own conviction that it is a more tolerant city than Hong Kong.[73] With the mainlandization of Macau in the past 20 years, one cannot be optimistic that people would become more tolerant of dissenting political views, which would not bode well for Macau's democracy in particular and China's democracy in general.

Political apathy continues to be a problem. A survey in 2009 of middle school students has found that 92.6% of them seldom or never talked with family members or friends about politics. Indeed, only 3 to 6% of the respondents believed that the definition of democracy includes rule of law, political checks and balances, and division of power.[74] A survey of the general population in 2009 finds that 54.3% of the respondents were not interested in politics, and only 4% were very interested and 41.8% somewhat interested. However, 51% would support universal suffrage for both the chief executive and the legislative assembly of the MSAR.[75] Our own research in 2014 found that 56% of the population favored universal suffrage.[76] Are people more interested in politics? It is hard to say, and one wonders whether they are going to be more conservative with increasing mainlandization.

Education plays an important role in raising people's political consciousness. Only when more people are aware of their civic responsibilities can they help improve the political system and make it more responsible and responsive.

Higher Education in Macau[77]

A Brief History of Higher Education in Macau

Higher education in Macau has a checkered past. The College of St. Paul was established by the Catholic missionaries in 1594 but was closed in 1762. There were attempts to build colleges again in the first half of the twentieth century. Gezhi College moved to Macau from mainland China in 1900, Yuehai Wen Shang (humanities and business) College was established in 1949, and Huaqiao (overseas Chinese) University, Huanan (south China) University, and Zhongshan College of Education were started in 1950. But they lasted only a few years for the lack of Portuguese Macau government and the Chinese social support. A major university, the University of East Asia, a private university started by Hong Kong businessmen, was not established until 1981. It was bought by the government in 1991 and renamed the University of Macau. Currently there are 10 post-secondary schools of various orientations and sizes (Table 7.8).

Four of the 10 institutions of higher education are public and the rest are private. The universities and colleges enrolling more than 1,000 students and having a larger faculty body are UM, MPI, IFT, CityU, USJ, and MUST. These are also higher education institutions (HEIs) that have seen great expansion in the numbers of both students and faculty members in the past ten years. (The 2006 data does not distinguish between part-time and full-time faculty.) CityU has seen some real consolidation after being bought by a businessman. It used to be criticized as a non-serious institution of higher education.

Vocationalization

Much of Macau's higher education is meant to train professionals in more applied disciplines. The five top fields students chose in 2016/2017 are business (administration) (25.18%), tourism and recreational services (21.33%), law (5.96%), language and literature (5.40%), and design and the arts (4.87%).[78] Of the 32,750 students, only 1,714 of them majored in social and behavioral sciences (p. 26). Meanwhile, 6.27% of them were pursuing a PhD degree, 17.26% an MA degree, and 75.23% a BA degree (p. 22).

Table 7.8 Higher education institutions (HEIs) in Macau in 2006 and 2016

	Year established	Number of students		Number of faculty members		Total		Nature of school
		2006	2016	Fulltime/ 2016	Part-time/ 2016	2006	2016	
University of Macau (UM)	1981 (UEA) 1991 (UM)	5,838/10,029		559	120	389/679		Public
Macau Polytechnic Institute (MPI)	1991	2,718/3,144		230	143	349/373		Public
Institute for Tourism Studies (IFT)	1995	840/1576		95	41	91/136		Public
Macau Security Force Superior School (MSFSS)	1988	41/37		2	34	23/36		Public
City University of Macau (CityU)	1992 (AIOU)* 2011 (CityU)	7,008/5,834		91	132	185/223		Private
University of St. Joseph (USJ)	1996 (IIUM)** 2009 (USJ)	256/1,063		67	79	68/146		Private
Kiang Wu Nursing College of Macau (KWNCM)	1999	271/279		27	9	38/36		Private
Macau University of Science and Technology (MUST)	2000	8,334/10,373		399	165	512/564		Private
Macau Institute of Management (MIM)	1984	349/215		2	25	33/27		Private
Macau Millennium College (MMC)***	2001	252/182		7	38	37/45		Private

Notes:
* AIOU stands for The Asia International Open University (Macau), the previous name of CityU.
** IIUM stands for The Inter-University Institute of Macau, a joint initiative by the Catholic University of Portugal and the Diocese of Macau. It is the previous name of USJ.
*** The Macau Millennium College's Chinese name is Zhong Xi Chuangxin Xueyuan (Sino-Western Innovation College), under the auspices of SJM (Sociedade de Jogos de Macau, S.A.), a corporation whose main business is gambling.
Data sources: Mark Bray et al., 2002, pp. 19-26; Tertiary Education Services Office of Macau Government 2007, *2006/2007 niandu jiao zhi yuan ji xuesheng renshu* (The number of teachers and students in 2006/2007), pp. 6-7, https://www.gaes.gov.mo/big5/book/stat2006/stat2006.pdf, accessed July 6, 2018; 2016, *Gao jiao tongji shuju huibian 2016* (Higher education statistical data collection 2016), pp. 10, 21, http://www.gaes.gov.mo/doc/2016/2016statistics-sc.pdf, accessed 30 June 30, 2018.

When the University of East Asia was established, it was for profits and for training in commerce and businesses. UM has inherited this tradition. MPI emphasizes applied and technical disciplines. IFT is similar. So are KWNCM, MSFSS, MIM, and MMC. UM, CityU, USJ, and MUST, while claiming to be comprehensive, all have large programs of business or public administration and other applied disciplines. Only in recent years have some larger institutions like UM and MUST begun to emphasize general education.

Internationalization

According to government statistics, 67.68% of the faculty members are local while 31.95% of them are from mainland China (350 people), Hong Kong (183), Taiwan (64), Europe (52), north America (63), south America (2), and Australia (8) (pp. 6, 11). It should be noted, though, that those who were recruited from outside Macau are treated as local if they have stayed in Macau for more than seven years and obtained permanent residency. As a result, more faculty members are from outside Macau than the numbers show. In other words, there are fewer faculty members originally from Macau. The language of instruction at the UM is English while in other colleges and universities, it is either Cantonese or mandarin Chinese.

About 53.20% (17,423) of the full-time students are local while 45.17% (14,792) of them are from outside Macau (p. 19). But 13,949 of the non-local students are from mainland China, and only 22 from north America, 26 south America, 4 Australia, 160 Europe, 108 Africa, 344 Hong Kong, 64 Taiwan, and 144 other parts of Asia (p. 19). Many are exchange students. One major reason why Macau's HEIs rank higher in internationalization is that mainland China, Hong Kong, and Taiwan students are viewed as international. (UM is ranked among the top 351–400 universities in the world according to the Times Higher Education's World University Rankings 2018.) This is a "political incorrectness" that few think about correcting since it boosts Macau's international ranking. The same is true for Hong Kong's HEIs.

Funding

Funding for colleges and universities is not transparent, but it is generally understood that all public institutions are amply funded by the government and student tuition is only supplementary. The funding for private institutions varies, but usually the government is quite generous in meeting their needs. For example, the large monetary donations by the government to MUST over the years have received a fair amount of criticism. People wondered whether personal connections played a major role. The old campus of UM was allocated to other universities after it moved to Hengqin Island, Zhuhai, adjacent to Macau. Although both IFT and MPI, as public institutions, received some properties, CityU and MUST obtained quite a number of buildings for free. USJ also received a substantial amount of funding for the building of its new campus in Qingzhou, Macau. The funding for R&D for Macau's HEIs, both public and private, is also ample.

Institutional Autonomy and Academic Freedom

The "one country, two systems" formula is supposed to give Macau plenty of autonomy. But as the political situation tightens in mainland China, Macau feels the pressure. Institutional autonomy and academic freedom are increasingly strained. Since 2016, the Office of the Secretary of Social Affairs and Culture of the Macau government, presumably under the direction of the Central Liaison's Office (the representative of the Central Government of China in Macau), has required UM faculty to report all their professional and academic activities with their colleagues in and from Taiwan. In May 2018 the rectors of UM and MUST wrote a letter to Xi Jinping, the Chinese Communist Party's general secretary and the paramount leader of China, allegedly on behalf of all the faculty members in colleges and universities in Macau, pledging to work hard to serve the nation's strategic goals of building a strong country with science and technology. In June, Xi Jinping's office wrote back conveying Xi's hope that Macau will train more and more students who love China and Macau. Thereafter, all major HEIs held meetings to study Xi's directives and wrote in the newspaper that they would follow Xi's instructions and conduct higher education in the "correct" way. The correct way, presumably, is the Party's way with little academic freedom.

There is no tenure system in Macau's HEIs, and no affective faculty associations. Decisions like the recruitment and appointment of rectors, deans, and department chairs are all made by the administration. Professors have little say in faculty recruitment and promotion and curricular design. After two faculty members were fired in 2014 for mostly being politically active (one from UM and the other from USJ), there are few dissident voices in higher education in Macau now.[79] Part-time faculty members have even less academic freedom: 65.30% of the faculty members are full-time while 34.70% of them are part-time (p. 10).

Future Challenges

Macau's Higher Education Law went into effect in August 2018. It stipulates institutional autonomy, but does not mention academic freedom. Apparently academic freedom will continue to be the most fundamental challenge to Macau's higher education. How it fares will depend on the flexibility of the political system in mainland China. For now it is not that promising. UM's ranking in the world may be a good sign, but Macau's HEIs, including UM, still have a long way to go regarding institutional autonomy and academic freedom. Only when they have true institutional autonomy and academic freedom will they be able to deal with other issues like funding and vocationalization and claim to be of true international standing.

As well as providing professional training, higher education also has to emphasize humanities and social sciences as a general requirement for all students. They should not produce what Weber calls "professionals without spirit, sensualists without heart."[80] The mission of a university is to train professionals with an understanding of liberal arts, of how the social world works, so that the graduates can help deal with social problems. Technological advances or a prosperous economy does not guarantee that people will live in a comfortable human and physical environment and be happy. Educational institutions, both middle and postsecondary schools, have yet to shoulder that part of their social responsibility.[81]

Above all the problem is the education of Macau history. As Wu Zhiliang, Clayton, and others point out, without a past, the city and its people would have no future, because they would not understand Macau and would not have a sense of belonging.[82] When Clayton did her studies at the end of the 20th century, she found that none of her interviewees could think of two schools where local history was being taught in any systematic way. It seemed that local history was viewed as being "at once too irrelevant (on certain 'global' scales) and too threatening (on certain 'national' scales) to be canonized as the subject of history."[83] Although this globalization (e.g., colonialism) and localization (e.g., nationalism) make Macau history most fascinating, they also make it most difficult to relate because of nationalist feelings of the Chinese, Macanese, and Portuguese parties involved. So any policies toward a more systematic and universal system of education regarding unified standards, curricula, school-leaving examinations, etc. are bound to meet with resistance from the schools themselves.[84] Facing a clash of civilizations and cultures, people resort to the Macau model, the laissez-faire approach. As a result, both the Chinese and Macanese (Portuguese) used their own educational system for the inculcation and reproduction of their own hegemonic cultural practices and identities.[85] Macau society therefore has become a fractured society in terms of identity and nationality between different ethnic groups.

So problems regarding the local Macau history education still remain: What is "local" (Chinese, Macanese, and/or Portuguese)? What are the proper contents of this history? What is the proper definition of the collective subject of that history? What are the reasons for teaching it? What is the significance of "history" in the process of "making subjects and citizens of a future state?"[86] To meet the political, economic, social, and cultural challenges of a fast-developing city, education in Macau needs to improve. The development of the city needs not only a great number of workers of various kinds, but workers of high caliber. The human resources, both in terms of number and quality, are already lacking in Macau. Without further development of education, Macau may find it even harder to survive in an increasingly competitive world.[87]

Civil Society and Public Sphere

Civil society is an ideal place where citizens will base their own happiness on the happiness of others in the same society, and where social interaction is characterized by mutual respect, tolerance, cooperation, and seeking for common good. It is what Georg Simmel calls "sociability," or what Hegel calls "civil society."[88] Mostly, though, civil society is often considered as the third sector between the state and business corporations, and composed of mostly non-profit and non-governmental organizations. The public sphere, on the other hand, will provide a forum for these social actors, i.e., the state, business corporations, and civil society organizations, to emphasize their commonalities, negotiate their differences, and come up with solutions to social problems. Civil society and public sphere will often serve as a balancing power against the state.[89] But can Macau's civil society and public sphere shoulder this responsibility?[90]

In Macau there are about 8,000 social organizations, an increase of 100% in the past 10 years,[91] including various neighborhood associations, workers' associations, women's associations, youth associations, business associations, and all kinds of Chinese, Macanese, or Portuguese associations. Zhao Xiangyang, the advisor to the Office of the Secretary of Administration and Legal Affairs, comments that although there are so many social organizations and they increase by one each day, none of them is a political organization. They are similar to one another, but no coordinated action between them.[92] Nonetheless, they have played important roles in protecting their members' own interests, although a majority of them are not very interested in fostering a civic consciousness or democratization in Macau.[93] Most of these organizations are managed by political, economic, and social elites who lack interest in democratization, believing that Macau is not ready for further development of it. They are the so-called "social organizations that love Macau and love China," or simply "patriotic social organizations."

There are few organizations that are interested in democratization, like Xin Aomen Xueshe (New Macau Association, or NMA) and Aomen Gongmin Liliang (Macau Civic Power, or MCP). The NMA was founded and made well-known by people like Antonio Ng Kuok Cheong, Au Kam San (both longtime legislators), Paul Chan Wai Chi (a former legislator), etc. It was later taken over by the new generation of leaders like Sulu Sou Ka Ho, Scott Chiang Meng Hin, and Jason Chao Teng Hei. Its current director-in-general is Kam Sut Leng, and Sulu Sou is vice director since he is now an elected legislator.[94] MCP is headed by Agnes Lam Lok Fong, a professor at the University of Macau and also a new legislator and it is less active as NMA in promoting democracy and counter-balancing the state. At any rate, pro-democracy organizations are few and far between to begin with.

In the section on class stratification and politics, we discussed social protests and demonstrations organized by various organizations. Sometimes they produced results. For example, on May 1, 2006, eight social groups organized a demonstration of about 3,000 people protesting the government's policies on importing migrant labor at the expense of Macau workers. Although it went out of order at certain points, the demonstration did press the government and businesses to come up with measures to deal with this sensitive issue. The demonstration in 2014 did press the government to withdraw its legislation that would have benefited the high-level government officials before and after retirement. It seems that if the protests are economic, they are more likely to succeed. If they are political in nature, like democracy, they tend to gain little or no progress as in the movements against the legislation of Article 23 of the Macau Basic Law and for democratization in 2007 and 2008. Sulu Sou led a demonstration against what they believed to be abuse of power by the chief executive, and he was sued for aggravated disobedience and almost lost his legislative position in 2018. Social protest movements are part of the civil society and public sphere. They are a way to coordinate social interests. They have mixed results but are important nonetheless.

As we discussed in chapter 5, the Church has been playing a much smaller role than it did before. The Catholic Church's newspaper, *Aomen Guancha Bao* (*The Observer of Macau*, 澳門觀察報), is often critical of the government on various economic, social, and political issues. But it is not clear how influential the paper is in Macau's politics. Macau's Church seems to be largely following the Macau model, and it remains to be seen whether it will be more active.

There are altogether 50 newspapers in Macau. Other major Chinese newspapers include 澳門日報 (*Macao Daily*), 華僑報 (*Va Kio Daily*, or overseas Chinese daily), 濠江日報 (*Hou Kong Daily*), 力報 (*Exmoo News*), 大眾報 (*Tai Chung Daily*, or people daily), 市民日報 (*Shimin Daily* or citizens' daily), 正報 (*Journal Cheng Pou*), 星報 (*Seng Pou*), 現代澳門日報 (*Today Macao*), 新華澳報 (*Journal San Wa Ou*, or new China and Macao daily), etc. 澳門勞動報 (*Macao Labor*), a critical newspaper, was published for only a short period of in 2008. There are also some weeklies, including 訊報 (*Son Pou*, or *Journal Informacao*, i.e., information weekly), 澳門脈搏 (*Pulso de Macau*, or Macao pulse), 澳門文娛報 (*Recreativo de Macau*, or recreation of Macau), 體育週報 (*Macau Sports Weekly*), etc. There are some monthly journals like 澳門月刊 (*Macao monthly*), 商訊 (*Business Intelligence*), and 九鼎雜誌 (*Jiuding* magazine).

Portuguese and English newspapers and magazines are becoming more and more important in providing a different political voice. There are five Portuguese newspapers: *Journal Tribuna de Macau* (Macau tribune), *Hoje Macau* (Macau today), *Ponto Final* (full stop newspaper), *O Clarim* (clarin), and *Plataforma Macau*

(Macau platform). *O Clarim* is trilingual (Portuguese, Chinese, and English), and *Plataforma Macau* is a new bilingual weekly (Portuguese and Chinese). There are two English newspapers: *Macau Daily Times* and *Macau Post*. In 2017 *Business Daily* shut down its operations after five years on the market. *Macau Business*, an English monthly, is fairly comprehensive in its coverage and critical of the government. There are 273 periodicals in various languages, but most of them are occupational, academic, professional, and governmental, unlike the newspapers and magazines mentioned above.[95] There are other mass media, such as Macau Television, Macau-Asia Television, Lotus Television, Macau Cable Company, Macau Satellite TV, Macau Radio, and various websites.

The news organizations seem numerous for a small place like Macau. Although some newspapers may only have a readership ranging from 1,500 to 3,000, others reach more than 10,000 readers. *Macao Daily* has a circulation of about 100,000 according to some estimates. Together these news organizations could exert a great influence, reflect the concerns of the citizens, and join in the effort to deal with problems. Indeed, they have done so to some extent.

The main problem, however, is that they are following the Macau model, not the improved Macau model. *Macao Daily* is making a special effort to maintain a very cordial relationship with the government and is seldom willing to rock the boat and voice criticism. In the editorial to celebrate its 51st anniversary in 2009, the paper said that it would "continue to correctly understand and propagate the Basic Law, and support the government in its administration based on the law." The editorial said that some people had ulterior motives when they followed the Hong Kong model and wanted to quicken the steps of democratization.[96] Its political stance is fairly clear. *Son Pou* (訊報) is often critical, but it has a small circulation. There is almost no conversation and negotiation of differences among the news organizations over social problems and issues, let alone between the news and other social organizations.[97] But I did hear from a key Portuguese journalist in Macau that the government does translate some Portuguese and English reports in the media into Chinese for the decision-makers' reference.

The fact that the news organizations are subsidized by the government (from MOP$15,000 to 50,000 per month) also makes it difficult for them to be critical. Other social organizations also get support from the government. But only when the various social organizations remain relatively independent and join in the building of a civil society and public sphere can they really make the political system work. The citizens will then be able to elect the most responsible and responsive decision-makers for the city's problems. The successful joint efforts of news and civic organizations in 2006 and 2007 to push the government to set height limits for new skyscrapers close to Songshan Light Tower to protect the values of historical relics are a good example of civil society making an impact on social and economic development. (See Figure 7.4 for a cartoon critical of the government allowing the building of high rises.) There are a couple of other such successful examples, including the protection of "small blue houses" (藍屋仔), houses left from the colonial times, and the redesign of the underground tunnel at the Tashi Square (塔石廣場), but they are still too few.[98]

Freedom of speech is increasingly strained in Macau. Kam Sut Leng, the current president or director-in-general of New Macau Association, was denied a contract at the Sacred Heart primary school in 2013 for her political activism.[99] As we mentioned earlier, two professors were let go in 2014 for their political activities. One student who held up a banner supporting the professor at the University of Macau was fired after three months on the job as a journalist. One reporter from TDM who had asked government officials tough questions was transferred to a desk job that did not allow him/her to do direct interviews. One fruit vendor who gave out free fruits to demonstrators on May 25, 2014 was denied business from GONGOs like neighborhood organizations. The lawyer who talked with one of the professors about a possible lawsuit suddenly stopped communicating with him. Two times in the past, this former professor at the University of Macau was stopped at the customs office at the Macau ferry terminal for an hour before being told to leave, saying that he looked like someone they were looking for.[100] Several journalists have been sued for reporting on various issues ranging from sexual harassment, criticism of business for wrongdoing, negative comments on public personnel, etc.[101]

In a meeting of Hong Kong and Macau studies scholars with the then vice president of the PRC, Li Yuanchao 李源潮, in 2014, Wu Zhiliang 吳志良, the

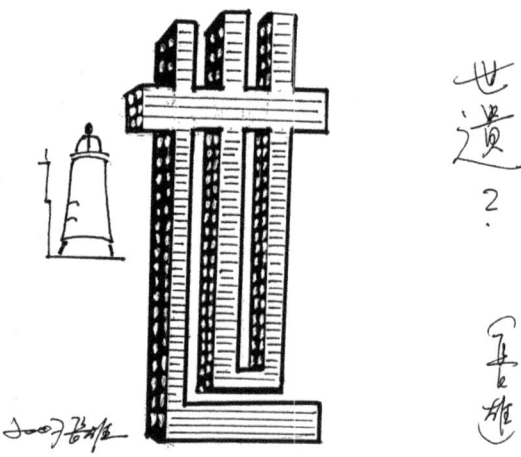

Figure 7.4
World heritages. Courtesy of Chou Cheong Hong.

president of the Macao Foundation (a government organization), claimed that they have already developed a team of academics who "love the country and love Macau." He said that for a long time they have studied, interpreted, and propagated the Macau Basic Law and the central government's policies in Macau with a clear banner and firm stand (旗幟鮮明、立場堅定). They have firmly controlled the way academic discourses go in Macau (牢牢地掌握了學術話語權) and influenced the direction where public opinion goes and where citizens' values are placed (影響了輿論導向和市民價值).[102] All of the above make civil society and public sphere almost impossible, although at least some people are still trying.

Conclusion

In this chapter, we focused only on a few social issues and problems, namely ethnic and class stratification and politics, casino-related crimes and deviance, middle school and postsecondary school education, and civil society and public sphere. There are many other social problems. For example, taxi drivers in Macau are notorious for their refusing to take customers (mostly for distances being too short) (1,574 cases in 2017), making detours so that they can charge more, or even going a normal route but still overcharging the customer (3,180 cases in 2017). The police processed 5,491 cases of taxi driver conduct violations in 2017.[103] The government promised in 2004 to renovate the old and dilapidated buildings, which are simply too many, but 15 years have passed and the government still has not figured out how to do it. Meanwhile, delaying and overspending on public works like the light rail or roads and bridges were widespread. Besides, despite the overspending, the work done is often shoddy and much of it has to be redone like the project on the University of Macau in Hengqin.

The solution to all the social problems we mentioned in this chapter and the coordination of interests between different social groups, ethnic, class or otherwise, depend on a healthy civil society and public sphere, and an effective education that can produce ethical and productive citizens. It also depends on a political system that has checks and balances. But from the discussion in this chapter on social issues and problems and in chapter 2 on politics, we can see that all of these are lacking in Macau. And mainlandization is only exacerbating the social problems, not really solving them. Recognizing the problems is the first step towards solving them. And after all some people from various walks of life are still trying. We will come back to the solution problem in the next chapter.

Plate 5.1

How Mazu saves people on the sea. 劉曉艷, 墉城妙韵, Beijing: 宗教文化出版社, 2008, p. 191.

Plate 5.2

Puji Chanyuan, one of the major Buddhist temples in Macau. Photo by Wang Xin and Zhang Kai.

Plate 5.3
Pictures of St. Mary and Jesus Christ in St. Dominic's Church in Macau. Photo by Jerry Wu.

Plate 5.4
Matteo Ricci and Xu Guangqi 利瑪竇與徐光啟, *Review of Culture* N°21 English Edition, Macau: Instituto Cultural de Macau, 1994, p. 103.

Plate 6.1

Rickshaw men in Macau. Ho Weng Hong, *The Past of Macau*, Macau: Macao Foundation, 1994, p. 162.

Plate 6.2

A contemporary scene of a Catholic procession. Photo by Raymond Wong.

Plate 6.3

Chinese opera singers. Photo by Pan Iok Kin. Camara Municipal das Ilhas, *Retrato das ilhas*, Macau: Camara Municipal das Ilhas, 1995, p. 34.

Plate 6.4
Two examples of the calligraphy as art at A-Ma Temple. Photos by Choi Lap San.

Plate 6.5
Wu Li's Lake, *Sky and Spring* 吳歷《湖天春色圖》. *Review of Culture* N°40 & 41, Macau: Instituto Cultural de Macau, 2000, p. 32.

Plate 6.7
The Bewitching Braid 《大辮子的誘惑》.
Wu Zhiliang and Ieong Wan Chong,
Enciclopedia de Macau, Macau: Macao
Foundation, 1999, p. 112.

Plate 6.6
One of the earliest Chinese painters of
Western style. Wong Yan-Tat, *Macau, As
Time Goes By*, Sunbright Publishing Co.,
1999, p. 115.

Plate 6.8
The Camões Garden by
William Daniell where Luis
de Camões once worked.
Luis Sa Cunha, *Macau di
nos-sa coracam*, Macau: Macao
Foundation, 1999, p. 2.

Plate 6.9
A portrait of George Chinnery. Wu Zhiliang and Ieong Wan Chong, *Enciclopedia de Macau*, Macau: Macao Foundation, 1999, p. 75.

Plate 6.10
Dr. Thomas R. Colledge and his patients. Chen Jichun, 錢納利與澳門 *Qian Nali yu Aomen*, Macau Foundation, 1995, p. 194.

Plate 6.11
The ruins of St. Paul's Cathedral and the vicinity by William Heine (1858). Lei Pang Chu, *Macao China*, Macau: Macao Daily News, 1999, p. 7.

Plate 6.12
A-Ma Temple by William Heine (1896). *Review of Culture* N°33, Macau: Instituto Cultural de Macau, 1997, p. 129.

Plate 6.13
Access to the Taipa island (1960s). Camara Municipal das Ilhas and Associacao de Historia de Macau, *Fotografias Antigas das Ilhas da Taipa e de Coloane*, Macau: Camara Municipal das Ilhas and Associacao de Historia de Macau, 1994, p. 49.

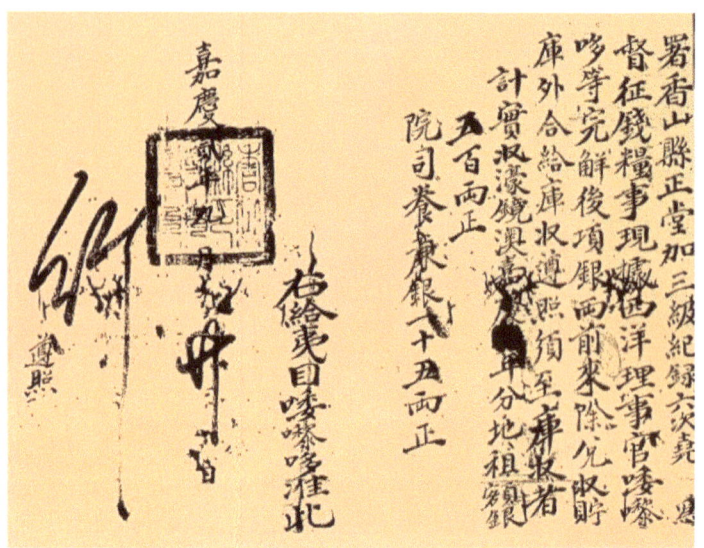

Plate 8.1

The rent receipt given to the Portuguese officials by the local Chinese government in Xiangshan. 孔繁壯, 陳伯良, 劉雅煌, *Macau*, Macau: 澳門出版社, 2002, p. 38.

Plate 8.2

The return of Macau to China. 兩國總理在交換簽署文本後握手致賀, ("Two premiers shake hands after exchanging the signed agreement") April 13, 1987. *Macao Daily News*, 澳門歷史的見證, Macau: Macao Daily News, 1987, p. 3.

8 Conclusions
Toward a Macauan Identity

> These days I have a U.S. passport and a Portuguese passport. I have a Hong Kong ID card and a Macau ID card. I have a Salvo-Conduto, which is a pass allowing Portuguese passport-holders to enter Hong Kong and stay for seven days. I have a *yihng biht jing* [認別證—a national ID card for Portuguese citizens, or Bilhete de Identidade de Cidadão Nacional], a U.S. Social Security card, a re-entry permit for Hong Kong, a re-entry permit for the U.S., a "home-returning" permit (回鄉證) for the mainland, four valid drivers' licenses (Macau, Hong Kong, U.S., and Canada) and one expired one (Taiwan).
>
> A middle-aged Macau Chinese businessman talking about some of his ID cards[1]

In light of a Macauan identity, the above quote shows that a person may not want to be pinned down to a single place, and it is advantageous to have many identities.[2] What is unique about Macau is its multiple identity, an identity similar to but also different from that of the mainland or Hong Kong. In this final chapter, we will discuss Macau's national/cultural, political, and economic identities, especially the reconstruction of them.

Defining National and Political Identities

When people use the term "national identity," they may mean either identification with a nation (民族), with a state (國家), and/or with a nation-state (民族國家). For Anderson, Smith, and others, the main characteristics of a nation are a relevant common history, shared cultural roots, pre-existing social networks, and a designated homeland.[3] Culture is also very important for Gellner: he thinks that people are in the same nation "if and only if they share the same culture, where culture in turn means a system of ideas and signs and associations and ways of behaving and communicating."[4] In addition, they have to recognize each other as belonging to the same nation. Underlying these characteristics are what we call primordial and perennial ethnic bonds filled with feelings and emotions.[5]

National identity can also mean identification with a state. From a Weberian point of view, the state is an organization that makes the rules and regulations within a given territory and that has the sole right to use violence in the enforcement of its order.[6] From a Marxian point of view, the state is a tool for one group of people to suppress other groups. From a traditional political science point of view, the state is composed of territory, people, government, and sovereignty.[7] Each state has a political system, which can be democratic, authoritarian, or totalitarian, that is, different ways of domination within a given territory.

A third kind of national identity is the identification with a nation-state. This could be a nation-state composed of only one's own nation, or of multiple nationalities. Less than 10% of all the nations in the United Nations are single nation-states, and most are multiethnic. Thus, broadly speaking, a nation-state is *"a state which the great majority of the citizens identify with to the extent of seeing it as their own"* (italics original).[8] One's national identity would be with both the nation and the state, where the state can be composed either of mostly one's own nation (單民族國家) or of multiple ethnicities (多民族國家).

In our discussion of national identity of the people in Macau, we will distinguish between these kinds of national identity: identification with a nation is *national identity*, and identification with a state is *political identity*. After the discussion of these two identities, we will see in what way *new national (socio-cultural)* and *political identities* might be built. Then we will discuss the *economic identity* of Macau. Finally, we will see whether a quasi nation-state, or *city-state*, defined as a political and cultural community where the national (socio-cultural) and the political are largely congruent, can be built. The characteristics of this community would distinguish Macau from other places in Greater China, i.e., mainland China, Hong Kong, or Taiwan.[9]

National Identity in Macau

Clayton asked the middle-aged Macau Chinese businessman quoted above whether he would prefer Macau to remain under Portuguese sovereignty rather than return to the PRC. "Well," the man replied with a smile:

> I'm not in the position [to answer your question]. All I know is that if you forced me to choose between calling myself American, Portuguese or Chinese, I would say that I am American. And if you really forced me, if you held a gun to my head and forced me to choose between being Portuguese and being a citizen of the PRC, I would have to call myself Portuguese. Even though I have not the slightest relation with anything Portuguese—I don't speak the language, I don't like the people or the Portuguese character. But if you forced me, that's the decision I would make.

You know the saying "*ren ru fu zhong*" (忍辱負重)—choosing the lesser of the two evils, there's not much of a choice.[10]

First, the man wants to be flexible, to choose the identity that most benefits him under the circumstance. Second, he is Chinese, with historical and cultural roots in China, and related to the Chinese by blood, i.e., the primordial bonds we mentioned above. He apparently speaks Cantonese, and uses a Chinese saying in the statement. His Chinese cultural identity is reinforced by his claim that he does not have the slightest relation with anything Portuguese. Third, he does not want to identify with the political term "PRC," which has vacillated between authoritarianism and dictatorship since the reform and opening. So politically he would rather identify with the United States or Portugal, which represents democracy.

His case might be typical of many Macau Chinese if they were given a choice. In a 2005 survey done on the quality of life in Macau, researchers found that only 41.4% of the respondents identified with China, while 37.5% identified with Macau, 20.2% identified with both, and 1.2% with neither.[11] The term "China" could refer to Chinese culture and history, or to Chinese politics, in which case it would mean the PRC. Culturally, over 95% of the people in Macau are Chinese. So according to our definition above, the "national identity" of over 95% of the people in Macau should be Chinese. There might be some Chinese who are almost entirely Americanized or Europeanized, but they are few. Others might identify to a certain extent with American or European cultures. The majority of the Chinese people in Macau can be said to identify with the Chinese culture and history to the greatest extent. *So we can say that the national identity of the Macau Chinese is by and large Chinese*, in spite of what the polls may say.

But the national identity of the Macanese would be different. In chapters 4, 5, and 6, we discussed the conflicted Macanese identity. They might feel Chinese—in addition to the mixed blood, they tend to speak Cantonese, although most of them do not write Chinese, and they follow some Chinese customs. But on the other hand, they tend to feel that they are Portuguese by culture and history. They mostly speak Portuguese and follow Portuguese customs. According to a 1998 survey, an overwhelming majority of Macanese thought that they were Portuguese all their lives, and should continue to be so after 1999. As one prominent Macanese woman commented,

> In my case, I have no doubts that … I will be Portuguese after 1999. I could never manage, culturally, to feel that I am Chinese, even though I can understand the Chinese way of being and have no problem in accepting Chinese values. Since childhood I have been taught at home that I am Portuguese, and people will not abandon their values simply because Macau is no longer a territory under Portuguese administration.[12]

Some thought that to ask them to choose nationality after the handover was ridiculous. "Nationality, like race, is something that cannot be 'chosen'; it is the basis for heritage, the truth behind culture, a fundamental and immutable building block of identity."[13] So even if the Macanese might feel conflicted sometimes, by and large *the Macanese national identity is Portuguese*, culturally and politically.

In sum, culturally and historically there should be no doubt that over 95% of the Macau population is by and large Chinese. The Macanese may experience some kind of ambiguity but they no doubt identify with Portuguese culture and history. For both groups, their political identity can be different from their cultural and historical identity.

State or Political Identity in Macau

State or political identity refers to the identification of a political system embodied by the state. For the most part of Macau's history, the state political system in Macau was characterized by joint sovereignty[14] and dual jurisdiction of Chinese and Portuguese control. As a result, just like the national identity, *the Chinese largely identified with the Chinese state, although there seem to be some changes in contemporary times, while the Portuguese and Macanese have largely identified with the Portuguese state*. Since there were no surveys done in the past, we base our judgment upon what we know from history.

As discussed in chapter 2, neither the Ming nor the Qing government of China ever gave up the total sovereignty of Macau to Portugal. The Portuguese government in Macau had been paying rent to the Chinese government for about 300 years until Amaral took power in Macau as its governor in 1846.[15] (See Plate 8.1 for an example of the rent receipt.) In the first 300 years of Portuguese control of Macau, the Chinese affairs in Macau were managed mainly by the Chinese government stationed either in Wangxia (Mong Ha), Macau, or in Qianshan in what is now Zhuhai. The Macau Chinese identified with the Chinese government more than with the Portuguese, as can be seen from the various conflicts throughout history such as the assassination of Amaral in 1849, which we discussed in chapter 2.

Even after the signing of the Luso-Chinese Treaty of Friendship and Trade in 1887 when the Chinese government allowed the Portuguese "perpetual occupation and government," there were border delineation issues that were never resolved.[16] In the 20th century, this sense of belonging to China, first the Republic of China (ROC), and later the People's Republic of China (PRC) on the part of many Chinese people, especially for the business elites, was even stronger. One might recall the scene of the Portuguese governor presenting the signed agreement in 1967 to the Chinese elites under the portrait of Mao and the Chinese national flag. A *pailou* would be built by the Chinese in celebration of the Chinese national holiday in

Macau even during Macau's relatively full colonial period in the 1960s. The fact that it was facing the Leal Senado has more than a symbolic meaning.

Part of this feeling of belonging may have to do with a dislike of the Portuguese government more than a fondness of the Chinese government. One of Clayton's interviewees says, "I mean that I still believe the Portuguese are invaders. I still consider them to be invaders. Whether by force, militarily, or economically, politically, religiously, whatever—they are invaders. This is not their place, but they have stayed here for four hundred years."[17] Many Macau Chinese people's enthusiastic welcome of the handover of Macau to China may be an indication of the same feeling. Here is Clayton's description of a crowd watching the ceremony on television: "When the camera zeroed in for the first time on the soldiers of the People's Liberation Army, a great cheer went up from the crowd. The first close-up of Jiang Zemin watching the soldiers elicited another long, loud cheer."[18] The Chinese in Macau for most of the 450 years of history were governed by a Chinese administration and they largely identified with the Chinese monarchy first, and then the ROC and PRC.

The Macau Chinese identification with the Chinese government and political system, however, was not uniform or consistent. There is no doubt that in contemporary times the Chinese identification with the Portuguese political system, which the MSAR has largely inherited, has also been extensive. That is why the 2005 survey found only 41.1% of the Chinese in Macau identifying with China—most likely in political terms, 37.5% with Macau, and 20.2% with multiple identities.[19] In a pre-1999 survey, researchers found that only 0.5% of the respondents felt proud of the PRC's socialist political system.[20]

In other words, a majority of the Macau Chinese do not identify with the PRC. In 2012, the Macau Federation of Trade Unions published a survey on Macau citizens' national identity. It showed that only 15.9% of the youths below 18 years old and 21% of the youths between 18 and 24 years old identified themselves as Chinese.[21] This apparently refers to their political identity rather than cultural and historical identity. Most people in Macau have a Chinese national identity, but not necessarily a Chinese state and political identity; some may hold a Portuguese passport (see Plate 8.2 for a picture symbolizing the formal return of Macau to China). That is probably what the middle-aged Macau Chinese businessman meant when he said he did not want to identify with the PRC.

That is exactly why the Party-state is making a great effort in securing the Macau Chinese people's loyalty by enticing the youths to attend higher education in mainland China, as we have discussed in chapter 7, and organize all kinds of activities for people from all walks of life in Macau to visit the mainland to be educated about what they believe to be the glorious history of the Party and the great achievements of the past 40 years. This way people in Macau will hopefully pledge their allegiance to the Chinese political state.

The state is successful to some extent but still, as a number of surveys find out, over 51% to 56% of the population continues to believe in universal suffrage.[22] Dictatorship or authoritarianism is still a hard sell in Macau despite the continuing mainlandization. For many Chinese, their Portuguese passports become more than a "travel document," different from what the Chinese government wanted to believe.[23] In other words, they may not like the mainland Chinese government, but they probably do not deny that they are Chinese, unlike some in Taiwan. Their Chinese national identity is fairly clear, before or after the return of Macau to China.[24] but their political identity is far from certain.

On the other hand, the Portuguese and the Macanese before 1999 were governed by a Portuguese administration and they identified with the Portuguese government. They generally would not identify with the Chinese monarchy, the ROC's or the PRC's dictatorship or authoritarianism. In fact, before the handover, they feared "that the Chinese government would consider the Macanese, by virtue of their Chinese ancestry and birth in a 'Chinese territory,' to be Chinese nationals, and thus subject to the same laws (read: the same restrictions on movement, religious activity, free speech, and so on) as any other Chinese citizen."[25] If they may be Chinese to some extent in terms of national identity, they were fairly certain that they did not want to become Chinese politically. As some Macanese explained:

> It's not that we don't like the Chinese … After all, we all have Chinese blood, we are part of Chinese, too. It's just that the communists have proven, time and again, that they can't be trusted. They promise one thing and then turn around and do the opposite.[26]

The reasons they consider themselves to be Chinese in some ways and not Chinese in other ways point to a difference between national and state/political identities.

Building a New National/Cultural Identity

Forming a new national/cultural identity requires that people increase the understanding of commonalities and appreciate each other's differences while defining the new identity, and that they be creative as cultural entrepreneurs in forming this new identity. This is the new Macau model we have been talking about.

First, there is a need to understand the shared cultural and historical heritages. Macau has a long and rich history. While serving as a trading center in Asia before the 19th century, Macau was also the center for cultural exchange in the East. Macau has contributed to the production of what we may call the first group of Sinologists as well as Westernologists, or what we call today the experts in China and Western studies. They include Michele Ruggieri (1543–1607), Matteo Ricci (1552–1610), both Italian Jesuits; Philippe Couplet and Ferdinand Verbiest, both Belgian Jesuits; Joseph Bahr and Johann Adam Schall von Bell (1591–1666), both German Jesuits;

Thomas Pereira, a Portuguese Jesuit; and Robert Morrison, a British Protestant. (See chapter 5.) These missionaries and scholars introduced Western culture to China and Chinese culture to the West, including philosophy, religion, literature, and science.

Macau contributed to the production of these scholars because the latter tended to have studied Chinese in Macau, and most of them were, in fact, graduates of St. Paul's College in Macau established in 1606, one of the first Western-style colleges in East Asia and certainly the first in China. Indeed, as we discussed in chapter 5, out of the 400 Jesuit missionaries in China during the Ming and Qing dynasties, 200 were graduates from this college. The college also trained about 40 Chinese missionaries, including the famous poet and painter, Wu Li. The first Western-style primary school was also established in Macau and it produced prominent figures in the cultural exchange between China and the West, such as Yung Wing and Huang Kuan.

Even though all of the above achievements seem to belong to the Portuguese, they would not have been possible without the participation and help of the Chinese. The Chinnery picture of two Chinese helping Morrison translate the Bible is more than symbolic of the cooperation between the two sides in the East-West cultural exchange. It is a source of pride in the cultural heritage.

In addition to producing scholars and officials of cultural exchange in its Western-style educational institutions, Macau as a cultural center has also witnessed the coexistence of Daoism, Buddhism, Christianity, and a number of other religions. Although interaction among the religions is limited, we do see occasional products of religious and cultural exchange. The façade of the Church of St. Paul, for example, embodies statues of the Virgin and saints, symbols of the Garden of Eden and the Cruxifixion, angels and the devil, Portuguese sailing ship, on the one hand, and a Chinese dragon and a Japanese chrysanthemum, and a pious warning inscribed in Chinese on the other hand. The church itself is a work of Western, Japanese, and Chinese architects.[27]

The emergence and existence of the Macanese community is probably the best example of such cultural integration. As explored in chapters 4 and 6, the Macanese are a result of interracial marriage, a form of social interaction.

Thus in terms of commonalities, Macau has the traditions of cultural exchange as embodied in Ricci, Morrison, Wu Li, and Yung Wing, of religious coexistence as embodied in the coexistence of St. Paul's Cathedral and the Temple of Nezha, and of cultural integration as embodied in the Macanese. These form their common history. It is characterized by cosmopolitanism notwithstanding all the conflicts that have occasionally erupted in Macau's long history. This is something that Macau needs to continue to cultivate, treasure, and expand.

Second, different ethnic groups and cultures may still have their own separate existence, but they need to appreciate each other's differences. For example, the Chinese have their own social organizations, with predominantly Chinese members.[28]

The Macanese/Portuguese have their organizations as well, such as Macau Home of Portuguese Association, Macau Club, Macanese Play Troupe, Macau Song and Dance Troupe, the Holy House of Mercy, the Oriental Foundation, the International Institute of Macau, and the Macanese Education Promotion Association.[29] All these social organizations are supposed to protect the political, economic, and social interests of their members, preserve their cultural characteristics and properties, cooperate with other social organizations in Macau, and work with the governmental organizations over issues of their concern.[30] But different organizations, especially from different ethnic groups, need to understand and appreciate each other's meaning and significance and be able to work together on social issues and problems, as an effective civil society and public sphere require.

When discussing the future of the Macanese community, Brookshaw points out, "The preservation of their identity through cultural and solidarity associations wherever they have settled, would indicate that they, like the Goans or even migrant Portuguese, are capable of blending attachment to roots with a pragmatically cosmopolitan attitude."[31] Similarly, Macau needs to reconcile tradition with modernity, and market itself as a center of culture, capitalizing on its different character, such as a multicultural, borderland personality, and emphasizing its cosmopolitanism, rather than being characterized by some sort of universal and culturally amnesic homogeneity under the forces of modernity and globalization or even "mainlandization."[32] The latter is a real threat.

Third, there will have to be some cultural entrepreneurs from all groups, who understand the issues involved and have the skills to execute solutions. They should then be able to create a new national/cultural, cosmopolitan identity that is characteristic of Macau, a multiple national identity with different ethnic and cultural emphasis but still characterized by cosmopolitanism. It is a Macauan national/cultural identity, sharing a relevant common history, cultural characteristics, social networks, and a designated homeland.

Postcolonialism can also shed some light on our study of the Macau story. Postcolonial theory asserts that Western knowledge and culture dominated the colonies in the past, and continue to dominate now. Orientalism, for example, viewed the West as rational and civilized, and the East as irrational, uncivilized, and lacking. This kind of thinking has become deeply rooted in the psyche of both the former colonizers and the colonized. The colonial discourse was, in fact, fractured, incomplete, contradictory, ambivalent, and undecided, as other postcolonial theorists point out. The West and the East were not binary distinctions. So the challenge for postcolonial theory is also our challenge, to produce alternative knowledge that will not reproduce the binary thinking of Orientalism.[33] Rather, it will be characterized by cosmopolitanism.

A new Macauan identity is still in the making, facing the challenge of reconciling the differences in the Chinese and Portuguese identities into one Macauan identity without sacrificing one's own ethnic identities, using their abundant historical heritages.³⁴ Such a rich and complex cultural and social identity of Macau can provide precious lessons for today's multicultural and multiethnic societies all over the world.

Building a New Political Identity in Macau

It seems that a majority of the people in Macau do not identify with the PRC political system. But within the constraints of the "one country, two systems" formula, there is still some room for Macau's own political design although that room is being challenged in the Xi Jinping era.

In terms of the political system, Macau's identity is not that clear, but it contains certain democratic elements. Since the 1970s, the Legislative Council became independent of the governor, and 6 of the 17 legislators were elected by the populace, 6 by functional constituencies, and 5 appointed by the governor. Since the return of Macau to China, the chief executive has also been elected, although he was elected by 300 to 400 representatives of functional constituencies only, not by the entire population. The number of popularly elected legislators has increased. Although Macau is not a full democracy yet, there has been more democracy than before.

At a youth meeting in Macau to commemorate the 55th anniversary of the founding of the People's Republic of China in 2004, Bai Zhijian, the director of the Central Liaison's Office in Macau, said that the number one historical mission of the young people in Macau is the building of democratic politics under the principle of "one country, two systems," where people from different ethnicities, classes, beliefs, and cultures can express their opinions and be heard.³⁵ He said that this system will be different from the one under the colonial rule, and different from China's.

But 15 years later, the way to building a democratic polity is still not clear. As we discussed in chapter 2, Macau's politics is moving away from democracy. Under such circumstances, can Macau still distinguish itself from the mainland? Can the "one country, two systems" principle survive? Can Macau build a civil society similar to that of Hong Kong, if not better?³⁶ Can people in Macau eventually select their chief executive and their legislators through popular elections, i.e., universal suffrage notwithstanding the current setbacks in Hong Kong and Macau?

In chapter 2, we discussed Chief Executive Edmund Ho's hope that he would clearly distinguish himself from the Portuguese administration. When commenting on the implementation of Article 23 in the Basic Law, he also said that he would not have to wait for Hong Kong to do something first. That, he did succeed at. But other than that, neither he nor his successor has done much to make Macau stand out. Even in the legislation of Article 23 Ho picked a much less urgent issue to legislate but left the urgent ones out. If anything, Macau is more and more like mainland China, and Hong Kong is more and more like Macau, politically. Government officials believe that they should be more responsible to the central government than to the people in Macau since they are appointed by the former, not the latter. The executive branch would be hesitant to pass laws that would restrict their power and the power of the capitalist class, no matter whether it is about universal suffrage or lawmaking related to legislative check on government spending or the collective bargaining power of workers.

In the past 20 years, the relationship between the Legislative Assembly and the executive branch simply has deteriorated compared with the Portuguese Macau period. Susana Chou, the chair of the Legislative Assembly, complained when retiring from the position in 2009 that before the handover, both the executive branch and the legislative branch could introduce bills, but after the handover, the latter has almost no power to introduce bills. Even when they did, they would be turned down by the executive branch on various pretexts.[37] That has not changed.

Many boast that Macau is a model of "one country, two systems." But without universal suffrage for both the chief executive and the legislative assembly, and without a strong civil society and public sphere, it is a questionable example. Rather, by resisting democratization and freedom of speech, it is already lagging behind Hong Kong, far behind Taiwan, and setting a poor example for a virtual Chinese confederation.

Indeed, Macau could help build a federal or confederal state of China in the future, with Taiwan included, by correcting all these problems.[38] With Macau and Hong Kong governed by Macau and Hong Kong people respectively and a high degree of autonomy, the "one country, two systems" formula is already resembling federalism, or even confederalism, since the two systems have vast differences in political arrangements, economic rules and regulations, and legal codes.[39] Macau and Hong Kong also have a fair amount of international relations.[40] But whether Macau can build a better political system within a virtual Chinese confederation is not clear. Politically Macau has yet to form a progressive identity.

What Macau has difficulty doing now contradicts its image in the past. In the 450 years of history, in addition to the role of cultural exchange, Macau also played a commendable political role. For example, both the Ming and Qing governments used Macau as a place for asylum for foreigners. Following the signing of the Nanjing Treaty in 1842, several foreign ministers even settled in Macau.[41] For several centuries, Macau also took in those who were fleeing from religious and political persecution in China and Japan.[42] At the end of the Qing dynasty, the reformers established their newspaper in Macau, *Zhi Xin Bao* (知新報), advocating Western culture and politics and calling for reforms in China. Zheng Guanying wrote his famous book "Warnings to the prosperous age" here in Macau. Both the families of Kang Youwei and Liang Qichao took refuge in Macau when their reform failed. In the Nationalist Revolution, Sun Yat-sen and his comrades planned their movements in Macau and received various support in Macau.[43]

Conclusions

During World War II, Macau provided a refuge to not only the mainlanders, but also Hong Kongers and Hong Kong Portuguese. Coates describes World War II as Macau's "finest hour" because it gave help "to untold thousands of Hong Kong People reduced to destitution and starvation…."[44] Over 40,000 people sought refuge in Macau—"The city was filled with refugees."[45] It hosted intellectuals supporting the Chinese Communist Party (CCP), including Fan Changjiang, Liang Shumin, Xia Yan, Jin Shan, Liang Zhonghua, who later went back to the mainland via Macau. Macau also provided medical assistance to the CCP army's resistance against Japan and sanctuary for the Nationalists.[46] There were in Macau representatives of both the Nationalists of the KMT and Wang Jingwei's Nanjing government that cooperated with the Japanese in their occupation of China. Even in 1946 to 1948, the KMT exerted dominant influence over 30 social organizations in Macau.[47] Although that influence was subsiding after the founding of the PRC, it did not completely disappear until 1966 when the 12-3 Incident changed the political landscape.[48]

Indeed, Macau's politically helpful role in the development of events in China throughout its history is more than commendable. The reason why the CCP government did not want to take Macau back after the founding of the PRC is that Macau did serve a function to break the economic blockade of China by the Western powers. "Macao became a passageway for enormous amounts of products that were indispensable for the survival of Mao's regime: petrol, metals, cars, chemical products, etc. These were purchased by the PRC's representative in the Territory, the Nam Kwong Consortium."[49] One of those important products was gold, which China needed to purchase on the international markets. Mr. Ho Yin had the monopoly in dealing gold in Macau, which partly explains his exceptional relationship with the CCP.[50] (Ho Yin was Edmund Ho's father.) So Mao himself said that they were not in a hurry to solve the problems of Hong Kong and Macau, especially because they could use these territories to develop foreign relations and foreign trade. And the PRC policy was to "make long term plans [with Hong Kong and Macau] and make the best use of them" (長期打算，充分利用).[51]

Macau could certainly do better than it does now politically. It has refused entry of democracy activities, writers, journalists, and academics whom the government thinks are threatening its rule or the rule of the mainland government.[52] But it does not have to. Instead, it should strive to be a model "province" of Greater China in its openness, tolerance, and democratization. Idealistic as it may sound, Macau could stand out as a positive model as long as it can truly utilize its tradition and make wise transformations. Macau could be famous for its culture and politics, not just for its gambling industry.

Building a New Economic Identity in Macau

As we discussed in chapters 3 and 7, Macau is known for being a gambling city; gambling contributes to about 80% of the city's revenues. But the gaming industry can vastly improve itself in responsible gaming and Macau's service sector can expand to include more tourist attractions.

Responsible Gambling and Corporate Social Responsibility

Blaszczynski et al. define responsible gambling as "policies and practices designed to prevent and reduce potential harms associated with gambling; these policies and practices often incorporate a diverse range of interventions designed to promote consumer protection, community/consumer awareness and education, and access to efficacious treatment."[53] As it is practiced now, its main target is individuals who have a gambling problem, and the gambling operator's responsibility is to properly inform the gamblers about the risks. Similarly, Victorian Gaming Machine Industry says that responsible gaming is for the industry to offer products and services in a way that facilitates customers' ability to enjoy gaming and for each person to exercise a rational and sensible choice while playing.[54]

But as we argued in chapter 7, while it is the gambler's own action, gaming providers have to exercise "a duty of care" and take reasonable and necessary steps in preventing problem gambling. They "must not knowingly exploit or take advantage of any player, in particular, vulnerable individuals manifesting characteristics associated with gambling-related problems."[55] In order for the player to make rational choices, gambling providers must inform the player of the probabilities and likelihood of winning, and payout schedules. Their advertising and promotional activities should present no misleading information or misrepresentation of the likelihood of winning. Above all, they should do much more intervention.

Others have also discussed how casino operators may interact with the community. Pitcher, for example, discusses what they do with community interest groups, including 1) high profile sponsorships of theater, music, ballet, entertainment and sporting events; 2) ongoing fund-raising for many charities in the city; 3) funds for problem gambling handled by an independent trust, used by local treatment providers; and 4) promotion of sensible gambling by working closely with local problem gambling treatment providers and offering to pay for the first consultation of problem customers.[56]

Responsible gambling is dealing with the relationship between the corporation and the customer and community, but ideally it would fulfill the requirements as set forth by the principles of corporate social responsibility (CSR), which answer to all the seven stakeholders. As we discussed in chapter 3, they are shareholders, employees, customers, suppliers, competitors, government, and civil society organizations (or the community). Here is the summary of the obligations of casinos (specifically those in Macau) to CSR's seven stakeholders:[57]

Shareholders: These are the investing companies and individuals. Casinos are supposed to make money for them, and in Macau, they do. In fact Macau has surpassed Las Vegas in its gambling earnings. They were doing very well in this regard even in times of financial difficulties in 2008/09.

Employees: Casinos are supposed to provide fair pay, decent benefits, good working conditions (e.g., non-smoking environment), problem gambling prevention programs, 24-hour hot-lines for help, etc. Macau casinos pay better than most other industries and provide more decent benefits and working conditions, especially after the liberalization of the gaming industry, and there is now some competition in attracting employees. The casinos in Macau have problem gambling prevention programs for their employees but their effectiveness is questionable, as we discussed in chapter 7.

Customers: As we discussed in chapter 7, casinos in Macau have programs that help gamblers to prevent problem gambling, but they are not effective. Gamblers are yet to be informed of the likelihood of winning and losing and helped with problem gambling. Some casinos do donate money to social organizations that help prevent problem gambling or treating problem gamblers. But first of all, such help centers are too few in Macau. Second, they can help only a very small number of addicted gamblers. Third, most of the problem gamblers are from the mainland, and help is almost not available to them. Fourth, most importantly there are no effective intervention programs as those discussed in chapter 7. Casinos have a long way to go in fulfilling their obligations to the gamblers while taking money from their pockets.

Suppliers: Casinos are supposed to make sure that suppliers are following the supplier codes of conduct, whether these are contractors building casinos for them, or suppliers of human labor, gaming machines, or food, and make sure that no human rights violations are involved in the supply chain. When construction workers for casino companies complain that they do not get their pay in time, or when mainland workers are still charged a fee every month by the employment agencies, casino companies have an obligation to help redress these issues. But they do not seem to care about them because they are not directly involved in their contractors' business. CSR requires, however, that they should be concerned and take action of some kind.

Competitors: How to cooperate while competing with other companies within the industry is another challenge for casinos. Casino operators in Macau have established their own business association but it does not really function. Rather, it should regulate their practices such as how much commission they will give to the middlemen and women who bring in VIP customers. More importantly, the association should research and coordinate their gambling prevention and intervention programs. Whether the association will do all of these things remains to be seen, but it is something they have to do as socially responsible companies. The government should step in if the casinos do not do them.

The government: Are casinos maintaining a professional relationship with the government, with little or no corrupt practices, or are they colluding with corrupt officials for their own gain? We discussed these in chapter 3 and the picture is not nice. The lack of transparency in the relationship between the casinos and the government makes one doubt whether casinos play a positive role in building a clean and responsible government.

Community interest groups or the community as a whole: Casinos need to maintain cordial relationships with the community, to be responsive to their complaints, and to have concrete measures to help improve the quality of life in the community. One of the difficulties that arises from the development of the casino industry is the traffic jams. As responsible corporations, casinos need to be engaging the community in finding ways to solve this and other problems.

Only when casinos have done the above can we consider Macau's gaming industry as an exemplar of success in responsible gambling. Macau will then have an admirable new economic identity as far as gaming is concerned. That of course is not enough, hence the following expansions of the service sector to build a city of culture and a world destination of tourism and recreation (世界旅遊休閒中心).

To Build a City of Culture and a World Class Destination of Tourism and Recreation

In December 2008 the National Committee on Development and Reform (國家發展和改革委員會) issued an outline on the development of the Pearl River Delta from 2008 to 2020, and subsequently in June, the State Council passed an outline for the development of Hengqin, inviting Macau to join in the project. According to the national development outline, Macau will be built into a world destination of tourism and recreation. These new developments should provide an opportunity for Macau to evolve into a city of culture rather than a city of sin.

We might be able to envision some things that Macau can do, and they should all be part of Macau's cultural and tourist industry.[58] For example, among other things, Macau can have:

> A museum that features Macau's history and society, the history of Macau's role in the cultural exchange between the East and the West, the history of the relationship between Macau and other world powers and between Macau and

mainland China, the emergence and development of the Macanese, as well as the ups and downs of Macau's economic development.

A museum on gambling, featuring Macau's gambling history as well as the probability of winning and losing on the part of the casinos and the gamblers respectively. There should be hands-on game playing facilities to demonstrate the probability of winning and losing. There should also be presentations of problem gambling stories, on international best practices of problem gambling prevention and intervention, and on casino-related crimes and deviance.

A tourist route that includes the restored ancient government houses, shipyards, hotels, pawnshops, prisons, casinos, etc. This should give people a physical impression of the history of Macau's politics, economics, culture, and society.[59]

A tourist route that features all kinds of streets that exhibit Macau history. Examples include those that represent trade and industrial development (Avenida Infante D. Henrique 殷皇子大馬路, Ruo do Chunabeiro 燒灰爐街, Ruo das Estalagens 草堆街, Rua da Felicidade 福隆新街), and military and political development (the Portuguese boarder gate 關閘拱門, streets and places named after Amaral and Mesquita, the street where the ancient Chinese customs house was 關前正街, and Estrada da Vitoria or Victory Road 得勝大馬路), etc.[60]

Religious tourism that will feature Macau's churches and temples, including a "tourist route" that will connect them and with their histories explained to tourists.

In its MICE (Meetings, Incentives, Conferences, Events) industry, Macau can hold conventions that feature religion—to bring different religions together—cultural exchanges, post-colonial development, etc., in addition to gaming and other commercial meetings.[61]

Manufacturing and selling of tourist gifts based on Macau's history, culture, and society.

These are in addition to the food festivals, music festivals, sports festivals, fireworks festivals, film festivals, car races (Macau Grand Prix), various trade fairs, as well as other traditional Chinese and Western festivals. They would be in addition to what Zhuhai would build in Hengqin, such as theme parks and golf courses. In fact, the tourist industry from the neighboring areas like Zhuhai and Hong Kong should be able to complement each other, each with its own features unique to the city.

In 2005, the UNESCO placed Macau's historic sites on its World Heritage List. There has been a momentum to do something about Macau's history and culture, but people seem uncertain as to what. In fact, many have long called for developing a tourist industry. João Manuel Costa Antunes 安棟樑, the former director of

Macau Government Tourism Office, states that the most valuable heritage that the Portuguese have left in Macau is the people, i.e., the Macanese.[62] Maria Helena de Senna Fernandes 文綺華, the current director of the Tourism Office, hopes that the Portuguese language, social organizations, food, etc. will be preserved; otherwise, Macau would lose its characteristics.[63] But it is also a challenge to put the maintenance and preservation of Macanese culture in practical terms and to make it part of the tourist industry.

Most importantly, developing more cultural integration does not mean just playing Portuguese folk songs with Chinese instruments, as Manuel Goncalves points out.[64] It is not only about cultural transformation and cultural reconstruction, as claimed by Jin Guoping and Wu Zhiliang, but also about cultural presentation.[65] That presentation should also feature the Chinese historical heritages, including the restoration of some ancient government houses, shipyards, hotels, pawnshops, prisons, and casinos.[66]

This cultural industry needs also the support of other development, including the improvement in human and physical environment. If Macau is going to be more and more like mainland China politically, i.e., more authoritarian and less democratic (see Figure 8.1), and if the public transportation continues to be as bad as it is now, with too many impolite bus drivers and errant taxi drivers, Macau will not be able to do what we have suggested above to attract tourists, and the so-called world destination of tourism and recreation center will only remain a dream. An emphasis on economic progress should not overshadow the importance of culture.[67] Building a Macauan identity is a holistic project.

Macau's economic identity can be much more than just gambling.[68] There are more attractions that can be built along the lines of cultural and religious tourism.

Figure 8.1

A *pailou* built in front of Leal Senado in Macau to celebrate the Chinese national holiday in the 1960s, courtesy of *Macao Daily*, September 25, 2004.

Economically, Macau can be known for its cultural sophistications as well as its socially responsible gambling fortifications.[69] Only then can we say that Macau has an admirable economic identity.

Conclusions: "A City of Sin" Competing with "a City of Culture"

Before the handover of Macau to China, the Portuguese Macau government had already begun to develop cultural tourism. The idea was that cultural tourism would "provide a corrective to the economic overdependence on gambling, … [and] a corrective to the overwhelming image that the territory's association with gambling had generated in the international media: the image of Macau as a 'cultural desert' (文化沙漠), a stepping stone for a highly mobile and materialistic population, a haven for vice-mongers, smugglers, and illiterates, a city built on and characterized by criminality, decadence, and corruption."[70] So the challenge was, and still is, to make a "city of sin" into a "city of culture."

Indeed, it is up to the people in Macau to build a Macauan identity in which they can take pride. This identity has national, political, cultural, social and economic aspects. And neither of the aspects can stand alone; they complement each other. This identity is similar to a nation-state identity, similar to a Chinese or a Portuguese identity, but it is a multinational identity, the improved Macau model of cosmopolitanism.[71] To build such an identity can help Macau "to recapture certain of its near half-millennium luster as gate-way to China and as bridge between east and west, not only in commerce, but also in the flow of ideas and technology."[72]

We will end by quoting W. H. Auden, an English poet, whose poem below may give us some insights. Written in 1938 during his visit to Macau,[73] it is about the reconciliation of the differences and contradictions in Macau, about a Macauan identity. The poem may be sarcastic, but the issues it raises, and other issues we have discussed in this chapter, require our careful study if we want to build a Macauan identity that can again put Macau on the map of the world.

> A weed from Catholic Europe, it took root
> Between the yellow mountains and the sea,
> And bore these gay stone houses like a fruit
> And grew in China imperceptibly.
>
> Rococo images of Saint and Saviour
> Promise her gamblers fortunes when they die;
> Churches beside the brothels testify
> That faith can pardon natural behaviour.
>
> This city of indulgence need not fear
> The major sins by which the heart is killed,
> And governments and men are torn to pieces:

Religious clock will strike; the childish vices
Will safeguard the low virtues of the child
And nothing serious can happen here.

Rather than "nothing serious can happen here," it is more a matter of the right and appropriate actions taking place.

Appendix: A Chronicle of Events in Macau History and Society

1277	When the Mongols conquered China and established the Yuan dynasty (1206–1368), they fought the remnants of the Song dynasty (960–1279) over the waters of Taipa.
1279	Wen Tianxiang 文天祥 (1236–83), a famous poet, patriot, and general, wrote the well-known poem "Guo Lingding Yang" 過零丁洋 (Passing the Lingding ocean) while fighting the Yuan army in this area.
1405–1431	Seven maritime expeditions led by Zheng He (1371–1435), a eunuch, in the Ming dynasty (1368–1644), mostly during the Yongle emperor's reign (1403–25).
1415–1511	Henry the Navigator (Prince Dom Henrique) conquered the North African Moorish city of Ceuta in 1415. Then the Portuguese mariners reached Madeira in 1420, Cape Bojador in 1434, Cape Branco in 1441, Cape Verde in 1445, and Gambia in 1446. Then Diogo Cao arrived at the mouth of Zaire in 1485, and Bartolomeu Dias sailed around the Cape of Good Hope in 1487. Vasco da Gama arrived in Calicut on the Malabar coast of India in 1498. Afonso de Albuquerque conquered Ormuz and Goa of India in 1507 and 1510 respectively. The he took Malacca in 1511, by which he gained access to the China Sea.
1443	The Portuguese began their human trafficking, when they bought and sold African slaves to Europe.
1465–1487	A-Ma Temple was first built, and there were most likely only a few thatched cottages at first.
1513	Jorge Álvares set foot on the China coast from Malacca, and his ship anchored in Tunmen (屯門, Tămáu, or Tămáo).
1515	Rafael Perestrelo made the second Portuguese mission to China from Malacca.
1517	The viceroy of Goa, Lopo Soares de Albergaria, sent a fleet of eight ships to China, led by Fernão Peres de Andrade. Along with the fleet was Tome Pires, an ambassador to Beijing. The trip failed.
1521	The Portuguese were expelled from Tunmen. The Battle of Tunmen (屯門海戰) was engaged and the Portuguese were defeated by the Chinese.

1522	The Battle of Xicaowan (西草灣之戰) was engaged and again the Portuguese were defeated.
1549–1553	Portuguese traders and missionaries settled in Shangchuan.
1553–1557	Portuguese settled in Langbaiao and Macau.
1555, 1614	The earliest records of Macau in the Portuguese language were by Fernão Mendes Pinto.
1563	There were about eight Jesuits from the Society of Jesus (耶穌會), who baptized about 600 Chinese believers either from Macau or from other parts of Guangdong.
1568	The city wall was built.
1569	The Jesuits founded the ancient charitable organization in Macau, the Santa Casa da Misericórdia (仁慈堂 or the Holy House of Mercy).
1579	Michel Ruggieri 羅明堅 (1543–1607), an Italian Jesuit, came to Macau.
1580–1640	Portugal was under Spanish rule.
1580	The first chief judge (王室大法官), Rui Machado, known as an *ouvidor*, representing the royal court, was appointed, and he presided over the Senate elections, and made judicial decisions. The position was suspended in 1642 and resumed again in 1702.
1582	Matteo Ricci 利瑪竇 (1552–1610), another Italian Jesuit, came to Macau.
1583	The Senate (議事會) was established.
1584	Ricci and Ruggieri compiled a Portuguese Chinese dictionary, setting off the movement of East-West exchange.
1586	With different religious orders established in Macau, the city was designated as the "City of the Name of God of Macau in China."
1594–1762	St. Paul's College was in existence.
1601	A Dutch fleet of six ships came to Macau, and the conflicts between the Portuguese and the Dutch began. The Portuguese executed 17 of the captives and let three of them go.
1602	The annals of Guangdong (廣東通誌) discussed how the Portuguese borrowed Macau to dry their goods. Macau was part of Xiangshan county.
1610	There had already been 54 incidents related to the conflict between the Chinese and Catholic missionaries, mostly in Guangdong and of small scale.
1616	The Ming dynasty emperor decided to expel all the Jesuits from the mainland to Macau. The Controversy of Rites deepened.
1622	The Dutch attacked Macau and was defeated.
1623	The first governor was appointed. Macau's gun foundry was started.
1625	One report by Jesuits at the time claimed that many wives of Portuguese men had already been Chinese or had Chinese blood.
1636	The Japanese expelled the Portuguese from Japan.

Appendix: A Chronicle of Events in Macau History and Society

1637	The first British fleet of four ships led by Captain John Weddell came to Macau and anchored around what are now Taipa and Coloane, then rocky and grass-covered islands.
1644	The number of Christians in China increased to 150,000.
1655–1684	The Qing government forbade trade and even fishing on the sea as a way to constrain Zheng Chenggong (Koxinga) in Taiwan.
1676	Schall von Bell's successor, Father Ferdiand Verbiest, became the president of the Board of Astronomy in Beijing.
1680	Wu Li came to study religion in Macau.
1685	Kangxi, the Qing emperor, decided to open China's ports to foreigners.
1685	Most ships coming from India and the South Seas carried opium among their other cargos.
1689	Another English ship, *Defence*, led by William Heath, came to Macau. In a skirmish between the Chinese and the English, one person from each side died, and some were wounded.
1692	Kangxi issued an edict that tolerated Christianity.
1699	The British East India Company saw that there was some opening in China trade and sent their ship *Macclesfield* to the Pearl River. Then they sent more ships to Canton, Xiamen (Amoy), Fuzhou (Foochow), and Ningbo. Their tonnage dues were determined at Macau, and mostly they sold woolen cloth and bought silk.
1702–1714	The War of Spanish Succession, and the rivalry between the Dutch and the Portuguese ended, and Holland and Portugal became allies.
1729, 1799	Opium was made contraband by Emperors Yongzheng and Jiangqing. From 1729 on, the Portuguese were also exporting opium to China through Macau.
1731	The Chinese set up a local government headed by Xian Cheng 縣丞 in Qian Shan Zhai (前山寨) or what is now Xiangzhou, Zhuhai, under Xiangshan county, to manage the affairs in Macau, both Chinese and Portuguese.
1735	*The History of the Ming Dynasty—The Story of Portugal in Macau* (明史・佛郎機傳), an official record finished, about 2,500 words.
1735	There were 300,000 Christians in mainland China.
1742	A British warship led by Captain George Anson came to visit Macau and wanted to sail upstream for repairs.
1744	The Chinese government added another layer of government above the Xiangshan county, Macau Coast Military and Civilian Government (澳門海防軍民同知), which governed four counties of Panyu, Dongguan, Shunde, and Xiangshan. The chief official was called Tongzhi 同知. The authors of *The Annals of Macau* (澳門記略), Yin Guangren and Zhang Rulin, were the first and third officials to hold the position.
1747	The beating death of two Chinese vagrants by Portuguese soldiers caused a crisis between the Chinese and Portuguese governments in Macau.

1749	Nossa Senhora do Amparo, the Church of Our Lady of Defense, a Chinese Christian Church (唐人廟) was closed.
1751	Yin Guangren 印光任 and Zhang Rulin 張汝霖 wrote 澳門記略 (*The Annals of Macau*), the first encyclopedic work of Macau.
1773	The Jesuits were disbanded by the pope under the pressures of the Portuguese, French, and Spanish governments.
1792	The British sent George Macartney as an ambassador to China. The mission failed.
1805	Protestantism came to Macau with a British missionary named Robert Morrison 馬禮遜 (1782–1834).
1805	Smallpox vaccine was first introduced in Macau and later to the mainland.
1808	The British troops forced their way into in Macau, led by Rear-Admiral William Drury, in the name of protecting their interests in China, and of "defending" Macau from possible French and Spanish attacks.
1820	In Portugal, the constitutional monarchy was established and a constitution was passed to include all Portuguese colonies as part of Portugal.
1827	Thomas R. Colledge, a British missionary in Macau, established an eye hospital in Macau.
1832	Anders Ljungstedt published his work, *An Historical Sketch of the Portuguese Settlements in China*.
1832	The first lithograph press was introduced to Macau.
1838	Macau and the islands in Lingding had become an opium depot for the merchants and the amount of opium reaching China increased to 40,000 chests.
1839	The First Opium War broke out with the Battle of Chuanbi (Chuenpe, 川鼻).
1839	The first Protestant elementary school was set up.
1840	Bremer declared a blockade of Canton, sailed northward to take Dinghai of Zhoushan, came to Tianjin, and presented to Qishan, the governor of Zhili, the British dispatch for his transmission to Beijing. Lin Zexu was dismissed.
1841	The third Battle of Chuanbi broke out. Admiral Guan Tianpei died in battle, and Qishan was dismissed and was led in chains to Beijing. The Treaty of Canton was signed. Sanyuanli peasant uprisings broke out. Malaria and a big typhoon struck Hong Kong. Elliot was dismissed, and his successor, Sir Henry Pottinger, launched another battle to take over Xiamen (Amoy), Chinhai, Ningbo, and Zhoushan in August 1841. This was a bloody process.
1842	The British troops occupied Wusung and Shanghai. The Treaty of Nanjing was signed.
1844	The first Sino-American treaty was signed in Macau.
1846	João Maria Ferreira Amaral became governor.
1847	The Portuguese formally licensed the gambling houses, like the *fantan* saloon.

Appendix: A Chronicle of Events in Macau History and Society

1849	A British teacher, James Summers, from Hong Kong was arrested by Amaral, the governor, because he did not take off his hat while watching a Catholic procession.
1849	Amaral was assassinated.
1849	There were about 4,000 Portuguese and 34,000 Chinese living in Macau.
1856–1860	The Second Opium War broke between China on one hand and the British and the French on the other, with the close support of the United States and Russia.
1856–1873	There were 180,061 coolies exported to Cuba and Peru from Macau.
1860	A formal government office was set up to regulate the agencies doing coolie trade in Macau.
1869	Macau and Timor became one province and a governor-general of the province was appointed.
1872	The British government prohibited gambling in Hong Kong, and gamblers traveled to Macau for it.
1873	The coolie trade was officially forbidden after protests and outcries from the Chinese as well as international communities, but it continued secretly. The British took over the trade through Hong Kong.
1880	There were 400 gambling parlors and many made their fortunes in that field and later became *du wang* 賭王, or "gambling tycoons."
1887	The Luso-Chinese Treaty of Friendship and Trade was signed.
1896	There were already 1,075 commercial and industrial enterprises owned by the Chinese, with 6,803 workers.
1902	Montalto de Jesus published his work, *Historic Macau*.
1908	A Chinese merchant in Macau hired a Japanese boat (二辰丸) to smuggle weapons to China, and the boat was intercepted by the Chinese naval forces off the waters of Coloane. It set off a crisis in foreign relations between China, Portugal, and Japan.
1910	The Portuguese answered the call for help from Chinese families whose children were kidnapped by bandits in Coloane. This led to what many see as the "Luhuan Massacre."
1918	Macau still made 667,600 dollars from the opium trade, although it declined to 181,900 dollars in 1925.
1919	The Provincial Organization Charter of Macau stipulated that there would be an Administrative Council composed not only of government officials but also senators.
1920	The legislative part was separated from the Administrative Council and a Legislative Council was established. There were 1,800 boats and 40,000 people, or 28% of the population involved in the fishing industry, either out on the sea or doing trading on land.

1922	On May 29, the Portuguese soldiers shot 70 Chinese to death. People had been protesting against a black soldier's disorderly conduct towards a Chinese woman and things had gone out of hand.
1934	Zhang Tianze 張天澤 published his *Sino-Portuguese Trade from 1514–1644*, a Ph.D. dissertation he did in Holland.
1934	The government granted exclusive rights to the Taixing Company for casino-style gambling.
1937	Zhou Jianglian 周景濂 published his 《中葡外交史》 (The history of Chinese-Portuguese diplomatic relations).
1939	A large number of refugees came to Macau, and the population in Macau swelled to 240,000.
1946	Liu Shaowu 劉紹武, one of the KMT army officers stationed in Zhongshan, Guangdong, led his troops into Macau to protest the Portuguese occupation,
1952	In July 25, the PLA troops clashed with the Portuguese troops at the border with casualties on both sides. This is the Guanzha Incident.
1962	Stanley Ho's Macau Tourism and Entertainment Company (Sociedade de Turismo e Diversões de Macau, or STDM) won the gambling monopoly.
1966	12-3 Incident on December 3, which led to 8 Chinese deaths and the injury of 212 people by December 5.
1976	The Organic Statute of Macau was put into practice. The Legislative Council became fully independent of the governor.
1980s	Textiles and garments dominated the industrial sector and employed 64% of the total labor force.
1984	The Chinese Macau basically had already dominated the directly and indirectly elected members of the legislature.
1993	The Basic Law of the Macau Special Administrative Region of the People's Republic of China was passed.
1999	Macau was handed over to China. The Portuguese colonial rule ended.
2001	The SAR government decided to open the industry to competition rather than the monopoly by STDM.
2002	The government granted two new licenses in addition to the one to STDM: Wynn Resorts and Galaxy Group of Hong Kong each won a license.
2004	Las Vegas Sands opened Sands Macao.
2006	Wynn Resorts opened Wynn Macau.
	The Galaxy Group opened its first flagship casino StarWorld Galaxy Macau.
	Ao Man Long—the first Secretary for Transport and Public Works of the Macau SAR—was arrested for corruption charges, making him the highest-ranking official arrested in the history of Macau.
2007	For crowd control purposes at a May 1 demonstration, a policeman fired several shots in the air and one of them accidentally hit a motorcyclist some distance away, wounding him but not fatally.

Appendix: A Chronicle of Events in Macau History and Society

	SJM opened the Grand Lisboa.
	Las Vegas Sands opened Venetian Macao.
	Melco PBL opened Crown Casino in Taipa, the name of which was later changed into Altira when it opened another casino, City of Dreams on the Cotai Strip.
	MGM Grand Macao opened on the Macau peninsula.
2008	SJM opened Casino Ponte 16.
	Las Vegas Sands opened the Plaza Macao in Cotai.
	The Labor Law was revised and passed.
	Ao Man Long was sentenced to 27 years in prison.
2009	The legislation of Article 23 of the Basic Law on national security was passed, addressing the prevention of subversion of the state.
	Melco PBL opened the City of Dreams in Cotai.
2012	Macau SAR initiated political reform without changing the basic power structure.
	Los Vegas Sands opened Sands Cotai Central in Cotai.
2014	Macau SAR proposed legislation to protect the interests of the chief executive and principal government officials before and after office but withdrew the bill after protest demonstrations by about 30,000 people.
2015	The Galaxy Group opened Galaxy Macau and Broadway Macau in Cotai.
2016	Las Vegas Sands paid Sands China's former chief executive, Steve Jacobs, US$75 million to settle a wrongful termination lawsuit.
	Las Vegas Sands paid US$9 million (less than two days of profit for the company) fine to end a U.S. Securities and Exchange Commission's probe into the company's possible violation of U.S. federal anti-bribery laws.
	Wynn Resorts opened Wynn Palace in Cotai.
	Las Vegas Sands opened the Parisian Macao in Caotai.
	The law on minimum wage for cleaners and security guards went into effect: MOP30 per hour, MOP240 per day, MOP6,240 per month.
2017	According to The World Bank, with a GDP per capita of US$80,892.8, Macau became the second richest territory in the world in 2017, trailing only Luxembourg.
	Ho Chio Meng, the first Prosecutor General of Macau SAR, was sentenced to 21 years of prison for 1,092 crimes including establishing criminal gangs, aggravated money laundering, and defrauding.
	Las Vegas Sands agreed to pay US$7 million criminal penalty to end a probe by the U.S. Department of Justice into whether the company violated anti-bribery laws when obtaining its license in Macau
	On August 23, 10 people died when Macau was hit by Typhoon Hato.

Notes

Introduction

1. Anthony Giddens, *Capitalism and Modern Social Society: An Analysis of the Writings of Marx, Durkheim, and Max Weber* (Cambridge: Cambridge University Press, 1971), p. 64.
2. In John K. Fairbank and Edwin O. Reischauer, *China: Tradition and Transformation* (Taipei: Caves Books, Ltd., 1986), p. 328. Robert Hart (1835–1911), an Englishman and inspector general of China's Maritime Customs (中國海關總稅務司) for 48 years, including two years of acting inspector general from 1861–63, was a controversial figure. Believing in China's potential, as the quote shows, he was instrumental in China's modernization efforts especially in maritime issues, such as charting the China coast; installing lighthouses, beacons, markers; managing port facilities; and publishing trade statistics and commercial and scientific reports. But he was also instrumental in a number of "unequal treaties" between China and Western powers, including the 1885 Sino-French treaty, which caused China to lose Annam (Vietnam) as its suzerainty, and the 1887 treaty between China and Portugal, which granted Portugal the right to permanently govern Macau (Fairbank and Reischauer, China, pp. 329, 354; see also a Chinese version of the 1989 revised edition of their book: *Zhongguo: Chuantong yu Bianqian*, translated by Zhang Pei, Zhang Yuan, and Gu Sijian (Beijing: Shijie Zhishi Chubanshe, 2002), pp. 352–3, 371–4, 404.
3. For the development of the capitalist world-system, see also Alvin Y. So, *Social Change and Development: Modernization, Dependency, and World-System Theories* (Newbury Park, California: Sage Publications, 1990); Immanuel Wallerstein, *The Modern World System: Capitalist Agriculture and the Origins of the European World Economy in the Sixteenth Century* (New York: Academic Press, 1976); and his *The Capitalist World-Economy* (New York: Cambridge University Press, 1979).
4. Richard Mertens, "China on the Rise," in *The University of Chicago Magazine*, August 2006, Volume 98, Issue 6.
5. "Macau" is the Portuguese spelling and "Macao" is the English spelling. We use the former in this book because we are discussing the history and society of Portuguese and Chinese mainly. However, according to Jin Guoping, "Macao" is the spelling in ancient Portuguese, and it was later adopted by the English. The latter, however, is beginning to use "Macau" now. See Jin Guoping, "Aomen yuan kao" (A study on the origin of Macau), in Wu Zhiliang, Jin Guoping, and Tang Kaijian (eds.) *Aomen Shi Xin Bian* (A new history of Macau), Vol. 1 (Macau: Macau Foundation, 2008), p. 46.
6. For the same point, see also Wu Zhiliang, "Xu" 序 (Preface), in Jin Guoping, *Xifang Aomen Shiliao Xuancui* (Selected Western records on Macau) (Guangzhou: Guangdong Remin Chubanshe, 2005), pp. 11–4.

7. Huang Wenkuan, "Guanyu Aomen shi de kaoding" (Reexamination of some issues in Macau history), in Huang Qichen and Deng Kaisong (eds.) *Zhong Wai Xuezhe Lun Aomen Lishi* (Studies on Macau history by Chinese and foreign scholars) (Macau: Macau Foundation, 1995), pp. 98–101; R. D. Cremer, "From Portugal to Japan: Macau's Place in the History of World Trade," in *Macau: City of Commerce and Culture* (Hong Kong: UEA Press Ltd., 1987), pp. 23–4.
8. The seventh and last expedition in 1431–33 was under Emperor Xuande.
9. For discussions on Zheng He's expeditions, see the following works: Timothy Brook, "Communications and Commerce," in Denis Twitchett and Frederick W. Mote (eds.) *The Cambridge History of China Volume 8: The Ming Dynasty, 1368–1644, Part 2* (New York: Cambridge University Press, 1998), pp. 615–7; Hok-Lam Chan, "The Chien-wen, Yung-lo, Hung-hsi, and Hsuan-te Reigns, 1399–1435," in Frederick W. Mote and Denis Twitchett (eds.) *The Cambridge History of China Volume 7: The Ming Dynasty, 1368–1644, Part 1* (New York: Cambridge University Press, 1998), pp. 232–6; Wang Gongwu, "Ming Foreign Relations: Southeast Asia," in Twitchett and Mote (eds.) *The Cambridge History of China*, pp. 320–4; and Yang Yunzhong (ed.) *Zheng He yu Hai shang Sichou zhi Lu* (Zheng He and the Silk Road on the sea) (Macau: Center for Macau Studies, the University of Macau, 2005). See also Cremer, "From Portugal to Japan," p. 25, for three more reasons for the discontinuation of Zheng He's expeditions: the completion of the Grand Canal in 1411 connecting Beijing to Ningbo, making it less necessary to continue exploiting the coastal sea routes, which were constantly threatened by Japanese pirates; a general anti-foreign policy; and the Ming's determination to restore the traditional Chinese culture after overthrowing the Mongolian Yuan dynasty.
10. For the mentioning of such descriptions of Macau, see Cathryn Hope Clayton, "*If We Are Not Different, We Will Cease to Exist*": *Culture and Identity in Transition-Era Macau* (Ann Arbor, Michigan: UMI Dissertation Services, 2001), p. 65; R. D. Cremer, "Introduction," in R. D. Cremer (ed.) *Macau: City of Commerce and Culture*, p. 1; Liu Denghan, "Hou ji" (Afterword), in Liu Denghan (ed.) *Aomen Wenxue Gaiguan* (A general view of literature in Macau) (Fuzhou: Lujiang Chubanshe, 1998), p. 384; Jill McGivering, *Macao Remembers* (Hong Kong: Oxford University Press, 1999), pp. xi–xii, 72–3, 148; João de Pina-Cabral, *Between China and Europe: Person, Culture and Emotion in Macao* (London, New York: Continuum, 2002), pp. xi, 29, 60, 205; Donald Pittis and Susan J. Henders (selected and edited), *Macao: Mysterious Decay and Romance, an anthology* (Hong Kong: Oxford University Press, 1997), pp. 4, 48, 67.
11. Cremer, "Introduction," in *Macau*, p. 1.
12. Clayton, "*If We Are Not Different*," p. 65.
13. As a corrective to the image of "the city of sin," the slogan "Macau: City of Culture" is engraved in stone in the exit hall of the Museum of Macau (Clayton, "*If We Are Not Different*," p. 260).
14. For both these descriptions, see McGivering, *Macao Remembers*, p. xi.
15. Ibid., p. 72.
16. Ibid., p. xii.
17. Because "Macanese" ("Macaense" in Portuguese) has a special meaning in Macau, I use a neologism in English, "Macauan," for the diverse members of this community, symbolizing a new identity, which they richly deserve. See more on this in chapter 8.
18. See, for example, the speeches given at a symposium on Macau's culture and humanism in *Macao Daily*, August 19, 2006, B1.
19. Pina-Cabral, *Between China and Europe*, p. 3.
20. Liu Denghan, *Aomen Wenxue Gaiguan*, p. 384.
21. McGivering, *Macao Remembers*, p. 148.

22. Clayton, "*If We Are Not Different*," p. 65.
23. Pina-Cabral, *Between China and Europe*, p. xi.
24. Ieong Hoi Keng, *Aomen Tese Wenxian Ziyuan Yanjiu* (A study of the documents, papers, books, and archives specifically on Macau) (Beijing: Beijing University Press, 2003), p. 18. For more on the research literature on Macau, see also Ieong Hoi Keng, "Suiyue de jianzheng: Aomen wenxian ziyuan" (The evidence of history: the sources of documents on Macau), and Wong Kuok Keung, "Aomen lishi yanjiu zhi Zhongwen shumu" (The Chinese works on Macau history studies), both in Wu Zhiliang, Jin Guoping, and Tang Kaijian (eds.) *Aomen Shi Xin Bian*.
25. See Ieong Hoi Keng, *Aomen Tese Wenxian Zhiyuan Yanjiu*, pp. 12–3.
26. For more of the above information, see Wu Zhiliang, "Aomen shi yanjiu shuping" (A review of Macau historical studies), in *Xingzheng* (Administration), (a journal of the Macau government), Vol. 9, No. 2 (June 1996): 509–10.
27. Wu Zhiliang, "Aomen shi yanjiu shuping," pp. 511–2.
28. Ieong Hoi Keng, *Aomen Tese Wenxian Ziyuan Yanjiu*, p. 239; Wu Zhiliang, "Aomen shi yanjiu shuping," pp. 514–8; Huang Qichen, "Fulu: Aomen lishi yanjiu zhuyao cankao ziliao mulu" (The main references in Macau studies), in Huang Qichen and Deng Kaisong (eds.) *Zhong Wai Aomen Lishi*, pp. 365–85. For a discussion on exploring historical documents, see Jin Guoping and Wu Zhiliang, *Jing Hai Piaomiao* (The misty Macau history) (Macau: Chengren Jiaoyu Xuehui Adult education association), pp. 1–12; Wu Zhiliang, "Xu," in Jin Guoping, *Xifang Aomen Shiliao Xuancui*, pp. 1–11; Huang Qichen and Deng Kaisong, "Aomen lishi yanjiu gaishu" (A general survey of Macau studies), in Huang Qichen and Deng Kaisong (eds.) *Zhong Wai Xuezhe Lun Aomen*, pp. 1–5; Lin Faqin, *Aomen Shigao* (Papers on Macau history) (Macau: Aomen Jindai Wenxue Xuehui, Association for Macau modern literature, 2005), pp. 1–49. See also various works online at http://www.macaudata.com.
29. For this quote, see David M. Kennedy, "What History Is Good For," *The New York Times*, July 19, 2009.

Chapter 1

1. In Geoffrey C. Gunn, *Encountering Macau: A Portuguese City-State on the Periphery of China, 1557–1999* (Boulder, Colorado: Westview Press, 1996), p. 15.
2. See also Andrew Webster, *Introduction to the Sociology of Development*, second edition (London: The MacMillan Press Ltd., 1990), pp. 70–9.
3. For a brief summary of the Portuguese maritime expansion, see Renelde Justo Bernardo da Silva, *The Macanese Identity* (Macau: International Institute of Macau, 2001), pp. 119–23.
4. For this part of history, see also Luo Rui Luo (Rui Manuel Loureiro), "Putaoyaren xunzhao Zhongguo: cong Maliujia dao Aomen" (Portuguese looking for China: from Malacca to Macau), in Wu Zhiliang, Jin Guoping, Tang Kaijian (eds.) *Aomen Shi Xin Bian*, Vol. 1. For all the places the Portuguese conquered during the 15th and 16th centuries, see Li Changsen, *Mingqing Shiqi Aomen Tusheng Zuqun de Xingcheng Fazhan yu Bianqian* (The emergence, development and transformation of the Macanese in the Ming and Qing dynasties) (Beijing: Zhonghua Shuju, 2007), pp. 42–5. For more on the Portuguese history, see also a journalistic yet informative book by Martin Page, *The First Global Village: How Portugal Changed the World* (Lisbon: Editorial Noticias, 2002).
5. Both Álvares and his son were buried in Tunmen later. See also Clive Willis (ed.) *China and Macau* (Aldershot: Ashgate, 2002), pp. 15–6.

6. For a description of the earlier encounters of the Portuguese with the Chinese related in these paragraphs, see B. V. Pires, "Origins and Early History of Macau," in R. D. Cremer (ed.) *Macau: City of Commerce and Culture* (Hong Kong: UEA Press Ltd., 1987), pp. 9–10; Zhao Liren, "Putaoya ren ruju qian de Guangdong yu Aomen" (Guangdong and Macau before the Portuguese settlement), in Deng Kaisong, Wu Zhiliang, and Lu Xiaomin (eds.) *Yue Ao Guanxi Shi* (The relationship between Guangdong and Macau) (Beijing: Zhongguo Shudian, 1999), pp. 21–66.
7. Willis (ed.) *China and Macau*, pp. xvii–xviii.
8. Ibid., pp. xix, 13–4.
9. For more information about Pires and his mission, see also the letters by two of his inmates in Canton, as described by Zhao Liren, "Putaoya ren ruju qian de Guangdong yu Aomen," p. 43. See also Willis (ed.) *China and Macau*, pp. 18–21.
10. Jin Guoping (ed. and trans.) *Xifang Aomen Shiliao Xuancui*, pp. 149–57; Willis (ed.) *China and Macau*, p. xix; Zhao Liren, "Putaoya ren ruju qian de Guangdong yu Aomen," pp. 38–42.
11. Jin Guoping, *Xifang Aomen Shiliao Xuancui*, pp. 35–42; Zhao Liren, "Putaoya ren ruju qian de Guangdong yu Aomen," pp. 46–9.
12. For more discussion on St. Francis Xavier's experience in China, see Liu Ranling, *Wenming de Boyi: 16 zhi 19 Shiji Aomen Wenhua Chang Boduan de Lishi Kaocha* (The game of civilizations: a longitudinal study of Macau's cultural history) (Guangzhou: Guangdong Renmin Chubanshe, 2008), pp. 84–6; Pittis and Henders (selected and edited) *Macao: Mysterious Decay and Romance*, pp. 224–8; Tang Kaijian, "Ming Qing shiqi Aomen tianzhujiao de fazhan yu xingshuai" (The development and decline of the Catholic Church in the Ming and Qing dynasties), in Wu Zhiliang, Jin Guoping, and Tang Kaijian (eds.) *Aomen Shi Xin Bian*, Vol. 4.
13. Zhao Liren, "Putaoya ren ruju qian de Guangdong yu Aomen," pp. 58–61; B. V. Pires, "Origins and Early History of Macau," in R. D. Cremer (ed.) *Macau: City of Commerce and Culture*, p. 10.
14. Silva, *The Macanese Identity*, p. 124.
15. Zhao Liren, "Putaoya ren ruju qian de Guangdong yu Aomen," pp. 61–3; Pires, "Origins and Early History of Macau," p. 10; Lin Zisheng, *Shiliu zhi Shiba Shiji Aomen yu Zhongguo zhi Guanxi* (The relationship between Macau and China from the 16th to 18th centuries) (Macau: Macau Foundation, 1998), pp. 17–20.
16. This is a later model of the temple the Portuguese saw when they first came here. It was almost 300 years later, but one may still get an idea of what it might have been like at the time.
17. Some questioned whether the temple was here when the Portuguese came, but as Lamas points out, even if this temple was not here, other similar shrines or temples probably were. See Rosmarie Wank-Nolasco Lamas, *History of Macau: A Student's Manual* (Macao: Institute of Tourism Education, 1998), p. 17. For the name of the place, see also C. R. Boxer, *Fidalgos in the Far East 1550–1770* (Hong Kong, London, New York: Oxford University Press, 1968), pp. 3–4; Clayton, *"If We Are Not Different,"* pp. 117–8; Jin Guoping and Wu Zhiliang, *Guo Shizi Men* (Passing Macau) (Macau: Chengren Jiaoyu Xuehui or Adult education association, 2004), pp. 73–109; Jonathan Porter, *Macau: The Imaginary City: Culture and Society, 1557 to the Present* (Boulder, Colorado: Westview Press, 1996), p. 41; Jin Guoping, "Aomen yuan kao," pp. 46–8.
18. The Chinese words on the flag of the ship, 利涉大川, are a line in the *Book of Changes* (or *Yijing*, an ancient Chinese book often used in fortune telling), meaning it is the right time to cross rivers (and seas).

19. Zha Canchang, *Zhuanxing, Bianxiang yu Chuanbo: Aomen Zaoqi Xiandaihua Yanjiu—Yapian Zhanzheng zhi 1945Nian*) (Transformation, variables, and communication: a study of Macau's modernization in the early days—from the Opium War to 1945) (Guangzhou: Guangdong Renmin Chubanshe, 2006), pp. 21–4.
20. Zha Canchang, *Zhuanxing*, pp. 25–6.
21. Yan Zhongming and Ye Nong, "Aomen chengshi de xingjian yu fazhan" (The rise and development of the city of Macau), in Wu Zhiliang, Jin Guoping, and Tang Kaijian (eds.) *Aomen Shi Xin Bian*, Vol. 3, pp. 770–1.
22. Jin Guoping and Wu Zhiliang, *Jing Hai Piaomiao* (The misty Macau history) (Macau: Chengren Jiaoyu Xuehui or Adult education association, 2001), pp. 247–56. For the legend of villages on the Macau peninsula, see also Tan Shibao, "Estudos sobre a Lenda das Aldeias: na Península de Macau antes da suo Fundação" (The legend of the villages on the Macao peninsula before the founding of Macao), *Review of Culture*, international edition 1, January 2002.
23. Huang Qichen, *Aomen Tongshi* (A general history of Macau) (Guangzhou: Gongdong Jiaoyu Chubanshe, 1999), pp. 18–22; see also Deng Kaisong and Xie Houhe, *Aomen Lishi yu Shehui Fazhan* (Macau history and social development) (Zhuhai: Zhuhai Chubanshe, 1999), p. 7.
24. Here as elsewhere in the book, I am mostly only translating the main ideas of the poems I quote. I hope that is enough for the reader who does not read Chinese. What I am omitting, as in this case, for example, are poetic descriptions of the weather, wind, feelings, etc. that convey the atmosphere. But they do not affect the reader's basic understanding of the substantive meanings of the poem. I have made some substantive revision and expansion of the translations, though, upon one reviewer's comments.
25. See also Jin Guoping and Wu Zhiliang, *Jing Hai Piaomiao*, pp. 218–46, for a more detailed discussion of the name "Aomen."
26. Lamas, *History of Macau*, p. 21.
27. Tan Shibao and Cao Guoqing believe that, on the contrary, Wang was an exemplary official at the time. See their paper "Nova Avaliação de Wang Bo: e do Primeiro Acordo Sino-Portugues" (A new evaluation of Wang Bo and the first Sino-Portuguese agreement), *Review of Culture*, international edition 1, January 2002.
28. See Jin Guoping and Wu Zhiliang, *Guo Shizi Men*, pp. 1–21, for a more detailed discussion of the situation under which the Chinese government decided to open Macau to the Portuguese; see also Clayton, *"If We Are Not Different,"* pp. 117–26; Deng Kaisong and Xie Houhe, *Aomen Lishi yu Shehui Fazhan*, pp. 15–6; Lin Zisheng, *Shiliu zhi Shiba Shiji Aomen yu Zhongguo zhi Guanxi*, pp. 23–6, 42–3; Rui Manuel Loureiro, "As Origens de Macau nas Fontes Ibéricas" (The origins of Macao in Iberian historical sources), *Review of Culture*, international edition 1, January 2002; Tereza Sena, "Historical Background of Macau with Particular Focus on the First Americans in China," in Ieda Siqueira Wiarda and Lucy M. Cohen (eds.) *Macau: Cultural Dialogue towards a New Millenium* (Philadelphia, PA: Xlibris, 2004), pp. 23–8.
29. For the records and legend on the Portuguese helping the Chinese to expel pirates, see Lin Faqin, *Aomen Shi Gao* (Papers on Macau history) (Macau: Aomen Jindai Wenxue Xuehui, 2005), pp. 128–36; Lin Zisheng, *Shiliu zhi Shiba Shiji Aomen yu Zhongguo zhi Guanxi*, pp. 31–41; Guo Jixiu, *Fei Liqi Xiaoshuo Yanjiu ji Qita* (The studies on the short stories by Henrique de Sanne Fernandos and other papers) (Macau: Aomen Wenhua Guangchang, 2002), pp. 18–27; Tang Kaijian, *Weiliduo "Baoxiao Shi Mo Shu" Jianzheng* (Study notes on Vereador's, i.e., Procurador's memorial to the Ming emperor) (Guangzhou: Guangdong Remin Chubanshe, 2004), pp. 49–59, 85–99.

30. Austin Coates, *Macao and the British 1637–1842: Prelude to Hong Kong* (New York: Oxford University Press, 1966), p. 4; *A Macao Narrative* (Hong Kong: Heinemann, 1978), p. 23.
31. Pittis and Henders (selected and edited), *Macao: Mysterious Decay and Romance*, pp. 125–6, citing Pierre Sonnerat.
32. Jin Guoping and Wu Zhiliang, *Zaoqi Aomen Shi Lun* (Essays on early Macau history) (Guangzhou: Guangdong Renmin Chubanshe, 2007), p. 130.
33. Jin Guoping and Wu Zhiliang, *Zaoqi Aomen Shi Lun*, pp. 20–1, 27–95, 134–40.
34. Pires, "Origins and Early History of Macau," p. 7. One reviewer's comment on this issue is worth quoting. He/she says that in the fifteenth and sixteenth centuries, "poverty and misery were quite the same all over Europe, but the Portuguese were the first ones to push beyond the known world into the awesome and awful unknown, mapping the world and carrying back and forth merchandise and knowledge from all over the world." See also Martin Page, *The First Global Village*, for more information on this. According to one estimate, in the 1500s and the first part of the 1600s, 600,000 Portuguese left Portugal to find a living by trade or otherwise overseas. See Liu Ranling, *Wenming de Boyi*, p. 56.
35. For the reasons, see Renelde Justo Bernardo da Silva, *The Macanese Identity*, pp. 124–5; Zha Canchang, *Zhuangxing, Bianxiang yu Chuanbo*, pp. 39, 48.
36. Teng and Fairbank, *China's Response to the West*, p. 1.
37. Clayton, "If We Are Not Different," pp. 125–6.

Chapter 2

1. Pina-Cabral, *Between China and Europe*, pp. 51, 70.
2. Ibid., p. 53.
3. See reports on his election activities in *Macao Daily*, August 26, 2004.
4. See *Macao Daily*, August 27, 2004.
5. Roderich Ptak, "Aomen lishi gaishu" (A survey of Macau history), in Huang Qichen and Deng Kaisong (eds.) *Zhong Wai Xuezhe Lun Aomen Lishi*, pp. 32–7, 45. The Amsterdam sale yielded 3.5 million guilders, and Chinese porcelain came to be known in Holland as *Kraakporselein* or "Carrack-porcelain" because of the kind of large sailing ship that *Santa Catarina* was. For more information on this and other conflicts between the Dutch and the Portuguese, see Boxer, *Fidalgos in the Far East 1550–1770*, pp. 49–51; Lin Faqin, "Aomen zaoqi dui wai zhanzheng yu junshi fangyu" (The wars against invaders and the military defense in early Macau), in Wu Zhiliang, Jin Guoping, and Tang Kaijian (eds.) *Aomen Shi Xin Bian*, Vol. 3.
6. Pittis and Henders (selected and edited) *Macao: Mysterious Decay and Romance*, p. 166, cited in an account by C. R. Boxer.
7. Silva, *The Macanese Identity*, pp. 149–52; see also Boxer, *Fidalgos in the Far East 1550–1770*, pp. 72–92; Austin Coates, *A Macao Narrative* (Hong Kong: Heinemann, 1978), pp. 44–6; and Lin Faqin, *Aomen Shigao*, pp. 76–122. The latter work and Boxer in Pittis and Henders above have a more detailed description and analysis of the 1622 battle. But Boxer's account claims that the lucky cannon-ball struck not the ammunition ship but "a barrel of gunpowder which exploded in the midst of the Dutch formation with devastating results." See Pittis and Henders (selected and edited) *Macao: Mysterious Decay and Romance*, p. 166.
8. Silva, *The Macanese Identity*, pp. 156–60.
9. Coates, *Macao and the British*, p. 31.
10. Ibid., p. 42.
11. For the British story here, see Coates, *Macao and the British*, pp. 1–27; Coates, *A Macao Narrative*, p. 57; Ptak, "Aomen lishi gaishu," pp. 42–3.

12. Coates, *Macao and the British*, p. 2.
13. For more on the English experience in Macau and China, see also Pu Jia (Rogerio Miguel Puga), "Yingguo ren chu han Aomen" (The first voyages of the Brits to Macau), in Wu Zhiliang, Jin Guoping, and Tang Kaijian (eds.) *Aomen Shi Xin Bian*, Vol. 2.
14. Coates, *Macao and the British*, pp. 35–6.
15. Ibid., pp. 32–7.
16. Ibid., pp. 48–52.
17. See also Deng Kaisong and Xie Houhe, *Aomen Lishi yu Shehui Fazhan*, p. 39.
18. Coates, *Macao and the British*, pp. 83–91.
19. Coates, *Macao and the British*, pp. 92–101; see also Deng Kaisong and Xie Houhe, *Aomen Lishi yu Shehui Fazhan*, pp. 39–40; Wei Qingyuan, *Aomen Shi Lungao* (Papers on Macau history) (Guangzhou: Guangdong Remin Chubanshe, 2005), pp. 163–4.
20. For the opium crisis and the wars between the Chinese and the British, see Coates, *Macao and the British*, pp. 123–224; Peter Ward Fay, *The Opium War 1840–1842* (New York: The Norton Library, 1976); Frederic Wakeman, Jr., *The Fall of Imperial China* (New York: The Free Press, 1975), pp. 135–7, 156–9.
21. Coates, *Macao and the British*, p. 203.
22. Fay, *The Opium War*, p. 269.
23. Coates, *Macao and the British*, pp. 205–6.
24. Fay, *The Opium War*, p. 303. Some Chinese sources would say that several hundreds of the British soldiers were killed. It was not clear how many Chinese were killed.
25. Coates, *Macao and the British*, p. 215.
26. Fay, *The Opium War*, p. 320.
27. Ibid., p. 321.
28. Ibid., p. 353.
29. Coates, *A Macao Narrative*, p. 99.
30. Wakeman, *The Fall of Imperial China*, p. 156.
31. Ibid., p. 158.
32. Ibid., p. 158.
33. For more on the Opium Wars, see also Fay, *The Opium War 1840–1842*; Wakeman, *The Fall of Imperial China*, pp. 135–7, 156–9.
34. For that possible scenario, see Fay, *The Opium War*, pp. xii–xiii.
35. Brook, "Communications and Commerce," p. 617.
36. Cited in Rosmarie W. N. Lamas, *Everything in Style: Harriett Low's Macau* (Hong Kong: Hong Kong University Press, 2006), p. 180.
37. Fairbank and Reischauer, *China: Tradition and Transformation*, pp. 177–8.
38. Coates, *Macao and the British*, p. 54.
39. Ibid., p. 208.
40. See Clayton for a discussion on the Macau formula, originally summarized by Fok Kaicheong. This was "a strategy developed by the Ming as a way of reconciling two contradictory imperatives: the need for strong coastal defense and the profitability of foreign trade" (Clayton, *"If We Are Not Different,"* p. 126. We mentioned the Macau model at the end of chapter 1.
41. Many simply did not think that China needed change. See Fay, *The Opium War*, pp. 363–4.
42. Coates, *Macao and the British*, pp. 66, 77, 79–82.
43. Ibid., pp. 137, 144.
44. Teng and Fairbank, *China's Response to the West*, p. 85.
45. Ibid., p. 29. For a description of Lin and his job, see also Fay, *The Opium War*; Liu Ranling, *Wenming de Boyi*, pp. 333–7.
46. Fay, *The Opium War*, pp. 344–7.

47. Excerpted in Teng and Fairbank, *China's Response to the West*, p. 28.
48. See excerpts in Teng and Fairbank, *China's Response to the West*, pp. 50–5. Feng was an assistant to Lin Zexu and secretary to Li Hongzhang.
49. Excerpted in Teng and Fairbank, *China's Response to the West*, pp. 121–2.
50. Lord Elgin's dictum might have a grain of truth in it: "The Chinese yield nothing to reason and everything to force." Of course it is not entirely true, but it is one strand of thought in political science: political realism. There are always people who believe in reason, and those who believe in force. Lord Elgin was the one who ordered the complete destruction of Yuan Ming Yuan. See Boxer, *Fidalgos in the Far East*, p. 77.
51. Fairbank and Reischauer, *China: Tradition and Transformation*, p. 420.
52. Ibid., p. 311.
53. Ibid., p. 350.
54. Wu Zhiliang defines seven periods. In addition to the three above, he has four more: 1) the early relationship between the Chinese and the Portuguese (1514–83) followed by the Senado period above; 2) the period of declining Senado (1783–1849) followed by the colonial period above; 3) the district autonomy period (1976–88); and 4) the transition period (1988–99), followed by the Chinese period above. See Wu Zhiliang, *Shengcun zhi Dao: Lun Aomen Zhengzhi Zhidu yu Zhengzhi Fazhan* (The way to survive: the political system and the political development in Macau) (Macau: Aomen Chengren Jiaoyu Xuehui, 1998), pp. 13–4. I am focusing on the main defining periods.
55. He Baogang, "The Question of Sovereignty in the Taiwan Strait: Re-examining Peking's Policy of Opposition to Taiwan's Bid for UN Membership," in *China Perspectives*, Number 34, 2001, p. 7; Roger Scruton, *A Dictionary of Political Thought* (New York: Hill and Wang, 1982), p. 441.
56. See Clayton, *"If We Are Not Different,"* p. 116, citing Richard Handler.
57. David Held, *Democracy and the Global Order* (Stanford, California: Stanford University Press, 1995), p. 315; for what seems to be necessary impingements on national sovereignty by international organizations, see also Yang Zewei, *Zhuquan Lun: Guoji Fa shang de Zhuquan Wenti jiqi Fazhan Qushi Yanjiu* (On sovereignty: a study on the issues of sovereignty in international law and the tendencies of their development) (Beijing: Beijing University Press, 2006).
58. Clayton, *"If We Are Not Different,"* p. 116; see also Gunn, *Encountering Macau*, pp. 57–70 on the sovereignty issue.
59. Clayton, *"If We Are Not Different,"* pp. 119–20; Montalto de Jesus, *Lishi shang de Aomen* (Historic Macao), translated by Huang Hongzhao and Li Baoping (Macau: Macau Foundation, [1902] 2000), pp. 14–23.
60. Pina-Cabral, *Between China and Europe*, p. 59.
61. See, for example, Zha Canchang, *Zhuanxing, Bianxiang yu Chuanbo*, pp. 260, 282.
62. See, for example, Anders Ljungstedt, *Zaoqi Aomen Shi* (*An Historical Sketch of the Portuguese Settlements in China*), translated by Wu Yixiong, Guo Deyan, and Shen Zhengbang (Beijing: Dongfang Chubanshe, [1832] 1997), p. 1; Pina-Cabral, *Between China and Europe*, p. 13; Silva, *The Macanese Identity*, pp. 109–10.
63. For more discussion on the sovereignty of Macau, see also Camoes C. K. Tam, *Aomen Zhuquan Wenti Shi Mo (1553–1993)* (Disputes concerning Macau's sovereignty between China and Portugal, 1553–1993) (Taipei: Yongye chubanshe, 1994); Wei Qingyuan, *Aomen Shi Lungao*, pp. 126, 140–1; Wu Zhiliang, *Shengcun zhi Dao*, pp. 122–34; Zha Canchang, *Zhuanxing, Bianxiang yu Chuanbo*, pp. 221–8, 236–68, 274–83.
64. Fairbank and Reischauer, *Tradition and Transformation*, p. 324; Cathryn H. Clayton, *Sovereignty at the Edge: Macau and the Question of Chineseness* (Cambridge and London: The Harvard University Asia Center, 2009).

65. See also Clayton, *"If We Are Not Different,"* p. 294, for a discussion on "joint sovereignty," which is a similar idea.
66. Russia obtained hundreds of thousands of square miles of territory from China by the Treaty of Aigun in 1860. See Wakeman, *The Fall of Imperial China*, p. 138.
67. Samuel Huntington, cited by Ted Lewellen, *Dependency and Development: An Introduction to the Third World* (Westport, Connecticut and London: Bergin & Garvey, 1995), p. 147.
68. Huang Qichen, *Aomen Tongshi*, pp. 92–3.
69. Gunn, *Encountering Macau*, pp. 35–6.
70. Coates, *A Macao Narrative*, p. 26.
71. Huang Qichen, *Aomen Tongshi*, p. 239.
72. Ljungstedt, *Zaoqi Aomen Shi*, pp. 78–9.
73. Zha Canchang, *Zhuanxing, Bianxiang yu Chuanbo*, pp. 261–8. For more discussion on the roles of this military position and the names of the appointees from 1550–1770, see Boxer, *Fidalgos in the Far East 1550–1770*, especially Appendices A and B.
74. See Huang Qichen, *Aomen Tongshi*, pp. 238–9; Montalto de Jesus, *Lishi shang de Aomen*, p. 27; Steve Shipp, *Macau, China: A Political History of the Portuguese Colony's Transition to Chinese Rule* (Jefferson, North Carolina, and London: McFarland & Company, Inc., Publishers, 1997), p. 36; and Wu Zhiliang, *Shengcun zhi Dao*, p. 54.
75. Tang Kaijian, *Weiliduo*, p. 24.
76. Gunn, *Encountering Macau*, p. 36. See also Liu Ranling, *Wenming de Boyi*, pp. 225–6.
77. Huang Qichen, *Aomen Tongshi*, pp. 238–41.
78. For a fairly complete description of the Senate, see Wu Zhichang, "Aomen zhimin zhengzhi de yanbian" (The transformation of Macau's colonial political system), in Deng Kaisong, Huang Hongzhao, Wu Zhiliang, and Lu Xiaomin (eds.) *Aomen Lishi Xinshuo* (New research on Macau history) (Shijiazhuang: Huashan Wenyi Chubanshe, 2000), pp. 514–9; see also Deng Kaisong and Xie Houhe, *Aomen Lishi yu Shehui Fazhan*, pp. 28–31.
79. Jesus, *Lishi shang de Aomen*, pp. 29–31, 110; Shipp, *Macau, China*, p. 37.
80. Ljungstedt, *Zaoqi Aomen Shi*, pp. 79–80.
81. Huang Qichen, *Aomen Tongshi*, p. 240.
82. See also Boxer, *Fidalgos in the Far East 1550–1770*, p. 272.
83. Jesus, *Lishi shang de Aomen*, pp. 108–10.
84. Ibid., p. 113. For more on the internal struggles between the Portuguese themselves, see also Wu Zhiliang, "Mingdai Aomen Zhengzhi Shehui" (The politics and society in the Ming dynasty), in Wu Zhiliang, Jin Guoping, and Tang Kaijian (eds.) *Aomen Shi Xin Bian*, Vol. 1, pp. 101–4.
85. Ljungstedt, *Zaoqi Aomen Shi*, pp. 78–9.
86. Coates, *Macau and the British*, pp. 47–8.
87. See Porter, *Macau, the Imaginary City*, pp. 46–7 as well as a map showing the geography of the area.
88. The building is mainly of Chinese architectural style, but the front walls have Portuguese characteristics. This is where the two-story building of the Senate was later constructed in 1783. See Jin Guoping and Wu Zhiliang, *Guo Shizi Men*, pp. 149–70, and their *Zaoqi Aomen Shi Lun*, pp. 284–311 for a more detailed discussion of the history of the building, including the controversy over the ownership of it. There are even controversies over whether the building actually existed. Tang Kaijian believes that although there was probably a city hall built by the Portuguese, the city hall in the Chinese architectural style as seen in the picture probably did not exist, because he could not find such a building in the maps from the 16th and 17th centuries (Tang Kaijian, *Weiliduo*, pp. 18–22). He thinks that it might be an imaginary product by Yin Guangren and Zhang Rulin. See Yin and Zhang, *Aomen Jilue Jiaozhu* (An edited version of *The Annals of Macau*), edited by Zhao Chunchen (Macau:

Aomen Wenhua Si or Macau Culture Department, [1751] 1992), pp. 218–9. But Jin Guoping and Wu Zhiliang think that the building did exist and the architectural style is a good example of cultural integration. For this issue, see also Tong Qiaohui, *Aomen Chengshi Huanjing yu Wenmai Yanjiu* (A study on the city environment and cultural traits in Macau) (Guangzhou: Guangdong Renmin Chubanshe, 2008), p. 110.

89. Huang Qichen, *Aomen Tongshi*, pp. 73–90.
90. Ibid., pp. 78, 82–90. For the various kinds of rules the Chinese set for the Portuguese, see also Deng Kaisong and Xie Houhe, *Aomen Lishi yu Shehui Fazhan*, pp. 23–25.
91. Huang Qichen, *Aomen Tongshi*, pp. 211–2, 215–6.
92. For more on the Chinese political structure, see also Lou Shenghua, "Hunhe, duoyuan yu zizhi: zaoqi Aomen de xingzheng" (Hybridity, plurality, and autonomy: public administration in early Macau), in Wu Zhiliang, Jin Guoping, and Tang Kaijian (eds.) *Aomen Shi Xin Bian*, Vol. 1.
93. Huang Qichen, *Aomen Tongshi*, pp. 221–4.
94. For more examples of the Chinese tactics, see later sections. For a previous example, in 1645, the Chinese cut off the Portuguese food supplies to punish them for their tolerance of the English (see Lamas, *History of Macau*, p. 43).
95. For an account of this event, see also Jesus, *Lishi Shang de Aomen*, pp. 113–4; Liu Ranling, *Wenming de Boyi*, pp. 212–3; Ljungstedt, *Zaoqi Aomen Shi*, pp. 126–7; Yin Guangren and Zhang Rulin, *Aomen Jilue Jiaozhu*, pp. 4–5, 87–94.
96. Wu Zhiliang, *Shengcun zhi Dao*, p. 126.
97. Huang Qichen, *Aomen Tongshi*, pp. 258–60; for that part of the history, see also Jin Guoping and Wu Zhiliang, *Guo Shizi Men*, pp. 188–208; Zhang Guogang, *Cong Zhong Xi Chushi dao Liyi Zhizheng: Ming Qing Chuan Jiao Shi yu Zhong Xi Wenhua Jiaoliu* (From the meeting of China and the West to the Controversy of Rites: the missionaries in the Ming and Qing dynasties and the cultural exchange between China and the West) (Beijing: People's Press, 2003).
98. For an account of this event, see Huang Qichen, *Aomen Tongshi*, p. 256; Jesus, *Lishi shang de Aomen*, p. 118; Ljungstedt, *Zaoqi Aomen Shi*, pp. 128–9; Yin Guangren and Zhang Rulin, *Aomen Jilue Jiaozhu*, pp. 81–4.
99. Huang Qichen, *Aomen Tongshi*, pp. 101–6; Lamas, *History of Macau*, p. 42; Wu Zhiliang, *Shengcun zhi Dao*, p. 68.
100. Huang Qichen, *Aomen Tongshi*, pp. 243–54; Wu Zhiliang, *Shengcun zhi Dao*, pp. 106–21.
101. Pina-Cabral, *Between China and Europe*, p. 226.
102. Wu Zhiliang, *Shengcun zhi Dao*, pp. 132–47.
103. Ibid., pp. 138–47.
104. The statue of Amaral was later wrapped up and shipped back to Portugal. In 1990, Lu Ping, director of the Chinese State Council's Hong Kong and Macau Affairs Office, said that the statue was a despised symbol of colonialism and should be removed by 1999. It was removed in 1991.
105. Coates, *A Macau Narrative*, p. 89; for more on Amaral, see Liu Ranling, *Wenming de Boyi*, pp. 344–8.
106. Zhang Guogang, *Cong Zhong Xi Chushi dao Liyi zhi Zheng*, p. 56.
107. See Huang Qichen, *Aomen Tongshi*, pp. 278–84; Wu Zhiliang, *Shengcun zhi Dao*, pp. 148–64; Shipp, *Macau, China*, pp. 71–2.
108. Quoted in Pina-Cabral, *Between China and Europe*, p. 62.
109. Coates, *A Macau Narrative*, p. 90.
110. For more on Amaral, see also Coates, *A Macau Narrative*, pp. 88–94; Pina-Cabral, *Between China and Europe*, pp. 60–3.

111. Pina-Cabral, *Between China and Europe*, p. 63. The statue of Colonel Mesquita was made in 1940 and was placed in front of the Senate, but it was destroyed during the riots in 1966. See Pina-Cabral, *Between China and Europe*, p. 68; and Gunn, *Encountering Macau*, p. 69. Several streets are still named after him, though. See also Tong Qiaohui, *Aomen Chengshi Huanjing yu Wenmai Yanjiu*, p. 108. According to a report by *The Times* of London in 1849, it was said that 74 Chinese were killed in the battle. See Pittis and Henders (selected and edited) *Macao: Mysterious Decay and Romance*, p. 171.
112. For more discussion on Amaral and his rule, see also Fei Chengkang, "Yamaliu shidai yu Putaoya guanzhi Aomen de kaiduan" (The times of Amaral and the beginning of the Portuguese rule), in Wu Zhiliang, Jin Guoping, and Tang Kaijian (eds.) *Aomen Shi Xin Bian*, Vol. 1.
113. For a more complete discussion of the disputes over the territory, see Hung Hongzhao, "Qing mo min chu Aomen huajie zhi jiaoshe" (The negotiations on the border delineation in Macau in the end of Qing and the beginning of the Republic of China), in Wu Zhiliang, Jin Guoping, and Tang Kaijian (eds.) *Aomen Shi Xin Bian*, Vol. 1.
114. For the issues surrounding the treaty, see Gunn, *Encountering Macau*, pp. 63–8; Huang Qichen, *Aomen Tongshi*, pp. 287–307; Lin Yun, "Yapian zhanzheng jieshu dao 'Zhong Pu Hehao Tongshang Tiaoyue' qianding shiqi Yue Ao guanxi de zhongda zhuanzhe" (The serious turn of events in the relationship between Guangdong and Macau during the period from the end of the Opium War to the signing of the Luso-Chinese Treaty of Friendship and Trade), in Deng Kaisong, Wu Zhiliang, and Lu Xiaomin (eds.) *Yue Ao Guanxi Shi*, pp. 244–67; Shipp, *Macau, China*, pp. 71–2; Wu Zhiliang, *Shengcun zhi Dao*, pp. 164–206; Xu Suqin, "Zhong Pu 'Hehao Tongshang Tiaoyue' de qianding" (The signing of the Luso-Chinese Treaty of Friendship and Trade), in Deng Kaisong, Huang Hongzhao, Wu Zhiliang, and Lu Xiaomin (eds.) *Aomen Lishi Xinshuo*, pp. 248–76.
115. Xu Suqin, "Qing mo zhengzhi fengyun zhong Yue Ao liang di de xianghu yingxiang yu Yue Ao jie wu fenzheng" (The relationship between Guangdong and Macau in the politics in the end of Qing and the conflicts regarding the boarders between Guangdong and Macau), in Deng Kaisong, Wu Zhiliang, and Lu Xiaomin (eds.) *Yue Ao Guanxi Shi*, pp. 344–74.
116. For more of them, see Xu Suqin, "Minguo chu zhi sanshi niandai Yue Ao guanxi de dongdang qifu" (The ups and downs of the Guangdong-Macau relations from the beginning of the Republic of China to the 1930s), in Deng Kaisong, Wu Zhiliang, and Lu Xiaomin (eds.) *Yue Ao Guanxi Shi*, pp. 378–436. See also Jin Guoping and Wu Zhiliang, *Jinghai Piaomiao*, pp. 122–47.
117. Huang Qichen, *Aomen Tongshi*, pp. 308–11; Wu Zhiliang, *Shengcun zhi Dao*, pp. 206–35; Camoes C. K. Tam, *Aomen Zhuquan Wenti Shi Mo (1553–1993)*, pp. 214–6. Tam puts the number of deaths in the incident at 170.
118. Huang Qichen, *Aomen Tongshi*, p. 495; Wu Zhiliang, *Shengcun zhi Dao*, pp. 244–50.
119. Fei Mao Shi (Moisés Silva Fernandes), "1952 nian guanzha shijian: guoji chengnuo yu dangdi xianzhi tiaojian zhijian de chongtu" (The Guanzha Incident in 1952: the conflict between international commitment and the constraints of the local conditions), in Wu Zhiliang, Jin Guoping, and Tang Kaijian (eds.) *Aomen Shi Xin Bian*, Vol. 1. Fernandes has a fuller description of the events, including the skirmishes for a couple of months before July 25, with no casualties, and the difficult negotiations after the event, with the help of the prominent Chinese elites in Macau like He Xian (Ho Yin) and Ma Wan Qi, who ran between Macau and the mainland trying to reconcile the two sides.
120. Huang Qichen, *Aomen Tongshi*, pp. 495–6; Wu Zhiliang, *Shengcun zhi Dao*, pp. 255–6.
121. McGivering's interview of Victor Ng Wing-lok in McGiverning, *Macao Remembers*, p. 38.

122. Guan Zhendong and Chen Shurong, *He Xian Zhuan* (A biography of Ho Yin) (Macau: Macau Press, 1999); Huang Qichen, *Aomen Tongshi*, pp. 498–501; Shipp, *Macau, China*, pp. 87–9; Wu Zhiliang, *Shengcun zhi Dao*, pp. 259–86.
123. Shipp, *Macau, China*, p. 89.
124. Lo Shiu Hing, *Political Development in Macau* (Hong Kong: The Chinese University Press, 1995), p. 68.
125. Wu Zhiliang, *Shengcun zhi Dao*, pp. 214–7.
126. For more on the democratization process, see Lo Shiu Hing, *Political Development in Macau*, pp. 31–41. For more on the political system in Macau at the time, see Herbert S. Yee, *Macau in Transition: From Colony to Autonomous Region* (New York: Palgrave, 2001), pp. 22–37.
127. Shipp, *Macau, China*, pp. 178–93 for the Organic Statute of Macau; see also Wu Zhiliang, *Shengcun zhi Dao*, pp. 321–4.
128. Wu Zhiliang, *Shengcun zhi Dao*, p. 334.
129. Ibid., pp. 324, 333–40; Wu Zhiliang, "Jiangou Aomen de shimin shehui" (The construction of Macau's civil society), in Wu Zhiliang and Chen Xinxin, *Aomen Zhengzhi Shehui Yanjiu* (A study of Macau's politics and society) (Macau: Macau Adult Educational Association, 2000), pp. 144–57.
130. R. Afonso and F. G. Pereira, "The Constitution and Legal System," in Cremer (ed.) *Macau: City of Commerce and Culture*, p. 189.
131. See Wu Zhiliang, *Shengcun zhi Dao*, p. 324, for a description of the problems of the old system.
132. Cheang Hong Kuong, *Aomen Tebie Xingzheng Qu "Xingzheng Zhudao" Zhengce zhi Youlai yu Shijian* (The origin and practice of Macao SAR's "executive led" policy), MA thesis, the University of Macau, 2003, p. 69.
133. See Zhidong Hao, "Social Stratification and Ethnic and Class Politics in Macao before and after the Handover in 1999" in *China: An International Journal*, Vol. 13, No. 1 (April 2015), p. 82.
134. Dai Yongru, "Cong lifahui xuanju kan zheng shang guanxi" (The relationship between the government and businesses as seen from the election of the legislators), *Shang Xun* (Business intelligence), No. 49, September 2009, p. 9. Hao, "Social Stratification and Ethnic and Class Politics," pp. 82–83.
135. Shipp, *Macau, China*, p. 155.
136. "Cao Qizhen [Susana Chou]: yihan ren nei wei lifa" (Cao Qizhen is sorry that they did not make the law), *Macao Daily*, July 24, 2009. Cao was the three-term president of the Legislative Assembly, and retired from the post of legislator in 2009.
137. Lo Shiu Hing, *Political Development in Macau*, pp. 205–7.
138. Herbet Yee, *Macau in Transition*, p. 37; and "Xianggang de gao guan wenze zhi jiqi dui Aomen zhengzhi gaige de qishi" (The responsibility system of the higher officials in Hong Kong and the implication of the practice for Macau's political reform), in Herbert Yee (Yu Zhen), Eilo Yu (Yu Yongyi), and Bruce Kwan (Kuang Jinjun) (eds.) *Shuang Cheng Ji II: Huigui hou Gang Ao de Zhengzhi, Jingji ji Shehui Fazhan* (A tale of two cities II: the political, economic and social development in Hong Kong and Macau after their return to China) (Macau: Aomen Shehui Kexue Xuehui), p. 129.
139. Hao Zhidong, "Aomen zhengzhi yu shehui fazhan de fengfeng yuyu" (The ups and downs in Macau's political and social development), *Jiuding*, September 2008.
140. Herbert Yee, *Macau in Transition*, pp. 38, 152.
141. Liu Bolong, "Huigui yihou Aomen duiwai guanxi de huigu yu zhanwang," in *Aomen 2002* (Macau in 2002) (Macau: Macau Foundation, 2002), at http://www.macaudata.com/macauweb/book269/.

142. For the issues around Article 23, see Chen Xinxin and Zheng Zijie, "Cong gang Ao tequ 'Jiben Fa 23 Tiao' lifa kan shehui de jihua yu zhenghe" (Polarization and integration in society as a result of the possible legislation of Article 23 of the Basic Law), in Herbert Yee (Yu Zhen), Eilo Yu (Yu Yongyi), and Bruce Kwan (Kuang Jinjun) (eds.) *Shuang Cheng Ji II*, pp. 437–58.
143. Yael Tamir, "Who Is Afraid of a Global State?" in Kjell Goldmann, Ulf Hannerz, and Charles Westin (eds.) *Nationalism and Internationalism in the Post-Cold War Era* (London and New York: Routledge, 2000), pp. 245–6; and again He Baogang, "The Question of Sovereignty in the Taiwan Strait," pp. 7–8.
144. Jin Guoping and Wu Zhiliang, *Jing Hai Piaomiao*, pp. 86–121, discuss a similar point when they talk about the "foreign settlements" (蕃坊) and "dual loyalty" (雙重效忠), referring to the Chinese arrangements in Macau and the Portuguese relationship with China respectively.

Chapter 3

1. Clayton, *"If We Are Not Different,"* pp. 362–3.
2. One of the anonymous reviewers points out that it might be problematic to divide the periods of Macau's economy into non–*pin mun* businesses before the First Opium War and *pin mun* businesses after it. Indeed, it is hard to say what is legal and what is illegal, especially from the sociological point of view of the social construction of reality. We are going by the normal understanding of the issues here. But I agree with the reviewer that indeed both legality and division of the periods can be open to questioning. Macau's economic history is more characterized by a wavelike pattern of ups and downs instead of a single, deep incision. I look forward to more discussion on this.
3. The date of the founding of the gun foundry is not clear. Some say 1557 (Huang Qichen, *Aomen Tongshi*, p. 57). But Jin Guoping and Wu Zhiliang say that 1557 might be too early a date for the industry, and put the date at 1623 (Jin and Wu, *Jinghai Piaomiao*, p. 278; see also their *Zaoqi Aomen Shi Lun*, pp. 312–21). Gunn mentioned, though, that from 1612 "guns caste in Macau by Bocarro were much in demand from Japan to China as were Portuguese specialists in military technology" (see Gunn, *Encountering Macau*, p. 40). Tang Kaijian thinks also that before 1621, Macau was already producing cannons (see Tang Kaijian, *Weliduo*, pp. 102–11). For more on the gun foundry, see also Richard J. Garrett, *The Defences of Macau: Forts, Ships and Weapons over 450 Years* (Hong Kong: Hong Kong University Press, 2010), pp. 146–9.
4. C. R. Boxer, "Shiliu—shiqi shiji Aomen de zongjiao he maoyi zhongzhuan gang zhi zuoyong" (Macau as a religious and trading entrepot in the 16th–17th centuries), in Huang Qichen and Deng Kaisong (eds.) *Zhong Wai Xuezhe Lun Aomen Lishi* (Studies on Macau history by Chinese and foreign scholars) (Macau: Macau Foundation, 1995), pp. 190–1.
5. As Boxer comments, had it not been for the help of the Jesuits in Beijing, the Qing rulers might have taken it on the Portuguese in Macau for their support of the falling Ming dynasty. After all, Macau did send out soldiers to help fight the invading Qing army. See Boxer, *Fidalgos in the Far East*, p. 155.
6. Lin Zesheng, *Shiliu zhi Shiba Shiji Aomen yu Zhongguo zhi Guanxi*, pp. 210–23. See also Li Xiangyu, *Aomen Sheng Baolu Xueyuan Yanjiu* (A study on the St. Paul's College in Macau) (Macau: Macao Daily Press, 2001), p. 24.
7. Huang Qichen, *Aomen Tongshi*, pp. 56–63; Jin Guoping and Wu Zhiliang, *Jinghai Piaomiao*, pp. 275–83.
8. For more discussion on the Portuguese trade starting in 1542, see Boxer, *Fidalgos in the Far East*, pp. 7–8; Liu Ranling, *Wenming de Boyi*, pp. 145–53; Rui D'Ávila Lourido, "The

Portuguese, the Maritime Silk Road and Macao's Connection with the Philippines in the Late Ming Dynasty," *Review of Culture*, No. 2, April 2002; Willis (ed.) *China and Macau*, p. xxiii.
9. For more discussion on the trade at the time, see Cremer, "From Portugal to Japan," pp. 23–37; Deng Kaisong and Xie Houhe, *Aomen Lishi yu Shehui Fazhan*, pp. 43–50; Huang Qichen, *Aomen Tongshi*, pp. 36–49; Gunn, *Encountering Macau*, pp. 13–33; Lamas, *History of Macau*, pp. 24–27; Ljungstedt, *Zaoqi Aomen Shi*, pp. 100–4, 140–2; Ptak, "Macau: A Historical Perspective," pp. 29–46; Quan Hansheng, "Ming dai zhongye hou Aomen de haiwai maoyi" (Macau's overseas trade after the middle of Ming dynasty), in Huang Qichen and Deng Kaisong (eds.) *Zhong Wai Xuezhe Lun Aomen Lishi* (Studies on Macau history by Chinese and foreign scholars) (Macau: Macau Foundation, 1995), pp. 148–74; and Zhang Guogang, *Cong Zhong Xi Chu Shi dao Liyi zhi Zheng*, pp. 65–8.
10. Lamas's description of the trading season: "The trading season lasted from October to March, when the ships sailed home. During the following 'dead season' the men could spend more time in Macau, except for the opium traders, who business thrived all year long." See Lamas, *Everything in Style*, p. 313.
11. Huang Qichen, *Aomen Tongshi*, pp. 167–85.
12. For the Portuguese trade in Macau, see also George Bryan Souza, "The Portuguese Merchant Fleet at Macao in the 17th and 18th Centuries," *Review of Culture*, international edition 13, January 2005. For more discussion on the trade between Macau and other places in the world, see Lamas, *Everything in Style*, chapter 6, and the following articles in Wu Zhiliang, Jin Guoping, and Tang Kaijian (eds.) *Aomen Shi Xin Bian*, Vol. 2: Wan Ming, "Ming dai Aomen maoyi" (Trade in Macau in the Ming dynasty); Pu Ta Ke (Roderich Ptak), "Ming dai Aomen yu Dong Nan Ya de maoyi" (Trade between Macau and South East Asia in the Ming dynasty); Luo Li Lu (Rui Lourido), "16–18 shiji de Aomen maoyi yu shehui" (Trade and society in Macau from 16th to 18th centuries); Qi Yinping, "Zaoqi Ao Ri maoyi" (Early trade between Macau and Japan); Meng An Na (Anabela Monteiro), "1640–1680 zhijian de Aomen maoyi" (Macau trade between 1640 and 1680); Lu Xiaomin and Deng Kaisong, "Yapian zhanzheng qian de Yue Ao guanxi" (The relationship between Guangdong and Macao before the Opium War); Su Sa (George Bryan Souza), "Aomen yu Pu Shu Yindu: zhimin zhili, xingzheng guan ji shangye, yi yancao wei li" (Macau and the Portuguese India: colonial administration, government officials, and commerce, with tobacco as an example); Jia Er Xi Ya (José Manuel Garcia), "Aomen yu Feilubin zhi lishi guanxi" (The historical relations between Macau and the Philippines); Bo Si (Arie Pos), "'Yi yi zhi yi': Mingdai de Ao He guanxi" ("To use foreigners to control foreigners": the relationship between Macau and Holland); Su Yi Yang (Ivo Carneiro de Sousa), "Aomen yu Diwen: zhimin guanli, maoyi ji chuan jiao" (Macau and Timor: colonial administration, trade, and missionary work); Luo Li Lu (Rui Lourido), "Aomen yu Baxi de zaoqi guanxi" (The early relations between Macau and Brazil); Su Yi Yang (Ivo Carneiro de Sousa), "Aomen yu Yindunixiya: siren maoxian, chaye ji zhimin sixiang" (Macau and Indonesia: individual risk taking, tea, and colonial thinking).
13. Coates, *Macao and the British*, p. 65. For the early records of opium use for medicinal purposes, see also Deng Kaisong, "Yapian zhanzheng qian Aomen de zousi maoyi yu lin zexu zai Aomen jin yan," in Huang Qichen and Deng Kaisong (eds.) *Zhong Wai Xuezhe Lun Aomen Lishi*, p. 327.
14. Huang Qichen, *Aomen Tongshi*, p. 189.
15. Shipp, *Macau, China*, p. 69.
16. See also Lamas, *Everything in Style*, pp. 181–9, for more discussion on the discovery of opium as substitute for silver and its nefarious consequences on the Chinese; Lintin Island as

center of opium smuggling; American opium dealers and abstainers; and opium consumption in the West.
17. Coates, *Macao and the British*, pp. 65–6; also Deng Kaisong, "Yapian zhanzheng qian Aomen de zousi maoyi yu lin zexu zai Aomen jin yan," pp. 327, 339.
18. Coates, *Macau Narrative*, p. 73.
19. Tang Kaijian, Chen Wenyuan, and Ye Nong (eds.) *Yapian Zhanzheng hou Aomen Shehui Shenghuo Jishi: Jindai Baokan Aomen Ziliao Xuancui* (Life in Macau after the Opium War: excerpts from modern newspapers) (Guangzhou: Huacheng Chubanshe, 2001), pp. 136–44; see also Deng Kaisong, "Yapian zhanzheng qian Aomen de zousi maoyi yu lin zexu zai Aomen jin yan," p. 335; Lamas, *Everything in Style*, pp. 181–8 on the discovery of opium as substitute for silver, Lintin Island as center of opium smuggling, American opium dealers and abstainers, and opium consumption in the West.
20. Shipp, *Macau, China*, pp. 68–9.
21. Jesus, *Lishi shang de Aomen*, p. 303.
22. Huang Hongzhao, *Aomen Jian Shi* (A brief history of Macao) (Hong Kong: Sanlian Press, 1999), p. 221; Quan Hansheng, "Ming dai zhongye hou Aomen de haiwai maoyi," p. 155.
23. A. H. de Oliveira Marques, *History of Portugal, Volume I: From Lusitânia to Empire* (New York: Columbia University Press, 1972), p. 468.
24. See Gunn, *Encountering Macau*, p. 73. For more discussion on the coolie trade, see also Jin Guoping and Wu Zhiliang, *Guo Shizi Men*, pp. 227–40; Wang Zhaoming, "Yapian zhanzheng qian hou Aomen diwei de bianhua" (The status change of Macau around the Opium War), in Huang Qichen and Deng Kaisong (eds.) *Zhong Wai Xuezhe Lun Aomen Lishi*, p. 210. Some estimates put the number of baracoons well over 200 to 300. See also Deng Kaisong and Xie Houhe, *Aomen Lishi yu Shehui Fazhan*, p. 138; Deng Kaisong, Yu Siwei, and Lu Xiaomin, *Aomen Cangsang* (The vicissitudes of Macao) (Zhuhai: Zhuhai Press, 1999), pp. 64–7; Huang Hongzhao, *Aomen Jian Shi*, pp. 225–8; Huang Qichen, *Aomen Tongshi*, pp. 192–7.
25. Huang Qichen, *Aomen Tongshi*, p. 199.
26. See Coates, *Macao and the British*, pp. 131–2; Pina-Cabral, *Between China and Europe*, p. 24; Pittis and Henders (selected and edited) *Macao: Mysterious Decay and Romance*, pp. 77–80, citing Russell H. Conwell's work on people for sale. Conwell was an American publisher and Baptist minister who campaigned against the coolie trade.
27. See excerpts from *The Cuba Commission Report: A Hidden History of the Chinese in Cuba*, the Original English-Language Text of 1876 (Baltimore: Johns Hopkins University Press, 1993). At https://cla.umn.edu/sites/cla.umn.edu/files/cuba_commission_report_exerpts.pdf, accessed October 9, 2018.
28. See Deng Kaisong, Yu Siwei, and Lu Xiaomin, *Aomen Cangsang*, pp. 64–7; Huang Qichen, *Aomen Tongshi*, pp. 198–209; Jin Guoping and Wu Zhiliang, *Guo Shizi Men*, pp. 227–40; for newspaper reports on the coolie trade at the time, see Tang Kaijian, Chen Wenyuan, and Ye Nong (eds.) *Yapian Zhanzheng hou Aomen Shehui Shenghuo Jishi*, pp. 209–11, 241–53. For the accounts of the coolies themselves, see especially *The Cuba Commission Report: A Hidden History of the Chinese in Cuba*, the Original English-Language Text of 1876 (Baltimore: Johns Hopkins University, 1993).
29. The information on pilots is from Paul Arthur Van Dyke, *Port Canton and the Pearl River Delta, 1690–1845*, Vol. 1, Ph.D. dissertation in history (University of Southern California, 2002), pp. 114–5, 123, 126–30, 154–63.
30. Ibid., p. 116. On p. 532, Van Dyke reports 22 by the 1930s.
31. Ibid., p. 163.
32. Cited in ibid., p. 126.
33. Ibid., p. 130.

34. Ibid., pp. 185, 221–2, 225. Closely related to compradors were interpreters or linguists. But because of a lack of data, I would simply refer the reader to Van Dyke's discussion of linguists in Canton in the same book to have an idea of the linguists in Macau. Fay also mentions the linguists in Canton who "kept on the go day and night, hurrying from warehouse to warehouse to examine and check out teas, arranging for chop boats, settling various obligations at the Hoppo's yamen" (Fay, *The Opium War*, p. 35).
35. Cited in Nan P. Hodges and Arthur W. Hummel (eds.) *Lights and Shadows of a Macao Life: The Journal of Harriett Low, Traveling Spinster*, Part One: 1829–1832, Part Two: 1832–1834 (Woodinville, WA: The History Bank), p. 70.
36. Gunn, *Encountering Macau*, p. 42. See also Coates, *A Macau Narrative*, pp. 35, 39; Cremer, "From Portugal to Japan," p. 35; Manuel Teixeira, "Yi ba wu si nian Meiguo haijun zhunjiang Peili kandao de Aomen" (The Macau seen by an American commander Perry in 1854, or originally in Portuguese: Macau Visto pelo Comodoro Perry em 1854), in Huang Qichen and Deng Kaisong (eds.) *Zhong Wai Xuezhe Lun Aomen Lishi* (Studies on Macau history by Chinese and foreign scholars) (Macau: Macau Foundation, 1995).
37. For workers to be a formal class, organization is needed. See Zhidong Hao, *Intellectuals at a Crossroads: The Changing Politics of China's Knowledge Workers* (Albany, New York: State University of New York Press, 2003), pp. 262–5. Since there was generally no organization, these groups of workers can only be referred to loosely as part of the working class. That same applies to the craft workers whom we will discuss below.
38. Cited in C. R. Boxer (ed. and trans.) *Seventeenth Century Macau in Contemporary Documents and Illustration* (Hong Kong: Heinemann, Asia, 1984), p. 15.
39. Wu Zhiliang, *Shengcun zhi Dao*, pp. 85–6.
40. Hoges and Hummel (eds.) *Lights and Shadows of a Macao Life*, p. 90; underlining original.
41. Porter, *Macau: The Imaginary City*, p. 137. The quote within the quote was from Yin Guangren and Zhang Rulin, *Aomen Jilue Jiaozhu*, p. 144. The original words are: 食余，傾於一器，如馬槽，黑奴男女以手搏食。See pp. 135–41 for more examples of the Portuguese upper class life in Macau.
42. Lamas, *Everything in Style*, p. 232.
43. Ibid., p. 233.
44. Wu Zhiliang, *Shengcun zhi Dao*, p. 226.
45. Ibid., p. 255.
46. Hodges and Hummel, *Lights and Shadows*, p. 69.
47. Cited in Van Dyke, *Port Canton and the Pearl River Delta*, p. 208.
48. McGivering, *Macau Remembers*, pp. 12, 65, 86, 121, where some talked about having "lots of servants" and drivers.
49. Van Dyke, *Port Canton and the Pearl River Delta*, pp. 209–12.
50. Lamas, *Everything in Style*, p. 158.
51. Gunn, *Encountering Macau*, pp. 89–90.
52. Jules Itier reporting on the contraband port in Pittis and Henders (selected and edited) *Macao: Mysterious Decay and Romance*, p. 84.
53. Ibid., pp. 148–9.
54. Ibid., pp. 147–8.
55. Ibid., pp. 130–1.
56. Ibid., p. 140. This excerpt was by George Wingrove Cooke in a report in 1858 on "European pirates."
57. Ibid., pp. 139–42.
58. For a drawing of fishing families' boatdwellings in Macau, see also C. Guillen-Nunez, "Macau through the Eyes of Nineteenth Century Painters," in R. D. Cremer (ed.) *Macau: City of Commerce and Culture* (Hong Kong: UEA Press Ltd., 1987), p. 66.

59. Cited in Rogério Miguel Puga, "Macao through the American Female Gaze: The Epistolary Diaries of Harriett Low (1829–1834) and Rebecca Chase Kinsman (1843–1847)," a talk given at the University of Macau, 2003, excerpts from the handout.
60. Boxer, *Seventeenth Century Macau*, p. 48.
61. McGiverning, *Macao Remembers*, p. 201.
62. Ibid., p. 202.
63. Macau Government Statistics Bureau, at http://www.dsec.gov.mo/index.asp?src=/chinese/indicator/c_ie_ indicator.html, last accessed on February 16, 2006.
64. Zha Canchang, *Zhuanxing, Bianxiang yu Chuanbo*, pp. 175–6. There were 145,000 persons in Macau at that time. Another figure puts the number of the fishing population at 60,000 or 71% of the population. See Yang Renfei, *Aomen Jindai Hua Licheng* (The modernization of Macao) (Macao: Macao Daily Press, 2000), p. 178. Yang was probably citing Huang Qichen, *Aomen Tonshi*, p. 321. But Zha thinks that the number is too high. Gunn, on the other hand, reports that Macau statistics for 1927 show that the almost half of the Macau population of 157,175 persons were classified as maritime. That is about 50%, which is higher than Zha's number, although they were a few years apart, and it is lower than that of Huang's. But by whatever counts, fishing was a very important trade in the 1920s and was a main employer of labor in the prewar years, with its products constituting a quarter of Macau's total exports in 1930. See Gunn, *Encountering Macau*, p. 79.
65. McGiverning, *Macao Remembers*, p. 193.
66. Ibid., pp. 149–50; *Macao Daily*, "Xiu yu qi ming jieshu yuchuan zhengzhuang dai fa" (Summer break for fishing ends tomorrow and boats are ready to go), July 31, 2006. The newspaper articles mentions that 300 boats had finished repairs, got their provisions, and were ready to go fishing on the sea. The number might give us an idea of how many ships there are now and the number of people in the trade. It also mentions that a large number of hired hands from the mainland had also returned to their ships.
67. Yang Renfei, *Aomen Jindaihua Licheng*, pp. 175–6.
68. Ibid., p. 177.
69. Zha Canchang, *Zhuanxing, Bianxiang yu Chuanbo*, pp. 177–81; Yang Renfei, *Aomen Jindaihua Licheng*, pp. 177–80. A cement factory was established in 1886 but was moved to Hong Kong in early 1930s. There used to be in the 1880s 15 tea factories. See Deng Kaisong and Xie Houhe, *Aomen Lishi yu Shehui Fazhan*, p. 142; and Gunn, *Encountering Macau*, pp. 74–5. See also Tang Kaijian, *Bei yiwang de "gongye qifei": Aomen gongye fazhan shi gao 1557–1941* (The forgotten "rise of industry": A history of Macau's industrial development 1557–1941) (Macau: Macau Bureau of Cultural Affairs, 2014).
70. See Zheng Caihong, "Danzai paozhu ye de huihuang suiyue" (The glorious days of the firecrackers industry in Taipa), pp. 100–7, in Zhang Zhuofu (ed.) *Haidao Fengyun* (The life in Macao) (Macau: Aomen Jindai Wenxue Xuehui, or Macao association of modern history, 2001), pp. 101–5. See also Deng Kaisong and Xie Houhe, *Aomen Lishi yu Shehui Fazhan*, p. 142.
71. Yang Renfei, *Aomen Jindaihua Licheng*, pp. 158–69.
72. Huang Qichen, *Aomen Tongshi*, p. 333.
73. Yang Renfei, *Aomen Jindaihua Licheng*, pp. 169–81.
74. Gunn, *Encountering Macau*, p. 144.
75. Yang Renfei, *Aomen Jindaihua Licheng*, p. 173.
76. For more on the development of Chinese capitalists in Macau, see also Lin Guangzhi, "Wan Qing Aomen hua shang de jueqi jiqi shehui diwei de bianhua" (The rise of Chinese businessmen in Macau in the late Qing era and their transformation in social status), in Wu Zhiliang, Jin Guoping, and Tang Kaijian (eds.) *Aomen Shi Xin Bian*, Vol. 1.

77. Gunn, *Encountering Macau*, pp. 138–9. See also R. Feitor, "Macau's Modern Economy," in R. D. Cremer (ed.) *Macau: City of Commerce and Culture* (Hong Kong: UEA Press Ltd., 1987), pp. 139–53; Fung Kwan, "Gang Ao jingji fazhan shouru suode fengpei" (The income distribution amidst the economic development in Hong Kong and Macau), in Yu Zhen (ed.) *Shuang Cheng Ji: Gang Ao de Zhengzhi, Jingji ji Shehui Fazhan* (A tale of two cities: the political, economic and social development in Hong Kong and Macau) (Macau: Macau Social Sciences Association, 1998), pp. 265–6.
78. Deng Kaisong and Xie Houhe, *Aomen Lishi yu Shehui Fazhan*, p. 199.
79. Huang Qichen, *Aomen Tongshi*, p. 578.
80. Cited in Huang Qichen, *Aomen Tongshi*, p. 177. For more on the development of the gaming industry in Macau, see Hu Gen, *Aomen Jindai Bocai Ye Shi* (Macau's gaming industry in the modern times) (Guangzhou: Guangdong Renmin Chubanshe, 2009).
81. Jesus, *Lishi shang de Aomen*, pp. 234, 263. This reminds one of a similar situation in the latter half of the 18th century. The following poem, though uncomplimentary about Macau, can give us an idea of what it was like in Macau then: A government without power, a similar bishop, / a den of virtuous nuns, / three monasteries of friars, five thousand / *nhons* [Macanese] and Chinese Christians who behave very badly. // A cathedral that today is exactly the same, / fourteen penniless canons, / many poor people, many base women; / one hundred Portuguese, packed altogether as if in a stable. // Six forts with no soldiers, but one drummer / three parishes ornamented only in wood / a vicar general without assistant / Two colleges, one of them very bad, / a Senate that is above everything / is as much as Portugal has in Macao. The poem was written by the Portuguese poet Manuel Maria Barbosa do Bocage (1765–1805) after his brief stay in Macau from 1789 to 1790. See Pittis and Henders (selected and edited) *Macao: Mysterious Decay and Romance*, pp. 191–2.
82. Pina-Cabral, *Between China and Europe*, pp. 87–103; A. Pinho, "Gambing in Macau," in R. D. Cremer (ed.) *Macau: City of Commerce and Culture* (Hong Kong: UEA Press Ltd., 1987), pp. 155–64.
83. Guangdong Sheng Dang'an Guan (ed.) *Gaundong Aomen Dang'an Shiliao Xuan Bian* (Selected documents on Guangdong and Macau history) (Beijing: Zhongguo Dang'an Chubanshe, 1999), p. 346.
84. See the Macau Data Website, at http://www.macaudata.com/macauweb/book082/, last accessed February 16, 2005.
85. Pina-Cabra, *Between China and Europe*, p. 88, citing Steward Culin, *The Games of the Orient: Korea, China, Japan* (Rutland: Charles E. Tuttle, 1958, reprint of 1891).
86. Zha Canchang, *Zhuanxing, Bianxiang yu Chuanbo*, pp. 146–7.
87. Yang Renfei, *Aomen Jindai Hua Licheng*, p. 142.
88. One estimate of the gambling facilities in Macau was by Zheng Guanying, and the number was 200. But Zhao Lifeng and Hu Gen believe it was an exaggeration. See Zhao Lifeng and Hu Gen, "Wan Qing Aomen bocai ye de xingqi yu fazhan" (The rise and development of the gambling industry in Macau during the late Qing era), in Wu Zhiliang, Jin Guoping, and Tang Kaijian (eds.) *Aomen Shi Xin Bian*, Vol. 3, p. 736. This is a fairly comprehensive article on the development of the gambling industry in Macau. For the number of *fantan* in the latter part of the 19th century, see also Pittis and Henders (selected and edited) *Macao: Mysterious Decay and Romance*, p. 49. They cited a travel book by Frederic Courtland Penfield entitled *The Monte Carlo of the East* and the number of licensed *fantan* places reported in the work, published in 1907, was 20.
89. Pina-Cabral, *Encountering Macau*, p. 81.
90. See also W. R. Eadington and Ricardo C. S. Siu, "Between Law and Custom—Examining the Interaction between Legislative Change and the Evolution of Macao's Casino Industry,"

International Gambling Studies, 2007, 7(1): 1–28. See also their description on the coolie trade.
91. Pina-Cabral, *Encountering Macau*, p. 144.
92. See Peter Wells, "Crown Exits Macau Casino JV with Melco," Financial Times, May 8, 2017, at https://www.ft.com/content/dcf82ebe-eec0-3b91-9670-a9fef13179b2, accessed October 15, 2018; Aaron Patrick, "James Packer's Macau Retreat Costs Crown Investors $2.5b," *The Australian Financial Review*, January 16, 2018.
93. See the Macau government's Gaming Inspection and Coordination Bureau's website at http://www.dicj.gov.mo/web/en/information/DadosEstat/2018/content.html#n5, accessed October 14, 2018. SJM's own website says that it has 20 casinos, but the government website says that it has 22.
94. See Sandy Li, "PBL and Melco Pay US$900m for Final License," *South China Morning Post*, March 7, 2006, at https://www.scmp.com/article/539378/pbl-and-melco-pay-us900m-final-licence, accessed October 14, 2018.
95. See Robert Johnson, "Las Vegas, Macau Casino Revenue Comparison Report (with Infographic), *Casino News Daily*, February 21, 2018, at http://www.casinonewsdaily.com/2018/02/21/las-vegas-macau-casino-revenue-comparison-report-infographic/, accessed October 14, 2018.
96. The World Bank, "GDP Per Capita (Current US$)," 2017, at its website at https://data.worldbank.org/indicator/NY.GDP.PCAP.CD?view=map, accessed October 14, 2018.
97. See Institute for the Study of Commercial Gaming, University of Macau, *Interim Review of Gaming Liberalization for Games of Fortune: Economic, Social, Livelihood Impacts and Operating Conditions of the Concessionaires*, 2016, p. 221 at Gaming Inspection and Coordination Bureau of Macau Government website http://www.dicj.gov.mo/web/en/news/Year-2016/mid-report/index.html, accessed October 17, 2018. The original is in both Chinese and Portuguese.
98. See Farah Master, "Las Vegas Sands Settles with Former CEO of Macau Casino Unit," Reuters, March 31, 2016, at https://www.reuters.com/article/us-lasvegassands-lawsuit/las-vegas-sands-settles-with-former-ceo-of-macau-casino-unit-idUSKCN0YN30X, accessed October 15, 2018; Jonathan Stempel, "Las Vegas Sands Pays $9 Million to End SEC Probe into China, Macau," Reuters, April 7, 2016, at https://www.reuters.com/article/us-lvsc-sec/las-vegas-sands-pays-9-million-to-end-sec-probe-into-china-macau-idUSKCN0X42CZ, accessed October 15, 2018; Asia Gaming Brief, "Las Vegas Sands Settles Lawsuit with Former Macau CEO," June 1, 2016, at https://agbrief.com/headline/las-vegas-sands-settles-lawsuit-with-former-macau-ceo/, accessed October 15, 2018; Asia Gaming Brief, "LVS Settles Criminal Bribery Case with $7 Million," January 20, 2017, at https://agbrief.com/headline/lvs-settles-criminal-bribery-case-with-7-million/, accessed October 15, 2018.]
99. Matt Isaacs, Lowell Bergman, and Stephen Engelberg, "Inside the Investigation of Leading Republican Money Man Sheldon Adelson," ProPublica and PBS Frontline, July 16, 2012, at https://www.propublica.org/article/inside-the-investigation-of-leading-republican-money-man-sheldon-adelson, accessed October 15, 2018. For casino politics and casino-related crimes around the handover, see also Lo Shiu Hing, "Casino Politics, Organized crime and the Post-Colonia State in Macau," *Journal of Contemporary China*, 2005, 14(43), and *Political Change in Macao* (London and New York: Routledge, 2008).
100. For the Taiwanese case, see Farah Master, "Former Macau Partner Gets Court Nod to Sue Las Vegas Sands for Billions," April 2, 2016, Reuters at https://www.reuters.com/article/us-macau-sands-trial/former-macau-partner-gets-court-nod-to-sue-las-vegas-sands-for-billions-idUSKCN0X000L, accessed October 26, 2018.
101. Office of the Secretary of Economy and Finance, Press Release, "The 'Interim Review of Gaming Liberalization for Games of Fortune' Research Report Released Today" May 11,

Notes to pp. 79–83

2016, at the Gaming Inspection and Coordination Bureau website, http://www.dicj.gov.mo/web/en/news/Year-2016/mid-report/press/press-1.htm, accessed October 17, 2018.
102. In addition to chapter 7, see also Beatrice Leong and Lo Shiu Hing (eds.), *Zhongguo aomen tequ bocai ye yu shehui fazhan* (Casino development and its impact on Macau SAR) (Hong Kong: City University of Hong Kong Press, 2010).
103. According to Macau government statistics, by April 2004, there were 1,117 industrial enterprises with 539 of them employing 1–9 workers and staff, 263 of them employing 10–49, 122 of them employing 50–99, 172 of them employing 100–499, 20 of them employing 500–1,000, and one of them employing over 1,000 (see Guo Yongzhong at the *Macao Daily* website, at http://www.macaodaily.com, accessed on September 26, 2004.

Chapter 4

1. Samuel P. Huntington, "The Clash of Civilizations?" in Lawrence E. Sneden (ed.) *Globalization and Conflict*, vol. II (Dubuque, Iowa: Kendall/Hunt Publishing Company, [1993] 2000), pp. 23–4.
2. Jonathan Porter, *Macau: The Imaginary City: Culture and Society, 1557 to the Present* (Boulder, Colorado: Westview Press, 1996), p. 67.
3. Huntington, "The Clash of Civilizations?" pp. 21–44; *Wenming de Chongtu yu Shijie Zhixu de Chongjian* (The clash of civilizations and the remaking of world order), translated by Zhou Qi, Liu Fei, Zhang Liping, and Wang Yuan (Beijing: Xinhua Chubanshe, [1996] 2002); *Who Are We? The Challenges to America's National Identity* (New York: Simon & Schuster, 2004). The concept can also be used to refer to the clash between subcultures, as in the case of Macau, Hong Kong, Taiwan, and the mainland.
4. Huntington, "The Clash of Civilizations?" pp. 24–5.
5. For a number of criticisms against the Huntingtonian arguments, see Edward Said, "The Clash of Ignorance," *Bulatlat*, Issue No. 35, October 14–20, 2001 at Bulatlat Philippine's Alternative Weekly Online News Magazine website, at http://www.bulatlat.com/archive/035us-said.html, last accessed on February 19, 2005; Elgin I. Erdem, "'The Clash of Civilizations': Revisited after September 11," *Alternatives: Turkish Journal of International Relations*, Vol. 1, No. 2, 2002 at Turkish Journal of International Relations website, at http://www.alternativesjournal.net/volume1/number2/erdem.htm, last accessed on February 19, 2005. The critics are especially unhappy with his "us" vs. "them" kind of argument, and they are afraid that what he says will become self-fulfilling prophecy.
6. Elaine Scarry, "The Difficulty of Imagining Other People," in Joshua Cohen (ed.) *For Love of Country: Debating the Limits of Patriotism* (Boston: Beacon, 1996), pp. 98–110. This may sound pre-determinist, but to understand human limitations is the first step to overcoming them. Besides, the limitations do exist, as we will see later.
7. Huntington, *Wenming de Chongtu yu Shijie Zhixu de Chongjian*, p. 134.
8. Martin N. Marger, *Race and Ethnic Relations: American and Global Perspectives*, fifth edition (Wadsworth, Thomson Learning, 2000), pp. 26–7, 69–88.
9. Herbet Blumer, *Symbolic Interactionism: Perspective and Method* (Berkeley, California: University of California Press, 1969); Erving Goffman, "Stigma and Social Identity," in Henry N. Pontell (ed.) *Social Deviance: Readings in Theory and Research* (Upper Saddle River, NJ: Prentice Hall, 1999), pp. 56–74.
10. Boxer, *Fidalgos in the Far East*, pp. 99–100.
11. Wu Zhiliang, *Shengcun zhi Dao*, pp. 85–6.
12. For a discussion of the composition of the population in Macau in the old days, see also Porter, *Macau, The Imaginary City*, pp. 129–35; Liu Ranling, *Wenming de Boyi*, pp. 238–42.

But see especially Su Yi Yang (Ivo Carneiro de Sousa), "Qian gongyehua Aomen de jumin ji renkou tixi (16–19 shiji)" (The people and their composition in pre-industrialized Macau), in Wu Zhiliang, Jin Guoping, and Tang Kaijian (eds.) *Aomen Shi Xin Bian*, Vol. 3.
13. There were people who did not think much of Western technology and called it *qi ji yin qiao* 奇技淫巧, or odd and wanton technique, as in the later self-strengthening movement. See Zhidong Hao, *Intellectuals at a Crossroads*, p. 39.
14. Yin Guangren and Zhang Rulin, *Aomen Jilue Jiaozhu*, pp. 171–86. See also Porter, *Macau: The Imaginary City*, pp. 141–6 for a discussion of the latest technology and mechanical devices of the West, which foreigners brought to Macau, including clocks, optical devices, astronomical instruments, and firearms. We will discuss these more in chapter 5 on religion. We will discuss the Western books and paintings foreigners also brought here in chapter 6 on literature and arts.
15. Yin Guangren and Zhang Rulin, *Aomen Jilue Jiaozhu*, p. 171.
16. Ibid., pp. 154–70.
17. Ibid., pp. 149–52.
18. Ibid., p. 143.
19. For a discussion on Yin and Zhang's use of derogatory words to refer to foreigners, see also Zhang Wenqin, *Aomen yu Zhonghua Lishi Wenhua* (Macau and Chinese history and culture) (Macau: Macau Foundation, 1995), p. 174.
20. Quoted in Yin Guangren and Zhang Rulin, *Aomen Jilue Jiaozhu*, p. 66, by Zhao Chunchen, the editor. Pang of the Ming dynasty was a Guangdong government official at the time.
21. Yin Guangren and Zhang Rulin, *Aomen Jilue Jiaozhu*, p. 238.
22. Ibid., p. 67.
23. Ibid., p. 249.
24. Yin Guangren and Zhang Rulin, *Aomen Jilue Jiaozh*, pp. 252–3.
25. Huang Qichen, *Aomen Tongshi*, p. 194. See also Kazunori Fukuda, "The Relations between China and Portugal in the Early Sixteenth Century: Some Observations on the Yue Shan Cong Tan," *Review of Culture*, international edition 1, January 2002. For more descriptions of how Portuguese ate children, see also Liu Ranling, *Wenming de Boyi*, p. 63.
26. Chen Xichang 陳熙昌 of the Ming dynasty, cited in Tang Kaijian, *Weiliduo*, p. 28.
27. Wang Xiwen 王希文 of the Ming dynasty, cited in ibid.
28. Boxer, *Fidalgos in the Far East*, p. 223.
29. Excerpted in Teng and Fairbank, *China's Response to the West*, p. 115.
30. Ibid., p. 35.
31. Cited in Teng and Fairbank, *China's Response to the West*, p. 36.
32. Ibid., p. 36.
33. Ibid., p. 190. Reverend Marshall Broomhall of the China Inland Mission set up in 1865 by the British Protestant missionary societies reported that 135 of the Mission's members and 53 of their children were killed in 1900 by the Boxers. See Colin Mackerras (selected and edited) *Sinophiles and Sinophobes: Western Views of China*, an anthology (New York: Oxford University Press, 2000), p. 93.
34. For example, see again Fay, *The Opium War*, pp. 320, 353.
35. See Mackerras (selected and edited), *Sinophiles and Sinophobes*, p. 93.
36. A country ship was one that was independent of the British East India Company, although the latter would still get involved in cases of dispute, as here. Generally a country trader used to belong to the East India Company but later left it to do business on his own. See Coates, *Macao and the British*, p. 62.
37. Ibid., p. 80. For a somewhat different version of the *Lady Hughes* incident, see Fay, *The Opium War*, p. 37. Fay's story says that the original gunner was submitted to the Chinese authorities.

38. Fay, *Opium War*, pp. 38–9. For another example of Chinese justice in strangling a convicted Chinese opium dealer, which caused protests among the foreigners in Canton, see ibid., pp. 133–4.
39. Tang Kaijian, *Weiliduo*, p. 28. For more of what Lin says, see also Liu Ranling, *Wenming de Boyi*, pp. 64–5.
40. Tang Kaijian, *Weiliduo*, p. 28.
41. Ibid., p. 85.
42. Pittis and Henders (selected and edited) *Macao: Mysterious Decay and Romance*, p. 208.
43. Ibid., pp. 208–9.
44. Excerpted in Teng and Fairbank, *China's Response to the West*, p. 38.
45. Ibid., pp. 38–9.
46. Ibid., p. 37. See also Zhang Wenqin's evaluation of Qiying in Zhang Wenqin, *Aomen yu Zhonghua Lishi Wenhua*, pp. 35–50.
47. Fay, *The Opium War*, p. 299.
48. Teng and Fairbank, *China's Response to the West*, p. 35.
49. Mackerras (selected and edited) *Sinophiles and Sinophobes*, pp. xxv–xxvi.
50. See Zhang Guogang, *Cong Zhong Xi Chushi dao Liyi zhi Zheng: Ming Qing Chuanjiaoshi yu Zhong Xi Wenhua Jiaoliu* (From the meeting of China and the West to the Controversy of Rites: the missionaries in the Ming and Qing dynasties and the cultural exchange of China and the West) (Beijing: People's Press, 2003), pp. 150, 165, 266, 271, 279.
51. Voltaire, cited in Mackerras (selected and edited) *Sinophiles and Sinophobes*, p. 39.
52. Ibid., pp. 169, 182.
53. See Hodges and Hummel (eds.) *Lights and Shadows of a Macao Life,* p. 125, underlining original.
54. Hodges and Hummel, *Lights and Shadows of a Macao Life*, pp. 141–2.
55. William Gascoyne-Ceci and Florence Cecil, cited in Mackerras (selected and edited) *Sinophiles and Sinophobes*, pp. 97–8.
56. Zhang Guogang, *Cong Zhong Xi Chusi Dao Liyi zhi Zheng*, pp. 266, 287, 291, 297, 302, 307.
57. See Wu Zhiliang, *Dong Xi Jiaohui Kan Aomen* (The East meets the West in Macau), the chapter on "Shiliu shiji Putaoya de Zhongguo guan" (The Portuguese view of China in the 16th century) (Macau: Macau Foundation, 1996b); you can also find his book at the Macau Data Website, at http://www.macaudata.com/macauweb/book025/, last accessed on February 19, 2005. Cruz's book is entitled *Tranchado das Cousas da China e de Ormuz*《中國概説》.
58. See excerpts in Jin Guoping (edited and translated) *Xifang Aomen Shiliao Xuancui (15–16 Shiji)* (Selected historical documents from the West, 15th–16th centuries) (Guangzhou: Guangdong Remin Chubanshe, 2005), p. 18.
59. Zhang Guogang, *Cong Zhong Xi Chushi dao Liyi zhi Zheng*, pp. 159, 161, 165, 169, 175–7.
60. Hodges and Hummel, *Lights and Shadows of a Macao Life*, pp. 460–1, underlining original; Lamas, *Everything in Style*, p. 199.
61. Hodges and Hummel, *Lights and Shadows of a Macao Life*, pp. 513–4; Lamas, *Everything in Style*, p. 232.
62. Lamas, *Everything in Style*, p. 220.
63. See P. Benjamim Antonio Videira Pires, *Shutu Tonggui: Aomen de Wenhua Jiaorong* (Reaching the same goal by different routes: the cultural exchange and integration in Macau) (Macau: The Cultural Institute of Macau, 1992), p. 173. The book is translated into Chinese by Su Qin from Portuguese, *Os Extremos Conciliam-se: Tramscultura'ao em Macau*, published by Macau Cultural Institute in 1987.
64. Montesquieu, cited in Mackerras (selected and edited) *Sinophiles and Sinophobes*, p. 44.

65. Ibid., pp. 26–7, 57, 67, 70–1, 79.
66. Ibid., p. 115.
67. Ibid., p. 84.
68. Ibid., p. 123.
69. Ibid., pp. 129–30.
70. Fay, *The Opium War*, pp. 108–9. This is Fay's summary of the Western views of the Chinese.
71. Ibid., p. 229.
72. Ibid., p. 241.
73. See Li Xiangyu, *Aomen Sheng Baolu Xueyuan Yanjiu*, pp. 137–8.
74. Boxer, "Shiliu—Shiqi Shiji Aomen de Zongjiao he Maoyi Zhongzhuan Gang zhi Zuoyong," pp. 186–7.
75. Yang Renfei, "Aomen minsu: yifu xuanli duozi de huajuan" (Local customs in Macau: a picture of multiple characteristics), in Wu Zhiliang, Jin Guoping, and Tang Kaijian (eds.) *Aomen Shi Xin Bian*, Vol. 4, p. 1139.
76. Ibid., pp. 1141–2.
77. By no means am I saying that Ms. Low or Father Pires transformed from one stage to another—they did not. But some have, and will continue to do so. In addition, I am by no means saying that this kind of thing will not happen among people of the same race and ethnic groups—they do, as has been powerfully evidenced by the Chinese revolutions in the 20th century. The key here is that whenever there is prejudice, it can easily and quickly translate into racism, sexism, or classism, etc., which in turn easily and quickly translates into discrimination and even more serious consequences like killings, e.g., genocide.
78. Liu Xianbing, Chen Shurong, Wang Guoqiang, and Xian Weikeng (eds.) *Tupian Aomen Jin Xi* (Macau history in pictures) (Hong Kong: Sanlian Press, 1999), pp. 28–9; see also newspaper reports in Tang Kaijian, Chen Wenyuan, and Ye Nong (eds.) *Yanpian Zhanzheng hou Aomen Shehui Shenghuo Jishi*, pp. 341–61, 656–7.
79. Pina-Cabral, *Between China and Europe*, pp. 66–7.
80. See Marger, *Race and Ethnic Relations*, pp. 29–32 for a fuller discussion on the development of racism.
81. Edward Said, *Orientalism* (New York: Vintage Books Edition, 1979).
82. Hodges and Hummel, *Lights and Shadows of a Macao Life*, p. 349, underlining original.
83. Ibid., p. 509.
84. Mackerras (selected and edited) *Sinophiles and Sinophobes*, pp. 58–9.
85. Cited in Gu Wei-min, "Cooperation and Contradiction: Portugal and the Holy See in the Ecclesiastical Affairs of China in the 17–18th Centuries," *Review of Culture*, international edition, No. 2, April 2002, p. 92; Zhang Guogang, *Cong Zhong Xi Chushi dao Liyi zhi Zheng*, pp. 432–33.
86. Mackerras (selected and edited) *Sinophiles and Sinophobes*, p. 112.
87. An explanation of the picture: "In 1838 and 1839, as part of Andrew Jackson's Indian removal policy, the Cherokee nation was forced to give up its lands east of the Mississippi River and to migrate to an area in present-day Oklahoma. The Cherokee people called this journey the 'Trail of Tears,' because of its devastating effects. The migrants faced hunger, disease, and exhaustion on the forced march. Over 4,000 out of 15,000 of the Cherokees died" (see the PBS Online TV Programs website, at http://www.pbs.org/wgbh/ aia/part4/4narr4.html, last accessed on September 15, 2005). The original painting by Robert Lindneux hangs in the Woolaroc Museum in Bartlesville, Oklahoma.
88. Marger, *Race and Ethnic Relations*, pp. 108–40.
89. For a full discussion of the Macanese, see Li Changsen, *Mingqing Shiqi Aomen Tusheng Zuqun de Xingcheng Fazhan yu Bianqian*.

90. Xu Jieshun and Tang Kaijian, "Guanyu Aomen tusheng puren wenti de sikao" (On the issue of Macanese), in Yu Zhen, Zheng Weiming, and Cui Baofeng (eds.) *Aomen Lishi, Wenhua yu Shehui* (Macau history, culture, and society) (Macau: Macau Chengren Jiaoyu Xiehui, 2003), p. 129.
91. Ibid., p. 130.
92. Ibid., pp. 131–2.
93. Ibid., p. 135.
94. Harald Bruning, "Tusheng puyu—Aomen binwei de 'tianmi yuyan'" (The Macanese language: a "sweet language" that is in the danger of extinction), *Aomen Zazhi*, No. 40, June 2004, p. 9.
95. Jia Yuan (João de Pina Cabral) and Lu Lingsuo (Nelson Lourenço), *Taifeng zhi Xiang: Aomen Tusheng Zuqun Dongtai* (The place of Typhoon: the dynamics of the ethnic Macanese) (Macau: Cultural Institute of Macau, 1995), p. 15. The original book is in Portuguese, *Em Terra De Tufões: Dinâmicas da Eternidade Macaense*, translated into Chinese by Chen Jieyin. See also Huo Zhizhao, *Aomen Tusheng Puren de Zongjian Xinyang* (Macanese religious beliefs) (Beijing: Social Science Academic Press, 2009), pp. 46–60.
96. Dra Ana Maria Amaro, *Dadi zhi Zi: Aomen Tusheng Puren Yanjiu* (The children of the earth: a study of Macanese), translated by Jin Guoping (Macau: Aomen Wenhua Sishu, 1993), p. 64; Bruning, "Tusheng Puyu," pp. 5, 9; Xu Jieshun and Tang Kaijian, "Guanyu Aomen tusheng Puren wenti de sikao," p. 138.
97. Bruning, "Tusheng Puyu," p. 9. See also J. M. R. Lume, "Center for Portuguese Language and Culture," in R. D. Cremer (ed.) *Macau: City of Commerce and Culture* (Hong Kong: UEA Press Ltd., 1987), pp. 119–21; Alan Baxter, "O português em Macau: contato e assimilação," a paper in English forthcoming in Portuguese forthcoming in Ana Carvalho (ed.) *Português em contato* (Frankfurt: Vervuert Publishers).
98. See Jia Yuan and Lu Lingsuo, *Taifeng zhi Xiang*, p. 138.
99. J. A. Berlie, "Society and Economy," in J. A. Berlie (ed.) *Macao 2000* (Oxford University Press, 1999), p. 25.
100. Jia Yuan and Lu Lingsuo, *Taifeng zhi Xiang*, p. 129.
101. Yang Renfei, "Aomen minsu," p. 1149.
102. See also Jia Yuan and Lu Lingsuo, *Taifeng zhi Xiang*, p. 15; Xu Jieshun and Tang Kaijian, "Guanyu Aomen tusheng Puren wenti de sikao," p. 141.
103. See Huo Zhizhao, *Aomen Tusheng Puren de Zongjiao Xinyang*.
104. João de Pina Cabral and Nelson Lourenço, "Macanese Ethnicity and Family: A Methodological Prologue," *Review of Culture*, No. 11/12 (September 1990): 99.
105. Article by Todd Crowell from Macau, entitled "A Proud People" at Asiaweek.com, December 24, 1999, Vol. 25, No. 51, at http://www-cgi.cnn.com/ASIANOW/asiaweek/magazine/99/1224/sr.macanese.html, last accessed on February 11, 2010.
106. Jia Yuan and Lu Lingsuo, *Taifeng zhi Xiang*, p. 178.
107. Ibid., p. 47.
108. Bruning, "Tusheng Puyu," p. 10. See also Lume, "Center for Portuguese Language and Culture."
109. Zheng Shuxian, "Tusheng tuhua huaju tuan yi yishu yanxu tuyu shengming" (The Macanese drama troupe's efforts to prolong the life of the Macanese language), *Aomen Zazhi*, No. 40, June 2004.
110. Zheng Shuxian, "Dona Aida he tade tusheng cai shitang" (Dona Aida and her Macanese restaurant), *Aomen Zazhi*, No. 40, June 2004.
111. Jia Yuan and Lu Lingsuo, *Taifeng zhi Xiang*, p. 164; see also Amaro, *Dadi zhi Zi*, p. 31.
112. See Amaro, *Dadi zhi Zi*, p. 9.

113. Feng Bangyan, *Puguo Chetui qian de Aomen* (Macau before the retreat of Portugal) (Guangzhou: Guangdong Jingji Chubanshe, 1999), pp. 241–2.
114. Yang Renfei, *Aomen Jindai Hua Licheng* (The modernization of Macao) (Macao: Macao Daily Press, 2000), p. 230.
115. Jia Yuan and Lu Lingsuo, *Taifeng zhi Xiang*, p. 56.
116. See Liu Xianbing, Chen Shurong, Wang Guoqiang, and Xian Weikeng (eds.) *Tupian Aomen Jin Xi* (Macau history in pictures) (Hong Kong: Sanlian Press, 1999), p. 84; see also Feng Bangyan, *Puguo Chetui qian de Aomen*, p. 244.
117. Liu Xian-bing, *Aomen Jiaoyu Shi* (A history of education in Macao) (Beijing: Renmin Jiaoyu Chubanshe, 1999), pp. 275–83.
118. Song Boniang, Zheng Miaoxian, and Huang Yanhong, *Aomen Wenhua Fangtan Lu* (Interviews on Macau culture) (Macau: Macau Polytechnic Institute, 2006), pp. 13, 20, 55.
119. Song Boniang, Zheng Miaoxian, and Huang Yanhong, *Aomen Wenhua Fangtan Lu*, pp. 65–75.
120. See Porter, *Macau: The Imaginary City*, p. 67.
121. Ibid., p. 67.
122. See, for example, Marreiros's discussion of the two cities and the role of Monte Fortress as a defense against territorial attacks from the north. C. Marreiros, "Traces of Chinese and Portuguese Architecture," in R. D. Cremer (ed.) *Macau: City of Commerce and Culture* (Hong Kong: UEA Press Ltd., 1987), p. 89. For more description of the wall, see also Lin Faqin, "Aomen zaoqi dui wai zhanzheng yu junshi fangyu"; Yan Zhongming and Ye Nong, "Aomen chengshi de xingjian yu fazhan," pp. 784–8. Garrett in *The Defences of Macau* (pp. 54–7) also discusses the purposes of the Northern Wall.
123. Arthur H. Cheng, "Macau as Metropolis: Heritage and Preservation towards the Future," in Ieda Siqueira Wiarda and Lucy M. Cohen (eds.) *Macau: Cultural Dialogue towards a New Millenium* (Philadelphia: Xlibris Corporation, 2004), pp. 84, 126; Gunn, *Encountering Macau*, p. 40; Lin Faqin, *Aomen Shi Gao*, pp. 15, 137–42; Lin Zisheng, *Shiliu zhi Shiba Shiji Aomen yu Zhongguo zhi Guanxi*, pp. 51–2.
124. Clayton, *"If We Are Not Different,"* pp. 365–6. See also Lamas, *Everything in Style*, p. 30.
125. See McGivering's interview with Henrique de Senna Fernandes in McGivering, *Macao Remembers*, p. 93.
126. Clayton, *"If We Are Not Different,"* pp. 365–6.
127. Ibid., p. 343.
128. Ibid., pp. 346, 348.
129. Ibid., p. 348.
130. Ibid., p. 368.
131. McGivering's interview with Sir Roger Lobo in McGivering, *Macao Remembers*, pp. 73–4. See also the observations of one of Pina-Cabral's interviewees in Pina-Cabral, *Between China and Europe*, p. 171. Mrs. Anabela Ritchie, another of McGivering's interviewees, also commented that the contact they had with the Chinese community was not great. See McGivering, *Macao Remembers*, p. 22.
132. See Tong Qiaohui, *Aomen Chengshi Huanjing yu Wenmai Yanjiu*, p. 157, citing the words of a Portuguese architect working in Macau for over 17 years.
133. McGivering, *Macao Remembers*, p. 87.
134. See McGivering's interviews with Stanley Ho and Mrs. Chen in ibid., pp. 111, 176.
135. See McGivering's interviews with Gary Ngai, Jorge Smith, and Father Peter Chung in ibid., pp. 158, 184, 220.
136. Lo Shiu Hing, *Political Development in Macau*, p. 147.
137. Clayton, *"If We Are Not Different,"* p. 406.
138. Lo Shiu Hing, *Political Development in Macau*, pp. 124–5.

139. Cited in Song Bonian, Zheng Miaoxian, and Huang Yanyong (eds.) *Aomen Wenhua Fangtan Lu*, p. 61.
140. Clayton's interview with Ng Kuok Cheong in Clayton, "*If We Are Not Different*," p. 83.
141. Coates, *A Macao Narrative*, p. 105.
142. Pina-Cabral, *Between China and Europe*, p. 3; see also Zha Canchang, *Zhuanxing, Bianxiang yu Chuanbo*, pp. 330–1.
143. Garry Ngai also discusses a Macau model. He says, "Macau is indeed a multi-racial and multi-cultural society, a melting pot of East and West. The interaction and blending of them is based on mutual respect and tolerance, implying more harmony than conflict, more checks and balances than confrontation, more reconciliation than alienation, and maintaining stability in plurality. This can be called the 'Macau model,' different from the Hong Kong model, which is Anglo-Saxon, with more conflict and confrontations." See Ngai, "Macau Communities: Past, Present and Future," in Ieda Siqueira Wiarda and Lucy M. Cohen (eds.) *Macau: Cultural Dialogue towards a New Millenium* (Philadelphia: Xlibris Corporation, 2004), p. 108. His Macau model sounds more idealistic than what we actually see. It emphasizes the appearance of harmony and downplays conflicts. What we develop here is a more complex model, and an improved one as well.
144. Fay, *The Opium War*, p. 98.
145. Ibid., p. 99.
146. Lo, *Political Development in Macau*, pp. 121, 130, 191.
147. See McGivering's interview with Dr. Sales Marques in McGivering, *Macao Remembers*, p. 31.
148. R. A. Zepp, "Interface of Chinese and Portuguese Cultures," in R. D. Cremer (ed.) *Macau: City of Commerce and Culture* (Hong Kong: UEA Press Ltd., 1987), p. 134.
149. See Liu Denghan, "Wenhua shiye zhong de Aomen juqi wenxue" (The cultural perspective of Macau and its literature), in Liu Denghan (ed.) *Aomen Wenxue Gaiguan*, p. 15.
150. Zepp, "Interface of Chinese and Portuguese Cultures," p. 135.
151. Liu Ranling, *Wenming de Boyi*, p. 29.
152. See McGivering's interview with Jorge Rangel in McGivering, *Macao Remembers*, p. 18.
153. Coates, *Macao and the British*, pp. 26, 57, 208.
154. Elaine Scarry, "The Difficulty of Imagining Other People," in Joshua Cohen (ed.) *For Love of Country: Debating the Limits of Patriotism* (Boston: Beacon, 1996), pp. 100, 98–110. This reminds one of a photo from the U.S. war on Iraq in 2003, which depicts a solder sitting there reading the Bible. On his helmet is written, "Kill'em All." It would be easier to kill people from other races and ethnic groups, even if we are religious people, since we do not feel the same pain as we would in our own people.
155. Ibid., pp. 102–3. In my other works, I have also used this example in understanding the cultural differences between people in Taiwan and mainland China.
156. Scarry, "The Difficulty of Imagining Other People," 103. Italics original.
157. See Huntington, *Wenming de Chongtu*, pp. 134, 301; Han Fei Zi (ca. 280–233 B.C.E.), one of the ancient Chinese philosophers, tells the story of a man who had a wall of his house broken down by rain. His son asked him to mend the wall, or the house might be visited by a thief. A neighbor also said the same to him. Indeed, the house was broken into. The man praised his son for being so smart, but he suspected that the neighbor must be the thief. It is easy to distrust the "other" (see chapter 12 of *Han Fei Zi*, Vol. 4).
158. Huntington, *Wenming de Chongtu*, p. 134.
159. See Xu Jieshun and Tang Kaijian, "Guanyu Aomen tusheng Puren wenti de sikao," pp. 144–5; see also Box 4.1.
160. See Alan Cowell, "Blair Criticizes Full Islamic Veils as 'Mark of Separation'," *New York Times*, October 18, 2006 at www.nytimes.com.

161. Our Macau model has some similarities with "the Macau model" that has been used to refer to the strategy of negotiations between Taiwan and mainland China regarding the exchange between the two sides such as direct charter flights between Taiwan and mainland cities. Before the KMT came to power in 2008, all flights would have to go through Hong Kong or Macau, and they could not fly directly between Taiwan and mainland cities. The negotiations of these issues were done in Macau, hence "the Macau model." The key to the model is to ask non-governmental organizations to do the negotiations, and they will not have to deal with sovereignty issues, which governmental talks would otherwise have to deal with. They do get the backing of their respective governments, though, in their talks. This is really a strategy of avoidance, similar to our Macau model. It is: "I don't bother with your sovereignty issue and you don't bother with my sovereignty issue." An improved Macau model would not avoid the tough issues, but will seek to understand each other and work out a compromised solution that will benefit both while preserving each party's own identity.

Chapter 5

1. For the first quote, see Emile Durkheim, *The Elementary Forms of the Religious Life* (New York: The Free Press, 1965), p. 62. For the second quote, see Durkheim, *Selected Writings*, edited by Anthony Giddens (Cambridge: Cambridge University Press, 1972), p. 250.
2. Hoiman Chan and Ambrose Y. C. King, "Religion," in Robert E. Gamer (ed.) *Understanding Contemporary China* (Boulder, London: Lynne Rienner Publishers, 1999); Lin Yutang, *My Country and My People* (New York: The John Day Company, 1936); Max Weber, *From Max Weber* (eds.) H. H. Gerth and C. Wright Mills (New York: Oxford University Press, 1946). In addition to what we mentioned above and among other things, Confucianism also believes in the hierarchical order of the social world and benevolent government.
3. Taoist Culture & Information Centre website, at http://www.gb.taoism.org.hk/content.htm, last accessed on February 16, 2005.
4. Zheng Weiming and Huang Qichen, *Aomen Zongjiao* (Religions of Macau) (Macao: Macau Foundation, 1994), at http://www.macaudata.com/macauweb/book128/, last accessed on February 16, 2005. Others believe the temple was built much later. See the disputes on the date of the founding of the temple in Xu Xiaowang, "Aomen de Mazu xinyang" (The belief in Mazu in Macau), in Wu Zhiliang, Jin Guoping, and Tang Kaijian (eds.) *Aomen Shi Xin Bian*, Vol. 4, pp. 1047–8.
5. Taoist Culture & Information Centre website, at http://www.gb.taoism.org.hk/taoist-immortal/pg3-8-4.htm, last accessed on February 16, 2005.
6. Zheng Weiming and Huang Qichen, *Aomen Zongjiao*.
7. Jean A. Berlie, "Macau's Overview at the Turn of the Century," *American Asian Review*, Vol. XVIII, No. 4 (Winter, 2000): 25–68, especially 32.
8. Pina-Cabral, *Between China and Europe*, p. 34.
9. See Zhidong Hao, Shun Hing Chan, Wen-ban Kuo, Yik Fai Tam, and Ming Jing. "Catholicism and Its Civic Engagement: Case Studies of the Catholic Church in Hong Kong, Macau, Taipei, and Shanghai," *Review of Religion and Chinese Society*, 2014, Vol. 1, No. 1, pp. 48–77.
10. Ji Fahan, Xu Shunping, and Song Hongyin, "Zhu xing wu chang, zhu fa wu wo: Fojia wenhua jiqi lixiang renge" (The uncertainty of actions and the forgetting of oneself in the Buddhist principles: the Buddhist culture and its ideal personality), in Jin Yuanpu, Tan Haozhe, and Lu Xueming (eds.) *Zhongguo Wenhua Gailun* (A general introduction to Chinese culture) (Beijing: Shouduo Shida Chubanshe [Capital Normal University Press], 1999), p. 406.

11. See Zheng Weiming and Huang Qichen, *Aomen Zongjiao*. For Macau's temples and shrines, see also Porter, *Macau: The Imaginary City*, pp. 161–86.
12. Roger Scruton, *A Dictionary of Political Thought* (New York: Hill and Wang, 1982), p. 412.
13. Huang Qichen, *Aomen Tongshi*, pp. 111–2.
14. St. Lazarus Church: "The first building on this site was the Hermitage of Our Lady of Hope, or more popularly St. Lazarus, established in 1570 to serve lepers. At the same time a settlement for lepers was built outside the old city walls. (This was transferred to D. João Island in 1882 and to Coloane in 1947, where it is today.) The present St. Lazarus was built in 1895 and renovated in 1966. In the forecourt is the Cross of Hope from the original chapel" (Hotel Travel website, at http://www.hoteltravel.com/.../ guides/sightseeing.htm, accessed on February 16, 2005).
15. The persecution and expelling of Catholics in Japan in the late 16th century to the first half of the 17th century sent many Japanese Christians to Macau. The persecution can be seen from a letter by the Japanese officials to the Portuguese government in Macau telling the latter that they had killed most of the delegation of 57 members they sent to Japan to negotiate with the Japanese: "… in spite of this strict command, your people came again to this land under the pretence of peace negotiations, but the government officials have no proof that this is their real intention. We therefore had no alternative but to obey the existing order and could not spare their lives. We therefore destroyed the ship; arrested those on board; exposed the heads of the several chiefs in the market-place; and killed all the others, young and old, except some sailors and the surgeon whose offence was not so grave in comparison with the several chiefs who were beheaded, and whom we ordered to report the facts to your country. They were therefore spared from execution, and it was arranged that they should be sent back in a small ship in order to bring this letter to Macao." See Pittis and Henders (selected and edited) *Macao: Mysterious Decay and Romance*, p. 233. About the 1835 burning of the church, see also ibid., pp. 240–1.
16. Carlos Baracho, "The Churches of Macau and Their Placement in Urban Space and within the City's Architectonic Context," *Macau Focus* 1:3 (2001): 29–45; Huang Qichen, *Aomen Tongshi*, pp. 111–7; Macao City Guide website, at http://www.cityguide.gov.mo/tg/church/macau_list_e.htm, last accessed on February 16, 2005; Zheng Weiming and Huang Qichen, *Aomen Zongjiao*; OlaMacauGuide website, at http://www.olamacauguide.com/catholic-churches.html, last accessed on February 16, 2005; for a fuller discussion of the development of the Catholic Church in Macau, see Tang Kaijian, "Ming Qing shiqi Aomen tianzhujiao de fazhan yu xingshuai."
17. Huang Qichen, *Aomen Tongshi*, p. 255.
18. Ibid., p. 261.
19. Ibid., p. 269.
20. Ibid., p. 272.
21. Ibid., pp. 274–5.
22. For the influence of religion in people's lives, see Lin Yutang, *Zhongguo Ren*, pp. 109–38.
23. Macau City Guide website, at http://www.cityguide.gov.mo/tg/church/c_detaile.asp?lc=2&lkey=02021400000000000000, last accessed on February 11, 2005.
24. Macau City Guide website, at http://www.cityguide.gov.mo/tg/church/c_detaile.asp?lc=2&lkey, last accessed on February 11, 2005.
25. Ibid.
26. Ibid.
27. Lou Shenghua, "Xiaoshi yu xinsheng: Aomen minjian jieshe de bianqian jiqi xiansuo" (Disappearances and births: the traces of transformation of Macau's social organizations), in Wu Zhiliang, Jin Guoping, and Tang Kaijian (eds.) *Aomen Shi Xin Bian*, Vol. 3.
28. Gunn, *Encountering Macau*, p. 39.

29. Teixeira, "The Church in Macau," p. 41.
30. Pires, "Origins and Early History of Macau," p. 11.
31. Jin Guoping and Wu Zhiliang, *Guo Shi Zi Men*, p. 203.
32. Coates, *A Macao Narrative*, pp. 63, 72; Pires, "Origins and Early History of Macau," p. 11; Zha Canchang, *Zhuanxing, Bianxiang yu Chuan Bo*, p. 233.
33. Coates, *Macau and the British*, pp. 47–8.
34. Coates, *A Macao Narrative*, p. 92. See also Ye Nong, "Cong 1840 zhi 1860: Ao Gang guanxi zuichu 20 nian" (From 1840 to 1860: the relations between Macau and Hong Kang in the first twenty years), in Wu Zhiliang, Jin Guoping, and Tang Kaijian (eds.) *Aomen Shi Xin Bian*, Vol. 2, pp. 491–5. The event led to the British invasion of the Portuguese prison at the Leal Senado. They rescued Summers but killed one Portuguese soldier in the process. Amaral made strong protests, and the British foreign minister apologized for what they did and compensated for the death of the soldier.
35. Lin Faqin, *Aomen Shigao*, pp. 137–9.
36. See again Coates, *A Macao Narrative*, p. 45.
37. Gunn, *Encountering Macau*, p. 39.
38. Liu Xining reports that in terms of the number of students, Catholic schools recruited about 43% to 44% of them in Macau in 1993 through 1998. See Liu Xining, *Aomen Jiaoyu Shi*, pp. 114–5.
39. McGivering's interview with Father Luis Sequeira, in McGivering, *Macao Remembers*, p. 211.
40. McGiverning's interview with Stanley Ho, in McGivering, *Macao Remembers*, pp. 115–6.
41. Pina-Cabral, *Between China and Europe*, p. 36.
42. Liang Jiefen, "Gang Ao huigui hou de zheng jiao (tianzhu jiao) guanxi" (The relationship between church and state after the return of Hong Kong and Macao to China), in Yu Zhen, Yu Yongyi, and Kuang Jinjun (eds.) *Shuang Cheng Ji II: Huigui hou Gang Ao de Zhengzhi, Jingji ji Shehui Fazhan* (A tale of two cities II: the political, economic and social development in Hong Kong and Macau after their return to China) (Macau: Aomen Shehui Kexue Xuehui).
43. Zhidong Hao, et al., "Catholicism and Its Civic Engagement."
44. See Huang Qichen, *Aomen Tongshi*, pp. 118–9. For Ruggieri's, Ricci's, Morrison's, and other Jesuits' efforts in studying the Chinese language and culture, and their influence on the Chinese people and society, including Wu Li and Yung Wing, see also Porter, *Macau: The Imaginary City*, pp. 109–25. We will discuss these important figures in the following pages. For the Portuguese contribution to the Jesuit missions in China, see also Willis (ed.) *China and Macau*, pp. 65–73.
45. Gunn, *Encountering Macau*, p. 39, citing Ljungstedt, *An Historical Sketch*, p. 51.
46. Zhang Wenqin, *Aomen yu Zhonghua Lishi Wenhua*, pp. 110–1.
47. For more information about the St. Paul's College, see Li Xiangyu, *Aomen Sheng Baolu Xueyuan Yanjiu*; Liu Xianbing, *Aomen Jiaoyu Shi*.
48. See Huang Qichen, *Aomen Tongshi*, pp. 119–27; Li Xiangyu, *Aomen Sheng Baolu Xueyuan Yanjiu*, pp. 193–202; Lin Zisheng, *Shiliu zhi Shiba Shiji Aomen yu Zhongguo zhi Guanxi*, pp. 125–6. Tang Kaijian questions whether there were these many Jesuit graduates from St. Paul's College. See Tang Kaijian, "Ba" (Afterword), in Jin Guoping and Wu Zhiliang, *Jing Hai Piaomiao* (The misty Macau history) (Macau: Chengren Jiaoyu Xuehui [Adult education association], 2001), p. 305. For Wu's life in Macau and his thoughts on the conflict between Chinese beliefs and Catholicism, see Zhang Wenqin, "The Life and Works of Wu Yushan [Wu Li]," *Review of Culture*, international edition 13, January 2005. For one thing, he was critical of Confucianism for not talking about the origin of life. See also Gu Weimin,

"Wu Yushan and His Pursuit of Faith in the Great Dynastic Transition," *Review of Culture*, international edition 13, January 2005.
49. Zhang Wenqin, *Aomen yu Zhonghua Lishi Wenhua*, p. 113.
50. Ibid., pp. 115, 117–8.
51. Lin Zisheng, *Shiliu zhi Shiba Shiji Aomen yu Zhongguo zhi Guanxi*, p. 132. For more examples of the success of Christianity in China, see also Huang Qichen, *Aomen Tongshi*, p. 127.
52. Huang Qichen, *Aomen Tongshi*, p. 257.
53. Lin Faqin, *Aomen Shigao*, pp. 168–9.
54. Huang Qichen, *Aomen Tongshi*, p. 128.
55. Ibid., p. 128; Lin Faqin, *Aomen Shigao*, pp. 166–72.
56. Huang Qichen, *Aomen Tongshi*, p. 128.
57. For more on the Controversy of Rites, see Jin Guoping and Wu Zhiliang, *Guo Shizi Men*, pp. 188–209; Li Tiangang, "Aomen yu Zhongguo liyi zhi zheng" (Macau and the Controversy of Rites), in Wu Zhiliang, Jin Guoping, and Tang Kaijian (eds.) *Aomen Shi Xin Bian*, Vol. 1; Lin Zisheng, *Shiliu zhi Shiba Shiji Aomen yu Zhongguo zhi Guanxi*, pp. 155–70; Manuel Teixeira, "The Church in Macau," in R. D. Cremer (ed.) *Macau: City of Commerce and Culture* (Hong Kong: UEA Press Ltd., 1987), pp. 43–4; Teng and Fairbank, *China's Response to the West*, p. 18; Wei Qingyuan, *Aomen Shi Lungao*, pp. 106–15.
58. Huang Qichen, *Aomen Tongshi*, pp. 258–9; see also Pina-Cabral, *Between China and Europe*, p. 36.
59. Zhang Wenqin, *Aomen yu Zhonghua Lishi Wenhua*, pp. 120–34, 163–6.
60. Liu Ranling, *Wenming de Boyi*, p. 314.
61. Huang Qiche, *Aomen Tongshi*, pp. 260–1.
62. See An Ximeng, "A Cultural Reflection on the Controversy of Rites," at http://www.xslx.com/ htm/zlsh/zjyj/2004-06-17-17000.htm, accessed February 16, 2005.
63. Jin Guoping and Wu Zhiliang, *Guo Shizi Men*, p. 209; *Zaoqi Aomen Shi Lun*, pp. 455–81; see also Zhang Guogang, *Cong Zhong Xi Chushi dao Liyi zhi Zheng*; Boxer, *Fidalgos in the Far East*, pp. 163–72.
64. See Jonathan D. Spence, *The Search for Modern China* (New York: W. W. Norton & Company, 1990), p. 72.
65. Zha Canchang, *Zhuanxing, Bianxiang yu Chuanbo*, p. 327.
66. Lin Faqin, *Aomen Shigao*, p. 165. For the early days of European Sinology in Macau and Manila, see also Rui Manuel Loureiro, "Primórdios da Sinologia Europeia: entre Macau e Manila em Finais do Século XVI" (The early days of European Sinology in Macau and Manila in the late 16th century), *Review of Culture*, international edition, No. 2, April 2002.
67. Huang Qichen, *Aomen Tongshi*, pp. 132–9; Liu Xianbing, *Aomen Jiaoyu Shi*, p. 71; Zha Canchang, *Zhuanxing, Bianxiang yu Chuanbo*, pp. 327–9.
68. Huang Qichen, *Aomen Tongshi*, p. 152.
69. Lin Zisheng, *Shiliu zhi Shiba Shiji Aomen yu Zhongguo zhi Guanxi*, p. 186. See also Zha Canchang, *Zhuanxing, Bianxiang yu Chuanbo*, p. 321.
70. Teixeira, "The Church of Macau," p. 47.
71. Ibid., p. 46.
72. Cited in Zha Canchang, *Zhuanxing, Bianxiang yu Chuanbo*, p. 322.
73. Zha Canchang, *Zhuanxing, Bianxiang yu Chuanbo*, p. 321.
74. For a discussion of the Eastern and Western architecture in Macau, see Liu Xianjue and Chen Zecheng (eds.) *Aomen Jianzhu Wenhua Yichan* (The architectural heritage in Macao) (Nanjing: Dongnan Daxue Chubanshe, 2005), pp. 17, 32–3, 42, 46–7, 58–60, 102–3, 112–3, 136.
75. Coates, *Macao and the British*, p. 104; Deng Kaixong and Xie Houhe, *Aomen Lishi yu Shehui Fazhan*, p. 51.

76. Zha Canchang, *Zhuanxing, Bianxiang yu Chuanbo*, pp. 323–6. See also Coates, *A Macao Narrative*, pp. 32–3; Gunn, *Encountering Macau*, pp. 44–5.
77. Teixeira, "The Church of Macau," p. 47. For more on the relationship between Kangxi and the Jesuits and his study of Western science, see Han Qi, "Yesu huishi he Kangxi shidai lisuan zhishi de chuanru" (The Jesuits and the introduction of Western calendar and mathematics to China in the Kangxi era), in Wu Zhiliang, Jin Guoping, and Tang Kaijian (eds.) *Aomen Shi Xin Bian*, Vol. 3.
78. Pina-Cabral, *Between China and Europe*, p. 56.
79. Coates, *Macao and the British*, p. 31.
80. For more discussion on missionaries' contribution to East and West exchange, see also Li Zisheng, *Shiliu zhi Shiba Shiji Aomen yu Zhongguo zhi Guanxi*, pp. 185–9; Liu Xian-bing, *Aomen Jiaoyu Shi* (A history of education in Macao) (Beijing: Renmin Jiaoyu Chubanshe, 1999), pp. 42–8; Teng and Fairbank, *China's Response to the West*, pp. 12–7.
81. Gunn, *Encountering Macau*, p. 48.
82. Huang Qichen, *Aomen Tongshi*, p. 271; See also the Harvard Divinity School website, at http://www.hds.harvard.edu/library/exhibitb/6.html, last accessed on February 16, 2005.
83. For more on the cemetery, see Pittis and Henders (selected and edited) *Macao: Mysterious Decay and Romance*, pp. 245–7, an article on the Protestant burial ground in the *Chinese Repository*.
84. See Coates, *A Macao Narrative*, pp. 75–9.
85. Coates, *Macao and the British*, p. 113.
86. Ibid., p. 223.
87. Cited in ibid., p. 110.
88. Wei Qingyuan, *Aomen Shi Lungao*, p. 101.
89. Huang Qichen, *Aomen Tongshi*, p. 273.
90. According to Liu Xianbing, Yung Wing was not the first Chinese who studied and graduated in the United States. Another young man named Wang from Guangzhou went to study in a church school in the United States in 1818. And the first Chinese who went to study in the West was Zheng Manuo, who was sent to study in Rome in 1650. See Liu Xianbing, "Aomen jiaoyu de fazhan, bianhua yu xiandaihua" (The development, change, and modernization of education in Macau), in Wu Zhiliang, Jin Guoping, and Tang Kaijian (eds.) *Aomen Shi Xin Bian*, Vol. 3, p. 913.
91. See also Teng and Fairbank, *China's Response to the West*, pp. 91–5.
92. Fay, *The Opium War*, pp. 92–3.
93. Gunn, *Encountering Macau*, p. 49.
94. Ibid., p. 50.
95. Huang Qichen, *Aomen Tongshi*, p. 106.
96. See Jonathan D. Spence, *The Search for Modern China* (New York: W. W. Norton & Company, 1990), p. 72.
97. See Zheng Weiming and Huang Qichen, *Aomen Zongjiao*.
98. See Jin Guoping and Wu Zhiliang, *Jing Hai Piaomiao*, p. 203 for a similar discussion on the dual tracks of culture.
99. See César Guillen-Nuñez, *Macao's Church of Saint Paul: A Glimmer of the Baroque in China* (Hong Kong: Hong Kong University Press in conjunction with Macau Bureau of Cultural Affairs, 2009), p. 130.
100. For more on Nu Wa and the temple, see Christina Miu Bing Cheng, "Matriarchy at the Edge: The Mythic Cult of Nu Wa in Macao," *Review of Culture*, international edition 13, January 2005. For more on the debate on the symbol of St. Mary standing on the dragon, see Liu Ranling, *Wenming de Boyi*, p. 266; Kou Sai Luo (Gonçalo Couceiro), "Da Sanba paifang de zhuangshi yishu" (The decorative arts on the façade of St. Paul's), in Wu Zhiliang,

Jin Guoping, and Tang Kaijian (eds.) *Aomen Shi Xin Bian*, Vol. 4; Tong Qiaohui, *Aomen Chengshi Huanjing yu Wenmai Yanjiu*, p. 149.
101. Here is more of the story regarding that controversy: "In 1707 the Dominicans sided with the Pope against Macau's bishop in the Rites Controversy. When local soldiers tried to enforce an excommunication order on them, the friars locked themselves in the church for three days and pelted the soldiers with stones. In 1834 the monastic orders were suppressed and for a time the church was used by the government as a barracks, stable and public works office" (see the explanation of the St. Dominic's Church at the Macao City Guide website, at http://www.cityguide.gov.mo/tg/church/macau_list_e.htm, accessed on February 16, 2005).
102. Zheng Weiming and Huang Qichen, *Aomen Zongjiao*.
103. Her diary in Hodges and Hummel (eds.) *Lights and Shadows of a Macao Life*, pp. 508–9, underlining (italics) original. See also Lamas, *Everything in Style*, p. 79.
104. See Wang Xiaochao's article on "Raising Civic Morality among Chinese Citizens in the New Century: The Role of Christian Values," *Chinese Cross Currents*, January–March 2004.
105. See Zhidong Hao and Yan Liu, "Mutual Accommodation in Church-State Relationship in China? A Case Study of the Sanjiang Church Demolition in Zhejiang," *Review of Religion and Chinese Society*, No. 5, 2018, pp. 26–42.

Chapter 6

1. The first quote is from Leo Lowenthal, "On Sociology of Literature," in *Literature and Mass Culture. Communication in Society*, Vol. 1 (Transaction Books, [1948] 1984), at http://www.marxists.org/reference/archive/lowenthal/, last accessed on February 16, 2005. Lowenthal (1900–93) was a sociologist and one of the leading figures in the Frankfurt School of critical theorists. Here he is commenting on the sociology of literature. The second quote is from Lowenthal's *An Unmastered Past: The Autobiographical Reflections of Leo Lowenthal* (Berkeley: University of California Press, 1987), p. 169, at http://ark.cdlib.org/ark:/13030/ft8779p24p/, last accessed on February 16, 2005. Theodore Adorno (1903–69) was one of his colleagues in the same school of thoughts.
2. Pittis and Henders (selected and edited) *Macao: Mysterious Decay and Romance*, p. 202.
3. Zhang Wenqin, *Aomen Shici Jianzhu (Ming Qing Juan, Wan Qing Juan)* (Annotated volumes of poems about Macau: Ming and Qing dynasties, late Qing dynasty) (Zhuhai and Macau: Zhuhai Chubanshe; Macau government Bureau of Culture, Macau SAR, 2003).
4. Ibid., Volume on Ming and Qing dynasties, Introduction, p. 16; Text, pp. 5–6.
5. Ibid., Introduction, p. 14; Text, pp. 172–4.
6. Ibid., pp. 28–9.
7. Ibid., Text, pp. 104–9.
8. The pipe organs built in China have not survived. See David Francis Urrows, "Pipe Organ Building and the Jesuits in China," a lecture at the Macau Ricci Institute, January 25, 2005. For more information on the history of music in Macau, see Dai Dingcheng, "Aomen yinyue jianshi" (A brief history of the music in Macau), in Wu Zhiliang, Jin Guoping, and Tang Kaijian (eds.) *Aomen Shi Xin Bian*, Vol. 4.
9. Zhang Wenqin, Volume on Ming and Qing dynasties, Text, pp. 14–5. Zhang thinks that "*ju ke*" here means Wu and his colleagues. But it may also mean people in Macau, which is my interpretation.
10. Ibid., p. 29.
11. Ibid., p. 34.
12. Ibid., p. 201.

13. See Zhang Wenqin, Volume on the Late Qing dynasty, p. 116.
14. Ibid., p. 219.
15. Ibid., p. 324. We see a repeat of such events in the modernization efforts in the 1990s and early 21st century in mainland China.
16. Ibid., p. 330.
17. Ibid., p. 23.
18. Ibid., p. 94.
19. Ibid., pp. 249, 251, 252–3, 256–7.
20. Zhang Wenqin, *Aomen Shici Jianzhu (Ming Qing Juan, Wan Qing Juan)* (Annotated volumes of poems about Macau: Republic of China era 1 and 2) (Zhuhai and Macau: Zhuhai Chubanshe; Macau Government Bureau of Culture, Macau SAR 2003).
21. Ibid., pp. 202–3.
22. Ibid., p. 253.
23. Tao Li and Zhuang Wenyong, "Aomen de xin shi chuangzuo" (Macau's new poetry), in Liu Denghan (ed.) *Aomen Wenxue Gaiguan*, pp. 116–7.
24. Ibid., p. 123.
25. Ibid., p. 149.
26. Liao Zixin, "Aomen de sanwen chuangzuo" (The essay writing in Macau), in ibid., pp. 171, 188.
27. See ibid.
28. Tao Li, "Aomen de xiaoshuo chuangzuo" (Macau's short stories and novels), in ibid., pp. 212–21.
29. See Tang Kaijian, Chen Wenyuan, and Ye Nong (eds.) *Yapian Zhanzheng hou Aomen Shehui Shenghuo Jishi: Jindai Baokan Aomen Ziliao Xuancui* (Life in Macau after the Opium War: excerpts from modern newspapers) (Guangzhou: Huacheng Chubanshe, 2001), p. 570.
30. Zheng Weiming, "Aomen de xiju huodong yu chuangzuo" (Macau's plays and the writing of plays), in ibid., pp. 224–5. For more on opera, dance, and movies in Macau, see Mu Xinxin, "Aomen xiju, wudao yu dianying" (Operas, plays, dance, and movies in Macau), in Wu Zhiliang, Jin Guoping, and Tang Kaijian (eds.) *Aomen Shi Xin Bian*, Vol. 4.
31. Zheng Weiming, "Aomen de xiju huodong yu chuangzuo," p. 234.
32. Ibid., pp. 235–8.
33. Ibid., p. 247.
34. See Isaac Pereira, "Fun, Appealing and Better," *Macau Magazine*, June 2001.
35. See Graça Marques and Veiga Jardim, "Opera in Macau (I)," and "Opera in Macau (II)," *Macau Magazine*, September and December 2002.
36. See Bradley Winterton, *Falstaff in Macau* (Hong Kong: Fairfield Books, 1995).
37. Zhang Wenqin, *Aomen yu Zhonghua Lishi Wenhua*, p. 264.
38. See also Jin Guoping and Wu Zhiliang, *Guo Shizi Men*, pp. 165–8.
39. "Heritage Excellence," *Macau Focus*, Vol. I, N. 3 (December 2001): 62.
40. See David W. Kowal, "Jesuit Buildings in Asia: Reflections on the Practice of Architectural Accommodation," a paper presented at an international symposium on "Culture, Art, and Religion: Wu Li (1632–1718) and His Inner Journey," Macau Ricci Institute, November 27–29, 2003. For more discussion of the façade, see also Porter, *Macau: The Imaginary City*, pp. 72–4; Marreiros, "Traces of Chinese and Portuguese architecture," p. 100; Liu Xianjueand Chen Zecheng (eds.) *Aomen Jianzhu Wenhua Yichan*.
41. See Li Puwen, "Wu Li de xinlu licheng jiqi huihua yishu" (Wu Li's thought processes and artistic skills), a paper presented at an international symposium on "Culture, Art, and Religion: Wu Li (1632–1718) and His Inner Journey," Macau Ricci Institute, November 27–29, 2003. Li does not think that Wu's paintings were influenced by Western styles. But Mo Xiaoye does. See Mo's "Wu Li shidai de dong xi fang yishu jiaoliu" (The exchange of

arts between the East and the West during Wu Li's times), a paper presented at the above symposium. Gu Weimin says that unlike Jesuits in China such as Giuseppe Catiglione and Denis Attirer, who dedicated to the assimilation of Chinese and Western styles of painting, Wu Li never used Western techniques in his paintings. See Gu Weimin, "Wu Yushan and His Pursuit of Faith in the Great Dynastic Transition."

42. Guillen-Nunez, "Through the Eyes of Nineteenth Century Painters," p. 64.
43. See also Chen Jichun, *Qian Nali yu Aomen* (Chinnery and Macau), the chapter on Lin Gua, at http://www.macaudata.com/macauweb/book127/, February 16, 2005. Rebecca Chase also discusses her encounter with Lamgua when she asked him to paint a portrait of her little daughter. See Cecília Jorge, "Rebecca Chase: An American in Macau," *Macau Magazine*, September 2002. See also Paulo Carmo, "China and the West: Images of a Meeting," *Macau Magazine*, December 2001.
44. For the above discussion, see Wang Chun, "Aomen de tusheng wenxue" (Macau's Macanese literature), in Liu Denghan (ed.) *Aomen Wenxue Gaiguan*, pp. 335–6.
45. Ibid., pp. 343–4.
46. The movie is full of descriptions of civilizational and cultural clashes in spite of the interracial marriage between the two protagonists. For an English translation of the book, see Henrique de Senna Fernades, *The Bewitching Braid*, translated by David Brookshaw (Hong Kong: Hong Kong University Press, 2004). For a Chinese translation, see Fei Li Qi, *Da Bianzi de Youhuo*, translated by Yu Huijuan (Macau: Institute of Culture, and Shijiazhuang, Huashan Wenyi Chubanshe, 1996).
47. There is no doubt that Chinese men marry Portuguese or Macanese women, too. We see it in the *Macau Bride* above. See also, for example, the story of Carmen in "Neither Meat nor Fish: Three Macanese Women in the Transition," by Ian E. Watts, a paper presented at a conference on Macau and its neighbors, 1997, at the Yahoo GeoCities website, at http://www.geocities.com/Tokyo/Temple/4735/fish.html, accessed on February 16 2005. But those cases are fewer.
48. Transcribed by Pina-Cabral, *Between China and Europe*, p. 162. Pina-Cabral's description of *cheong-sam*: "The tight-collared, side-buttoned, slit-skirted dress that was characteristic of Chinese women during the first half of the twentieth century and that Deolinda da Conceicao used as the name of her book and the symbol of the condition of the women she depicts." (See ibid., p. 236.) It is similar to what the woman in Figure 6.2 wears.
49. Ibid., p. 163.
50. Wang Chun, "Aomen de tusheng wenxue," pp. 346–7.
51. David Brookshaw, *Visions of China: Stories from Macau* (Hong Kong: Hong Kong University Press, 2002), pp. 14–8. This work is a collection of short stories by writers such as Deolinda da Conceição, Henrique de Senna Fernandes, Maria Ondina Braga, and Fernanda Dias.
52. Wang Chun, "Aomen de tusheng wenxue," pp. 347–8, 354–6.
53. A *Time Magazine* article describes Fernandes's work this way: "In 1993, Julie de Senna Fernandes had an idea. She decided to try to revive the Macanese patúa (dialect), which had long fallen into disuse. The last theater play in the dialect had been written at least 16 years previously. So she and some like-minded friends formed a group called the Dóci Papiaçam di Macau (The Sweet Language of Macau) to try to keep their patúa from going the way of many other dead languages. 'Very few people speak it today,' she says." (See the *Time Magazine* website, at http://www.asiaweek.com/asiaweek/magazine/99/1224/sr.macanese.html, last accessed on February 16, 2005.)
54. Wang Chun, "Aomen de tusheng wenxue," pp. 359–60, 367. See also Zheng Shuxian, "Tusheng tuhua huaju tuan yi yishu yanxu tuyu shengming" (The Macanese drama troupe's efforts to prolong the life of the Macanese language), *Aomen Zazhi*, No. 40, June 2004.

55. In one of those days, the glass windows of her family house were shattered by mobs, and as a little girl, she was intimidated by Chinese men when her A-Mah took her to a market. See Watts, "Neither Meat nor Fish."
56. Wang Chun, "Aomen de tusheng wenxue," pp. 351, 372–7. Adé (1919–93) was a prolific writer: he wrote 18 books of poetry, prose, plays, operettas, and radio shows in Patua. He also wrote, directed, and acted in his own productions.
57. Ibid., pp. 351–3.
58. For a number of stories by Fernanda Dias, see Brookshaw, *Visions of China*, pp. 191–20.
59. I would like to thank one of the anonymous reviewers for reminding me of the important contributions made by these institutions and individuals in preserving and propagating the Macanese culture.
60. Bartleby website, at http://www.bartleby.com/65/ca/Camoes.html, last accessed on February 16, 2005.
61. See also Porter, *Macau: The Imaginary City*, pp. 102–4; Coates, *A Macao Narrative*, pp. 26–7.
62. Pittis and Henders (selected and edited) *Macao: Mysterious Decay and Romance*, p. 194.
63. José Augusto Seabra, "Camilo Pessanha and the Mirage of Writing," *Review of Culture*, No. 11/12 (September 1990): 142.
64. David Brookshaw, *Perceptions of China in Modern Portuguese Literature: Border Gates* (Lewiston, New York: The Edwin Mellen Press, 2002), pp. 10, 26–27.
65. Ibid., p. 29.
66. Jia Le An (Rodrigo Leal de Carvalho), *Huan Hun Qu* (Requiem por Irina Ostrakoff, or a story of revival after death), translated by Yu Huijuan, and commented by Lin Baona (Ana Paula Laborinho) (Macau and Hainan: Instituto Cultural de Macau, Instituto Português do Oriente, Editora de Hainan, and Sanhuan Chubanshe, 1999).
67. Brookshaw, *Perceptions of China in Modern Portuguese Literature*, p. 131.
68. Tao Li, "Aomen de xiaoshuo chuangzuo," p. 220; Brookshaw, *Visions of China*, p. 18.
69. Brookshaw, *Visions of China*, p. 170. The excerpt is from her short story, "The Pedicab Driver."
70. The Sabores website, at http://spg.sapo.pt/XdR/445867.html, accessed on February 16, 2005. For a true love story of a Chinese woman and a British man, see Austin Coates's *City of Broken Promises* (Oxford: Oxford University Press, 1967).
71. Guillen-Nunez, "Through the Eyes of Nineteenth Century Painters," pp. 60–3.
72. Coates, *Macao and the British*, p. 147.
73. Cited in Coates, *Macao and the British*, p. 148. See also See Lamas, *Everything in Style*, p. 208, for more description of Chinnery by Harriett Low.
74. Chen Jichun, *Qian Na Li yu Aomen* (Chinnery and Macau) (Macau: Macau Foundation), at http://www.macaudata.com/macauweb/book127/, accessed February 16, 2005.

Chapter 7

1. C. Wright Mills, "The Promise," in Susan J. Ferguson, *Mapping the Social Landscape: Readings in Sociology* (Boston: McGraw Hill, 2002), pp. 1–2.
2. C. Wright Mills, *The Sociological Imagination* (New York: Oxford University Press, 2000).
3. For a book on social problems in the 1990s, see Chen Xin-xin (ed.) *Aomen Shehui Wenti* (Social problems in Macau) (Hong Kong: Guangjiaojing Chubanshe, 1995). This collection of papers deals with social problems in youth, education, security, traffic, pollution, the elderly, and cross-border crimes.

4. The parts on ethnic and class stratification and politics are originally published as part of an article "Social Stratification and Ethnic and Class Politics in Macau before and after the Handover in 1999," *China: An International Journal*, 13(1) (2015): 66–92. The information in these parts is now updated.
5. In fact, the percentage of Macanese holding director- or chief-rank civil servant positions had declined from 34.8% in 1987 to 14.5% in 1995, according to Herbert S. Yee, *Macau in Transition: From Colony to Autonomous Region* (New York: Palgrave, 2001), p. 55.
6. "Xu Weikun ze yiyuan pohuai shehui hexi" (Xu Weikun accuses one legislator of sabotaging social harmony), *Macao Daily*, August 12, 2009, p. B5.
7. *Aomen Tebie Xingzheng Qu Fayuan sifa niandu nianbao 2016–2017* (The annual report of the court of Macau Special Administrative Region 2016–2017), pp. 57–59, at http://www.court.gov.mo/ebook/2016-2017/index.html#_2016-2017/page/58-59, accessed October 30, 2018.
8. Li Huangjiang, "Aomen lushi ye gaikuang he fazhan jiyu" (The current status of Macau's legal field and opportunities for its development), *Macao Daily*, October 25, 2017. Li is a registered lawyer in Macau.
9. Catarina Brites Soares, "Falu jie xuanzhan" (Election battle in the legal field over the position of AAM president), October 19, 2018, Plataforma Macau, at http://www.plataformamacau.com/zh-hant/, accessed October 31, 2018.
10. See reports on this issue in *Macao Daily*, October 18, 2013, p. A3.
11. See reports on this issue in *Macao Daily*, November 18, 2008, p. A1.
12. Only 10 judges were added in the nine years after the return of Macau to China according to a report in *Macao Daily*, November 19, 2008, p. A2.
13. See reports on this issue in *Macao Daily*, October 20, 2013, p. A7.
14. See reports on Chan Chak Mo's speech in *Macao Daily*, November 19, 2008, p. A2.
15. For the new development discussed in this and the next two paragraphs, see Farah Master, unless cited otherwise, "In Macau, Portuguese Elites Feel Squeezed out by Chinese Influence," October 5, 2018, Reuters, at https://www.reuters.com/article/us-macau-china-law/in-macau-portuguese-elites-feel-squeezed-out-by-chinese-influence-idUSKCN1MF0OQ?il=0, accessed October 30, 2018.
16. Catarina Brites Soares, "Falu jie xuanzhan."
17. Catarina Brites Soares, "Falu jie xuanzhan."
18. José Carlos Matias, "Qian Lifahui yiyuan Leonel Alves piping Lifahui citui falu guwen Jian Tiantong he Dai Baolu de jueding" (Former legislator Leonel Alves criticize the decision of the legislature to dismiss Paulo Taipa and Paulo Cardinal), August 24, 2018, Plataforma Macau at http://www.plataformamacau.com/zh-hant/, accessed October 31, 2018. In an interview with the press, Ho Iat Seng denied all these allegations, saying that the two lawyers' work was highly valued, but they do not retain people because of good work, and do not dismiss people because of bad work. He sounded as if the two left the job of their own volition. But that is not true. At least one of them in Matias's article says that he was surprised to receive the end-of-contract letter. For Ho's interview, see "Renyuan likai shu zhengchang" (It is normal for people to leave), *Macao Daily*, September 11, 2018.
19. See Chen Xinxin, "Xianggang he Aomen de shehui jieji jiegou" (Social Class Structure in Hong Kong and Macau), in *Shuang cheng ji: Gang Ao de zhengzhi, jingji ji Shehui Fazhan* (A Tale of Two Cities: The Political, Economic, and Social Development in Hong Kong and Macau), ed. Yu Zhen (Macau: Association for the Study of Social Sciences, 1998), pp. 281–301.
20. See website of the Macao Chinese Chamber of Commerce (MCCC), at http://www.acm.org.mo/, accessed November 7, 2013.

21. See website of the Macao Federation of Trade Unions (MFTU), at http://www.faom.org.mo/portal.php, at November 7, 2013.
22. Lou Shenghua, *Zhuanxing shiqi Aomen shetuan yanjiu: Duoyuan shehui zhong fatuan zhuyi tizhi jiexi* (A Study of Macao's Social Organizations in the Period of Transition: An Analysis of Corporatism in a Multicultural Society) (Guangzhou: Guangdong renmin chubanshe, 2004), p. 147.
23. See website of Association for Civil Servants in Macao (ATFPM), at http://www.atfpm.org.mo/, November 7, 2013.
24. See the 2012 research report by the Institute of Social and Cultural Studies, Macau University of Science and Technology. The survey was done in 2011 by conducting door-to-door interviews of a representative sample of 1,200 respondents aged 18 years old and above.
25. These include the chiefs of departments (*Ting*), bureau chiefs (*Ju*), secretaries (*Si*), and the Chief Executive of Macao, in ascending order.
26. In 2013, 14 legislators were directly elected, 12 indirectly elected by occupational groups, and seven appointed by the chief executive. Indirect election involves only the social organizations of each of the following pre-defined occupations: (i) industry, commerce, and finance with four positions; (ii) labor with two positions; (iii) professional groups with three positions; (iv) social services and education with one position; and (v) culture and sports with two positions. In direct elections, 20 political groups competed for 14 positions. There was no competition in the indirect elections, however, and no known competition for the appointed positions.
27. For more details on Macau's legislative elections, see Lao Ritian, "Aomen lifahui xuanju zhidu zhi yanjiu" (On the electoral system of the Legislative Assembly in Macau), MA thesis, Department of Public Administration and Policy, National Jinan International University, Taiwan, 2007.
28. Guo Jixiu, *Dangdai Aomen toushi* (*An Analysis of Modern Macau*) (Macau: Jiuding yuekan, 2009), pp. 49–51.
29. Hao Zhidong, *Zouxiang minzhu yu hexie: Aomen, Taiwan yu Dalu shehui jinbu de jiannan licheng* (On the Way to Democracy and Harmony: Difficulties in Social Progress in Macau, Taiwan, and mainland China) (Macau: Jiuding chuanbo chubanshe, 2008), pp. 48–49.
30. Hao Zhidong, "Xiao cheng bing bu pingjing" (The Little Town Is Not Quiet), *Jiuding yuekan*, no. 9, 2008.
31. Lo, *Political Development in Macau*, pp. 32–33.
32. Op. cit., pp. 204–15.
33. Hao Zhidong, "Dui weilai Aomen zhengzhi tizhi gaige de zhanwang" (Future Prospects for Macau's Political Reform), *Aomen yuekan* (*Macao monthly*), no. 5, 2012.
34. Hao Zhidong, "Aomen jibenfa di ershisan tiao lifa de tiaojian yu shiji" (The condition and timing of the legislation of Article 23 of the Macau Basic Law), *Yazhou zhoukan* (*Asia weekly*), November 16, 2008, vol. 22, no. 45.
35. Clayton, "*If We Are Not Different*," pp. 66–9. For more information on the triads, see McGivering's interview of one former member, in McGivering, *Macao Remembers*, pp. 134–7, and Pina-Cabral, *Between China and Europe*, pp. 201–21.
36. See Office of the Secretary for Security, "Baoan Sizhang jiao gei chuanmei de wenjian" (The document distributed to the mass media by the Secretary for Security about the number of crimes in year 2017), February 9, 2018 at the Office's website https://www.gss.gov.mo/pdf/2017_C_full.pdf, accessed October 22, 2018.
37. "Macau Casinos Look to Insure Themselves against Rising Threat of Kidnappings," September 1, 2015, *Asia Gaming Brief*, at https://agbrief.com/headline/macau-casinos-look-to-insure-themselves-against-rising-threat-of-kidnappings/, accessed October 26, 2018.

38. "Sifa jingcha ju ying chun zuotanhui" (Spring festival symposium organized by the Judiciary Police), January 30, 2018 at the Judiciary Police's own website http://www.pj.gov.mo/Web//u/cms/www/201801/ 30155327rbel.pdf, accessed October 22, 2018. See also their corresponding report of the same title but for 2016 made on January 16, 2017, p. 2; The Office of the Secretary of Security, "2017 nian Aomen bocai ye fazhan dui Aomen zhian yingxiang de pinggu yijian" (An evaluation of the impact of the development of the gambling industry on Macau's public security), February 9, 2018 at https://www.gss.gov.mo/pdf/talk20180209b.pdf, accessed October 23, 2018; and Nelson Moura, "Macau: Gaming Related Crime Cases Drop in 2017," *Macau Business* at http://www.macaubusiness.com/macau-gaming-related-crime-cases-drop-slightly-2017/, accessed October 26, 2018.
39. See Zhidong Hao, Linda Hancock, and Bill Thompson, "In Search of Best Practices in Responsible Gambling (RG): A Report on a Comparative Study of RG among Macau, Las Vegas, and Melbourne." This is a report done in 2012 and 2013 for the Macau government's Gaming Inspection and Coordination Bureau, available through the author.
40. "Du shou die bocai zuian zeng" (Gambling revenue down and crime rate related to gambling up), *Macao Daily*, January 27, 2016.
41. Macau Interview Notes #2, and #19.7.
42. Melbourne Interview Notes #5.
43. For more on how the VIP system works in Macau, see Wang, Wuyi, and Peter Zabielskis, "Making Friends, Making Money: Macao's Traditional VIP Casino System" in *Global Gambling: Cultural Perspectives on Gambling*, ed. Sytze F. Kingma (London: Routledge Criminology, 2010).
44. Sheeraz Raza, "Las Vegas and Macau Casino Revenue Comparison Report," February 27, 2018, ValueWalk at https://www.valuewalk.com/2018/02/las-vegas-and-macau-casino-revenue-comparison/, accessed October 26, 2018.
45. "Du shou yu qibai yi, wu cheng si guibing ting" (Gambling revenue is MOP$70 billion, and 54% are from the VIP rooms), *Macao Daily*, October 23, 2018.
46. Zeng Zhonglu, "Neidi fu Ao haodu ke tezheng fenxi" (The characteristics of high rollers from mainland China), a paper manuscript, 2008.
47. "Macau Junkets Vulnerable to Money Laundering Says U.S. Report," March 9, 2016, *Asia Gaming brief* at https://agbrief.com/headline/macau-junkets-vulnerable-to-money-laundering-says-u-s-report/, accessed October 26, 2018.
48. See Davis Fong and Wu Meibao, "Aomen jumin canyu bocai huodong diaocha 2010" (A study on Macau residents' participation in gambling 2010), at the website of MSAR's Bureau of Social Work at http://www.ias.gov.mo/wp-content/themes/ias/tw/stat/download/dfccvf_rs2010.pdf, accessed October 26, 2018.
49. See "Bocai yuangong mi du qiu zhu zhan sancheng" (Casino employees constitute one third of those who seek help for problem gambling), *Macao Daily*, September 27, 2017.
50. The following is from Zhidong Hao et al., "In Search of Best Practices in Responsible Gambling."
51. Macau Interview Notes #13.
52. See Melbourne Interview Notes #5.
53. Las Vegas Interview Notes #41.
54. For more problem gambling prevention measures, see Zhidong Hao et al., "In Search of Best Practices."
55. Melbourne Interview Notes #5.
56. Las Vegas Interview Notes #3.
57. For the differences between the two cities, see above cited Sheeraz Raza, "Las Vegas and Macau Casino Revenue Comparison Report."

58. Robert Johnson, "Las Vegas, Macau Casino Revenue Comparison Report," *Casino News Daily*, at http://www.casinonewsdaily.com/2018/02/21/las-vegas-macau-casino-revenue-comparison-report-infographic/, accessed October 26, 2018.
59. For more on casino-related problems and remedies, see Hao Zhidong (forthcoming), "Aomen duye de wenti yu zhengfu he yunying shang de zeren" (The problems of Macau's gambling industry and the responsibility of the government and casino operators), a special issue of Er Shi Yi Shiji (The twenty-first century) to commemorate the twentieth anniversary of the return of Macau to China. This is a journal published by the Chinese University of Hong Kong.
60. Clayton, *"If We Are Not Different,"* pp. 213, 219–25. See also Garry Ngai, "Macau Communities," pp. 108–9.
61. Cathryn Hope Clayton, "History *of* and *for* Macao: Some Observations on Teaching Local History and Identity in Macao's Middle Schools," *Review of Culture*, international edition, No. 2 (April 2002): 174.
62. Clayton, *"If We Are Not Different,"* pp. 214, 226–7. See also Liu Xianbing, *Aomen Jiaoyu Shi*, pp. 8–57.
63. The data of this section on middle schools in Macau are from Zhidong Hao, "Aomen de jiaohui xuexiao zai aomen shehui fazhan zhong de zuoyong: Zhongdeng jiaoyu zhong jiaohui yu fei jiaohui xuexiao de duibi yanjiu" (The role of religious schools in the social development of Macau: A comparative study of religious and non-religious middle schools), a paper presented at a conference entitled "Jidujiao yu jindai Zhongguo jiaoyu" (Christianity and education in modern China), Shanghai University, October 29–30, 2016.
64. John Tan Kang, "Secondary School History Curricula," in Mark Bray and Ramsey Koo (eds.), *Education and Society in Hong Kong and Macao*, p. 216.
65. Ibid.
66. See the example of Kam Sut Leng discussed in an article by Xiao Jiayi, "Aomen 'guo jiao' xilie zhi er: Bi hong di geng kepa de . . ." (The second article on Macau's 'national education': Something more scary than the red background), August 17, 2015, The Standnews at https://thestandnews.com/, accessed November 11, 2018.
67. "Taiwan ge daxue jiu du Aomen xuesheng zhuangkuang diaocha yanjiu baogao (A report on a study of Macau students in Taiwan universities), organized and published by Macao Youth Research Association, Macao New Chinese Youth Association, and General Association of Chinese Students of Macao, July 2010, p. 19 at http://www.myra.org.mo/wp-content/uploads/2010/08/, last accessed October 28, 2018.
68. See Education and Youth Affairs Bureau's reports on 2012/2013, 2013/2014, 2014/2015, 2015/2016, 2016/2017 xuenian Aomen gaozhong biye sheng shengxue diaocha jian bao (Academic year reports on Macau graduating high school students' enrollment in colleges and universities).
69. "Ba daibiao: xiuding gaokao zhaosheng ming'e fenpei" (Eight representatives to the National People's Congress: Need to revise the quota distribution for college admissions). *Macao Daily*, March 13, 2017.
70. *Macao Daily*, "Chan Hong: The state values Macau and students from Macau are fortunate," November 10, 2016, A02.
71. "San daibiao: Ji kuo shou sheng jiaqiang guoqing jiaoyu" (Three representatives: Take advantage of expanding enrolment to strengthen national education). *Macao Daily*, March 13, 2017.
72. Yu Zhen, "Gang Ao shimin de zhengzhi canyu he minzhu jiazhi" (Political participation and democratic values in the citizens in Hong Kong and Macau), in Herbert Yee (Yu Zhen), Eilo Yu (Yu Yongyi), and Bruce Kwan (Kuang Jinjun) (eds.) *Shuang Cheng Ji II: Huigui hou Gang Ao de Zhengzhi, Jingji ji Shehui Fazhan* (A tale of two cities II: the political, economic and

73. social development in Hong Kong and Macau after their return to China) (Macau: Aomen Shehui Kexue Xuehui, 2003), p. 167.
73. For more discussion on the civic culture in Macau, see Herbert Yee, *Macau in Transition*, pp. 83–106.
74. Li Jiazeng, "Yige po kan wanwei de diaocha jieguo" (Survey findings that should make people think), *Macao Daily*, August 19, 2009, p. F2.
75. Shang Xun, "Minzhu husheng gao manyi du fantan" (A louder voice for democracy and people are less satisfied in general), *Business Intelligence*, No. 48, August 2009.
76. Zhidong Hao, "Social Stratification and Ethnic and Class Politics in Macao before and after the Handover in 1999," p. 89.
77. This part is based on my article "Higher Education Systems and Institutions, Macau," in Teixeira P. and Shin J. (eds.), *Encyclopedia of International Higher Education Systems and Institutions* (Dordrecht: Springer, 2018) at https://doi.org/10.1007/978-94-017-9553-1.
78. Tertiary Education Services Office of Macau Government, 2016, p. 20. Note that all the numbers below are from this source, too.
79. For this and other information on Macau's higher education, see also Zhidong Hao, "In Search of a Professional Identity: Higher Education in Macau and the Academic Role of Faculty," *Higher Education* 72(1) (2016): 101–13.
80. Max Weber, *The Protestant Ethic and the Spirit of Capitalism* (New York: Charles Scribner's Sons, 1958), pp. 181–2.
81. Seventeen tons of garbage was collected by sanitation workers after people's moon watching in the Mid-Autumn festival in 2004. This indicates the importance of an all-rounded education.
82. Clayton, "*If We Are Not Different*," p. 168.
83. Ibid., pp. 169, 171.
84. Ibid., pp. 181, 190–1, 194–5, 197–9.
85. Ibid., pp. 168, 177. See also Clayton, "History *of* and *for* Macao."
86. See Clayton, "*If We Are Not Different*," pp. 186–7, 195–6, 201.
87. For the future development of Macau's education, see also Gu Dingyi, "Guodu qi Gang Ao de jiaoyu fazhan" (The development of education in the transition periods in Hong Kong and Macau), in Yu Zhen (ed.) *Shuang Cheng Ji: Gang Ao de Zhengzhi, Jingji ji Shehui Fazhan* (A tale of two cities: the political, economic and social development in Hong Kong and Macau) (Macau: Macau Social Sciences Association, 1998), pp. 327–45.
88. Cited in Zhidong Hao, "Ye lun shimin shehui yu gonggong lingyu: jian ping Lii Ding Tzann deng suo zhu *Gonggong Lingyu zai Taiwan*" (On civil society and public sphere, and a review of Lii Ding Tzann et al.'s book *Public sphere in Taiwan*), *Sixiang* (Reflexion) (Taiwan), 2006, No. 2: 168–9.
89. For more on civil society and public sphere, see Georg Simmel, *The Sociology of Georg Simmel*, edited by Kurt Wolff (New York: The Free Press, 1950); Jürgen Habermas, "Citizenship and National Identity: Some Reflections on the Future of Europe," *Praxis International*, 12:1 (April 1992): 1–19.
90. For more on civil society in Macau, see Zhidong Hao, "Aomen gongming shehui zhishu chutan" (An exploratory study on the index of Macao's civil society), *Macao Daily*, October 27, p. E9, continued in the following four weeks.
91. "Zhao Xiangyang san jianyi youhua xieshang minzhu" (Zhao Xiangyang makes three suggestions to better consultative democracy), *Macao Daily*, March 30, 2017.
92. Ibid. See also Hao Zhidong, "Cong shetuan dao zhengtuan dao zhengdang: Du 'Liang Qingting fangtang lu' ye tan Aomen de zhengzhi tizhi gaige" (From civic associations to political associations to political parties: Reading "An interview with Leong Heng Teng" and thinking about political reform in Macau) in *Jiuding*, January 2010, Issue 27.

93. For a full discussion on social organizations in Macau and how they operate, see Lou Shenghua, *Zhuanxing Shiqi Aomen Shetuan Yanjiu* (A study of Macau's social organizations in the period of transition) (Guangzhou: Guangzhou Renmin Chubanshe, 2004), especially p. 7; Lou Shenghua, "Disappearances and births"; see also Aomen Fazhan Celue Yanjiu Zhongxin (Center for the study of development strategies in Macau), "Aomen shetuan de xianzhuang yu qiangzhan" (The current status and future prospects for Macau's social organizations), in Yu Zhen, Cui Bao-feng, and Zheng Wei-ming (eds.) *Aomen Lishi, Wenhua yu Shehui* (Macau history, culture, and society) (Macau: Macau Foundation, 2003), pp. 7–20; Wu Zhiliang's article on building a civil society in Macau and Penny Chan (Chen Xin-xin)'s article on sociopolitical forces in Macau in articles in Wu Zhiliang and Chen Xin-xin, *Aomen Zhengzhi Shehui Yanjiu* (A study of politics and society in Macau) (Macau: Macau Association for Adult Education, 2000), pp. 204–17. Chen analyzes the relationship between the middle class and democratization, and social forces such as A. the traditional left; B. the religious; C. the Macanese; and D. the democratic advocates, a framework based on Ngo Kuo-chang's analysis. For the reform of the government, see Bill K. P. Chou, "Public Sector Reform in Macau after the Handover," *China Perspectives*, No. 52 (March–April 2004): 56–63.
94. Sou Hei Lam, "Wo jueding le danren zhege zhiwu, ye jiu zhineng jinshen dian" (Once I decide to take this position, I'll have to be a bit cautious), November 17, 2017, Plataforma Macau, at http://www.plataformamacau.com/zh-hant/, accessed November 3, 2017.
95. For the information on mass media in Macau, see Wu Mei, "Mass Media in Macau," a presentation at the Fulbright Forum at the University of Macau, February 28, 2005. I did the English translation of the names to give the reader an idea of the message they want to convey, at least the message they want the reader to believe that they convey. For more on the development of Macau's publication history and the history of its news organizations, see Lin Yufeng, "Aomen xinwen chuban si bai nian" (Four hundred years of Macau's mass media publications), in Wu Zhiliang, Jin Guoping, and Tang Kaijian (eds.) *Aomen Shi Xin Bian*, Vol. 4; Manuel Teixeira, "Early Newspapers in Macau," *Review of Culture*, No. 11/12, September 1990.
96. "Qingchun haoqi zou qian shan: qingzhu ben bao chuan kan 51 zhounian" (Our youthful spirit will carry us forward: a commemoration of the 51st anniversary of the founding the *Macao Daily*), *Macao Daily*, August 15, 2009, p. A9.
97. See also Cai Qi'en, "Gang Ao liangdi chuanmei shengtai pingxi" (Comments on the ecology of the mass media in Hong Kong and Macau), in Yu Zhen, Yu Yongyi, and Kuang Jinjun (eds.) *Shuang Cheng Ji II*, pp. 395–406.
98. See Yu Hui-ying 余惠鶯, "Cujin gongmin canyu gong jian hexie shehui" (Promote civic participation and construct a harmonious society), *Macao Daily*, February 21, 2007, p. E5.
99. Sou Hei Lam, "Wo jueding le danren zhege zhiwu, ye jiu zhineng jinshen dian."
100. Personal conversation with one of the professors.
101. David Chan, "Guanzhu xinwen ziyou ji yanlun ziyou zhe ying guanzhu jiqi an" (Those who are concerned about press freedom and freedom of speech should pay attention to several lawsuits), September 14, 2018, *Plataforma Macau*, at http://www.plataformamacau.com/zh-hant/, accessed November 3, 2018.
102. "Li Yuanchao: Jiaqiang yan Gang Ao xin wenti" (Strengthen the studies of the new problems in Hong Kong and Macau), *Macao Daily*, September 29, 2014.
103. Baoan sizhang bangongshi (The office of the Secretary of Security, Macau government), "2017 nian quan nian aomen zuian tongji he zhifa gongzuo shuju jianbao" (A brief report on the statistics on crimes in Macau and the cases we handled in 2017), p. 3, at https://www.gss.gov.mo/pdf/talk20180209a.pdf, accessed November 3, 2019.

Chapter 8

1. Quoted in Clayton, *"If We Are Not Different,"* p. 161. Clayton interviewed him before 1999, so he did not have a Macau SAR passport yet.
2. See ibid., p. 164.
3. Benedict Anderson, *Imagined Communities: Reflections on the Origin and Spread of Nationalism*, revised edition (London and New York: Verso, 1991), pp. 6–7; Anthony D. Smith, *Nationalism and Modernism: A Critical Survey of Recent Theories of Nations and Nationalism* (London and New York: Routledge, 1998), p. 130.
4. Ernest Gellner, *Nations and Nationalism* (Oxford: Basil Blackwell, 1983), p. 7.
5. See also Craig Calhoun, *Nationalism* (Buckingham: Open University Press, 1997); Jürgen Habermas, "Citizenship and National Identity: Some Reflections on the Future of Europe," *Praxis International* 12(1)1-19 (April 1992): 3; Smith, *Nationalism and Modernism*, pp. 71, 83, 127–9, 245–70.
6. Weber, *From Max Weber*, p. 78; Lewellen, *Dependency and Development*, p. 133; Smith, *Nationalism and Modernism*, p. 70.
7. Liu I-chou and Tian Fang-hua, "Taiwan minzhong guojia rentong de leixing" (The types of national identity among people in Taiwan), a paper presented at Sun Yat-sen Institute of Humanities and Social Sciences, Academia Sinica, June 3, 2003.
8. Stein Tønnesson and Hans Antlöv, "Asia in Theories of Nationalism and National Identity," in Stein Tønnesson and Hans Antlöv (eds.) *Asian Forms of the Nation* (London: Curzon, 1996), p. 2.
9. Part of this section is based on my book on *Whither Taiwan and Mainland China: National Identity, the State, and Intellectuals* (Hong Kong: Hong Kong University Press, 2010).
10. Clayton, *"If We Are Not Different,"* p. 165.
11. Zhidong Hao, "Shehui kexue de zeren: lun dangqian Aomen de sheke yanjiu" (The responsibilities of social sciences: on the current social science research in Macau), *Aomen Yanjiu* (Macau studies), 2006, No. 33 (April): 118–29.
12. Clayton, *"If We Are Not Different,"* p. 143.
13. Ibid., p. 149.
14. Ibid., p. 294.
15. See also A. H. de Oliveira Marques, *History of Portugal, Volume I: From Lusitânia to Empire* (New York: Columbia University Press, 1972), pp. 234, 336, 477.
16. See Jin Guoping and Wu Zhiliang, *Jing Hai Piaomiao*, p. 136, for more discussion on the border issue.
17. Clayton, *"If We Are Not Different,"* p. 411.
18. See ibid., p. 427.
19. Zhidong Hao, "Shehui kexue de zeren," p. 118.
20. Herbet Yee, *Macau in Transition*, p. 70.
21. Li Zhenyu, "Tuiguang Jiben Fa yu guomin jiaoyu shi shizheng zhongxin" (To propagate the Basic Law and practice national education should be the focus of the government), *Macao Daily*, September 4, 2015.
22. For the number 51%, see "The end of Apathy," *Macau Business*, July 2009, p. 37. For the number 56%, see Zhidong Hao, "Social Stratification and Ethnic and Class Politics in Macao before and after the Handover in 1999," p. 89. Our survey in 2012 reported in this article found that on the average over 54.6% of the population favors universal suffrage: 66.1% of the middle class, 46.2% of the upper class, and 50.4% of the lower class. A 2009 survey found that over 80% of high school students believed that Macau should practice democracy although they did not really know what democracy really means. See "Xuesheng zantong minzhu, wei renshi buzu" (Students are in favor of democracy but do not really

know what it is), *Macao Daily*, May 29, 2009, p. A3. That number should be high even now among the whole population since democracy can be an abstract value while universal suffrage is a specific practice of democracy.
23. According to official explanations of the nationality question regarding Macau residents, those who have mixed blood could decide of their own accord whether they wanted to be Chinese or Portuguese national. And "all Chinese citizens in Macau holding Portuguese travel documents would be allowed to continue to use these documents to travel abroad, but would not have the right to consular protection from Portugal while in Macau or the PRC." See Clayton, *"If We Are Not Different,"* p. 145.
24. It would be interesting to compare the relationships between the mainland on one hand and Hong Kong, Macau, and Taiwan respectively on the other. One wonders to what extent each of the following factors influences people's nationalist feelings toward or national identity with the mainland: the proximity (the farther away from the mainland, the less attached emotionally to it), the nature of the colonizers (the Portuguese—least harsh, the British—harsh, and the Japanese—harshest), the political history of the Greater China (the communist revolution in China, refugees in Hong Kong, the neutral status of Macau in World War II), etc.
25. Clayton, *"If We Are Not Different,"* pp. 142–3.
26. Ibid., pp. 143–4.
27. The Macau City Guide website, at http://www.cityguide.gov.mo/tg/church/c_detaile.asp?lc=2&lkey= 02020900000000000000, last accessed on February 16, 2005. See also "Heritage Excellence," *Macau Focus* 1(3)59-64. December 2001. See more discussion on this issue in chapter 5.
28. Lou Shenghua, *Zhuanxing Shiqi Aomen Shetuan Yanjiu*.
29. Zhao Yanfang, *Puren Tusheng Fangtan* (Interviews with the Portuguese and Macanese in Macau) (Macau: International Institute of Macau, 2004), pp. 18, 25, 48, 54, 57, 95, 102, 110.
30. See, for example, the charter for Macau Chamber of Commerce (Chinese), and an interview with João Costa Antunes concerning the Macau Home of Portuguese Association, respectively in Lou Shenghua, *Zhuangxing Shiqi Aomen Shetuan Yanjiu*, pp. 363–4 and Zhao Yanfang, *Puren Tusheng Fangtan*, p. 18.
31. Brookshaw, *Perceptions of China in Modern Portuguese Literature*, p. 149.
32. See, for example, ibid., pp. 181–2.
33. For a discussion of postcolonial theory, see Julian Go, "Postcolonial Theory," in Bryan S. Turner (ed.) *The Cambridge Dictionary of Sociology* (Cambridge: Cambridge University Press, 2006); Said, *Orientalism*. For the Macau story in the eyes of postcolonialism, see also Tong Qiaohui, *Aomen Chengshi Huanjing yu Wenmai Yanjiu*, pp. 163–70.
34. See a fuller discussion on this issue, see Jin Guoping and Wu Zhiliang, pp. 201–14. See also chapter 7 for more discussion on race and ethnic relations.
35. Bai Zhijian, "Cheng youliang chuantong, ai guo ai Ao, li yuanda zhixiang, chuang ye jian gong: zai Aomen gejie qingnian qingzhu jianguo wu shi wu zhounian zuotanhui shang de jianghua" (Carry on the good tradition, love one's country, love Macau, set up high goals, and perform meritorious deeds: a talk at the meeting of Macau youths to celebrate the fiftieth anniversary of the founding of the People's Republic of China), *Macao Daily*, November 2, 2004, p. B6.
36. For a discussion on the formation of Hong Kong's political identity and a civil or political society, see Liu Zhaojia, "'Xianggang ren' huo 'Zhongguo ren': Xianggang huaren de shenfen rentong 1985–1995" ("Hongkongers" or "Chinese": The Hong Kong Chinese national identity 1985–1995); Kwan Hsin-chi, "Xianggang zhengzhi zhixu de xunqiu" (Looking for a political order), and "Xianggang zhengzhi shehui de xingcheng" (The formation of Hong

Kong's political society). All three articles are in Liu Qingfeng and Guan Xiaochun (eds.) *Zhuanhua zhong de Xianggang: Shenfen yu Zhixu de Zai Xunqiu* (Hong Kong in transition: looking again for identity and order) (Hong Kong: The Chinese University of Hong Kong Press, 1998), pp. 3–30, 73–113. See also Wu Zhiliang, "Jiangou Aomen de shimin shehui" (The construction of Macau's civil society), and Chen Xinxin, "Aomen de zhongchan jieji yu minzhu hua" (Macau's middle class and democratization), both in Wu Zhiliang and Chen Xinxin (eds.) *Aomen Zhengzhi Shehui Yanjiu* (A study of Macau's politics and society) (Macau: Macau Adult Educational Association 2000), pp. 144–57, 204–17.
37. "Cao yu xingzheng lifa duo goutong" (Chou [Susana] calls on more interaction between the executive branch and the legislative branch), *Macao Daily*, August 15, 2009, p. A1.
38. In other words, can Macau contribute to China's democratic transformation by more fully democratizing itself or by helping to form a federation of some kind? See Zhidong Hao, *Whither Taiwan and Mainland China*; Wu Jiaxiang, *Lianbang Hua: Zhongguo Di San Gongheguo zhi Lu* (Federation: the way to a third Chinese republic) (Hong Kong: The Mirror Press, 2004).
39. See also Clayton, *"If We Are Not Different,"* pp. 132, 173.
40. Liu Bolong, "Huigui yihou Aomen duiwai guanxi de huigu yu zhanwang"; Gunn, *Encountering Macau*, p. 188.
41. Tereza Sena, "Historical Background of Macau with Particular Focus on the First Americans in China," p. 77.
42. See, for example, Zhang Wenqin, *Aomen yu Zhonghua Lishi Wenhua*, pp. 119–21.
43. Xu Suqin, "Qing Mo zhengzhi fengyun zhong Yue Ao liang di de xianghu yingxiang yu Yue Ao jie wu fenzheng," pp. 315–21, 326–38. See also Deng Kaisong and Xie Houhe, *Aomen Lishi yu Shehui Fazhan*, pp. 124–33; Gunn, *Encountering Macau*, pp. 96–103.
44. See also Coates, *A Macao Narrative*, pp. 103–4.
45. Pina-Cabral, *Between China and Europe*, p. 26. See also Guangdong Sheng Dang'an Guan (ed.) *Guangdong Aomen Dang'an Shiliao Xuan Bian*, pp. 380–5.
46. Jiang Minrui, "Kang Ri zhanzheng yu jiefang zhanzheng xin xingshi xia Yue Ao guanxi de xin neirong" (The new relationship between Guangdong and Macau in the war of resistance against the Japanese and the civil war), in Deng Kaisong, Wu Zhiliang, and Lu Xiaomin (eds.) *Yue Ao Guanxi Shi* (The relationship between Guangdong and Macau) (Beijing: Zhongguo Shudian, 1999), pp. 444–7; F. A. Silva, *The Sons of Macao, Their History and Heritage* (California: UMA, Inc, 1979), p. 40. For the war time Macau and Macau as a *de facto* sanctuary for the KMT refugees, see also Gunn, *Encountering Macau*, pp. 120–7, 154.
47. Lou Shenghua, *Zhuangxing Shiqi Aomen Shetuan Yanjiu*, pp. 78–88. See also *Aomen Jinri zhi Qiao Yun* (The overseas Chinese movements in Macau today) (Aomen Shijie Chubanshe, 1948).
48. See also McGivering's interview with Kung Yick, a KMT member who came to Macau after 1949, in McGivering, *Macau Remembers*, p. 131. He discusses how the Macau community was divided into pro-Communist and pro-Nationalist communities until the 12-3 Incident.
49. Pina-Cabral, *Between China and Europe*, p. 135.
50. Lou Shenghua, *Zhuanxing Shiqi Aomen Shetuan Yanjiu*, p. 280; Pina-Cabral, *Between China and Europe*, pp. 135–6;
51. Lu Xiaomin, "Xin Zhongguo chengli zhi 'Wenhua Da Geming' jieshu Yue Ao guanxi de quzhe fazhan" (The twists and turns in the Guangdong-Macau relations from the founding of new China to the end of the Cultural Revolution," in Deng Kaisong, Wu Zhiliang, and Lu Xiaomin (eds.) *Yue Ao Guanxi Shi*, pp. 506–7. See also Xie Houhe, *Aomen Lishi yu Shehui Fazhan*, pp. 176–7.
52. On December 20, 2008, the Macau government refused entry of some Hong Kong legislators who came to Macau to support the democracy movements against the legislation of

Article 23 (see Zhidong Hao, "Shaonian Aomen renge taiguo cuiruo" (Young Macao and its vulnerabilities in personality), *Asia Weekly*, No. 1, Vol. 23, January 4, 2009). It refused entry to Wuer Kaixi, a Chinese democracy activist, who wanted to enter Macau as a symbolic entry of China. He lives in Taiwan now. He is not allowed to go back to China because he was one of the student activists in the 1989 democracy movement. He came on June 3, 2009, the eve of the 20th anniversary of the June Fourth crackdown on demonstrators in 1989. Journalists from Hong Kong were denied entry after Typhoon Hato in 2017 for fear that they might say bad things about the Macau government's ability to handle natural disasters (see Sou Ka Ho, "Feng zai hexie yiyuan tingzhi tong lie shijie renquan wudian, shiqu mian ju ziyou longzhao ziwu shencha nai zhiming shang" or "After Typhoon, a legislator is suspended and this becomes a stain on Macau's human rights record; it is a fatal wound to lose the freedom of fear and practice self-censorship," Lun Jin Meiti [All about media] in *Son Pou*, March 2, 2018). Three writers were denied entry in 2018 for a literature festival: James Church, Jung Chang, and Suki Kim (see Liao Kong, "Sanwei zuojia bei ju rujing canyu wenyue jie, Aomen xingxiang shou sun biaoda ziyou qianjiang kan you" or "Three writers were denied entry for a literature festival, Macao's image is damaged, and the future of freedom of expression is in danger," *Son Pou*, page B2.) Michael Hsin-Huang Hsiao, a pro-independence academic from Academia Sinica in Taiwan, was denied entry in Macau in 2016 even though he was coming to attend a research workshop at the University of Macau, a project sponsored by the Hong Kong government. These are only few examples among many.

53. Alex Blaszczynski, Robert Ladouceur, and Howard J. Shaffer, "A Science-Based Framework for Responsible Gambling: The Reno Model," *Journal of Gambling Studies*, Vol. 20, No. 3: 308.
54. Mark Dickerson, "Exploring the Limits of 'Responsible Gambling': Harm Minimization or Consumer Protection?" proceedings of the 12th Annual Conference of the National Association for Gambling Studies, Melbourne, 2003.
55. For this quote and other information in this paragraph, see Blaszczynski et al., "A Science-Based Framework for Responsible Gaming," pp. 311–2.
56. Arthur Pitcher, "Responsible Promotion of Gaming and Dealing with Problem Gamblers," *Journal of Gambling Studies*, Vol. 15, No. 2: 156.
57. Zhidong Hao, "Cong qiye shehui zeren de shijiao kan fuzeren bocai: Yi Aomen weili" (Responsible gambling from the perspective of corporative social responsibility: The case of Macau), *Zhongguo shehui kexue neibu wengao* (Chinese social sciences: Restricted version), 2010, No. 5.
58. See also Kang Ping, "Jingji 'shidu duoyuan' kongjian henda" (There is big room for improvement in "appropriate diversification"), *Shang Xun* (Business intelligence), May 2009.
59. See Lam Fat Iam (ed.), *Aomen lishi jianzhu de gushi* (The stories of Macau's historical buildings) (Macau: Aomen Peidao Zhongxue Lishi Xuehui, 2005); Lei Kun Min and Lam Fat Iam, *19–20 shiji minxinpian zhong de Aomen* (Macau in postcards in the 19th and 20th centuries) (Macau: Aomen Lishi Jiaoyu Xuehui 2008).
60. See Zhdiong Hao (forthcoming), "Macau's Natural and Social Environments and Their Historical Backgrounds," in Haruhiko Fujita, Christine Guth, and Wendy Siuyi Wong (eds.) *The Encyclopedia of Asian Design* (London: Bloomsbury Publishing). See also Jason Wordie, *Macao: People and Places, Past and Present* (Hong Kong: Angsana Limited, 2013); Lam Fat Iam (ed.), *Aomen jiedao de gushi* (Stories of Macau's streets) (Macau: Aome Peidao Zhongxue Lishi Xuehui, 2005; Xiao Yu, "Aomen 1200 duo tiao jiedao, zhexie jiedao qu shi bendiren dou weibi zhi" (Over 1200 streets in Macau whose interesting stories locals may not know), FreeWeChat at https://freewechat.com/a/MjM5MTAzODIxNA==/2651486727/1 and Miya, "Xiqi guguai de Aomen lupai—Luanhuan" (Strange street names in Macau—Coloane) at https://mp.weixin.qq.com/s/nXQ3Kf4zCiMEFO4zahoGSw?##, accessed

November 9, 2018. For the challenges of heritage development in Macau, see Peter Zabielskis, "Challenges of Heritage Development Projects in Macau and Penang: Preservation and Anti-preservation" in *Dynamics of Community Formation: Developing Identity and Notions of Home*, edited by Robert W. Compton, Jr., Ho Hon Leung, and Yaser Robles (New York: Palgrave Macmillan, 2018).

61. One of the anonymous reviewers of the first edition points out that the Macau Government Tourist Office intends to help diversify Macau's economy by developing not "cultural tourism," but "business tourism." In other words, it will render its active support to a number of MICE activities. The reviewer points out, "The cultural attractions are a valuable asset to achieve this goal. The huge investments in Macau's infrastructure over the past few years, of more than 20 billion US$, have led to the emergence of state-of-the-art convention and exhibition facilities, among the biggest in the world, to numerous luxurious hotels and shopping malls (with more to come …), which have to be filled for more than one night. Business travellers, on the contrary to many cultural tourists, will stay longer in town and spend more money. This very recent change of direction, or planned change of direction, means a huge challenge for Macau, because the demand for labour, housing, health, food, etc. has reached proportions hitherto unknown." That is very true, and the government support of MICE activities can very well include cultural events. It is a direction that the government should seriously think about.
62. See an interview with Auntunes in Song Bonian, Zheng Miaoxian, and Huang Yanhong, *Aomen Wenhua Fangtan Lu*, p. 25.
63. See an interview with Maria Helena de Senna Fernades in Song Bonian, Zheng Miaoxian, and Huang Yanhong, *Aomen Wenhua Fangtan Lu*, pp. 11–2.
64. See an interview with Goncalves in Song Bonian, Zheng Miaoxian, and Huang Yanhong, *Aomen Wenhua Fangtan Lu*, p. 33.
65. See Jin Guoping and Wu Zhiliang, *Jinghai Piaomiao*, pp. 207–9.
66. See Cheng Tijie, "Tigao Aomen luyou ye de wenhua cengci" (Raise the cultural standards of Macau's tourist industry), in Herbert Yee (Yu Zhen), Eilo Yu (Yu Yongyi), and Bruce Kwan (Kuang Jinjun) (eds.) *Shuang Cheng Ji II*, p. 303.
67. C. Marreiros, "Traces of Chinese and Portuguese Architecture," p. 101.
68. See also Zhidong Hao, "Dependent development? Macao's Gaming Industry: Its Problems and Prospects," *Macau Studies*, No. 51 (April): 64–77.
69. For Macau's role in China's development, see also Gary Ngai's article "Macau—An Ideal Base to Develop Sino-Latin Ties" *Macau Focus*, Vol. 1, No. 3, December 2001.
70. Clayton, *"If We Are Not Different,"* p. 259.
71. As for the difficulties of forming one's identity, the Hong Kong example is again very illuminating. For more discussions on the formation of a Hong Kong identity, see Ren Hai, "Kan de bianzheng: zhanlan chu zhong de Xianggang" (The dialectics of watching: the Hong Kong in the exhibition windows), and Ma Jiewei, "Zaizao Xianggang: dianshi jiangou de xianggang jiyi" (The reconstruction of Hong Kong: the Hong Kong memory as construed in television), both articles in Liu Qingfeng and Guan Xiaochun (eds.) *Zhuanhua zhong de Xianggang: Shenfen yu Zhixu de Zai Xunqiu* (Hong Kong in transition: looking again for identity and order) (Hong Kong: The Chinese University of Hong Kong Press, 1998), pp. 195–235. Both articles describe how people purposefully forget or ignore things that are inconvenient for their political stance. For how national identity issues were reflected in history teaching curricula, see Edward Vickers, *In Search of an Identity: The Politics of History as a School Subject in Hong Kong, 1960s–2002* (New York & London: Routledge, 2003.) For how the youths of Macau, Hong Kong, and Goa think about their colonial heritage, see Ratna Ghosh, "Colonization and the Construction of Identity: A Comparison of Teenage Identity in Macao, Hong Kong and Goa," *Review of Culture*, international edition 1, January

2002. Young people in Macau, for example, do not know much about the Portuguese heritage, and do not care about knowing it, either. That is a typical attitude of young people in these former colonies.
72. Gunn, *Encountering Macau*, pp. xiii–xiv. See also Jin Guoping and Wu Zhiliang, *Guo Shizi Men*, p. 24, for a similar point.
73. See the Lycos Tripod website, at http://members.lycos.co.uk/macau1999/features/poems/macao.htm, last accessed on February 16, 2005. For a translation of the poem, see Tao Li and Zhuang Wenyong, "Aomen de xin shi chuangzuo" (Macau's new poetry), in Liu Denghan (ed.) *Aomen Wenxue Gaiguan*, p. 117. This is not a very accurate translation, though.

Selected Bibliography

Afonso R. and F. G. Pereira. 1987. "The Constitution and Legal System," in R. D. Cremer (ed.) *Macau: City of Commerce and Culture*, pp. 185–98. Hong Kong: UEA Press Ltd.

Amaro, Dra Ana Maria 安娜. 瑪裏亞. 阿馬羅. 1993. *Dadi zhi Zi: Aomen Tusheng Puren Yanjiu* 大地之子：澳門土生葡人研究 (The children of the earth: a study of Macanese). Translated by Jin Guoping 金國平. Macau: Aomen Wenhua Sishu 澳門文化司署.

An Ximeng 安希孟. 2005. "A Cultural Reflection on the Controversy of Rites" 對禮儀之爭的文化反思. At http://www.xslx.com/ htm/zlsh/zjyj/2004-06-17-17000.htm, last accessed February 16, 2005.

Anderson, Benedict. 1991. *Imagined Communities: Reflections on the Origin and Spread of Nationalism*. Revised edition. London and New York: Verso.

Aomen Fazhan Celue Yanjiu Zhongxin 澳門發展策略研究中心 (Center for the study of development strategies in Macau). 2003. "Aomen shetuan de xianzhuang yu qiangzhan" 澳門社團的現狀與前瞻 (The current status and future prospects for Macau's social organizations), in Yu Zhen, Cui Bao-feng, and Zheng Wei-ming (eds.) *Aomen Lishi, Wenhua yu Shehui* 澳門歷史、文化與社會 (Macau history, culture, and society), pp. 7–20. Macau: Macau Foundation.

———. 2006. *Aomen Tequ Jumin Suzhi Diaocha Baogao 2005* 澳門特區居民素質調查報告 2005 (A research report on the quality of residents in Macau SAR 2005). Macau: Aomen Fazhan Celue Yanjiu Zhongxin.

Aomen Jinri zhi Qiao Yun 澳門今日之僑運 (The overseas Chinese movements in Macau today). 1948. Macau: Aomen Shijie Chubanshe 世界出版社.

Baracho, Carlos. 2001. "The Churches of Macau and Their Placement in Urban Space and within the City's Architectonic Context." *Macau Focus* 1(3): 29–45.

Baxter, Alan N. 2009. "O português em Macau: contato e assimilação," in Ana Maria Carvalho (ed.) *Português em contato*, pp. 277–312. Madrid/Frankfurt: Iberoamericana/Editorial Vervuert.

Berlie, J. A. 1999. "Society and Economy," in J. A. Berlie (ed.) *Macao 2000*, pp. 20–52. Oxford University Press.

———. 2000. "Macau's Overview at the Turn of the Century." *American Asian Review*, Vol. XVIII, No. 4 (Winter): 25–68.

Blaszczynski, Alex, Robert Ladouceur, and Howard J. Shaffer. 2004. "A Science-Based Framework for Responsible Gambling: The Reno Model." *Journal of Gambling Studies*, 20(3): 301–17.

Blumer, Herbet. 1969. *Symbolic Interactionism: Perspective and Method*. Berkeley, California: University of California Press.

Bo Si 博斯 (Arie Pos). 2008. "'Yi yi zhi yi': mingdai de Ao He guanxi" '以夷制夷'：明代的澳荷關係 ("To use foreigners to control foreigners": the relationship between Macau and

Holland), in Wu Zhiliang, Jin Guoping, and Tang Kaijian (eds.) *Aomen Shi Xin Bian* 澳門史新編 (A new history of Macau), Vol. 2., pp. 561–78. Macau: Macau Foundation.

Boxer, C. R. 1968. *Fidalgos in the Far East 1550–1770*. Hong Kong, London, New York: Oxford University Press.

——— (ed. and trans.). 1984. *Seventeenth Century Macau in Contemporary Documents and Illustrations*. Hong Kong: Heinemann (Asia).

———. 1995. "Shiliu–shiqi shiji Aomen de zongjiao he maoyi zhongzhuan gang zhi zuoyong" 十六 —— 十七世紀澳門的宗教和貿易中轉港之作用 (Macau as a religious and trading entrepot in the 16th–17th centuries), in Huang Qichen 黃啟臣 and Deng Kaisong 鄧開頌 (eds.) *Zhong Wai Xuezhe Lun Aomen Lishi* 中外學者論澳門歷史 (Studies on Macau history by Chinese and foreign scholars), pp. 175–99. Macau: Macau Foundation.

Bray, Mark, with R. Butler, P. K. F. Hui, O. W. K. Kwo, and E. W. L. Mang. 2002. *Higher Education in Macau: Growth and Strategic Development*. Comparative Education Research Centre, The University of Hong Kong. At http://www.hku.hk/cerc/Publications/he-macau.htm, last accessed November 3, 2005.

Bray, Mark and Ramsey Koo. 2004. "Postcolonial Patterns and Paradoxes: Language and Education in Hong Kong and Macao." *Comparative Education* 40(2): 215–39.

Bray, Mark and Ramsey Koo (eds.). 2004. *Education and Society in Hong Kong and Macao: Comparative Perspectives on Continuity and Change*. Second edition. Hong Kong: Comparative Education Research Centre, The University of Hong Kong, and Dordrecht: Kluwer Academic Publishers.

Brook, Timothy. 1998. "Communications and Commerce," in Denis Twitchett and Frederick W. Mote (eds.) *The Cambridge History of China Volume 8: The Ming Dynasty, 1368–1644, Part 2*, pp. 579–707. New York: Cambridge University Press.

Brookshaw, David (selected and translated). 2002. *Visions of China: Stories from Macau*. Hong Kong: Hong Kong University Press.

———. 2002. *Perceptions of China in Modern Portuguese Literature: Border Gates*. Lewiston, New York: The Edwin Mellen Press.

Bruning, Harald. 2004. "Tusheng puyu—Aomen binwei de 'tianmi yuyan'" 土生葡語 — 澳門瀕危的"甜蜜語言." *Aomen Zazhi* 澳門雜誌, No. 40, June 2004.

Cabral, João de Pina and Nelson Lourenço. 1990. "Macanese Ethnicity and Family: A Methodological Prologue." *Review of Culture*, No. 11/12, September.

Cai Chang 蔡昌 and Gu Ding-yi 古鼎儀 (eds.). 2001. *Aomen Jiaoyu yu Shehui Fazhan* 澳門教育與社會發展 (Education and social development in Macao). Hong Kong: Department of Educational Policy and Administration, Hong Kong College of Education.

Cai Qi'en 蔡啟恩. 2003. "Gang Ao liangdi chuanmei shengtai pingxi" 港澳兩地傳媒生態評析 (Comments on the ecology of the mass media in Hong Kong and Macau), in Yu Zhen, Yu Yongyi, and Kuang Jinjun (eds.) *Shuang Cheng Ji II: Huigui hou Gang Ao de Zhengzhi, Jingji ji Shehui Fazhan* 雙城記 II：回歸後港澳的政治、經濟及社會發展 (A tale of two cities II: the political, economic and social development in Hong Kong and Macau after their return to China), pp. 395–406. Macau: Aomen Shehui Kexue Xuehui.

Calhoun, Craig. 1997. *Nationalism*. Buckingham: Open University Press.

Cao Qizhen (Susana Chou). 2009. "Aomen xingzheng yu lifa zhijian zenmala: *Lifahui Zhuxi Shinian Gongzuo Qingkuang de Zongjie Baogao*" 澳門行政與立法之間怎麼了：《立法會主席十年工作情況的總結報告》(What happened to the relationship between the executive and legislative branches: an excerpt of the summary report on the ten years of legislative work by the chair of the legislative assembly). *Jiuding* 九鼎, No. 24, September 2009.

Cai, Yongjun. 2013. "Cong lifahui de liyi daibiao dan huigui hou de shehui yundong" (Social movements after the handover as seen from legislators representing different interests), in *Yiguo liangzhi yanjiu* (Academic Journal of One country, Two Systems), No. 2.

Carmo, Paulo. 2001. "China and the West: Images of a Meeting." *Macau Magazine*, December.

Chan, Hoiman and Ambrose Y. C. King. 1999. "Religion," in Robert E. Gamer (ed.) *Understanding Contemporary China*, pp. 321–54. Boulder, London: Lynne Rienner Publishers.

Chan, Hok-Lam. 1988. "The Chien-wen, Yung-lo, Hung-hsi, and Hsuan-te Reigns, 1399–1435," in Frederick W. Mote and Denis Twitchett (eds.) *The Cambridge History of China Volume 7: The Ming Dynasty, 1368–1644, Part 1*, pp. 182–304. New York: Cambridge University Press.

Chan, Kwok Shing. 2011. Book Review of *Macau History and Society* by Zhidong Hao, *The China Review*, Vol. 11, No. 2.

Cheang Hong Kuong 鄭洪光. 2003. *Aomen Tebie Xingzheng Qu "Xingzheng Zhudao" Zhengce zhi Youlai yu Shijian* 澳門特別行政區"行政主導"政策之由來與實踐 (The origin and practice of Macao SAR's "executive led" policy). M.A. thesis, The University of Macau.

Chen, Arthur H. 2004. "Macau as Metropolis: Heritage and Preservation towards the Future," in Ieda Siqueira Wiarda and Lucy M. Cohen (eds.) *Macau: Cultural Dialogue towards a New Millenium*, pp. 123–32. Philadelphia: Xlibris Corporation.

Chen Jichun 陳繼春. 1995. *Qian Nali yu Aomen* 錢納利於澳門 (Chinnery and Macau). Macau: Macau Foundation. At http://www.macaudata.com/macauweb/book127/, last accessed Februay 16, 2005.

Chen Xinxin 陳欣欣 (Penny Chan). 1992. *Aomen Shenhui Chutan* 澳門社會初探 (A brief exploration of the Macao society). Hong Kong: Wan Shi Wei Chuban.

———. 1993. *Aomen Fazhan Xiankuang* 澳門發展現況 (The contemporary development in Macao). Hong Kong: Guangjiaojing Chubanshe.

——— (ed.). 1995. *Aomen Shehui Wenti* 澳門社會問題 (Social problems in Macao). Hong Kong: Guangjiaojing Chubanshe.

———. 2000. "Aomen de zhongchan jieji yu minzhu hua" 澳門的中產階級與民主化 (Macau's middle class and democratization), in Wu Zhiliang and Chen Xinxin, *Aomen Zhengzhi Shehui Yanjiu* 澳門政治社會研究 (A study of Macau's politics and society), pp. 204–17. Macau: Macau Adult Educational Association.

Chen Xinxin 陳欣欣 and Zheng Zijie 鄭子傑. 2003. "Cong Gang Ao tequ 'Jiben Fa 23 Tiao' lifa kan shehui de jihua yu zhenghe" 從港澳特區《基本法23條》立法看社會的極化與整合 (Polarization and integration in society as a result of the possible legislation of Article 23 of the Basic Law), in Herbert Yee (Yu Zhen), Eilo Yu (Yu Yongyi), and Bruce Kwan (Kuang Jinjun) (eds.) *Shuang Cheng Ji II: Huigui hou Gang Ao de Zhengzhi, Jingji ji Shehui Fazhan* 雙城記 II：回歸後港澳的政治、經濟及社會發展 (A tale of two cities II: the political, economic and social development in Hong Kong and Macau after their return to China), pp. 437–58. Macau: Aomen Shehui Kexue Xuehui.

Chen Xi-qiao 陳錫僑 and Tan Wei-guang 譚衛廣 (eds.). 2004. *Ershi Shiji de Aomen Huanjing* 二十世紀的澳門環境 (Macao's environment in the 20th century). Macau: Macao Association for Social Sciences.

Cheng, Christina Miu Bing. 2005. "Matriarchy at the Edge: The Mythic Cult of Nu Wa in Macao." *Review of Culture*, international edition 13, January 2005.

Cheng Tijie 程惕潔. 2003. "Tigao Aomen luyou ye de wenhua cengci" 提高澳門旅遊業的文化層次 (Raise the cultural standards of Macau's tourist industry), in Herbert Yee (Yu Zhen), Eilo Yu (Yu Yongyi), and Bruce Kwan (Kuang Jinjun) (eds.) *Shuang Cheng Ji II: Huigui hou Gang Ao de Zhengzhi, Jingji ji Shehui Fazhan* 雙城記 II：回歸後港澳的政治、經濟及社會發展 (A tale of two cities II: the political, economic and social development in Hong Kong and Macau after their return to China), pp. 295–307. Macau: Aomen Shehui Kexue Xuehui.

Chou, Bill K. P. 2004. "Public Sector Reform in Macau after the Handover." *China Perspectives*, No. 52, March–April 2004, pp. 56–63.

Clayton, Cathryn Hope. 2001. *"If We Are Not Different, We Will Cease to Exist": Culture and Identity in Transition-Era Macau*. Ann Arbor, Michigan: UMI Dissertation Services.
———. 2002. "History *of* and *for* Macao: Some Observations on Teaching Local History and Identity in Macao's Middle Schools." *Review of Culture*, international edition, No. 2, April.
———. 2009. *Sovereignty at the Edge: Macau and the Question of Chineseness*. Cambridge and London: The Harvard University Asia Center.
Coates, Austin. 1966. *Macao and the British 1637–1842: Prelude to Hong Kong*. New York: Oxford University Press.
———. 1978. *A Macao Narrative*. Hong Kong: Heinemann.
Correia, Francisco Nunes and Pedro Liberato. 1998. *Aomen Huanjing Zhuangkuang Pinggu ji Celuexing Jianyi* 澳門環境狀況評估及策略性建議 (An evaluation of the environment in Macao and suggestions on the strategies for its protection). Macau: Social Affairs and Budget Office, Macao Government.
Correios e Telecomunicoes de Macau 澳門郵電司 (ed.). 1990. *From the Sampan to the Jetfoil, from the Sedan Chair to the Car* (從轎子到汽車, 從舢舨到飛翔船). Text by Jorge Cavalheiro. Macao: Correios e Telecomunicoes de Macau.
Cowell, Alan Cowell. 2006. "Blair Criticizes Full Islamic Veils as 'Mark of Separation'." *New York Times*, October 18, 2006 at www.nytimes.com.
Cremer, R. D. 1987. "From Portugal to Japan: Macau's Place in the History of World Trade," in R. D. Cremer (ed.) *Macau: City of Commerce and Culture*, pp. 23–37. Hong Kong: UEA Press Ltd.
———. 1987. "Introduction," in R. D. Cremer (ed.) *Macau: City of Commerce and Culture*, pp. 1–4. Hong Kong: UEA Press Ltd.
Crowell, Todd. 1999. "A Proud People." Asiaweek.com, December 24, 1999, Vol. 25, No. 51.
Dai Dingcheng 戴定澄. 2008. "Aomen yinyue jianshi" 澳門音樂簡史 (A brief history of the music in Macau), in Wu Zhiliang, Jin Guoping, and Tang Kaijian (eds.) *Aomen Shi Xin Bian* 澳門史新編 (A new history of Macau), Vol. 4., pp. 1329–53. Macau: Macau Foundation.
Dai Yongru 戴詠如. 2009. "Cong lifahui xuanju kan zheng shang guanxi" 從立法會選舉看政商關係 (The relationship between the government and businesses as seen from the election of the legislators). *Shang Xun* 商訊 (Business Intelligence), No. 49, September.
Deng Kaisong 鄧開頌. 1995. "Yapian zhanzheng qian Aomen de zousi maoyi yu Lin Zexu zai Aomen jin yan," in Huang Qichen 黃啟臣 and Deng Kaisong 鄧開頌 (eds.) *Zhong Wai Xuezhe Lun Aomen Lishi* 中外學者論澳門歷史 (Studies on Macau history by Chinese and foreign scholars), pp. 326–54. Macau: Macau Foundation.
Deng Kaisong 鄧開頌 and Xie Houhe 謝厚和. 1999. *Aomen Lishi yu Shehui Fazhan* 澳門歷史與社會發展 (Macau history and social development). Zhuhai: Zhuhai Chubanshe.
Deng Kaisong 鄧開頌, Yu Siwei 余思偉, and Lu Xiaomin 陸曉敏. 1999. *Aomen Cangsang* 澳門滄桑 (The vicissitudes of Macao). Zhuhai: Zhuhai Press.
Durkheim, Emile. 1965. *The Elementary Forms of the Religious Life*. New York: The Free Press.
———. 1972. *Selected Writings*. Edited by Anthony Giddens. Cambridge: Cambridge University Press.
Eadington, W. R. and Ricardo C. S. Siu. 2007. "Between Law and Custom—Examining the Interaction between Legislative Change and the Evolution of Macao's Casino Industry." *International Gambling Studies*, 7(1): 1–28.
Edmonds, Richard Louis. 2011. Book Review of *Macau History and Society* by Zhidong Hao, *The China Quarterly*, No. 208, pp. 1060–2.
Fairbank, John K. and Edwin O. Reischauer. 1986. *China: Tradition and Transformation*. Taipei: Caves Books, Ltd 敦煌書局.

———. 2002. *Zhongguo: Chuantong yu Bianqian* 中國：傳統與變遷 (China: tradition and transformation). Translated by Zhang Pei 張沛, Zhang Yuan 張源, and Gu Sijian 顧思兼. Bijing: Shijie Zhishi 世界知識 Chubanshe.
Fay, Peter Ward. 1976. *The Opium War 1840–1842.* New York: The Norton Library.
Fei Chengkang 費成康. 2008. "Yamaliu shidai yu Putaoya guanzhi Aomen de kaiduan" 亞馬留時代與葡萄牙管治澳門的開端 (The times of Amaral and the beginning of the Portuguese rule), in Wu Zhiliang, Jin Guoping, and Tang Kaijian (eds.) *Aomen Shi Xin Bian* 澳門史新編 (A new history of Macau), Vol. 1, pp. 179–94. Macau: Macau Foundation.
Fei Li Qi (Henrique de Senna Fernandes). 1996. *Da Bianzi de Youhuo* 大辮子的誘惑. Translated by Yu Huijuan 喻慧娟. Macau: Institute of Culture 文化司署, and Shijiazhuang, Huashan Wenyi 花山文藝 Chubanshe.
Fei Mao Shi 費茂實 (Moisés Silva Fernandes). 2008. "1952 nian guanzha shijian: guoji chengnuo yu dangdi xianzhi tiaojian zhijian de chongtu" 1952年關閘事件：國際承諾與當地限制條件之間的衝突 (The Guanzha incident in 1952: the conflict between International commitment and the constraints of the local conditions), in Wu Zhiliang, Jin Guoping, and Tang Kaijian (eds.) *Aomen Shi Xin Bian* 澳門史新編 (A new history of Macau), Vol. 1, pp. 305–27. Macau: Macau Foundation.
Feitor, R. 1987. "Macau's Modern Economy," in R. D. Cremer (ed.) *Macau: City of Commerce and Culture*, pp. 139–53. Hong Kong: UEA Press Ltd.
Feng Bangyan 1999a. *Puguo Chetui Qian de Aomen* 葡國撤退前的澳門 (Macau before the retreat of Portugal). Guangzhou: Guangdong Jingji Chubanshe.
———. 1999b. *Aomen Gailun* 澳門概論 (An introduction to Macau). Hong Kong: Sanlian Press.
Feng Jia-chao 馮家超 and Wu Mei-bao 伍美寶. 2003. "Aomen jumin canjia bocai huodong diaocha" 澳門居民參與博彩活動調查 (A study on Macao citizens' participation in gaming). Macao: Institute for the Study of Commercial Gaming, University of Macau.
Feng Zengjun 馮增俊 and Li Yiming 黎義明 (eds.). 1999. *Aomen Jiaoyu Gailun* 澳門教育概論 (An introduction to Macao's education). Guangzhou: Guangdong Jiaoyu Chubanshe.
Fernandes, Henrique de Senna. 2004. *The Bewitching Braid*. Translated by David Brookshaw. Hong Kong: Hong Kong University Press.
Fukuda, Kazunori. 2002. "The Relations between China and Portugal in the Early Sixteenth Century: Some Observations on the Yue Shan Cong Tan." *Review of Culture*, international edition 1, January 2002.
Fukuyama, Francis. 2018. "Against Identity Politics: The New Tribalism and the Crisis of Democracy." *Foreign Affairs*, August 14.
Garrett, Richard J. 2010. *The Defences of Macau: Forts, Ships and Weapons over 450 Years.* Hong Kong: Hong Kong University Press.
Gellner, Ernest. 1983. *Nations and Nationalism.* Oxford: Basil Blackwell.
Ghosh, Ratna. 2002. "Colonization and the Construction of Identity: A Comparison of Teenage Identity in Macao, Hong Kong and Goa." *Review of Culture*, international edition 1, January 2002.
Giddens, Anthony. 1971. *Capitalism and Modern Social Society: An Analysis of the Writings of Marx, Durkheim, and Max Weber*. Cambridge: Cambridge University Press.
Go, Julian. 2006. "Postcolonial Theory," in Bryan S. Turner (ed.) *The Cambridge Dictionary of Sociology*, pp. 452–4. Cambridge: Cambridge University Press.
Goffman, Erving. [1963] 1999. "Stigma and Social Identity," in Henry Pontell (ed.) *Social Deviance: Readings in Theory and Research*, pp. 56–74. Upper Saddle River, NJ: Prentice Hall.
Gu Dingyi 古鼎儀. 1998. "Guodu qi Gang Ao de jiaoyu fazhan" 過渡期港澳的教育發展 (The development of education in the transition periods in Hong Kong and Macau), in Yu Zhen 余振 (ed.) *Shuang Cheng Ji: Gang Ao de Zhengzhi, Jingji ji Shehui Fazhan* 雙城記：港澳的

政治、經濟及社會發展 (A tale of two cities: the political, economic and social development in Hong Kong and Macau), pp. 327–45. Macau: Macau Social Sciences Association.

Gu Weimin 顧衛民. 2002. "Cooperation and Contradiction: Portugal and the Holy See in the Ecclesiastical Affairs of China in the 17–18th Centuries." *Review of Culture*, international edition, No. 2, April.

———. 2005. "Wu Yushan and His Pursuit of Faith in the Great Dynastic Transition." *Review of Culture*, international edition 13, January 2005.

Guan Zhendong 關振東 and Chen Shurong 陳樹榮. 1999. *He Xian Zhuan* 何賢傳 (A biography of Ho Yin). Macao: Macao Press.

Guangdong Sheng Dang'an Guan (ed.). 1999. *Guangdong Aomen Dang'an Shiliao Xuan Bian* 廣東澳門檔案史料選編 (Selected documents on Guangdong and Macau history). Beijing: Zhongguo Dang'an 檔案 Chubanshe.

Gunn, Geoffrey C. 1996. *Encountering Macau: A Portuguese City-State on the Periphery of China, 1557–1999*. Boulder, Colorado: Westview Press.

———. 2009. *Aomen Shi* (Macau history, a translation of *Encountering Macau*). Beijing: Central Compilation & Translation Press.

Guo Jixiu 郭濟修. 2002. *Fei Liqi Xiaoshuo Yanjiu ji Qita* 飛歷奇小說研究及其他 (The studies on the short stories by Henrique de Senna Fernandes and other papers). Macau: Aomen Wenhua Guangchang 澳門文化廣場.

Habermas, Jürgen. 1992. "Citizenship and National Identity: Some Reflections on the Future of Europe." *Praxis International* 12(1): 1–19, April.

Han Qi 韓琪. 2008. "Yesu huishi he Kangxi shidai lisuan zhishi de chuanru" 耶穌會士和康熙時代曆算知識的傳入 (The Jesuits and the introduction of Western calendar and mathematics to China in the Kangxi era), in Wu Zhiliang, Jin Guoping, and Tang Kaijian (eds.) *Aomen Shi Xin Bian* 澳門史新編 (A new history of Macau), Vol. 3, pp. 967–86. Macau: Macau Foundation.

Hao, Zhidong 郝志東. 2003. *Intellectuals at a Crossroads: The Changing Politics of China's Knowledge Workers*. Albany, New York: State University of New York Press.

———. 2006. "Shehui kexue de zeren: lun dangqian Aomen de sheke yanjiu" 社會科學的責任：論當前澳門的社科研究 (The responsibilities of social sciences: on the current social science research in Macau). 《澳門研究》雜誌 (Macau studies), No. 33 (April): 118–29.

———. 2006. "Ye lun shimin shehui yu gonggong lingyu: jian ping Lii Ding Tzann deng suo zhu *Gonggong Lingyu zai Taiwan*" 也論市民社會與公共領域：兼評李丁贊等所著《公共領域在臺灣》 (On civil society and public sphere, and a review of Lii Ding Tzann et al.'s book *Public sphere in Taiwan*). 《思想》雜誌 (Reflexion) (Taiwan), No. 2: 165–80.

———. 2008. "Aomen zhengzhi yu shehui fazhan de fengfeng yuyu" 澳門政治與社會發展的風風雨雨 (The ups and downs in Macau's political and social development). 《九鼎雜誌》 (*Jiuding*), September 2008.

———. 2008. "Aomen gongmin shehui zhishu chutan" 澳門公民社會指數初探 (An exploratory study on the index of Macao's civil society). 《澳門日報》 (*Macao Daily*), October 27, p. E9, continued in four weeks.

———. 2009. "Shaonian Aomen renge taiguo cuiruo" 少年澳門人格太過脆弱 (Young Macao and its vulnerabilities in personality). 《亞洲周刊》 (*Asia Weekly*) No. 1, Vol. 23, January 4.

———. 2009. "Aomen de chuzuche fuwu: cong dazao 'shijie luyou xiuxian zhongxi' tanqi" 澳門的出租車服務：從打造「世界旅游休閒中心」談起 (The taxis in Macao: on building an international resort destination). 《澳門日報》 (*Macao Daily*), February 16, p. E8.

———. 2009. "Dependent Development? Macao's Gaming Industry: Its Problems and Prospects." 《澳門研究》 (Macau studies), No. 51 (April): 64–77.

———. 2010. *Whither Taiwan and Mainland China: National Identity, the State, and Intellectuals*. Hong Kong: Hong Kong University Press.

———. 2010. "Cong qiye shehui zeren de shijiao kan fuzeren bocai: Yi Aomen weili" (Responsible gambling from the perspective of corporative social responsibility: The case of Macau). *Zhongguo shehui kexue neibu wengao* (Chinese social sciences: Restricted version), No. 5.

———. 2015. "Social Stratification and Ethnic and Class Politics in Macao before and after the Handover in 1999." *China: An International Journal*, Vol. 13, No. 1.

———. 2016. "In Search of a Professional Identity: Higher Education in Macau and the Academic Role of Faculty." *Higher Education* Vol. 72, No. 1.

———. 2016. "Aomen de jiaohui xuexiao zai aomen shehui fazhan zhong de zuoyong: Zhongdeng jiaoyu zhong jiaohui yu fei jiaohui xuexiao de duibi yanjiu" (The role of religious schools in the social development of Macau: A comparative study of religious and non-religious middle schools), a paper presented at a conference entitled "Jidujiao yu jindai Zhongguo jiaoyu" (Christianity and education in modern China), Shanghai University, October 29–30, 2016.

———. 2018. "Higher Education Systems and Institutions, Macau." In Teixeira P. and Shin J. (eds.) *Encyclopedia of International Higher Education Systems and Institutions*. Dordrecht: Springer.

———. Forthcoming. "Macau's Natural and Social Environments and Their Historical Backgrounds." In Haruhiko Fujita, Christine Guth, and Wendy Siuyi Wong (eds.) *The Encyclopedia of Asian Design*. London: Bloomsbury Publishing.

Hao, Zhidong, Linda Hancock, and Bill Thompson. 2014. "In Search of Best Practices in Responsible Gambling (RG): A Report on a Comparative Study of RG among Macau, Las Vegas, and Melbourne." This is a report done in 2012 and 2013 for the Macau government's Gaming Inspection and Coordination Bureau, available through the author.

Hao, Zhidong, Shun Hing Chan, Wen-ban Kuo, Yik Fai Tam, and Ming Jing. 2014. "Catholicism and Its Civic Engagement: Case Studies of the Catholic Church in Hong Kong, Macau, Taipei, and Shanghai," *Review of Religion and Chinese Society*, Vol. 1, No. 1.

Hao, Zhidong, and Yan Liu. 2018. "Mutual Accommodation in Church-State Relationship in China? A Case Study of the Sanjiang Church Demolition in Zhejiang." *Review of Religion and Chinese Society*, No. 5.

He Baogang. 2001. "The Question of Sovereignty in the Taiwan Strait: Re-examining Peking's Policy of Opposition to Taiwan's Bid for UN Membership." *China Perspectives*, 34: 7–18.

Held, David. 1995. *Democracy and the Global Order*. Stanford, California: Stanford University Press.

Hodges, Nan P. and Arthur W. Hummel (eds.). 2002. *Lights and Shadows of a Macao Life: The Journal of Harriett Low, Traveling Spinster*, Part One: 1829–1832, Part Two: 1832–1834. Woodinville, WA: The History Bank.

Hu Gen 胡根. 2009. *Aomen Jindai Bocai Ye Shi* 澳門近代博彩業史 (Macau's gaming industry in the modern times). Guangzhou: Guangdong Renmin Chubanshe.

Huang Hanqiang 黃漢強 and T. J. Cheng 程惕潔. 2005. *Xin Lai Ao Dingju zhi Neidi Yimin Lunxi* 新來澳定居之內地移民論析 (Analysis on Macao's new immigrants from mainland China). Macao: Center for Macao Studies, University of Macau.

Huang Hongzhao 黃鴻釗. 1999. *Aomen Jian Shi* 澳門簡史 (A brief history of Macao). Hong Kong: Sanlian Press.

———. 2008. "Qing Mo min chu Aomen huajie zhi jiaoshe" 清末民初澳門劃界之交涉 (The negotiations on the border delineation in Macau in the end of Qing and the beginning of the Republic of China), in Wu Zhiliang, Jin Guoping, and Tang Kaijian (eds.) *Aomen Shi Xin Bian* 澳門史新編 (A new history of Macau), Vol. 1, pp. 263–96. Macau: Macau Foundation.

Huang Jiushun 黃就順 and Li Jinping 李金平 (eds.). 1997. *Aomen Huanjing Baohu* 澳門環境保護 (Environmental protection in Macao). Macao: Macau Foundation.

Huang Qichen 黃啟臣. 1995. "Fulu: Aomen lishi yanjiu zhuyao cankao ziliao mulu" 附錄：澳門歷史研究主要參考資料目錄 (The main references in Macau studies), in Huang Qichen and Deng Kaisong (eds.) *Zhong Wai Xuezhe Lun Aomen Lishi* 中外學者論澳門歷史 (Studies on Macau history by Chinese and foreign scholars), pp. 365–85. Macau: Macau Foundation.

———. 1999. *Aomen Tongshi* 澳門通史 (A general history of Macau). Guangzhou: Gongdong Jiaoyu 廣東教育 Chubanshe.

Huang Qichen 黃啟臣 and Deng Kaisong 鄧開頌. 1995. "Aomen lishi yanjiu gaishu" 澳門歷史研究概述 (A general survey of Macau studies), in Huang Qichen and Deng Kaisong (eds.) *Zhong Wai Xuezhe Lun Aomen Lishi* 中外學者論澳門歷史 (Studies on Macau history by Chinese and foreign scholars), pp. 1–5. Macau: Macau Foundation.

Huang Wenkuan 黃文寬. 1995. "Guanyu Aomen shi de kaoding" 關於澳門史的考訂 (Reexamination of some issues in Macau history), in Huang Qichen 黃啟臣 and Deng Kaisong 鄧開頌 (eds.) *Zhong Wai Xuezhe Lun Aomen Lishi* 中外學者論澳門歷史 (Studies on Macau history by Chinese and foreign scholars), pp. 98–137. Macau: Macau Foundation.

Huntington, Samuel P. 1993. "The Clash of Civilizations?" *Foreign Affairs* 72(3): 22–49.

———. 2002. *Wenming de Chongtu yu Shijie Zhixu de Chongjian* 文明的衝突與世界秩序的重建 (The clash of civilizations and the remaking of world order). Translated by Zhou Qi 周琪, Liu Fei 劉緋, Zhang Liping 張立平, and Wang Yuan 王圓. Beijing: Xinhua 新華 Chubanshe.

Huo Zhizhao (Daniel Fok) 霍志釗. 2009. *Aomen Tusheng Puren de Zongjiao Xinyang: Cong "Danyi" dao "Duoyuan Hunrong" de Bianqian* 澳門土生葡人的宗教信仰：從"單一"到"多元混融"的變遷 (Macanese religious beliefs: from monotheism to polytheism). Beijing: Social Science Academic Press.

Ieong Hoi Keng 楊開荊. 2003. *Aomen Tese Wenxian Ziyuan Yanjiu* 澳門特色文獻資源研究 (A study of the specialized documents in Macao). Beijing: Beijing University Press.

———. 2008. "Suiyue de jianzheng: Aomen wenxian ziyuan" 歲月的見證：澳門文獻資源 (The evidence of history: the sources of documents on Macau), in Wu Zhiliang, Jin Guoping, and Tang Kaijian (eds.) *Aomen Shi Xin Bian* 澳門史新編 (A new history of Macau), Vol. 4, pp. 1387–426. Macau: Macau Foundation.

Ieong, S. L. 1994. "Reflections on the Language Issues in Macau: Policies, Realities, and Prospects," in R. Koo and H. T. Ma (eds.) *Macau Education: Continuity and Change*, pp. 60–9. Macau: Macau Foundation, in Chinese.

Institute for the Study of Commercial Gaming, University of Macau. 2016. *Interim Review of Gaming Liberalization for Games of Fortune: Economic, Social, Livelihood Impacts and Operating Conditions of the Concessionaires*. Gaming Inspection and Coordination Bureau of Macau Government website at http://www.dicj.gov.mo/web/en/news/Year-2016/mid-report/index.html, accessed October 17, 2018.

Jesus, Montalto de. [1902] 2000. *Lishi shang de Aomen* 歷史上的澳門 (Historic Macau). Translated by Huang Hongzhao and Li Baoping. Macau: Macau Foundation.

Ji Fahan 吉發涵, Xu Shunping 徐順平, and Song Hongyin 宋洪印. 1999. "Zhu xing wu chang, zhu fa wu wo: fojia wenhua jiqi lixiang renge" 諸行無常，諸法無我：佛家文化及其理想人格 (The uncertainty of actions and the forgetting of oneself in the Buddhist principles: the Buddhist culture and its ideal personality), in Jin Yuanpu 金元浦, Tan Haozhe 譚好哲, and Lu Xueming 陸學明 (eds.) *Zhongguo Wenhua Gailun* 中國文化概論 (A general introduction to Chinese culture). Beijing: Shoudu Shifan Daxue Chubanshe 首都師範大學出版社 (Capital Normal University Press).

Jia Er Xi Ya 加爾西亞 (José Manuel Garcia). 2008. "Aomen yu Feilubin zhi lishi guanxi" 澳門與菲律賓之歷史關係 (The historical relations between Macau and the Philippines), in Wu Zhiliang, Jin Guoping, and Tang Kaijian (eds.) *Aomen Shi Xin Bian* 澳門史新編 (A new history of Macau), Vol. 2, pp. 531–60. Macau: Macau Foundation.

Jia Le An 賈楽安 (Rodrigo Leal de Carvalho). 1999. *Huan Hun Qu* 還魂曲 (Requiem por Irina Ostrakoff, or A story of revival after death). Translated by Yu Huijuan 喻慧娟, and commented by Lin Baona 林寶娜 (Ana Paula Laborinho). Macau and Hainan: Instituto Cultural de Macau 澳門文化司署, Instituto Português do Oriente 東方葡牙學會, Editora de Hainan 海南出版社, and Sanhuan Chubanshe 三環出版社.

Jia Yuan 賈淵 (João de Pina Cabral) and Nelson Lourenço 陸淩梭. 1995. *Taifeng zhi Xiang: Aomen Tusheng Zuqun Dongtai* 颱風之鄉：澳門土生族群動態 (The place of typhoon: the dynamics of the ethnic Macanese). Translated into Chinese from Portuguese by Chen Jieying 陳潔瑩. Macau: Cultural Institute of Macau.

Jiang Minrui 江敏銳. 1999. "Kang Ri zhanzheng yu jiefang zhanzheng xin xingshi xia Yue Ao guanxi de xin neirong" 抗日戰爭與解放戰爭新形勢下粵澳關係的新內容 (The new relationship between Guangdong and Macau in the war of resistance against the Japanese and the civil war), in Deng Kaisong, Wu Zhiliang, and Lu Xiaomin (eds.) *Yue Ao Guanxi Shi* 粵澳關係史 (The relationship between Guangdong and Macau), pp. 437–504. Beijing: Zhongguo Shudian 中國書店.

Jin Guoping 金國平 (ed. and trans.). 2005. *Xifang Aomen Shiliao Xuancui (15–16 Shiji)* 西方澳門史料選萃 (15–16 世紀)(Selected historical documents from the West, 15th–16th centuries). Guangzhou: Guangdong Remin Chubanshe.

———. 2008. "Aomen yuan kao" 澳門源考 (A study on the origin of Macau), in Wu Zhiliang, Jin Guoping, and Tang Kaijian (eds.) *Aomen Shi Xin Bian* 澳門史新編 (A new history of Macau), Vol. 1, pp. 45–78. Macau: Macau Foundation.

Jin Guoping 金國平 and Wu Zhiliang 吳志良. 2001. *Jing Hai Piaomiao* 鏡海縹緲 (The misty Macau history). Macau: Chengren Jiaoyu Xuehui 成人教育學會 (Adult education association).

———. 2004. *Guo Shizi Men* 過十字門 (Passing Macau). Macau: Chengren Jiaoyu Xuehui 成人教育學會 (Adult education association).

Jorge, Cecília. 2002. "Rebecca Chase: An American in Macau." *Macau Magazine*, September.

Kang Ping 康平. 2009. "Jingji 'shidu duoyuan' kongjian henda" 經濟"適度多元"空間很大 (There is big room for improvement in "appropriate diversification"). *Shang Xun* 商訊 (Business intelligence), May.

Kennedy, David M. 2009. "What History Is Good For." *The New York Times Book Review*, July 19, 2009.

Kong, Travis. 2004. "Part III: A Study on the Needs of Sex Workers' Children in Hong Kong," in *A Report on Studies on Deprived Children*. The Social Work Professional Practice Centre, Department of Applied Social Sciences, Hong Kong Polytechnic University and Hong Kong Society for Protection of Children.

Kou Sai Luo 寇塞羅 (Gonçalo Couceiro). 2008. "Da Sanba paifang de zhuangshi yishu" 大三巴牌坊的裝飾藝術 (The decorative arts on the façade of the St. Paul's), in Wu Zhiliang, Jin Guoping, and Tang Kaijian (eds.) *Aomen Shi Xin Bian* 澳門史新編 (A new history of Macau), Vol. 4, pp. 1313–27. Macau: Macau Foundation.

Kowal, David W. 2003. "Jesuit Buildings in Asia: Reflections on the Practice of Architectural Accommodation." Paper presented at an international symposium on "Culture, Art, and Religion: Wu Li (1632–1718) and His Inner Journey." Macau Ricci Institute, November 27–29.

Kwan, Fung 關鋒. 1998. "Gang Ao jingji fazhan shouru suode fenpei" 港澳經濟發展收入所得分配 (The income distribution amidst the economic development in Hong Kong and Macau), in Yu Zhen 余振 (ed.) *Shuang Cheng Ji: Gang Ao de Zhengzhi, Jingji ji Shehui Fazhan* 雙城記：港澳的政治、經濟及社會發展 (A tale of two cities: the political, economic and social development in Hong Kong and Macau), pp. 261–80. Macau: Macau Social Sciences Association.

———. 2009. "Shouru fenpei yu pinqiong" 收入分配與貧窮 (Income distribution and poverty), in Wang Jiaying 王家英, Huang Shaolun 黃紹倫, Yin Baoshan 尹寶珊, and Zheng Hongtai 鄭宏泰 (eds.) *Aomen Shehui Xin Mao: Chengjiu yu Tiaozhan* 澳門社會新貌：成就與挑戰 (The new face of society in Macau: successes and challenges), pp. 1–19. Hong Kong: Hong Kong Institute of Asian and Pacific Studies of the Chinese University of Hong Kong.

Kwan Hsin-chi 關信基. 1998. "Xianggang zhengzhi shehui de xingcheng" 香港政治社會的形成 (The formation of Hong Kong's political society), in Liu Qingfeng 劉青峰 and Guan Xiaochun 關小春 (eds.) *Zhuanhua zhong de Xianggang: Shenfen yu Zhixu de Zai Xunqiu* 轉化中的香港：身份與秩序的再尋求 (Hong Kong in transition: looking again for identity and order), pp. 99–113. Hong Kong: The Chinese University of Hong Kong Press.

———. 1998. "Xianggang zhengzhi zhixu de xunqiu" 香港政治秩序的尋求 (Looking for a political order), in Liu Qingfeng 劉青峰 and Guan Xiaochun 關小春 (eds.) *Zhuanhua zhong de Xianggang: Shenfen yu Zhixu de Zai Xunqiu* 轉化中的香港：身份與秩序的再尋求 (Hong Kong in transition: looking again for identity and order), pp. 73–97. Hong Kong: The Chinese University of Hong Kong Press.

Lamas, Rosmarie Wank-Nolasco. 1998. *History of Macau: A Student's Manual*. Macau: Institute of Tourism Education.

———. 2006. *Everything in Style: Harriett Low's Macau*. Hong Kong: Hong Kong University Press.

Lam Fat Iam (ed.) 2005. *Aomen lishi jianzhu de gushi* (The stories of Macau's historical buildings). Macau: Aomen Peidao Zhongxue Lishi Xuehui.

——— (ed.) 2005. *Aomen jiedao de gushi* (The stories of Macau's streets). Macau: Aome Peidao Zhongxue Lishi Xuehui.

———. 2005. *Aomen Shigao* 澳門史稿 (Papers on Macau history). Macau: Aomen Jindai Wenxue Xuehui, Association for Macau modern literature.

———. 2008. "Aomen zaoqi dui wai zhanzheng yu junshi fangyu" 澳門早期對外戰爭與軍事防禦 (The wars against invaders and the military defense in early Macau), in Wu Zhiliang, Jin Guoping, and Tang Kaijian (eds.) *Aomen Shi Xin Bian* 澳門史新編 (A new history of Macau), Vol. 3, pp. 833–68. Macau: Macau Foundation.

Lei Kun Min 利冠棉 and Lam Fat Iam 林發欽. *19–20 Shiji Mingxinpian zhong de Aomen* 19–20 世紀明信片中的澳門 (Macau in postcards in the 19th and 20th centuries). Macau: Macao Association for Historical Education.

Lewellen, Ted C. 1996. *Dependency and Development: An Introduction to the Third World*. Westport, Connecticut and London: Bergin & Garvey.

Li Changsen 李長森. *Mingqing Shiqi Aomen Tusheng Zuqun de Xingcheng Fazhan yu Bianqian* 明清時期澳門土生族群的形成發展與變遷 (The emergence, development and transformation of the Macanese in the Ming and Qing dynsties). Beijing: Zhonghua Shuju.

Li Feng-yan 黎鳳燕. 1995. "Zhian wenti" 治安問題 (Security problems), in Chen Xin-xin (ed.) *Aomen Shehui Wenti* 澳門社會問題 (Social problems in Macao). Hong Kong: Guangjiaojing Chubanshe.

Li Pengzhu 李鵬翥. 1999. *Zhongguo Aomen* 中國澳門 (Chinese Macau). Macau: Macao Daily Press.

Li Puwen 李普文. 2003. "Wu Li de xinlu licheng jiqi huihua yishu" 吳歷的心路歷程及其繪畫藝術 (Wu Li's thought processes and artistic skills)." Paper presented at an international symposium on "Culture, Art, and Religion: Wu Li (1632–1718) and His Inner Journey," Macau Ricci Institute, November 27–29.

Li Tiangang 李天綱. 2008. "Aomen yu Zhongguo liyi zhi zheng" 澳門與中國禮儀之爭 (Macau and the controversy of rites), in Wu Zhiliang, Jin Guoping, and Tang Kaijian (eds.) *Aomen Shi Xin Bian* 澳門史新編 (A new history of Macau), Vol. 1, pp. 161–78. Macau: Macau Foundation.

Li Xiangyu 李向玉. 2001. *Aomen Sheng Baolu Xueyuan Yanjiu* 澳門聖保祿學院研究 (A study on the St. Paul's College in Macau). Macau: Macao Daily Press.

Liang Jiefen 梁潔芬. 2003. "Gang Ao huigui hou de zheng jiao (tianzhu jiao) guanxi" 港澳回歸後的政教（天主教）關係 (The relationship between church and state after the return of Hong Kong and Macao to China), in Yu Zhen, Yu Yongyi, and Kuang Jinjun (eds.) *Shuang Cheng Ji II: Huigui hou Gang Ao de Zhengzhi, Jingji ji Shehui Fazhan* 雙城記 II：回歸後港澳的政治、經濟及社會發展 (A tale of two cities II: the political, economic and social development in Hong Kong and Macau after their return to China), pp. 367–79. Macau: Aomen Shehui Kexue Xuehui.

Liang Jiefen and Lo Shiu Hing (eds.) 2010. *Zhongguo aomen tequ bocai ye yu shehui fazhan* (Casino development and its impact on Macau SAR). Hong Kong: City University of Hong Kong Press.

Liao Zixin 廖子馨. 1998. "Aomen de sanwen chuangzuo" 澳門的散文創作 (The essay writing in Macau), in Liu Denghan 劉登翰 (ed.) *Aomen Wenxue Gaiguan* 澳門文學概觀 (A brief introduction to Macau's literature). Xiamen: Lujiang 鷺江 Chubanshe.

Lin Guangzhi 林廣志. 2008. "Wan qing Aomen hua shang de jueqi jiqi shehui diwei de bianhua" 晚清澳門華商的崛起及其社會地位的變化 (The rise of Chinese businessmen in Macau in the the late Qing era and their transformation in social status), in Wu Zhiliang, Jin Guoping, and Tang Kaijian (eds.) *Aomen Shi Xin Bian* 澳門史新編 (A new history of Macau), Vol. 1. Macau: Macau Foundation.

Lin Yufeng 林玉鳳. 2008. "Aomen xinwen chuban si bai nian" 澳門新聞出版四百年 (Four hundred years of Macau's mass media publications), in Wu Zhiliang, Jin Guoping, and Tang Kaijian (eds.) *Aomen Shi Xin Bian* 澳門史新編 (A new history of Macau), Vol. 4, pp. 1189–241. Macau: Macau Foundation.

Lin Yun 林芸. 1999. "Yapian zhanzheng jieshu dao 'Zhong Pu Hehao Tongshang Tiaoyue' qianding shiqi Yue Ao guanxi de zhongda zhuanzhe 鴉片戰爭結束到《中葡和好通商條約》簽訂時期粵澳關係的重大轉折 (The serious turn of events in the relationship between Guangdong and Macau during the period from the end of the Opium War to the signing of the Luso-Chinese Treaty of Friendship and Trade), in Deng Kaisong, Wu Zhiliang, and Lu Xiaomin (eds.) *Yue Ao Guanxi Shi* 粵澳關係史 (The relationship between Guangdong and Macau), pp. 216–308. Beijing: Zhongguo Shudian.

Lin Yutang 林語堂. 1939. *My Country and My People*. New York: The John Day Company.

———. 2001. *Zhongguo Ren* 中國人 (The Chinese). Translated by Hao Zhidong and Shen Yihong from Lin's original English work *My Country and My People*. Shanghai: Xuelin 學林 Chubanshe.

Lin Zisheng 林子升. 1998. *Shiliu zhi Shiba Shiji Aomen yu Zhongguo zhi Guanxi* 十六至十八世紀澳門與中國之關係 (The relationship between Macau and China from the 16th to 18th centuries). Macau: Macau Foundation.

Liu Bolong 劉伯龍. "Huigui yihou Aomen duiwai guanxi de huigu yu zhanwang" 回歸以後澳門對外關係的回顧與展望, in Wu Zhiliang, Yang Yunzhong, et al. (eds.) *Aomen 2002* 澳門 2002 (Macau in 2002). Macau: Macau Foundation, 2002. At http://www.macaudata.com/macauweb/ book269/.

Liu Denghan 劉登翰. 1998. "Hou ji" 後記 (Afterword), in Liu Denghan (ed.) *Aomen Wenxue Gaiguan* 澳門文學概觀 (A general view of literature in Macau), pp. 384–6. Fuzhou: Lujiang 鷺江 Chubanshe.

———. 1998. "Wenhua shiye zhong de Aomen jiqi wenxue 文化視野中的澳門及其文學 (The cultural perspective of Macau and its literature), in Liu Denghan (ed.) *Aomen Wenxue Gaiguan* 澳門文學概觀 (A general view of literature in Macau), pp. 1–41. Fuzhou: Lujiang 鷺江 Chubanshe.

Liu, I-chou 劉義周 and Tian Fang-hua 田芳華. 2003. "Taiwan Minzhong Guojia Rentong de Leixing" 台灣民眾國家認同的類型 (The types of national identity among people in Taiwan). Paper presented at the Sun Yat-sen Institute of Humanities and Social Sciences, Academia Sinica, June 3.

Liu Ranling 劉然玲. 2008. *Wenming de Boyi: 16 zhi 19 Shiji Aomen Wenhua Chang Boduan de Lishi Kaocha* 文明的博弈：16至19世紀澳門文化長波段的歷史考察 (The game of civilizations: a longitudinal study of Macau's cultural history). Guangzhou: Guangdong Renmin Chubanshe.

Liu Xianbing 劉羨冰. 1999. *Aomen Jiaoyu Shi* 澳門教育史 (A history of education in Macao). Beijing: Renmin Jiaoyu Chubanshe.

———. 2008. "Aomen jiaoyu de fazhan, bianhua yu xiandaihua" 澳門教育的發展、變化與現代化 (The development, change, and modernization of education in Macau), in Wu Zhiliang, Jin Guoping, and Tang Kaijian (eds.) *Aomen Shi Xin Bian* 澳門史新編 (A new history of Macau), Vol. 3. Macau: Macau Foundation.

Liu Xianbing 劉羨冰, Chen Shurong 陳樹榮, Wang Guoqiang 王國強, and Xian Weikeng 洗為鏗 (eds). 1999. *Tupian Aomen Jin Xi* 圖片澳門今昔 (Macau history in pictures). Hong Kong: Sanlian Press.

Liu Xianjue 劉先覺 and Chen Zecheng 陳澤成 (eds.). 2005. *Aomen Jianzhu Wenhua Yichan* 澳門建築文化遺產 (The architectural heritage in Macao). Nanjing: Dongnan Daxue Chubanshe 東南大學出版社.

Liu Zhaojia 劉兆佳. 1998. "'Xianggang ren' huo 'Zhongguo ren': Xianggang huaren de shenfen rentong 1985–1995" "香港人"或"中國人"：香港華人的身份認同1985–1995 ("Hongkongers" or "Chinese": The Hong Kong Chinese national identity 1985–1995), in Liu Qingfeng 劉青峰 and Guan Xiaochun 關小春 (eds.) *Zhuanhua zhong de Xianggang: Shenfen yu Zhixu de Zai Xunqiu* 轉化中的香港：身份與秩序的再尋求 (Hong Kong in transition: looking again for identity and order), pp. 3–30. Hong Kong: The Chinese University of Hong Kong Press.

Ljungstedt, Anders. [1832] 1997. *Zaoqi Aomen Shi* 早期澳門史 (An historical sketch of the Portuguese settlements in China). Translated by Wu Yixiong, Guo Deyan, and Shen Zhengbang. Beijing: Dongfang 東方 Chubanshe.

Lo Shiu Hing. 1995. *Political Development in Macau*. Hong Kong: The Chinese University Press.

———. 2005. "Casino Politics, Organized Crime and the Post-Colonia State in Macau." *Journal of Contemporary China*, 14(43).

———. 2008. *Political Change in Macao*. London and New York: Routledge.

Lou Shenghua 婁勝華. 2004. *Zhuanxing Shiqi Aomen Shetuan Yanjiu* 轉型時期澳門社團研究 (A study of Macao's social organizations in the period of transition). Guangzhou: Guangzhou Renmin Chubanshe.

———. 2008. "Hunhe, duoyuan yu zizhi: zaoqi Aomen de xingzheng" 混合、多元與自治：早期澳門的行政 (Hybridity, plurality, and autonomy: public administration in early Macau), in Wu Zhiliang, Jin Guoping, and Tang Kaijian (eds.) *Aomen Shi Xin Bian* 澳門史新編 (A new history of Macau), Vol. 1, pp. 125–60. Macau: Macau Foundation.

———. 2008. "Xiaoshi yu xinsheng: Aomen minjian jieshe de bianqian jiqi xiansuo" 消逝與新生：澳門民間結社的變遷及其綫索 (Disappearances and births: the traces of transformation of Macau's social organizations), in Wu Zhiliang, Jin Guoping, and Tang Kaijian (eds.) *Aomen Shi Xin Bian* 澳門史新編 (A new history of Macau), Vol. 3. Macau: Macau Foundation.

Loureiro, Rui Manuel. 2002. "As Origens de Macau nas Fontes Ibéricas" (The origins of Macao in Iberian historical sources). *Review of Culture*, international edition 1, January 2002.

———. 2002. "Primórdios da Sinologia Europeia: entre Macau e Manila em Finais do Século XVI" (The early days of European Sinology in Macau and Manila in the late 16th century). *Review of Culture*, international edition, No. 2, April.

Lourido, Rui D'Ávila. 2002. "The Portuguese, the Maritime Silk Road and Macao's Connection with the Philippines in the Late Ming Dynasty." *Review of Culture*, No. 2, April.

Lowenthal, Leo. [1948] 1984. "On Sociology of Literature." *Literature and Mass Culture. Communication in Society*, Vol. 1. Leo Lowenthal, published by Transaction Books. At http://www.marxists.org/reference/archive/ lowenthal/, last accessed Februray 16, 2005.

———. 1987. *An Unmastered Past: The Autobiographical Reflections of Leo Lowenthal*. Berkeley: University of California Press. At http://ark.cdlib.org/ark:/13030/ft8779p24p/, last accessed February 16, 2005.

Lu Xiaomin 陸曉敏. 1999. "Xin Zhongguo chengli zhi 'Wenhua da Geming' jieshu Yue Ao guanxi de quzhe fazhan" 新中國成立至"文化大革命"結束粵澳關係的曲折發展 (The twists and turns in the Guangdong-Macau relations from the founding of new China to the end of the Cultural Revolution," in Deng Kaisong, Wu Zhiliang, and Lu Xiaomin (eds.) *Yue Ao Guanxi Shi* 粵澳關係史 (The relationship between Guangdong and Macau), pp. 505–38. Beijing: Zhongguo Shudian 中國書店.

Lu Xiaomin 陸曉敏 and Deng Kaisong 鄧開頌. 2008. "Yapian zhanzheng qian de Yue Ao guanxi" 鴉片戰爭前的粵澳關係 (The relationship between Guangdong and Macao before the Opium War), in Wu Zhiliang, Jin Guoping, and Tang Kaijian (eds.) *Aomen Shi Xin Bian* 澳門史新編 (A new history of Macau), Vol. 2, pp. 445–70. Macau: Macau Foundation.

Lume, J. M. R. 1987. "Center for Portuguese Language and Culture," in R. D. Cremer (ed.) *Macau: City of Commerce and Culture*, pp. 115–23. Hong Kong: UEA Press Ltd.

Luo Li Lu 羅利路 (Rui Lourido). 2008. "16–18 shiji de Aomen maoyi yu shehui" 16–18世紀的澳門貿易與社會 (Trade and society in Macau from 16th to 18th centuries), in Wu Zhiliang, Jin Guoping, and Tang Kaijian (eds.) *Aomen Shi Xin Bian* 澳門史新編 (A new history of Macau), Vol. 2, pp. 395–408. Macau: Macau Foundation.

———. 2008. "Aomen yu Baxi de zaoqi guanxi" 澳門與巴西的早期關係 (The early relations between Macau and Brazil), in Wu Zhiliang, Jin Guoping, and Tang Kaijian (eds.) *Aomen Shi Xin Bian* 澳門史新編 (A new history of Macau), Vol. 2, pp. 613–24. Macau: Macau Foundation.

Luo Rui Luo 洛瑞羅 (Rui Manuel Loureiro). 2008. "Putaoyaren xunzhao Zhongguo: cong Maliujia dao Aomen" 葡萄牙人尋找中國：從馬六甲到澳門 (Portuguese looking for China: from Malacca to Macau), in Wu Zhiliang, Jin Guoping, and Tang Kaijian (eds.) *Aomen Shi Xin Bian* 澳門史新編 (A new history of Macau), Vol. 1, pp. 17–30. Macau: Macau Foundation.

Ma Jiewei 馬傑偉. 1998. "Zaizao Xianggang: dianshi jiangou de Xianggang jiyi" 再造香港: 電視建構的香港記憶 (The reconstruction of Hong Kong: the Hong Kong memory as construed in televion), in Liu Qingfeng 劉青峰 and Guan Xiaochun 關小春 (eds.) *Zhuanhua zhong de Xianggang: Shenfen yu Zhixu de Zai Xunqiu* 轉化中的香港: 身份與秩序的再尋求 (Hong Kong in transition: looking again for identity and order), pp. 219–35. Hong Kong: The Chinese University of Hong Kong Press.

Macau Education and Youth Bureau. 2005. *2003 Nian Guzhu dui Bendi Zhongxue Biyesheng Biaoxian de Yijian Diaochao Baogao* 2003年雇主對本地中學畢業生表現的意見調查報告 (A report on a survey of employers regarding their employees who graduated from middle school). At http://www.dsej.gov.mo/~webdsej/www/reference/doc/report/2003_gra_ability.doc, last accessed August 28, 2005.

———. 2006. *Aomen Lishi* 澳門歷史 (A history of Macau). Macau: Macau Education and Youth Bureau. *Macau Focus*. 2001. "Heritage Excellence," Vol. I, No. 3, December.

Macau Public Administration and Civil Service Bureau. 2004. *2003 Nian Aomen Tebie Xingzheng Qu Gonggong Xingzheng Renli Ziyuan Baogao* 2003 年澳門特別行政區公共行政人力資源報告 (2003 public administration human resources in Macau). Macau: Public Administration and Civil Service Bureau.

Mackerras, Colin (selected and edited). 2000. *Sinophiles and Sinophobes: Western Views of China*, an anthology. New York: Oxford University Press.

Marger, Martin N. 2000. *Race and Ethnic Relations: American and Global Perspectives*. Fifth edition. Wadsworth, Thomson Learning.

Marques, A. H. de Oliveira. 1972. *History of Portugal, Volume I: From Lusitânia to Empire*. New York: Columbia University Press.

Marques, Graça and Veiga Jardim. 2002. "Opera in Macau (I)" and "Opera in Macau (II)." *Macau Magazine*, September and December.

Marreiros, Carlos. 1987. "Traces of Chinese and Portuguese Architecture," in R. D. Cremer (ed.) *Macau: City of Commerce and Culture*, pp. 87–102. Hong Kong: UEA Press Ltd.

McGivering, Jill. 1999. *Macao Remembers*. Hong Kong: Oxford University Press.

Meng An Na 孟安娜 (Anabela Monteiro). 2008. "1640–1680 zhijian de Aomen maoyi" 1640–1680之間的澳門貿易 (Macau trade between 1640 and 1680), in Wu Zhiliang, Jin Guoping, and Tang Kaijian (eds.) *Aomen Shi Xin Bian* 澳門史新編 (A new history of Macau), Vol. 2 pp. 431–44. Macau: Macau Foundation.

Mills, C. Wright. 2000. *The Sociological Imagination*. New York: Oxford University Press.

———. 2002. "The Promise," in Susan J. Ferguson, *Mapping the Social Landscape: Readings in Sociology*, pp. 1–7. Boston: McGraw Hill.

Mo Xiaoye 莫小也. 2003. "Wu Li shidai de dong xi fang yishu jiaoliu" 吳歷時代的東西方藝術交流 (The exchange of arts between the East and the West during Wu Li's times). Paper presented at an international symposium on "Culture, Art, and Religion: Wu Li (1632–1718) and His Inner Journey," Macau Ricci Institute, November 27–29.

Morrison, Keith. 2009. "A Poor City, in So Many Ways." *Macau Business*, June.

Mu Xinxin 穆欣欣. "Aomen xiju, wudao yu dianying" 澳門戲劇、舞蹈與電影 (Operas, plays, dance, and movies in Macau), in Wu Zhiliang, Jin Guoping, and Tang Kaijian (eds.) *Aomen Shi Xin Bian* 澳門史新編 (A new history of Macau), Vol. 4, pp. 1355–86. Macau: Macau Foundation.

Ngai, Gary. 2001. "Macau—An Ideal Base to Develop Sino-Latin Ties." *Macau Focus* 1:3 (December): 47–57.

———. 2004. "Macau Communities: Past, Present and Future," in Ieda Siqueira Wiarda and Lucy M. Cohen (eds.) *Macau: Cultural Dialogue towards a New Millenium*, pp. 101–21. Philadelphia: Xlibris Corporation.

Nuñez, César Guillén. 1987. "Macau through the Eyes of Nineteenth Century Painters," in R. D. Cremer (ed.) *Macau: City of Commerce and Culture*, pp. 53–69. Hong Kong: UEA Press, Ltd.

———. 2009. *Macao's Church of Saint Paul: A Glimmer of the Baroque in China*. Hong Kong: Hong Kong University Press in conjunction with Macau Bureau of Cultural Affairs.

———. 2012. "Book Review of *Macau History and Society* by Zhidong Hao." *Journal of the Royal Asiatic Society Hong Kong Branch*, Vol. 52, pp. 360–3.

Page, Martin. 2002. *The First Global Village: How Portugal Changed the World*. Lisbon: Editorial Noticias.

Patrick, Aaron. 2018. "James Packer's Macau Retreat Costs Crown Investors $2.5b." *The Australian Financial Review*, Jan. 16, at https://www.afr.com/news/james-packers-asia-retreat-has-cost-crown-investors-25b-20180114-h0i9f3 accessed October 14, 2018.

Pereira, Isaac. 2001. "Fun, Appealing and Better." *Macau Magazine*, June.

Pina, Joyce. 2008. "The Unhappiness Trade." *Macau Business*, April.

———. 2008. "When the Tables Turn." *Macau Business*, December.
Pina-Cabral, João de. 2002. *Between China and Europe: Person, Culture and Emotion in Macao*. London, New York: Continuum.
Pinho, A. 1987. "Gambling in Macau," in R. D. Cremer (ed.) *Macau: City of Commerce and Culture*, pp. 155–64. Hong Kong: UEA Press Ltd.
Pires, B. V. 1987. "Origins and Early History of Macau," in R. D. Cremer (ed.) *Macau: City of Commerce and Culture*, pp. 7–21. Hong Kong: UEA Press Ltd.
Pires, Father Benjamim António Videira 潘日明神父. 1992. *Shutu Tonggui: Aomen de Wenhua Jiaorong* 殊途同歸：澳門的文化交融 (Reaching the same goal by different routes: the cultural exchange and integration in Macau). Macau: The Cultural Institute of Macau. The book is translated into Chinese by Su Qin 蘇勤 from Portuguese, *Os Extremos Conciliam-se: Transculturação em Macau*, published by Macau Cultural Institute in 1987.
Pittis, Donald and Susan J. Henders (selected and edited). 1997. *Macao: Mysterious Decay and Romance*, an anthology. Hong Kong: Oxford University Press.
Porter, Jonathan. 1996. *Macau: The Imaginary City: Culture and Society, 1557 to the Present*. Boulder, Colorado: Westview Press.
Ptak, Roderich. "Aomen lishi gaishu" 澳門歷史概述 (A survey of Macau history), in Huang Qichen 黃啟臣 and Deng Kaisong 鄧開頌 (eds.) *Zhong Wai Xuezhe Lun Aomen Lishi* 中外學者論澳門歷史 (Studies on Macau history by Chinese and foreign scholars), pp. 15–53. Macau: Macau Foundation.
Pu Jia 普加 (Rogerio Miguel Puga). 2008. "Yingguo ren chu hang Aomen" 英國人初航澳門(The first voyages of the Brits to Macau), in Wu Zhiliang, Jin Guoping, and Tang Kaijian (eds.) *Aomen Shi Xin Bian* 澳門史新編 (A new history of Macau), Vol. 2, pp. 579–92. Macau: Macau Foundation.
Pu Ta Ke 普塔克 (Roderich Ptak). 2008. "Ming dai Aomen yu Dong Nan Ya de maoyi" 明代澳門與東南亞的貿易 (Trade between Macau and South East Asia in the Ming dynasty), in Wu Zhiliang, Jin Guoping, and Tang Kaijian (eds.) *Aomen Shi Xin Bian* 澳門史新編 (A new history of Macau), Vol. 2, pp. 365–94. Macau: Macau Foundation.
Puga, Rogério Miguel. 2003. "Macao through the American Female Gaze: The Epistolary Diaries of Harriett Low (1829–1834) and Rebecca Chase Kinsman (1843–1847)." Talk given at the University of Macau. Excerpts from the handout.
Qi Yinping 戚印平. 2008. "Zaoqi Ao Ri maoyi" 早期澳日貿易 (Early trade between Macau and Japan), in Wu Zhiliang, Jin Guoping, and Tang Kaijian (eds.) *Aomen Shi Xin Bian* 澳門史新編 (A new history of Macau), Vol. 2, pp. 409–30. Macau: Macau Foundation.
Quan Hansheng 全漢升. 1995. "Ming Dai zhongye hou Aomen de haiwai maoyi" 明代中葉後澳門的海外貿易 (Macau's overseas trade after the middle of Ming dynasty), in Huang Qichen 黃啟臣 and Deng Kaisong 鄧開頌 (eds.) *Zhong Wai Xuezhe Lun Aomen Lishi* 中外學者論澳門歷史 (Studies on Macau history by Chinese and foreign scholars), pp. 148–74. Macau: Macau Foundation.
Ren Hai 任海. 1998. "Kan de bianzheng: zhanlan chu zhong de Xianggang" 看的辯證：展覽櫥中的香港 (The dialectics of watching: the Hong Kong in the exhibition windows), in Liu Qingfeng 劉青峰 and Guan Xiaochun 關小春 (eds.) *Zhuanhua zhong de Xianggang: Shenfen yu Zhixu de Zai Xunqiu* 轉化中的香港：身份與秩序的再尋求 (Hong Kong in transition: looking again for identity and order), pp. 195–219. Hong Kong: The Chinese University of Hong Kong Press.
Ruan, Zirong, 2018. "Aomen Koushu Shi: Huo Huashi de Huiyi" (Macau oral history: The memory of a "living fossil"), The Paper website at https://www.thepaper.cn/newsDetail_forward_2463790, accessed October 9, 2018. The article is originally from Lin Faqin (ed.) *Longhuan chunqiu: Aomen lao jiefang koushu lishi* (A history of Macau: The oral history of Taipa's long-time residents), Guilin: Guangxi Teachers University Press.

Said, Edward. 1979. *Orientalism*. New York: Vintage Books Edition.
Scarry, Elaine. 1996. "The Difficulty of Imagining Other People," in Joshua Cohen (ed.) *For Love of Country: Debating the Limits of Patriotism*. Boston: Beacon, 1996.
Scruton, Roger. 1982. *A Dictionary of Poltical Thought*. New York: Hill and Wang.
Seabra, José Augusto. 1990. "Camilo Pessanha and the Mirage of Writing." *Review of Culture*, No. 11/12, September.
Sena, Tereza. 2004. "Historical Background of Macau with Particular Focus on the First Americans in China," in Ieda Siqueira Wiarda and Lucy M. Cohen (eds.) *Macau: Cultural Dialogue towards a New Millenium*, pp. 23–100. Philadelphia, PA: Xlibris.
Shang Xun. 2009. "Minzhu husheng gao manyi du fantan" 民主呼聲高滿意度反彈 (A louder voice for democracy and people are less satisfied in general). 《商訊》 (Business intelligence), No. 48, August.
Shipp, Steve. 1997. *Macau, China: A Political History of the Portuguese Colony's Transition to Chinese Rule*. Jefferson, North Carolina, and London: McFarland & Company, Inc., Publishers.
Silva, F. A. 1979. *The Sons of Macao, Their History and Heritage*. California: UMA, Inc.
Silva, Renelde Justo Bernardo da. 2001. *The Macanese Identity*. Translated from Portuguese by Rui Cascais. Macau: International Institute of Macau.
Simmel, Georg. 1950. *The Sociology of Georg Simmel*. Edited by Kurt Wolff. New York: The Free Press.
Smith, Anthony D. 1998. *Nationalism and Modernism: A Critical Survey of Recent Theories of Nations and Nationalism*. London and New York: Routledge.
So, Alvin Y. 1990. *Social Change and Development: Modernization, Dependency, and World-System Theories*. Newbury Park, California: Sage Publications.
Song Bonian 宋柏年, Zheng Miaoxian 鄭妙嫺, and Huang Yanhong 黃雁鴻. 2006. *Aomen Wenhua Fangtan Lu* 澳門文化訪談錄 (Interviews on Macau culture). Macau: Macau Polytechnic Institute.
Sou, Hei Lam. 2017. "Wo jueding le danren zhege zhiwu, ye jiu zhineng jinshen dian" (Once I decide to take this position, I'll have to be a bit cautious), November 17, 2017, Plataforma Macau, at http://www.plataformamacau.com/zh-hant/, accessed November 3, 2017.
Souza, George Bryan. 2005. "The Portugese Merchant Fleet at Macao in the 17th and 18th Centuries." *Review of Culture*, international edition 13, January 2005.
Spence, Jonathan D. 1990. *The Search for Modern China*. New York: W. W. Norton & Company.
Su Sa 蘇薩 (George Bryan Souza). 2008. "Aomen yu Pu Shu Yindu: zhimin zhili, xingzheng guan ji shangye, yi yancao wei li" 澳門與葡屬印度：殖民治理、行政官及商業—以烟草為例 (Macau and the Portuguese India: colonial administration, government officials, and commerce, with tobacco as an example), in Wu Zhiliang, Jin Guoping, and Tang Kaijian (eds.) *Aomen Shi Xin Bian* 澳門史新編 (A new history of Macau), Vol. 2, pp. 511–30. Macau: Macau Foundation.
Su Yi Yang 蘇一揚 (Ivo Carneiro de Sousa). 2008. "Aomen yu Diwen: zhimin guanli, maoyi ji chuan jiao" 澳門與帝汶：殖民管理，貿易及傳教 (Macau and Timor: colonial administration, trade, and missionary work), in Wu Zhiliang, Jin Guoping, and Tang Kaijian (eds.) *Aomen Shi Xin Bian* 澳門史新編 (A new history of Macau), Vol. 2, pp. 593–612. Macau: Macau Foundation.
———. 2008. "Aomen yu Yindunixiya: siren maoxian, chaye ji zhimin sixiang" 澳門與印度尼西亞：私人冒險、茶葉及殖民思想 (Macau and Indonesia: individual risk taking, tea, and colonial thinking), in Wu Zhiliang, Jin Guoping, and Tang Kaijian (eds.) *Aomen Shi Xin Bian* 澳門史新編 (A new history of Macau), Vol. 2, pp. 625–37. Macau: Macau Foundation.
———. 2008. "Qian gongyehua Aomen de jumin ji renkou tixi (16–19 shiji)" 前工業化澳門的居民及人口體系：16–19世紀 (The people and their composition in pre-industrialized

Macau), in Wu Zhiliang, Jin Guoping, and Tang Kaijian (eds.) *Aomen Shi Xin Bian* 澳門史新編 (A new history of Macau), Vol. 3, pp. 1007–44. Macau: Macau Foundation.

Tam, Camoes C. K. 1994. *Aomen Zhuquan Wenti Shi Mo (1553–1993)* 澳門主權問題始末 (1553–1993) (Disputes concerning Macau's sovereignty between China and Portugal, 1553–1993). Taipei: Yongye 永業 chubanshe.

Tamir, Yael. 2000. "Who Is Afraid of a Global State?" in Kjell Goldmann, Ulf Hannerz, and Charles Westin (eds.) *Nationalism and Internationalism in the Post-Cold War Era*, pp. 244–67. London and New York: Routledge.

Tan Ruomei 譚若梅 (May Tam), Gu Xuebin 古學斌 (Hok Bun Ku), and Jiang Shaoqi 江紹祺 (Travis Kong) (eds.). 2005. *Gongmin Shenfen de Zaisi yu Dazao: Huaren Shehui de Shehui Paichi yu Bianyuan Xing* 公民身份的再思與打造：華人社會的社會排斥與邊緣性 (Rethinking and recasting citizenship: social exclusion and marginality in Chinese societies). Hong Kong: Center for Social Policy Studies, The Hong Kong Polytechnic University.

Tan Shibao. 2002. "Estudos sobre a Lenda das Aldeias: na Península de Macau antes da suo Fundação" (The legend of the villages on the Macao peninsula before the founding of Macao). *Review of Culture*, international edition 1, January 2002.

Tan Shibao and Cao Guoqing. 2002. "Nova Avaliação de Wang Bo: e do Primeiro Acordo Sino-Portugues" (A new evaluation of Wang Bo and the first Sino-Portuguese agreement). *Review of Culture*, international edition 1, January 2002.

Tang Kaijian 湯開建. 2001. "Ba" 跋 (Afterword), in Jin Guoping and Wu Zhiliang, *Jing Hai Piaomiao* 鏡海縹緲 (The misty Macau history), pp. 303–6. Macau: Chengren Jiaoyu Xuehui 成人教育學會 Adult education association.

———. 2004. *Weiliduo "Baoxiao Shi Mo Shu" Jianzheng* 委黎多《報效始末疏》箋正 (Study notes on Vereador's, i.e., procurador's memorial to the Ming emperor). Guangzhou: Guangdong Remin Chubanshe.

———. 2008. "Ming Qing shiqi Aomen tianzhujiao de fazhan yu xingshuai" 明清時期澳門天主教的發展與興衰 (The development and decline of the Catholic Church in the Ming and Qing dynasties), in Wu Zhiliang, Jin Guoping, and Tang Kaijian (eds.) *Aomen Shi Xin Bian* 澳門史新編 (A new history of Macau), Vol. 4. Macau: Macau Foundation, 2008.

———. 2014. *Bei yiwang de "gongye qifei": Aomen gongye fazhan shi gao 1557–1941* (The forgotten "rise of industry": A history of Macau's industrial development 1557–1941). Macau: Macau Bureau of Cultural Affairs.

Tang Kaijian 湯開建, Chen Wenyuan 陳文源, and Ye Nong 葉農 (eds.) 2001. *Yapian Zhanzheng hou Aomen Shehui Shenghuo Jishi: Jindai Baokan Aomen Ziliao Xuancui* 鴉片戰爭後澳門生活記實 — 近代報刊澳門資料選粹 (Life in Macau after the Opium War: excerpts from modern newspapers). Guangzhou: Huacheng 花城 Chubanshe.

Tao Li 陶裏. 1998. "Aomen de xiaoshuo chuangzuo" 澳門的小說創作 (Macau's short stories and novels), in Liu Denghan 劉登翰 (ed.) *Aomen Wenxue Gaiguan* 澳門文學概觀 (A brief introduction to Macau's literature). Xiamen: Lujiang 鷺江 Chubanshe.

Tao Li 陶裏 and Zhuang Wenyong 莊文永. 1998. "Aomen de xin shi chuangzuo" 澳門的新詩創作 (Macau's new poetry), in Liu Denghan 劉登翰 (ed.) *Aomen Wenxue Gaiguan* 澳門文學概觀 (A brief introduction to Macau's literature), pp. 116–68. Xiamen: Lujiang 鷺江 Chubanshe.

Teixeira, Manuel. 1987. "The Church in Macau," in R. D. Cremer (ed.) *Macau: City of Commerce and Culture*, pp. 39–49. Hong Kong: UEA Press Ltd.

———. 1990. "Early Newspapers in Macau." *Review of Culture*, No. 11/12, September.

———. 1995. "Yi ba wu si nian Meiguo haijun zhunjiang Peili kandao de Aomen" 一八五四年美國海軍準將佩里看到的澳門 (The Macau seen by an American commander Perry in 1854, or originally in Portuguese: Macau Visto pelo Comodoro Perry em 1854), in Huang Qichen 黃啟臣 and Deng Kaisong 鄧開頌 (eds.) *Zhong Wai Xuezhe Lun Aomen Lishi* 中外

學者論澳門歷史 (Studies on Macau history by Chinese and foreign scholars), pp. 232–43. Macau: Macau Foundation.

Teng, Ssu-yu and John K. Fairbank. 1979. *China's Response to the West: A Documentary Survey 1839–1923.* Cambridge, Massachusetts: Harvard University Press.

Tong Qiaohui 童喬慧. 2008. *Aomen Chengshi Huanjing yu Wenmai Yanjiu* 澳門城市環境與文脉研究 (A study on the city environment and cultural traits in Macau). Guangzhou: Guangdong Renmin Chubanshe.

The Cuba Commission Report: A Hidden History of the Chinese in Cuba. 1993. The Original English-Language Text of 1876. Baltimore: Johns Hopkins University Press.

Tønnesson, Stein and Hans Antlöv. 1996. "Asia in Theories of Nationalism and National Identity," in Stein Tønnesson and Hans Antlöv (eds.) *Asian Forms of the Nation*, pp. 1–39. London: Curzon.

Urrows, David Francis. "Pipe Organ Building and the Jesuits in China." Lecture at the Macau Ricci Institute, Janury 25, 2005.

Van Dyke, Paul Arthur. 2002. *Port Canton and the Pearl River Delta, 1690–1845*, Vol. 1 and 2, Ph.D. dissertation in history. Los Angeles: University of Southern California.

Vickers, Edward. 2003. *In Search of an Identity: The Politics of History as a School Subject in Hong Kong, 1960s–2002.* New York and London: Routledge.

Wakeman, Frederic, Jr. 1975. *The Fall of Imperial China.* New York: The Free Press.

Wallerstein, Immanuel. 1976. *The Modern World System: Capitalist Agriculture and the Origins of the European World Economy in the Sixteenth Century.* New York: Academic Press.

———. 1979. *The Capitalist World-Economy.* New York: Cambridge University Press.

Wan Ming 萬明. 2008. "Ming dai Aomen maoyi" 明代澳門貿易 (Trade in Macau in the Ming dynasty), in Wu Zhiliang, Jin Guoping, and Tang Kaijian (eds.) *Aomen Shi Xin Bian* 澳門史新編 (A new history of Macau), Vol. 2, pp. 341–64. Macau: Macau Foundation.

Wang Chun 汪春. 1998. "Aomen de tusheng wenxue" 澳門的土生文學 (Macau's Macanese literature), in Liu Denghan 劉登翰 (ed.) *Aomen Wenxue Gaiguan* 澳門文學概觀 (A brief introduction to Macau's literature). Xiamen: Lujiang 鷺江 Chubanshe.

Wang Gongwu. 1998. "Ming Foreign Relations: Southeast Asia," in Denis Twitchett and Frederick W. Mote (eds.) *The Cambridge History of China Volume 8: The Ming Dynasty, 1368–1644, Part 2*, pp. 300–32. New York: Cambridge University Press.

Wang, Wuyi and Peter Zabielskis. 2010. "Making Friends, Making Money: Macao's Traditional VIP Casino System." In *Global Gambling: Cultural Perspectives on Gambling*, edited by Sytze F. Kingma. London: Routledge Criminology.

Wang Xiaochao 王曉朝. 2004. 基督教與新世紀中國公民道德建設 (Raising civic morality among Chinese citizens in the new century: the role of Christian values.) *Chinese Cross Currents*, January–March 2004.

Wang Yu. 2004. "Zhongwen shi Aomen tebie xingzheng qu de zhuyao zhengshi yuyan" 中文是澳門特別行政區的主要正式語文 (Chinese is the main formal language in Macau SAR). *Macao Daily*, August 22, 2004.

———. 2005. "Zai lun Zhongwen shi Aomen tebie xingzheng qu de zhuyao zhengshi yuyan" 再論中文是澳門特別行政區的主要正式語文 (Again on Chinese as the main and formal language in Macao SAR), June 5, 2005.

Wang Zhaoming 王昭明. 1995. "Yapian zhanzheng qian hou Aomen diwei de bianhua" 鴉片戰爭前後澳門地位的變化 (The status change of Macau around the Opium War), in Huang Qichen 黃啟臣 and Deng Kaisong 鄧開頌 (eds.) *Zhong Wai Xuezhe Lun Aomen Lishi* 中外學者論澳門歷史 (Studies on Macau history by Chinese and foreign scholars), pp. 200–31. Macau: Macau Foundation.

Watts, Ian E. 1999. "Neither Meat nor Fish: Three Macanese Women in the Transition." Paper presented at a conference on Macau and its neighbors, at http://www.geocities.com/Tokyo/Temple/4735/fish.html, last accessed on February 16, 2005.
Weber, Max. 1946. *From Max Weber*. Edited by H. H. Gerth and C. Wright Mills. New York: Oxford University Press.
———. 1958. *The Protestant Ethic and the Spirit of Capitalism*. New York: Charles Scribner's Sons.
Webster, Andrew. 1990. *Introduction to the Sociology of Development*. Second edition. London: The MacMillan Press Ltd.
Wei Qingyuan. 2005. *Aomen Shi Lungao* 澳門史論稿 (Papers on Macau history). Guangzhou: Guangdong Remin Chubanshe.
Willis, Clive (ed.) 2002. *China and Macau*. Aldershot: Ashgate.
Winterton, Bradley. 1995. *Falstaff in Macau*. Hong Kong: Fairfield Books.
Wong Kuok Keung 王國強. 2008. "Aomen lishi yanjiu zhi Zhongwen shumu" 澳門歷史研究之中文書目 (The Chinese works on Macau history studies), in Wu Zhiliang, Jin Guoping, and Tang Kaijian (eds.) *Aomen Shi Xin Bian* 澳門史新編 (A new history of Macau), Vol. 4, pp. 1427–56. Macau: Macau Foundation.
Wong, Timothy Ka-ying and Wan Po-san. 2009. "The Emerging Middle Class in Post-Colonial Macao: Structure, Profile, and Mobility." *Issues and Studies* Vol. 45, no. 2.
Wordie, Jason. 2013. *Macao: People and Places, Past and Present*. Hong Kong: Angsana Limited.
Wu Jiaxiang 吳稼祥. 2004. *Lianbang hua: Zhonghuo di san gongheguo zhi lu* 聯邦化：中華第三共和國之路 (Federation: the way to a third Chinese republic). Hong Kong: The Mirror Press.
Wu Mei. 2005. "Mass Media in Macau." Presentation at the Fulbright Forum at the University of Macau, February 28.
Wu Zhichang 吳志昌. 2000. "Aomen zhimin zhengzhi de yanbian" 澳門殖民政制的演變 (The transformation of Macau's colonial political system), in Deng Kaisong, Huang Hongzhao, Wu Zhiliang, and Lu Xiaomin (eds.) *Aomen Lishi Xinshuo* 澳門歷史新說 (New research on Macau history), pp. 514–85. Shijiazhuang: Huashan Wenyi 花山文藝 Chubanshe.
Wu Zhiliang. 1996a. "Aomen shi yanjiu shuping" 澳門史研究述評 (A review of Macau historical studies). *Xingzheng* 行政 (Administration) (a journal of Macau government), Vol. 9, Number 2 (June): 509–22.
———. 1996b. *Dong Xi Jiaohui Kan Aomen* 東西交匯看澳門 (The East meets the West in Macau). Macau: Macau Foundation.
———. 1998. *Shengcun zhi Dao: Lun Aomen Zhengzhi Zhidu yu Zhengzhi Fazhan* 生存之道：論澳門政治制度與政治發展 (The way to survive: the political system and the political development in Macau). Macau: Aomen Chengren Jiaoyu Xuehui 澳門成人教育學會.
———. 2000. "Jiangou Aomen de shimin shehui" 建構澳門的市民社會 (The construction of Macau's civil society), in Wu Zhiliang and Chen Xinxin, *Aomen Zhengzhi Shehui Yanjiu* 澳門政治社會研究 (A study of Macau's politics and society), pp. 144–57. Macau: Macau Adult Educational Association.
———. 2005. "Xu" 序 (Preface), in Jin Guoping 金國平, *Xifang Aomen Shiliao Xuancui* 西方澳門史料選萃 (Selected Western records on Macau), pp. 1–15. Guangzhou: Guangdong Remin Chubanshe.
———. 2008. "Mingdai Aomen zhengzhi shehui 明代澳門政治社會 (The politics and society in the Ming dynasty), in Wu Zhiliang, Jin Guoping, and Tang Kaijian (eds.) *Aomen Shi Xin Bian* 澳門史新編 (A new history of Macau), Vol. 1, pp. 79–123. Macau: Macau Foundation.
Wu Zhiliang and Chen Xin-xin. 2000. *Aomen Zhengzhi Shehui Yanjiu* 澳門政治社會研究 (A study of politics and society in Macao). Macao: Macao Association for Adult Education.
Xu Jieshun 徐傑舜 and Tang Kaijian 湯開建. 2003. "Guanyu Aomen tusheng Puren wenti de sikao" 關於澳門土生葡人問題的思考 (On the issue of Macanese), in Yu Zhen 余振, Zheng Weiming 鄭煒明, and Cui Baofeng 崔寶峯 (eds.) *Aomen Lishi, Wenhua yu Shehui*

澳門歷史、文化與社會 (Macau history, culture, and society), pp. 129–47. Macau: Macau Chengren Jiaoyu Xiehuia 澳門成人教育協會.

Xu Suqin 徐素琴. 1999. "Minguo chu zhi sanshi niandai Yue Ao guanxi de dongdang qifu" 民國初至30年代粵澳關係的動盪起伏 (The ups and downs of the Guangdong-Macau relations from the beginning of the Republic of China to the 1930s), in Deng Kaisong, Wu Zhiliang, and Lu Xiaomin (eds.) *Yue Ao Guanxi Shi* 粵澳關係史 (The relationship between Guangdong and Macau), pp. 378–436. Beijing: Zhongguo Shudian 中國書店.

———. 1999. "Qing mo zhengzhi fengyun Zhong Yue Ao liangdi de xianghu yingxiang yu Yue Ao jie wu fenzheng" 清末政治風雲中粵澳兩地的相互影響與粵澳界務紛爭 (The relationship between Guangdong and Macau in the politics in the end of Qing and the conflicts regarding the boarders between Guangdong and Macau), in Deng Kaisong, Wu Zhiliang, and Lu Xiaomin (eds.) *Yue Ao Guanxi Shi* 粵澳關係史 (The relationship between Guangdong and Macau), pp. 309–77. Beijing: Zhongguo Shudian 中國書店.

———. 2000. "Zhong Pu 'Hehao Tongshang Tiaoyue' de qianding" 中葡《和好通商條約》的簽訂 (The signing of the Luso-Chinese Treaty of Friendship and Trade), in Deng Kaisong, Huang Hongzhao, Wu Zhiliang, and Lu Xiaomin (eds.) *Aomen Lishi Xinshuo* 澳門歷史新說 (New research on Macau history), pp. 248–91. Shijiazhuang: Huashan Wenyi 花山文藝 Chubanshe.

Xu Xiaowang 徐曉望. 2008. "Aomen de mazu xinyang" 澳門的馬祖信仰 (The belief in Mazu in Macau), in Wu Zhiliang, Jin Guoping, and Tang Kaijian (eds.) *Aomen Shi Xin Bian* 澳門史新編 (A new history of Macau), Vol. 4, pp. 1045–82. Macau: Macau Foundation.

Yan Zhongming 嚴忠明 and Ye Nong 葉農. 2008. "Aomen chengshi de xingjian yu fazhan" 澳門城市的興建與發展 (The rise and development of the city of Macau), in Wu Zhiliang, Jin Guoping, and Tang Kaijian (eds.) *Aomen Shi Xin Bian* 澳門史新編 (A new history of Macau), Vol. 3, pp. 769–807. Macau: Macau Foundation.

Yang Renfei 楊仁飛. 2000. *Aomen Jindaihua Licheng* 澳門近代化歷程 (The modernization of Macao). Macao: Macao Daily Press.

———. 2008. "Aomen minsu: yifu xuanli duozi de huajuan" 澳門民俗：一幅絢麗多姿的畫卷 (Local customs in Macau: a picture of multiple characteristics), in Wu Zhiliang, Jin Guoping, and Tang Kaijian (eds.) *Aomen Shi Xin Bian* 澳門史新編 (A new history of Macau), Vol. 4, pp. 1135–56. Macau: Macau Foundation.

Yang Yunzhong (ed.) 2005. *Zheng He yu Hai shang Sichou zhi Lu* 鄭和與海上絲綢之路 (Zheng He and the silk road on the sea). Macau: Center for Macau Studies, The University of Macau.

Yang Zewei 楊澤偉. 2006. *Zhuquan Lun: Guoji Fa shang de Zhuquan Wenti jiqi Fazhan Qushi Yanjiu* 主權論：國際法上的主權問題及其發展趨勢研究 (On sovereignty: a study on the issues of sovereignty in international law and the tendencies of their development). Beijing: Beijing University Press.

Ye Nong 葉農. 2008. "Cong 1840 zhi 1860: Ao Gang guanxi zuichu 20 nian" 從1840至1860：澳港關係最初20年 (From 1840 to 1860: The relations between Macau and Hong Kang in the first twenty years), in Wu Zhiliang, Jin Guoping, and Tang Kaijian (eds.) *Aomen Shi Xin Bian* 澳門史新編 (A new history of Macau), Vol. 2, pp. 471–97. Macau: Macau Foundation, 2008.

Yee, Herbert S. 余振 (Yu Zhen). 2001. *Macau in Transition: From Colony to Autonomous Region*. New York: Palgrave.

———. 2003. "Gang Ao shimin de zhengzhi canyu he minzhu jiazhi quxiang" 港澳市民的政治參與和民主價值取向 (Political participation and democratic values in the citizens in Hong Kong and Macau), in Herbert Yee (Yu Zhen), Eilo Yu (Yu Yongyi), and Bruce Kwan (Kuang Jinjun) (eds.) *Shuang Cheng Ji II: Huigui hou Gang Ao de Zhengzhi, Jingji ji Shehui Fazhan* 雙城記 II：回歸後港澳的政治、經濟及社會發展 (A tale of two cities II: the political, economic and social development in Hong Kong and Macau after their return to China), pp. 155–73. Macau: Aomen Shehui Kexue Xuehui.

———. 2003. "Xianggang de gao guan wenze zhi jiqi dui Aomen zhengzhi gaige de qishi 香港的高官問責制及其對澳門政治改革的啟示 (The responsibility system of the higher officials in Hong Kong and the implication of the practice for Macau's political reform), in Herbert Yee (Yu Zhen), Eilo Yu (Yu Yongyi), and Bruce Kwan (Kuang Jinjun) (eds.) *Shuang Cheng Ji II: Huigui hou Gang Ao de Zhengzhi, Jingji ji Shehui Fazhan* 雙城記 II：回歸後港澳的政治、經濟及社會發展 (A tale of two cities II: the political, economic and social development in Hong Kong and Macau after their return to China), pp. 121–32. Macau: Aomen Shehui Kexue Xuehui.

Yin Guangren 印光任 and Zhang Rulin 張汝霖. [1751] 1992. *Aomen Jilue Jiaozhu* 《澳門記略校注》 (An edited version of *The Annals of Macau*, edited by Zhao Chunchen 趙春晨). Macau: Aomen Wenhua Si (Macau culture department).

Yu Hui-ying 余惠鶯. 2007. "Cujin gongmin canyu gong jian hexie shehui" 促進公民參與共建和諧社會 (Promote civic participation and construct a harmonious society). *Macao Daily*, February 21, 2007, p. E5.

Zeng Zhonglu 曾忠祿. 2006. "Bocai shichang fazhan 'Ji zhong Yi Huan'" 博彩市場發展"急中宜緩" (The gambling industry should go slowly). *Macao Daily*, September 3, 2006, p. A11.

Zepp, R. A. 1987. "Interface of Chinese and Portuguese Cultures," in R. D. Cremer (ed.) *Macau: City of Commerce and Culture*, pp. 125–36. Hong Kong: UEA Press Ltd.

Zha Canchang 查燦長. 2006. *Zhuanxing, Bianxiang yu Chuanbo: Aomen Zaoqi Xiandaihua Yanjiu—Yapian Zhanzheng zhi 1945 Nian* 轉型、變項與傳播：澳門早期現代化研究（鴉片戰爭至1945年）(Transformation, variables, and communication: a study of Macau's modernization in the early days—from the Opium War to 1945). Guangzhou: Guangdong Remin Chubanshe.

Zhang Guogang 張國剛. 2003. *Cong Zhong Xi Chushi dao Liyi zhi Zheng: Ming Qing Chuanjiaoshi yu Zhong Xi Wenhua Jiaoliu* 從中西初識到禮儀之爭：明清傳教士與中西文化交流 (From the meeting of China and the West to the Controversy of Rites: the missionaries in the Ming and Qing dynasties and the cultural exchange of China and the West). Beijing: People's Press.

Zhang Jian-hao 張建豪. 1995. "Jiaotong wenti" 交通問題 (Traffic problems), in Chen Xin-xin (ed.) *Aomen Shehui Wenti* 澳門社會問題 (Social problems in Macao). Hong Kong: Guangjiaojing Chubanshe.

Zhang Wenqin 張文欽. 1995. *Aomen yu Zhonghua Lishi Wenhua* 澳門與中華歷史文化 (Macau and Chinese history and culture). Macau: Macau Foundation.

———. 2003. *Aomen Shici Jianzhu (Ming Qing Juan, Wan Qing Juan, Min Guo Juan, Shang, Xia)* 澳門詩詞箋注（明清卷、晚清卷、民國卷上、下）(Annotated volumes of poems about Macau: Ming and Qing dynasties, Late Qing dynasty, and the Republican China Vol. 1 and 2). Zhuhai and Macau: Zhuhai Chubanshe; Macau government Bureau of Culture, Macau SAR.

———. 2005. "The Life and Works of Wu Yushan." *Review of Culture*, international edition 13, January 2005.

Zhao Lifeng 趙利峰 and Hu Gen 胡根. 2008. "Wan Qing Aomen bocai ye de xingqi yu fazhan" 晚清澳門博彩業的興起與發展 (The rise and development of the gambling industry in Macau during the late Qing era), in Wu Zhiliang, Jin Guoping, and Tang Kaijian (eds.) *Aomen Shi Xin Bian* 澳門史新編 (A new history of Macau), Vol. 3, pp. 715–67. Macau: Macau Foundation.

Zhao Liren 趙立人. 1999. "Putaoya ren ruju qian de Guangdong yu Aomen" 葡萄牙人入據前的廣東與澳門 (Guangdong and Macau before the Portuguese settlement), in Deng Kaisong 鄧開頌, Wu Zhiliang 吳志良, and Lu Xiaomin 陸曉敏 (eds.) *Yue Ao Guanxi Shi* 粵澳關

係史 (The relationship between Guangdong and Macau), pp. 1–66. Beijing: Zhongguo Shudian 中國書店.
Zhao Yanfang. 趙燕芳. 2004. *Puren Tusheng Fangtan* 葡人土生訪談 (Interviews with the Portuguese and Macanese in Macau). Macau: International Institute of Macau.
Zheng Caihong 鄭彩紅. "Danzai paozhu ye de huihuang suiyue" 氹仔炮竹業的輝煌歲月 (The glorious days of the firecrackers industry), in Zhang Zhuofu 張卓夫 (ed.) *Haidao Fenghua* 海島風華 (The life in Macao), pp. 100–7. Macao: Aomen Jindai Wenxue Xuehui (Macao association of modern history).
Zheng Shuxian 鄭淑賢. 2004a. "Tusheng tuhua huaju tuan yi yishu yanxu tuyu shengming" 土生土語話劇團以藝術延續土語生命 (The Macanese drama troupe's efforts to prolong the life of the Macanese language). *Aomen Zazhi* 澳門雜誌, No. 40, June 2004.
———. 2004b. "Dona Aida he tade tusheng cai shitang" Dona Aida 和她的土生菜食堂 (Dona Aida and her Macanese restaurant). *Aomen Zazhi* 澳門雜誌, No. 40, June 2004.
Zheng Weiming 鄭煒明. 1998. "Aomen de xiju huodong yu chuangzuo" 澳門的戲劇活動與創作 (Macau's plays and the writing of plays), in Liu Denghan 劉登翰 (ed.) *Aomen Wenxue Gaiguan* 澳門文學概觀 (A brief introduction to Macau's literature), pp. 222–60. Xiamen: Lujiang 鷺江 Chubanshe.
———. 2008. "Aomen wenxue: 1591–1999" 澳門文學：1591–1999 (Literature in Macau: 1591–1999), in Wu Zhiliang, Jin Guoping, and Tang Kaijian (eds.) *Aomen Shi Xin Bian* 澳門史新編 (A new history of Macau), Vol. 4, pp. 1157–87. Macau: Macau Foundation.
Zheng Weiming 鄭煒明 and Huang Qichen 黃啟臣. 1994. *Aomen Zongjiao* 澳門宗教 (Religions of Macau). Macao: Macau Foundation.
Zhong Li 鍾莉. 2009. "Aomen fayuan shi nian" 澳門法院十年 (The ten years of Macau's courts). *Jiuding* (九鼎), No. 23, September.
Zi Teng. 2000. *Research Report on Mainland Chinese Sex Workers: Hong Kong, Macau and Town B in Pearl River Delta*. Hong Kong: The University of Hong Kong.

Index

12-3 Incident 6, 42–44, 110–11, 126, 154, 174
5-29 Incident 42, 61, 110, 174

Adé 154–55, 266
Alves, Leonel Alberto 163–64, 167, 175–76
Amaral, João Maria Ferreira do 18, 32, 39–41, 100, 107, 143, 148, 221
  in the Summers incident 125
Anson, Captain Gorge 21, 93
Article 23 and its legislation 48, 50, 176, 178, 181–82, 202, 215

Bai Zhijian (白志健) 215
Basic Law of Macau 45–50, 162, 164, 166–67, 176, 178–79
Bewitching Braid, The 103, 151, 265
Boxers 85–86, 252
Buck, Pearl 95

Camões, Luís de 145, 156
Cao Qizhen (Susana Chou) 166
Carvalho, Rodrigo Leal de 157
Captain-major 31
Chief Judge 31–33
Chinese (*see also* Portuguese)
  political structure 27, 33–35, 45–50
  and Portuguese conflicts 35–44
  reasons for allowing the Portuguese to stay in Macau 16–17
Chinese learning as the foundation and Western learning for practical purposes (中學為體, 西學為用) 89
Chinnery, George 65, 132, 149, 157–58, 213
Chou Cheong Hong (曹長雄) 150, 204
Chui, José 63, 109

Church of Our Lady of Defense, the Chinese Christian Church (唐人廟) 135
City Hall (see *yi shi ting*)
Civil society and public sphere 77, 201–5, 216
Clash of civilizations and cultures 81–114 (*see also* Huntington; religion)
Class, social 47, 57–71, 79, 93, 168–84
Colledge, Thomas R. 133
Coloane (Luhuan) 12–13, 15, 20, 41, 97, 142
Coutinho, José Maria Pereira 163, 166–67, 169
Crime and deviance, gambling-related 184–89
Culture (*see* clash of civilizations and cultures; identity; and religion)

Daoguang, emperor 22, 27
d'Assumpção, Carlos 178
Democracy
  definition 31
  democratization 1, 4, 19, 29–31, 48–51, 126, 176, 178–79, 201–3, 216–17, 272–73
  election committee, the 46
  election of the legislature 47–49
  Portuguese 31–33
Dowager, Empress 28, 86
Dual jurisdiction 29–38

Economy of Macau 52–80
Education 90, 92, 126, 130, 133, 171–72
  higher education 196–201
  middle school 190–96
Ethnic stratification and politics 161–68
Elliot, Charles 22–24, 132

Fanfang (番坊) 2
Federalism 216
Feng Guifen 28, 89–90
Fernandes, Henrique de Senna 103, 105, 108–9, 151–53
Freedom of speech 31, 50, 113, 167, 204, 216, 276

Gambling 3, 52, 58, 71–79, 93, 143–46
    addicted/problem gambling 79, 187–89
    city of sin 223
    companies and personalities 74–76
    crimes and deviance 184–89
    corporate social responsibility 78–79, 218–20
    fantan 72–74
    legalization 72
    liberalization 74
    loan sharking 185
    museum 221
    reasons for the industry's rise 71–73
    responsible gambling 78–79, 188–89, 218–20
    VIP room 185–87
Guanzha Incident 42, 61, 242
Guo Songtao 28, 89–90

Han Fei Zi 257
Hart, Robert 1, 28, 41, 232
Ho, Edmund (何厚鏵) 18–19, 44, 46, 48, 52, 71, 215
Ho, Stanley (何鴻燊) 71, 74–76, 109, 126
Ho, Yin (He Xian, 何賢) 44, 69, 169, 174, 178, 217, 242
Huang Yu (黃瑜) 15
Huntington 5, 81–83, 106, 111–14, 127, 257

"I don't bother you, you don't bother me" 5, 109–12, 258
Identity 114, 258, 274, 277
    Chinese national and political identity in Macau 192
    economic 218–19, 223
    Macanese identity 152–55, 192
    Macauan identity 3–5, 155, 207, 214, 222–23
    Macauan national/cultural identity 155, 208, 212–15
    Macauan political identity 210–12, 215–17
    national 207–10

Jiang Zemin 192, 211

Kangxi, emperor 21, 26, 90, 130, 133
    and Catholicism 21, 36, 129, 131

Lady Hughes 87
Langbaijiao 12
Li Keqiang 192
Lin Gua (Lamqua) 149–50, 158
Lin Zexu (林則徐) 22–23, 27, 83, 86, 125, 134, 160
Literature and the arts about Macau 138–59
Liu Shaowu (劉紹武) 42
Longobardi, Nicolò 128
Low, Harriett 60–65, 91–94, 98, 110, 136–37, 148

Macanese 3, 100–105, 222
    as citizens of Macau 18, 30
    characteristics 45, 101–11
    defined by Carvalho 157
    ethnic stratification and politics (*see above*)
    future 112, 114, 157
    identity 153–54, 209–10, 212 (*see also* identity)
    in the 12-3 Incident 42
    interaction with others 111, 146–48, 153, 213
    literature and arts 150–56
    organizations 112, 214
Macartney, George 21, 98
Macau (*see also* clash of civilizations and cultures)
    characteristics 3–4
    in earlier times 12–16, 249
    geography 13–14
    history periodization 239
    model/formula 5, 17, 26–27, 40, 81, 109–14, 200, 203, 212, 216, 223, 238, 257–58
    name 232
    shi zi men (十字門) 13–15
Macau Coast Military and Civilian Government 34–35

Index

Macau model (*see* clash of civilizations; Macau)
Mainlandization 113–14, 166–67, 195–96, 205, 212, 214
Malacca 10–12, 19–20, 54, 92, 101
Marques, José Luis de Sales 102, 104–5
May 29 Incident (*see* 5-29 Incident)
Mesquita, Vicente Nicolau de 40, 221, 242
Montesquieu 94
Morrison, Robert 96, 123–24, 131–33, 157, 213

Nei Lingding Island 10–11
Ng, Kuok Cheong, 109, 167, 178, 201
Ningbo in the First Opium War 21, 24, 55, 65

One country, two systems
    and democracy 31, 51, 216
    as a theme of the book 5
    implementation 18, 113, 195, 199, 215
Opium 245–46 (*see also* Economy of Macau)
    history of use in China 55–56, 94
    role of officials in China 95
    trade in Macau 52, 55–57, 71
    use by Portuguese 156
Opium Wars 22–29, 38, 51
Orientalism 81, 98, 107, 214

Pereira, Thomas (徐日升) 130, 213
Pessanha, Camilo 156–57
Pinto, Fernão Mendez 9
Pires, Tomé 11, 27
Politics (*see* democracy; Chinese; Macanese; Portuguese)
Portuguese (*see also* Chinese; identity; literature and the arts; Macanese)
    arrival in Southern China and settlement in Macau 12–17
    colonial occupation 38–45
    conflicts with the Dutch, English, and Chinese 19–22
    maritime expansion 9–12
    political structure in Macau and the clash with the Chinese 31–38
Postcolonialism 214
Propaganda Fide (傳信部) of the Roman Catholic Church 99, 129

Qian Shan Zhai 34–35
Qianlong, emperor 21, 26, 129
Qishan 23, 88, 90
Qiu Fengjia (邱逢甲) 142
Qiying 38, 88–90

Race and ethnic relations (*see* ethnic stratification and politics)
Racism 61, 82, 93, 97–98, 100, 110, 113, 254
Rangel, Jorge Alberto Hagedorn (黎祖智) 63, 112, 178
Refugees 148, 157, 217
Religion (*see also* clash of civilizations and cultures)
    and the clash of civilizations 81–82, 84, 88, 99, 110
    and politics 33, 35–36
    and social development 115–37
    Buddhism 118–19
    Chinese 115–19
    Christianity and Catholicism 119–23
    Controversy of Rites 127–30
    Daoism 116–18
    Macanese 104 (*see also* Macanese)
    Mazu 116–17
    Nu Wa 117, 136
    Protestantism 123–24
    relationship between church and state 125–27
    role of religion 124–35
Ricci, Matteo 127–28, 130–31, 212–13
Ruggieri, Michel 127–28, 130, 212

Santa Catarina 19, 237
Sanyuanli 23, 85–86, 90
Shangchuan 9, 12–13
Shen Zhiliang (沈志亮) 40, 143, 148
Sou Ka Hou 48
Sovereignty 6, 18, 29–35, 38–40, 49, 51, 208, 210, 258
Spence, Jonathan 129, 134

Tang Xianzu (湯顯祖) 139
Teixeira, Diogo de Pinho (戴冰玉) 33
Toynbee 95
Treaty of Canton 23–24
Treaty of Nanjing 24
Treaty of Tianjin 24

Valente, Jorge Neto 165–67
Voltaire 90

Wang Bo (汪柏) 16
Wen Tianxiang (文天祥) 15–16
Wu Li (吳歷) 127, 140–41, 149–50, 158, 213

Xian cheng (縣丞) 34–36, 44
Xian Yuqing (冼玉清) 144
Xianfeng, emperor 24
Xi Zhongxun 178
Xu Guangqi 128, 130–31

Yi shi ting (City Hall 議事亭) 33–34, 149, 159, 240
Yongzheng, emperor 21–22, 27, 33, 90, 125
Yung Wing (容閎) 133–34, 213, 262

Zheng Chengong 55, 128
Zheng Guanying 84–86, 89, 216, 249
Zheng He 2, 26
Zheng Zhilong 128
Zhenjiang in the First Opium War 24

www.ingramcontent.com/pod-product-compliance
Ingram Content Group UK Ltd.
Pitfield, Milton Keynes, MK11 3LW, UK
UKHW021834210426
5322IPUK00018B/268